THE AVANT GARDENER

Carolus Linnaeus, 1707–1778 — the founder of modern botany, and the first avant gardener.

THE AVANT GARDENER

A Handbook and
Sourcebook
of All That's
New and Useful
in Gardening

Thomas and Betty Powell

HOUGHTON MIFFLIN COMPANY

BOSTON 1975

Dedicated with great respect and affection to Richard B. Farnham, a horticulturist whose ability to inspire accomplishment in gardening and communication is equaled only by his own achievements.

Library of Congress Cataloging in Publication Data

Powell, Thomas
    The avant gardener.

    Bibliography: p.
    Includes index.
    1. Gardening.   I. Powell, Betty   joint
author.   II. Title.
SB453.P66   635   74-34599
ISBN 0-395-20460-7

Printed in the United States of America

H 10 9 8 7 6 5 4 3 2 1

Acknowledgments

A great many people have contributed directly or indirectly to this book. To all the gardeners, growers, government agencies, institutions and manufacturers who supplied information and illustrations, our thanks for their help and cooperation.

Our special thanks to Rudolph Benjamin, who so generously provided the many fine photographs taken by his late wife, Hertha; Charles D. Webster, President of the Horticultural Society of New York, and Miss Elizabeth C. Hall, the Society's Senior Librarian; Harold Epstein, a horticulturist whose encouragement and advice have been unfailingly helpful; Ruth Shortell, Leslie L. Dawson and the late Rudolph F. Sudek for their unswerving confidence and support; and in special measure to our editor, Frances Tenenbaum, whose patience, skill and fortitude helped immeasurably in the preparation of this book.

CONTENTS

The German 'Fingerling' is unsurpassed for potato salad and German-fried potatoes.

INTRODUCTION

The past decade has wrought a remarkable change in gardening — remarkable because it is both renaissance and revolution. Not only has gardening come back in style, it has also radically altered its tools and techniques, indeed its very philosophy and style.

People have suddenly become aware of plants, of their importance to the environment and to man's sense of well-being. More people are gardening than ever before: a recent Gallup Poll showed that 30 million American households now have vegetable gardens . . . indoor gardening or "interior plantscaping" is the fastest-growing hobby in the country . . . the wholesale value of ornamental horticultural crops has tripled in the past ten years, and gardeners today spend over $4 billion annually on plants and supplies.

With this demand has come a vast array of new and improved plants, and new and better ways of growing them. Every major and many a minor flower, from daylilies and marigolds to peonies and penstemons, is being improved in color, form and environmental adaptability. Breeders are also responding to the explosion of interest in fruits and vegetables with a wide-ranging program aimed at developing higher-yielding, earlier-maturing and longer-bearing home garden crops, with greater insect and disease resistance and better flavor and nutritional and keeping qualities. Midget vegetables for the tiniest garden spaces have appeared, as well as new ornamental edibles and edible ornamentals.

In trees and shrubs, selection and breeding are producing an ever-increasing number of superior forms. Gardeners are learning to ask for 'Summershade' Norway maple or 'Purple Splendor' European beech rather than just a maple or beech tree. Finer flowering shrubs and low-maintenance evergreens — especially the fascinating and versatile dwarf types — have become available in almost bewildering variety.

Even more amazing is the new technology of gardening. For the first time, plant scientists are unlocking the "why" and "how" of the basic processes involved in plant-environment relationships, to discover and understand the factors that influence plant growth from day to day, even from moment to moment. They are beginning to place a solid scientific foundation under an art practiced by gardeners since gardening began — the art of growth control. The results are not only improvement in many time-honored horticultural practices through precise manipulation of the biophysical and biochemical activities involved, but also the development of totally new techniques that give almost incredible growth benefits.

The new "accelerated growth techniques," for example, make it possible to grow petunias from seed to flower in five weeks, or to triple the growth rate of trees. Drip irrigation, which maintains optimum moisture in the soil at all times, greatly stimulates plant growth and quality. Chemical growth-regulators speed rooting,

Trilliums are the most universally loved and easily domesticated deep-woods wildlings.

Less than two months after sowing, Pennisetum ruppelii is a handsome fountain of silver-blue leaves and coppery-rose plumes.

inhibit unwanted growth, promote flowering, give larger blooms, control fruit formation and provide numerous other beauty and labor-saving benefits. Slow-release fertilizers, soilless media, safe biological pest controls, mist propagation, aerial fertilization, totally automated climate control in plant rooms and greenhouses — these and many other innovations are bringing new excitement and opportunity for achievement in gardening.

This enormous volume of new information and products, has, however, created a problem. The professional horticulturist finds it increasingly difficult to keep up with the research and discoveries of other professionals. The gardener, with less access to the journals and bulletins that report the latest developments, is at an even greater disadvantage, for this new knowledge filters down very slowly to the general gardening publications. To everyone with more than a casual interest in gardening, rapid and accurate dissemination of information has become a prime need.

As practicing gardeners as well as garden writers and editors, we felt this need daily. The logical way to meet it, it seemed, was to provide an entirely new kind of publication — a modern-day hybrid, "The Avant Gardener," *a news service* X *magazine* X *digest.* Published twice monthly (*P.O. BOX 489, NEW YORK, NY 10028; $10 A YEAR*) in eight-page newsletter form, it has the primary aim of bringing gardeners the first news of new plants, new products, new techniques. But to keep all this data in perspective for

maximum usefulness to the reader, we decided to provide in-depth evaluations of the best of the old and the new, and to evaluate ongoing trends in horticulture (and perhaps even initiate new ones), thus rounding out the full spectrum of newsmagazine function.

Publishing "The Avant Gardener" has brought many pleasures and quite a few surprises; one of the latter is the reason for this book. There has been a constant demand for back copies, with many new readers who began their subscriptions as recently as Volume 6 requesting full sets of issues back through Volume 1. So it became obvious that "getting it all together" in one book might be a useful service. Thus this book is the sum of knowledge presented in "The Avant Gardener" since its first issue, which appeared on October 15, 1968.

Please note that while all sources and prices have been checked for accuracy up to the date of compilation of this book, inflation and rapid changes in the horticultural industry make it impossible to guarantee absolute dependability. It should also be noted that smaller firms and organizations may not be equipped to handle quickly the many inquiries resulting from their being mentioned in this book, and your patience is requested.

— *Thomas and Betty Powell*

ANNUALS

Annual Report

The more sophisticated the gardener, the less he seeks one-season satisfactions. He comes to value annuals as "accessory" plants, to supplement flowers and foliage of more durable disposition. Annuals are indispensable where a fast, prolonged and brilliant summer display is needed, and using them creatively in "annual redecorating" is one of gardening's most exciting challenges.

The list of major annuals that have been spectacularly improved and widely distributed is growing rapidly. Ten years ago Americans relied mainly on a quartet of annuals — marigold, petunia, zinnia and snapdragon. Although these are still tops, in this past decade breeding advances have resulted in a brilliant array of colors and forms in many other annual flowers as well. Growth habits, too, have been improved, to give a much more useful range of plant sizes, hybrid vigor, uniformity, earlier and longer flowering and disease and weather resistance.

So even the novice today has a wide choice. But the serious gardener will seek further, to find gems among the unimproved little-known annuals. These provide new opportunities for adventuring. Many of them are as useful as any of the major annuals for borders, beds, edging, screens, backgrounds, fillers in bulb and perennial areas, containers of all sorts and as sources of summer color in the rock garden and of flowers to cut and dry.

Pots of annuals provide constant or impromptu special-occasion color in a green garden or during lulls in bloom.

Picking Daisies

All-marigold, all-dahlia, even all-daisy bed and container schemes can be fun. In daisies, for example, at least a dozen genera provide a vast variety.

For edging or low massing, there is the 8″ ferny-leaved Dahlborg daisy, *Thymophylla tenuiloba*, blanketed with gold flowers beginning five months after sowing, and the charming blue marguerite, *Felicia bergeriana*. In the 10″ to 12″ range, the Tahoka daisy, *Machaeranthera tanacetifolia*, has yellow-centered lavender-blue flowers; *Charieis heterophylla* is a gold-centered light blue; and white, yellow, orange, bronze or salmon 3″ flowers are supplied by the two African daisies, *Dimorphotheca aurantiaca* and arctotis.

The 15″ Swan River Daisy, *Brachychome iberidifolia*, bears cineraria-like fall flowers in a fine color range — everything except yellow. Two 18″ plants are the gold-centered white lazy daisy, *Aphanostephus skirrobasis*, and sky-blue *Agathaea coelestis*. The 18″ to 24″ star of Texas, *Xanthisma texanum*, has bright yellow daisies.

Trumpeting Datura

Angel's-trumpet is an old-fashioned flower that has, most undeservedly, gone out of vogue. *Datura* is best known for *D. arborea* and *D. suaveolens*, showy large shrubs or small trees in southern gardens, but the annual forms are equally spectacular in flower, and bloom may be enjoyed from July to frost if seed is started early indoors. They are of easiest culture in full sun, many are sweetly scented and the spiny "thornapple" fruits are useful for arrangements.

A species extremely fragrant at night is *D. cornigera*, a 4′ plant with downy branches and long drooping white trumpets. *D. chlorantha*, usually offered as 'Golden Queen,' has beautifully ruffled double yellow flowers in shades of cream

Daturas never fail to attract attention with their huge single or double trumpets and very sweet scent.

From South Africa via South America, gazanias provide large, brilliant blooms in blazing sun and drought.

and yellow. The 3', downy-leaved *D. meteloides* has erect, single 8" rose-tinted white blooms, and should not be confused with *D. metel (D. fastuosa, D. cornucopia)*, which can grow to 5', with 8" leaves and 7" single or double flowers in white, yellow, blue, lavender or even varicolored.

Since seed is frequently offered in mixed colors only, save the seed of the plants you like best for next year. A source is GEO. W. PARK SEED CO. (GREENWOOD, SC 29647).

New Gayer Gazanias

The most popular bedding plant in South America is the South African gazania. There are about two dozen species, of which the best known is the coppery-gold *Gazania splendens*, grown occasionally as a perennial in California. But few gardeners know that gazanias can be grown as annuals anywhere, and that new strains of magnificent coloring are becoming available.

Few low-growing plants are as valuable for hot, dry sites. Given full sun and sandy soil that drains perfectly, gazanias bear large daisy flowers lavishly all summer on leafless stems rising above rosettes of narrow gray-green leaves. Plants set

12" apart on centers rapidly make solid groundcovers. Lifted before frost, the plants can be carried over in a greenhouse, and basal cuttings are easily rooted in sand. Seed may be sown any time of the year for pot plants.

Two exciting strains are the 8" 'Fire Emerald,' with 3½" flowers in shades and combinations of gold, pink and red, often with emerald green center rings, and the even more striking new 6" 'Sunshine Hybrids,' bearing 5" flowers, each with as many as 5 sharply defined colors. Both of these are now available from GEO. W. PARK SEED CO. (GREENWOOD, SC 29647). The first double gazania, bright yellow 'Moonglow,' has just been introduced by the wholesale SELECT NURSERIES (BREA, CA 92621), which reports that in California established plants bloom 365 days a year.

The Irene Geraniums

Some of the older varieties of zonal geraniums are fully as meritorious as any recent introductions. In an English gardening magazine, the Irene strain is hailed as "outstanding — exceptionally free-flowering, with a strong constitution and a natural free-branching habit, and perpetual flowering."

The original Irene, a beautiful soft red, was selected for its hybrid vigor from a large batch of seedlings by Charles Behringer, a grower in Warren, Ohio, 25 years ago, and was named for his wife. Irene "sports" readily, and David Adgate, who took over Mr. Behringer's nursery after his death, introduced many fine color variations. Some of the best are 'Dark Red,' 'Rose,' 'Salmon,' deep pink 'Penny,' white-centered rose-pink 'Genie,' 'Orange Fizz,' velvet red 'Show Girl,' delicate pink 'Party Dress,' white 'Modesty,'

scarlet 'Toyon' and the unusual orange and scarlet 'Lollipop' and 'Jolly Roger.'

All are compact plants bearing large heads of semi-double flowers on strong stems. Many are available from pelargonium specialists such as WILSON BROTHERS (ROACHDALE, IN 46172). A special value of the Irenes is their durability as cut flowers.

Introducing Meadowfoam

While studying ornamental plants for possible agronomic and industrial uses, the Agricultural Research Service has found a beautiful hardy annual that should be widely grown. A native of California and Oregon, meadowfoam, *Limnanthes douglasii*, grows to 7″ high with a spreading habit, and bears masses of showy white and yellow flowers.

Plant physiologist J. J. Higgins of the AGRICULTURAL MARKETING SERVICE (6525 BELCREST ROAD, HYATTSVILLE, MD 20782) reports that seed of meadowfoam is the best known source of an oil that can be converted into chemicals which can substitute for the recently banned sperm whale oil in some of its uses. Besides being a potential cash crop for farmers, it is both a good bee plant and a fine garden plant for moist situations in full sun.

A lovely new annual, meadowfoam is a northwestern native that produces masses of bright, fragrant flowers.

Annuals 3

In mild winter areas such as Washington, D.C., meadowfoam should be planted in the fall for vigorous growth and heavy flowering. In colder areas it is best sown in spring.

A source is CLYDE ROBIN (BOX 2091, CASTRO VALLEY, CA 94546; CATALOG $1).

Impatiens to be impatient for

The exciting new impatiens collected by the Agricultural Research Service–Longwood Foundation plant exploration of New Guinea in 1970 are greatly enhancing the variety and versatility of this popular bedding and window garden plant. Many have very large flowers in a wide range of colors; one group has marvelously colored and variegated foliage, and a number are unusually sun tolerant. The ARS PLANT GENETICS AND GERMPLASM RESEARCH INSTITUTE (BELTSVILLE, MD 20705) is rapidly releasing these to breeders.

The new Star Series of variegated-foliage Cyclone Hybrids developed by Iowa State University is an example of the fine impatiens of the future. 'Star Fire' has broad splashes of bright yellow to gold in the leaf centers, and bears bright orange flowers in light shade. 'Star Burst' is similar, but has cyclamen-purple flowers and grows well in sun or shade. Two that bloom from late summer through autumn are 'Star Dazzler,' with gold leaf centers and crimson flowers, and 'Star Dancer,' which has rose flowers and rose-pink accents on the leaves; both do well in light shade and are excellent for hanging baskets.

Creeping Zinnia

An unusually versatile annual is the creeping or trailing zinnia. As a groundcover or bedding, edging or rockery plant, *Sanvitalia procumbens* is neat and compact, growing no taller than 6″. The unobtrusive foliage is covered with 1″ bright golden double flowers with dark centers. In sunny, dry situations, it blooms lavishly all summer.

The new 'Gold Braid,' introduced by BODGER SEEDS (EL MONTE, CA 91734), is highly recommended for hanging baskets as well as edgings.

Beautiful Butterfly Flower

A delightful annual with an unfortunate reputation for poor performance under high temperatures is schizanthus, the poor man's orchid or butterfly flower.

However, botanist Alex D. Hawkes tells us he grows schizanthus successfully in his Coconut Grove, Florida, garden, "on the verge of the tropics," both in a bed of rich soil under a mango tree and in pots on his patio. And professional gardeners say that schizanthus needs only daily mist spraying to give extended bloom in hot weather.

New hybrids, including some marvelous ones from Germany, are extremely floriferous, range from dwarf to 24″ tall, and offer fabulous color — white, gold, crimson, salmon, violet. As Dr. Hawkes says, "With their wondrous fringed complexity — they do look much like tiny butterflies if one examines them closely — these unique flowers form a truly glorious addition to any garden or patio."

Two sources of the newest hybrids are GEO. W. PARK SEED CO. (GREENWOOD, SC 29647) and BURNETT BROTHERS, INC. (92 CHAMBERS STREET, NEW YORK, NY 10007).

Jewel of a Daisy

South Africa has yielded a stunning array of plants for American gardens. Growers' trade publications have recently called attention to

An example of improvement in neglected annuals is heliotrope 'Iowa,' Dr. Griffith J. Buck's new heat-resistant variety of the fragrant blue-flowered old favorite.

venidiums, South African jewel daisy or monarch-of-the-veldt, suggesting that they are ideal as a cut-flower crop. We think venidiums are also a superb annual deserving greater notice by gardeners.

Their flowers are very long lasting, and have the peculiarity of opening in the morning and closing at night even when cut. Best of the 18 known species is *V. fastuosum*, 30″ tall, with 4″ to 5″ flowers. The ray florets are glowing orange-banded purple at the base, and the disk is purplish-black. Hybrids are now available, in yellow, orange, salmon, cerise and buff.

Venidiums thrive in hot, sunny, dry situations. Rich soil is not required, but good drainage is essential. Seed a year old, a florists' magazine reports, will germinate better than fresh seed. Venidiums also make a fine greenhouse pot plant.

A source is GEO. W. PARK SEED CO. (GREENWOOD, SC 29647).

Versatile Annual Vinca

The pure white variety of Madagascar periwinkle, *Vinca rosea*, is a marvelously useful annual, says Mrs. J. Folsom Paul of Pennsylvania's Longwood Gardens.

Besides extensive bedding and border use, Longwood has interplanted this everbloomer in new groundcover beds of Bowles' vinca, to give color while the cover is becoming established, and also used it in large terra-cotta pots combined with blue 'Sky Magic' and pink 'Peach Tart' petunias, plus 'Amethyst' and coral 'Delight' verbenas. It does well in sun or part shade, will stand heat, dryness and considerable air pollution, and grows to 18″ (but can be kept lower by pinching).

Though perhaps not so versatile for color blending, the 18″ pink and red varieties and rosy-pink-with-red-eye 'Twinkles' are also delightful. The 10″ Little Series is equally colorful, from 'Little Pinkie' and white 'Little Blanche' to baby-pink, red-eyed 'Little Delicata' and glistening white, crimson-centered 'Little Bright Eye.' A dwarf creeping form, 'Rose Carpet,' is excellent for window boxes, hanging baskets and carpeting. All are available from DEGIORGI COMPANY (COUNCIL BLUFFS, IA 51501; CATALOG 25¢). For bloom by Memorial Day, seed should be started very early indoors.

Trying Wallflowers

Both the nomenclature and the culture of the much-desired wallflowers confuse even veteran gardeners. The true wallflower, *Cheiranthus cheiri*, prized in Europe for its lovely bloom in daffodil season, grows from 12″ to 30″, with showy spikes of very fragrant velvety ivory, yellow, yellow-brown, crimson or maroon flowers that resemble stock. In mild climes, it is grown as a perennial, the seed sown early in spring for bloom the following spring. In the North, wallflower is treated as a biennial, the seed started in spring to early summer, then carried over in a coldframe to be set out in spring, but some strains can be used as annuals, blooming in five months from sowing.

New hybrids of Dimorphotheca aurantiaca produce big glistening daisies in many colors.

The Siberian wallflower, commonly sold as *C. allionii*, is properly *Erysimum asperum*. It has fragrant, brilliant orange flowers, grows from 12″ to 24″, and is of easy culture as a perennial in the South, as a biennial or hardy annual in the North.

Wallflowers cannot stand excessive moisture in any season — sharp drainage and good air circulation are essential.

Reviewing Rarities

From our own experience, we would like to suggest a baker's dozen of rare, little-known, or undeservedly forgotten annuals worthy of wider use (the catalogs of PARK, DEGIORGI, HUDSON and foreign seedsmen offer many more):

Alonsoa warscewiczi, Peruvian mask flower — to 36″, brilliant red flowers in terminal clusters; var. *compacta* is 12″.

Anagallis coerulea, blue pimpernel — 9″, with 1″ indigo blue star flowers; 18″ *A. linifolia* is blue and blue-red.

Asclepias curassavica, Brazilian butterfly flower — glowing heads of gold, orange, or red-bronze on 30″ stems.

Bartonia aurea, blazing star — 18″; spectacular fragrant night-to-noon bloomer, yellow petals and long stamens.

Centratherum 'Manaos Beauty' — 24″; a sophisticated thistle with blue-green pineapple-scented foliage, 1″ lavender-blue flowers.

Diascia barberae, twin-spur — 12″; with dainty yellow-throated coral-pink snapdragon-like flowers in long terminal clusters.

Lavatera trimestris, tree mallow — 36″; very showy and easy to grow; 'Alba' is white, 'Loveliness' is rich rose, new compact tetraploid 'Tanagra' is rosy-pink.

Linum grandiflorum, annual flax — 12″ to 24″; a neglected beauty with white, glowing red or blue flowers for many months.

Oxypetalum coeruleum, southern star — arching sprays of lacquered turquoise star flowers from June to October on 15″ plants.

Phacelia, bluebell — 8″ to 30″; with racemes of white, bright blue or lavender flowers, very attractive to bees.

Saponaria vaccaria, soapwort — 30″; with airy cymes of satiny white, pink or rose blooms; very popular in Europe.

Senecio elegans — 24″; beautiful feathery foliage, heads of multicolored flowers, double in some varieties.

Silene pendula — a charming 10″ spreader, now available in 6″ dwarf forms with double flowers in many colors.

Use annuals imaginatively: prosaic petunias become poetic when grown in tiers of baskets for a summer wedding.

ANNUAL RESOURCES

"Annuals," by James Underwood Crockett, Time-Life Encyclopedia of Gardening ($6.95)

"Flower Gardening: A Primer," by James W. Wilson (Van Nostrand Reinhold, $7.95)

"Growing Flowering Annuals," USDA Home and Garden Bulletin 91 (10¢ from Superintendent of Documents, Washington, DC 20402)

"How to Grow and Use Annuals" (Sunset Books, Menlo Park, CA 94025; $1.95)

"The Picture Book of Annuals," by Arno and Irene Nehrling (Hearthside, $5.95)

ANNUAL SOURCES

Burnett Brothers, Inc., 92 Chambers Street, New York, NY 10007

W. Atlee Burpee Co., Philadelphia, PA 19132; Clinton, IA 52732; Riverside, CA 92504

Carter's Tested Seeds Ltd., Raynes Park, London, S.W. 20, England

DeGiorgi Company, Inc., Council Bluffs, IA 51501; catalog 35¢

Samuel Dobie & Son Ltd., 11 Grosvenor Square, Chester, England

Allen L. Goodwin, "Milford," Mangalore, Tasmania 7406, Australia

Joseph Harris Co., Moreton Farm, Rochester, NY 14624

J. L. Hudson, Seedsman, Box 1058, Redwood City, CA 94064; catalog 50¢

Jacks Nurseries, Meyerton, P.O. Box 81, Transvaal, South Africa

Kitagawa Seed Co., 356 West Taylor Street, San Jose, CA 95110

Geo. W. Park Seed Co., Greenwood, SC 29647

Pellett Gardens, Atlantic, IA 50022

Stokes Seeds, Inc., Box 548, Buffalo, NY 14240

Sutton & Sons, Ltd., Reading, Berks., England

Thompson & Morgan, Box 24, Somerdale, NJ 08083

W. J. Unwin Ltd., Histon, Cambridge, England

Vilmorin-Andrieux, Service Exportation, Boite Postale No. 30-01, 75-Paris-R.P., France

PERENNIALS

Perennial Prospectus

For a time, it seemed perennials were becoming obsolete. With a few major exceptions, such as daylilies, iris and phlox, the use of hardy herbaceous perennials was steadily declining in modern gardens.

This, of course, was part of a general trend. The recreation revolution of the fifties and sixties resulted in severe competition for leisure time and money, and gardening — especially its more dedicated aspects — was bypassed in favor of other activities. The public sought easy, inexpensive, long-blooming, low-maintenance plants, and fewer and fewer nurseries produced perennials, in diminishing variety.

Today, however, the new environmental awareness has brought with it a powerful resurgence of horticulture. Homeowners are developing a real interest in gardening and, most importantly, the willingness to acquire the knowledge necessary to garden well. The educational effort undertaken by many horticultural and some commercial groups is fostering rapid maturing in new gardeners, and with this growth, the gardener inevitably turns to perennials as the most fascinating and dependable source of flowering beauty in the garden.

Perennials Go Places

In their classic use, the herbaceous border, perennials present one of gardening's great challenges. A fine perennial border, which calls for a mating of artistic talent and horticultural skill, is the mark of a real gardener. This is as true in today's small gardens as it was when the concept originated a century ago in England and reached its zenith in magnificent borders hundreds of feet long and proportionately wide.

Even in much reduced scale, a border is still considered the best way to display perennials. The smallest property can accommodate a perennial border 2' to 3' wide along a fence, walk or driveway. And a narrow border can still offer the diversity of flowers — airy sprays, solid mounds, spires, bold single blooms, in all color combinations — and the succession of bloom that gives a perennial border unequaled charm and mystery.

A narrow border is also easy to work on, without heavy expenditure of time and labor. (A most often overlooked advantage of perennials over annuals is the fact that work with perennials is spread out through the season, rather than concentrated in spring when there are so many other demanding tasks.)

In addition to the pure perennial border, another rising concept is the mixed hardy border advocated 75 years ago by Gertrude Jekyll and William Robinson. This is simply a wider border, perhaps 6' to 10' — or even an "island bed" planting — that mingles small trees, dwarf to medium evergreen and flowering shrubs, perennials, bulbs and groundcovers. As a general rule, over the season the largest amount and length of bloom is provided by the perennials. These integrated herbaceous-woody groupings illustrate an ideal every gardener should hold as a prime objective — the elimination of artificial segregations of plants that fragment so many small gardens and weaken the concept of gardening as a true art form.

Perennials have other important uses. Low-growing types in complementary or contrasting colors add much to the charm of bulb groups. The rich blues of ajuga, white arabis and iberis, golden *Alyssum saxatile*, the pinks, crimsons and purples of aubretia, and white-blue-lilac found in *Phlox divaricata* and *P. subulata* are perfect foils for dramatic spring bulbs. Some perennials are ideal for massing — not only daylilies and chrysanthemums, but also such unusuals as glowing orange *Asclepias tuberosa* and the spectacular, long-blooming *Rudbeckia speciosa* 'Goldsturm,' which can be as rewarding as any annuals when planted in bold sweeps.

There is no corner of the garden to which perennials will not add substance. Many thrive in light to medium shade, and the less flamboyant of these blend well with wildflowers. Indeed, heuchera, helleborus, *Iberis sempervirens*, pulmonaria, meadow rue and others often appear so "natural" in woodlands they are thought of as wildflowers. Some border perennials make fine groundcovers — *Bergenia cordifolia* and *Cerato-stigma plumbaginoides*, for example. Others serve as focal points in patio gardens or along walls. Still others beautifully solve the problems of slopes or wet or arid spots, and some, as Sylvia Crowe suggests in her superb *"GARDEN DESIGN"* (HEARTHSIDE, $8.95), "can be grown in grass as they were in medieval times."

Border Lines

Much of the excitement of creating an herbaceous border lies in its great flexibility of design. In form, placement and plants, the contemporary border follows few rigid rules and allows fullest expression of the gardener's taste.

Where space permits, the traditional solid background of a hedge, shrubbery or a wall helps set off the flowers and serves as a windbreak to protect taller plants. But actually the modern border can be sited in any level area that has adequate light and drainage. It may be backed by an open fence or screen, or it may follow the property line, border a terrace, walk or drive, or serve as a divider between public and private areas of the garden.

A general rule, unless the garden is very spacious or formal, is to avoid a ruler-straight front edge. A gentle to bold sweeping curve — easily laid out with a hose — is best even along a fence, and the border can taper as it recedes from the main viewing point if an effect of distance is desired. A border outlined with bricks or flat stones set flush with the soil is better than a steeply cut lawn verge which must be trimmed after mowing. The edge will look neat if tidy plants like nepeta, iberis, *Dianthus plumarius* or other edging plants are used.

Bearing 2″ clearest gold flowers, the native Celandine poppy is one of the finest minimum-care perennials for light shade.

Miniature replicas of the florists' tender cyclamen, hardy species flower in spring, summer or fall in light to deep shade.

Even the advanced gardener finds it advantageous to plan a border to scale on graph paper. The hardest task — organizing the selection of plants — will be simplified if only two main "mass forms" are considered: drifts and clumps. Drifts are elongated groupings of a plant that flow more or less at an angle through sections of the border. Clumps consist of circular groupings of a variety, or a single large plant such as a peony. The length of drifts and the diameter of clumps, as well as their heights, should be varied for best effects, and the dimensions should always be in proportion to the overall size of the border.

In a narrow border, plant height is best limited to two-thirds the width of the border, e.g., no plants taller than 4' in a border 6' wide. Height lines should be broken up, too: letting some tall plants extend forward into the medium-height groups, with a few recessed clumps or drifts leading the eye back into the border, gives a much more natural effect than a "step" profile.

Arts and Wiles

The most logical way to choose plants is first by period of bloom, then by color and finally by height. This information is not difficult to glean from books on perennials and catalogs.

The only restrictions on any given plant will be environmental — a lack of ability to stand winter or summer temperature extremes, or special soil, moisture or light needs — and any limits the gardener must place on the time available for maintenance. Perennials demanding a minimum of care are comprehensively evaluated in a three-part series, *"PERENNIALS FOR LOW MAINTENANCE GARDENING,"* in the January, March and May *1971 "ARNOLDIA" (ARNOLD ARBORETUM, JAMAICA PLAIN, MA 02130; 60¢ EACH ISSUE).*

The enormous color range in perennials, plus their easy movability if a disharmony occurs, gives the gardener great latitude in choosing and combining colors. A border in tones of the same color can be effective, or several closely related colors may be used, or the border may be made wildly exuberant with a vast variety of hues in one or more seasons. The objective is a balanced composition in every season, with no section being at any time too heavily weighted with color, and the bloom so distributed that it always makes a pleasing pattern through the bed.

Many gardening books give excellent lists of compatible colors; these plus a garden notebook and camera are invaluable for planning and revising color schemes. For real floral artistry, it

Delphiniums thrive in the protective microclimate afforded by a wall, which also serves to set off their beauty.

is perhaps more important to consider intensity than hue — light tones placed near dark ones, or contrasting palest tones with the most intense, can give new interest and life to the border. Some colors are suitable only as dramatic accents: deep pure red clashes with almost everything (unless softened by dark green foliage), yet properly used it confers strength and depth.

White flowers and gray foliage are indispensable as separators of conflicting colors. Shasta daisies and white phlox and veronica, and silvery-leaved nepeta, dusty millers (artemisia, senecio, certain centaureas), alyssum, *Cerastium tomentosum*, lavender, echinops and *Stachys lanata* are some of the best for unifying opposite colors and giving homogeneity to the picture.

As a gardener grows adept at producing constant color harmony in the border, he becomes more aware of the roles played by plant forms and foliage. Good foliage is obviously vital in plants with short blooming periods. Peonies and gas plant, *Dictamnus albus*, are supreme in this respect. But achillea, eryngium, *Euphorbia polychroma* and many others with distinctive forms and foliage — airy and delicate, or strong and solid — are wonderfully useful for creating interest. So are ornamental grasses, roses, even handsome-foliaged vegetables like broccoli and asparagus.

Borders with strong hedge or shrub backgrounds will benefit from "buttressing," as the English call it, with solid-form or large-leaved shrubs of varying size brought forward occasionally into the border.

Two excellent aids to designing with perennials are *"THE NEGS FISHER COLOR CHART,"* the simplest and handiest color chart for garden work, used officially by several plant societies, and available for $1.50 unmounted or $3 mounted, from CHARLES T. BASLE (11 ROCKRIDGE ROAD, WALTHAM, MA 02154); and *"SEQUENCE OF BLOOM OF PERENNIALS, BIENNIALS AND BULBS,"* EXTENSION BULLETIN 1190, very helpful for planning continuous bloom; free to New York State residents, 15¢ to others, from COOPERATIVE EXTENSION, NEW YORK STATE COLLEGE OF AGRICULTURE, CORNELL UNIVERSITY (ITHACA, NY 14850).

Haute Flowerage

Searching for new perennials — new at least to the gardener — is one of gardening's most rewarding activities. While it is perfectly possible to build a fine border using only tried-and-true perennials, either alone or in a mixed border with annuals, biennials and tender bulbs, the greatest richness of beauty is achieved by going beyond the popular, by exploring the myriad variety of "forgotten" perennials. Many of these are as dependable, and some also as long-lived and long-blooming, as the garden mainstays. Others reputed to be "touchy" are often far less so if proper attention is paid to their basic needs. And quite a few have been improved by selection and breeding — though these rarely receive the publicity and dissemination given improved varieties of the major perennials or almost any annual.

Many gardeners expand their perennial horizons even farther, experimenting with nonborder perennials in the border. Wildflowers, rock garden plants like jasione and erysimum, even weeds such as the bonesets (*Eupatorium*), can add new dimensions to the border.

Many of the less popular perennials could be greatly improved in "stamina," ease of culture and adaptability to varied conditions. Numerous perennials are "temperamental," says horticulturist John P. Baumgardt, because their tolerance of our harsher climates was bred out of the native American species by European hybridizers working in a more equable climate. Breeders should go back to the original species and "re-improve" them to suit our many macroclimates.

A point that deserves repeated emphasis is that long-term success with perennials, just as with woody plants, depends upon providing a proper root environment. Liberal additions to at least 18″ depth of organic matter — compost, peat, rotted manure, old sod — and a high-phosphorus fertilizer in the lower levels, plus maintaining a coarsely granulated mulch of chips, bark, hulls or ground corncobs, will considerably enhance the growth, flowering and persistence of perennials.

'Moonlight' is a new anthemis that produces great numbers of 2 ½″ pale yellow daisies on 12″ plants.

CONNOISSEUR'S
PERENNIALS

Early

Adonis vernalis, pheasant's eye — 18″; ferny foliage and 3″ yellow flowers in earliest spring.

Amsonia tabernaemontana — 18″ to 30″; starry blue, stands shade.

Armeria, thrift — 6″ to 15″; white or pink globular heads.

Baptisia australis, false indigo — 4′; handsome foliage, blue pea flowers.

Bletilla hyacinthina, hardy orchid — 12″; amethyst blooms.

Brunnera macrophylla (Anchusa myosotidiflora), Siberian bugloss — 12″; purest blue.

Campanula glomerata 'Joan Elliott' — 18″; a new fine deep violet.

Chrysogonum virginianum, golden star — 8″; fine carpeter in light shade, 1″ bright yellow star flowers from May to September.

Cyclamen — hardy species such as *C. libanoticum, C. atkinsi, C. coum* and *C. repandum* bear white to red flowers in shade from February to May; other species bloom in summer and fall.

Doronicum 'Spring Beauty' — 2′; new double golden leopardbane from Germany.

Eremurus, foxtail lily — 3′ to 6′; superb white, yellow, orange or salmon spires in Shelford Hybrids, rose to cream in Ruiter's Hybrids; plant in early autumn, needs excellent drainage, give deep porous winter mulch.

Euphorbia polychroma, cushion spurge — 18″; mounded plant with large rose-shaped yellow bracts, crimson autumn foliage and seed capsules.

Helleborus orientalis, Lenten rose — easiest to grow of the hellebores, evergreen leaves to 12″ wide, 18″ stems bearing 3″ multicolored speckled flowers; finest colors are found in the Millet Hybrids.

Omphalodes verna, blue-eyed Mary — 8″; electric blue forget-me-nots.

Polemonium, Jacob's ladder — 12″ to 18″; white or blue, stands shade.

Primula auricula, auricula primrose — 8″; rich gold, crimson, lilac and pastel flowers, easy to grow in part shade.

Pulmonaria, lungwort — 10″; blue or rare scarlet-salmon, likes shade.

Saponaria ocymoides, soapwort — 1'; showy pink dianthus-like flowers.

Stylophorum diphyllum, Celandine poppy — 12" to 18"; bright yellow flowers, needs shade and moisture.

Trillium, wakerobin — 5" to 18"; white to yellow, red and rose-purple, one of the finest for cool, moist, deep shade.

Trollius, globe flower — 2' to 3'; brilliant gold to orange buttercups.

Midseason

Achillea, yarrow — good for hot, dry, infertile sites; silvery foliage, flat-topped flowers to 6" across; best are 18" rosy-red 'Fire King,' 24" yellow 'Moonshine,' and 36" yellow 'Coronation Gold'; white-flowered *A. ptarmica* varieties tend to be invasive.

Alchemilla vulgaris, Lady's mantle — 10"; soft gray-green leaves, clusters of tiny greenish-yellow flowers on forked stems.

Anchusa 'Royal Blue' — 3'; finest summer forget-me-not.

Anthemis, golden marguerite — 24" to 42"; big white or yellow daisies.

Aster frikarti — 'Wonder of Staffa' is one of the longest-flowering perennials, bearing large lavender daisies from June through October.

Astilbe — 6" to 36"; ever-growing number of fine white, pink, red, lilac forms.

Callirhoe involucrata, poppy mallow — 8"; pink to crimson.

Chelone lyoni, red turtlehead — 12"; 2" rose-purple blooms, likes some shade.

Coreopsis 'Baby Sun' — 16", and 'Sunburst' — 30"; brilliant gold daisies.

Dianthus gratianapolitanus (D. caesius), cheddar pink — 6"; mat-forming, fringed pink flowers, much longer lived than other perennial dianthus.

Dicentra eximia, summer-flowering bleeding heart — 24"; ferny foliage, rosy flowers, thrives in full sun to heavy shade.

Digitalis mertonensis — 3' to 4'; a perennial foxglove, strawberry-red.

Echinops 'Taplow Blue,' superb steely-blue globular thistles, 4'.

Erigeron, summer aster — 18"; many showy and double varieties in pink to purple.

Eryngium, sea holly — 1' to 2'; blue thistle heads over spiny leaves.

Filipendula hexapetala — 15"; airy heads of double white flowers.

Gaillardia 'Sun Dance' is a new 8" bicolor blanket flower.

Galega officinalis hartlandi, goat's rue — 30"; striking white and lavender blooms.

Geranium, cranesbill — 3" to 24"; many fine pink to blue species and cultivars.

Geum, avens — 8" to 30"; new hardier varieties in yellow to orange and scarlet.

Helianthus multiflorus, perennial sunflower — 4'; several double, golden, named varieties.

Heliopsis 'Gold Greenheart'—36", gold "sunflowers" with green centers.

Hesperis matronalis, sweet rocket — 30"; heavy heads of white or lilac.

Hibiscus — hardy giant hybrids produce 10" to 12" blooms on 3' to 6' plants, best grown as single specimens in the mixed border.

Inula, sunray — 1' to 4'; graceful yellow or orange daisies.

Kniphofia, red-hot poker — 24″ to 40″; new hardier whites, yellows, bicolors.

Limonium latifolium 'Violetta,' an 18″ sea lavender with violet-blue heads.

Linum 'Heavenly Blue' — 15″, longest-blooming, bluest flax.

Lychnis, campion — 12″ to 30″; white to fiery heads.

Lysimachia, loosestrife — 6″ to 36″; white and yellow.

Lythrum, purple loosestrife — 1′ to 5′; now in bright pink to purple Morden Series and others.

Malva alcea, vervain mallow — 4′; brilliant pink.

Monarda didyma, bergamot or beebalm — 30″ to 40″; brilliant red 'Adam' is new addition to fine varieties such as 'Croftway Pink,' 'Snow White,' 'Violet Queen.'

Oenothera, evening primrose — 10″ Tetragona Hybrids are very free-flowering.

Penstemon, beardtongue — 20″ to 30″; spectacular new hybrids in white, rose, purple (an excellent "Manual for Beginners" is available from THE AMERICAN PENSTEMON SOCIETY, MRS. F. J. SCHMEECKLE, SECRETARY, ROUTE 2, BOX 61, COZAD, NB 69130).

Primula japonica, candelabra primrose — 2′ to 3′; white to crimson flowers, thrives with light shade, excellent drainage, abundant moisture; many fine species, also superb Bartley Strain and Pagoda Hybrids.

Scabiosa caucasica, blue bonnet — 2′; needs high humus, lime, fertilizer.

Silene stellata, starry campion — 10″; white, one of the best of several white- or red-flowered perennial campions.

Thermopsis caroliniana, false lupine — 3′; long yellow spikes.

Tunica saxifraga rosea, coatflower — 9″; masses of dainty pink flowers.

Yucca, Spanish bayonet — dramatic plants with showy panicles of greenish-white to reddish bell flowers on 3′ to 6′ stalks; *Y. glauca* and *Y. elata* are hardy to southern Minnesota.

Late

Aconitum, monkshood — 2′ to 6′; white, yellow, rich blue hooded blooms.

Anaphalis yedoensis, 2′, white pearly everlasting.

Anemone japonica, fall windflower — 3′; showy white, pink, rose or lavender buttercup flowers above beautiful 3-leaflet leaves.

Asclepias tuberosa, butterfly weed — 2′; gives dazzling display in the driest summer, flat clusters of brilliant orange flowers.

Aster — 3′ to 6′ New York (*A. novi-belgi*) and New England (*A. novae-angliae*) asters, 18″ to 30″. *A. amellus* and others in many colors are invaluable for autumn beauty.

Boltonia latisquama nana, 2′ to 3′ form of the 4′ to 8′ giant aster.

Cichorium intybus, chicory — 3′ to 5′; sky-blue, a wildling that is much finer under cultivation.

Cimicifuga simplex, 3′, and *C. racemosa,* 6′, dramatic creamy fairy candles.

Clematis heracleaefolia davidiana — 30″; blue, and other herbaceous clematis.

Echinacea 'Robert Bloom' is a stunning new carmine-purple coneflower.

Gypsophila oldhamiana — 42″; rose-pink, finest late baby's breath.

Helenium autumnale — 1′ to 4′; glowing yellow, copper, mahogany daisies, more carefree than mums, and rivaling them in beauty.

Liatris, gayfeather — 18″ to 72″; striking flower spikes, many new white, pink, purple varieties.

Lobelia cardinalis, cardinal flower — 2′ to 4′; brilliant red flowers, stands sun if kept moist.

Meconopsis baileyi, Tibetan blue poppy — 3′ to 4′; brilliant blue flowers, must have coolness and deep, moist, woodsy soil; a challenge to grow: said the late Mrs. Clement Houghton, "The woman who grew meconopsis/Was asked to give a synopsis/How can I? she cried/When all of them died/Do more than describe their autopsies?"

Salvia pitcheri — 3′; a gentian-blue late sage.

Sidalcea, miniature hollyhock — 2′ to 3′; beautiful rose-pink.

Solidago, goldenrod — 18″ to 36″; fine named varieties in light to deepest yellow.

Thallictrum rochebrunianum — 3′ to 4′; a late meadow rue, lilac-red and yellow sprays.

Primroses, trilliums and other shade perennials around a pool create a tiny suburban woodland garden.

FOLIAGE PERENNIALS

Oriental Splendor

The ornamental values of bamboos are duplicated by no other plants. Their evergreen character and delicate supple beauty recommend them for screens and accents (some are marvelously handsome against walls), and a number of varieties are ideal for hedges or groundcovers. And we note increasing availability of subzero-hardy types for northern gardens.

Yellowgroove and golden bamboos (*Phyllostachys aureosulcata* and *P. aurea*) are hardy to at least −20°, and grow up to 30′. *P. nigra*, the black bamboo, is very unusual, with thin-walled but extremely strong canes that turn ebony-black their second year. At the other extreme of size are several species of *Sasa* ranging from 10″ to 3′. These and others are offered by PACIFIC BAMBOO GARDENS (4754 VISTA LANE, SAN DIEGO, CA 92116; CATALOG 35¢) and PALETTE GARDENS (26 WEST ZION HILL ROAD, QUAKERTOWN, PA 18951; CATALOG 50¢).

Bamboos require a deep, fertile soil with considerable organic matter, and all except black bamboo prefer full sun. Ample moisture, plus complete fertilizer in early and late spring and late summer, are important, as is a 12″ mulch of loose material applied after initial sprouting of a new planting. Planting depth is 1″ for dwarf types, 4″ for others. The rhizomes of runner-type bamboos often need confining by edging. Usually several years are required after planting for root development before the canes begin to attain their characteristic rapidity of growth. New canes are sent up if the old are killed in severe winters.

Most bamboos make fine pot plants, and *Phyllostachys aurea* is the best for bonsai culture. The genus *Phyllostachys* also provides the finest edible shoots to harvest in spring, for parboiling and then sautéeing or using in Oriental dishes.

Getting Cacti Down Cold

Cacti grow in Brooklyn — and in South Dakota. It's quite a revelation to find an impressive hardy cactus garden in a New York City borough (it belongs to a former President of the New York Cactus and Succulent Society), and an equally stunning collection at Claude Barr's Prairie Gem Ranch in Smithwick, South Dakota, where a temperature of −40° is frequently experienced.

Dozens of prickly pears (*Opuntia*), with bright green or purple pads and yellow, pink, carmine or red flowers, thrive in these gardens. "Ball" types such as *Coryphantha vivipara, Echinocereus viridiflorus* and *Neobesseya missouriensis* grow and bloom along with the "fish hook" *Sclerocactus whipplei* and "barrel" *Pediocactus simpsonii*. The variety of size, form and flower is amazing.

A superb garden can be created almost anywhere in northern areas by growing many of these with other desert-type and succulent plants such as yucca, sedums and sempervivums. Besides full sun and air circulation, their most absolute requirement is perfect drainage. Plant them on a hillside, in a raised bed or in a ground bed prepared with 2″ of gravel at the bottom, overlaid with 1″ of half-rotted compost, and topped with 6″ of sand. Mr. Barr advises adding some limestone chips and dust to the sand, and mulching

With full sun and perfect drainage, hardy opuntias give spectacular bloom far in the North.

with gravel or stone chips to reflect heat and light onto the plants.

A source of hardy cacti is PALETTE GARDENS (WEST ZION HILL ROAD, QUAKERTOWN, PA 18951; CATALOG 50¢). More details can be found in "SUCCULENT PLANTS," HANDBOOK 43 OF THE BROOKLYN BOTANIC GARDEN (BROOKLYN, NY 11225; $1.50).

Ferns for Sunny Sites

Ferns have a greater range of adaptability than most gardeners realize. Contemporary landscaping trends have given new prominence to these perennials of pleasing pattern and lowest maintenance — indeed, they have become recognized as an indispensable "supporting cast" in the rock garden, woodland and shaded foundation planting.

But the possibilities of ferns for sunny situations are generally overlooked. With ample moisture, many will stand more sun than they are usually given. Quite a few actually can thrive in full sunlight. The first group includes such dependables as the evergreen maidenhair spleenwort, *Asplenium trichomanes;* cinnamon fern, *Osmunda cinnamomea,* so useful for bold effects; and the lady fern, *Athyrium felix-femina,* connoisseurs of which hail the new crested English cultivars such as 12″ 'Christulatum' and 8″ 'Acrocladon' — the latter one of the most beautiful of all ferns.

In the highly sun-tolerant class are sensitive fern, *Onoclea sensibilis,* a luxuriant grower to 18″ in full sun; the hay-scented fern, *Dennstaedtia punctilobula,* 24″, adaptable to almost any soil and moisture conditions and an excellent groundcover for rough banks; the fascinating native climbing fern, *Lygodium palmatum,* an evergreen which climbs over low bushes in bright, moist, very acid situations; the dramatic Japanese painted fern, *Athyrium goeringianum*, to 24″, with wine-red and gray-green foliage; two cliff ferns, *Woodsia ilvensis* and *W. obtusa*, very easy to grow on dry rock ledges or walls; bracken and ostrich ferns, *Pteridium aquilinum* and *Pteretis nodulosa*, both too rampant-spreading for small gardens but perfect for waste areas; and two for very moist locations, the Virginia chain fern, *Woodwardia virginica*, 36″, and marsh fern, *Thelypteris palustris*, 24″.

A source is LOUNSBERRY GARDENS (BOX 135, OAKFORD, IL 62673). Rare ferns may be located through the AMERICAN FERN SOCIETY (DEPARTMENT OF BOTANY, UNIVERSITY OF RHODE ISLAND, KINGSTON, RI 02881).

Hospitable Hostas

Hostas offer greater variety of landscape effects than almost any other perennial. There are hostas for accents, facing down shrubs, edgings and groundcover use. They are also minimum-maintenance plants, requiring only the removal of faded flowers to prevent self-seeding — and even this can be eliminated by growing variegated forms in deep shade, where they will not flower but will add eye-catching gleams of gold and silver.

While *H. undulata* (good in sun) and *H. vilmoriana* are fine groundcovers, most hostas are best planted singly to display the handsome symmetry of the individual plant. Some are grown mainly for their flowers, such as the superb 'Betsy King' or fragrant 'Honeybells.' For foliar beauty, the huge heavy leaves of *H. sieboldiana*, silver-dusted 'Krossa Regal' or gold-leaved *H. lancifolia*, 'Kabitan,' are examples of the diversity available.

PALETTE GARDENS (26 WEST ZION HILL ROAD, QUAKERTOWN, PA 18951; CATALOG 50¢) offers many fine hostas. For more information on hostas, contact the AMERICAN HOSTA SOCIETY (MRS. NANCY MINKS, SECRETARY, 114 THE FAIRWAY, ALBERT LEA, MN 56007).

Grand Grasses

An almost universally neglected class of plants is the ornamental grasses. Actually, there are hundreds of members of the Graminiae or grass

Some hostas have large fragrant flowers that complement their impressive foliage (note the eyeglasses illustrating the leaf size).

family valuable for edging, specimen, screen, groundcover, border and foundation planting. Often an ornamental grass will fulfill a landscape purpose no other plant could serve as well. Yet, to our knowledge, no plantsman has specialized in investigating and offering these.

However, it is good to see expanded listings by two large nurseries, WAYSIDE GARDENS (MENTOR, OH 44060; CATALOG $2), and GEO. W. PARK SEED CO. (GREENWOOD, SC 29647). They offer tall, bold types — marvelous accents to modern architecture — such as the great reed, *Arundo donax*, and its variegated form, and the beautiful silky-plumed pampas grass, *Cortaderia selloana*, both growing up to 10′. In 3′ to 4′ heights, there are *Pennisetum ruppelii*, with striking coppery-rose spikes; blue lime grass, *Erianthus ravennae*, with 3′ leaves but 10′ silver plumes; and ruby grass, *Tricholaena rosea*, which produces stunning wine-colored panicles. Some of the best low-growing selections are the fascinating animated oats, *Avena sterilis*, and blue *A. sempervirens;* the very hardy white-striped *Carex morrowi variegata;* sheep's fescue, *Festuca ovina glauca*, an unusual groundcover or edging; and the woolly-headed hare's-tail grass, *Lagurus ovatus*.

A new WAYSIDE introduction is a fountain grass, *Miscanthus sinensis variegatus*, with 4′ gold-and-green-striped foliage and 5′ beige to pink plumes.

An evergreen perennial of great charm, Alchemilla vulgaris has gray-green leaves like pleated silk fans with scalloped edges.

Liberty Hyde Bailey, incidentally, called *Miscanthus* species the best permanent ornamental grasses for the North.

Many of these are fine pot or tub plants, and practically all supply worthy material for summer and winter bouquets. Their one essential cultural need: give them ample room for growth — crowded plants will not perform well.

An invaluable guide is *"ORNAMENTAL GRASSES FOR THE HOME AND GARDEN," INFORMATION BULLETIN 64 (30¢ FROM MAILING ROOM, BUILDING 7, RESEARCH PARK, CORNELL UNIVERSITY, ITHACA, NY 14850).*

The authors, Cooperative Extension Agent Mary Hockenberry Meyer and Prof. Robert G. Mower, note that at least 80 kinds of ornamental grasses, growing from 6″ to 20′, are suited to garden use. Of the 50 perennials for specimen, border and other uses, 80% are hardy to −20°. The annuals are equally attractive and versatile, and excellent for dried arrangements. The bulletin provides a key to 41 of the best, and detailed descriptions — including very complete indoor and outdoor use recommendations — for more than 30; many are illustrated. Directions on culture and drying, a glossary and reference and source lists are included.

Succulent Subject

For beauty, diversity and performance, sedums and sempervivums are truly modern plants. As limited-area groundcovers in poor, dry soil, or clinging in rock crannies in practically no soil, they provide mosaics of color and form. New varieties offer brilliant colors, most are hardy evergreens and all are easy to propagate — so easy that chopped leaves and stems are simply sprayed on roadsides in the Southwest.

Study the catalogs and you'll find hundreds of stonecrops and houseleeks with foliage ranging from tiny beads to needles to broad scalloped leaves, in lightest to deepest green, gray, intense bronze, richest maroon, often edged in red or pink or turning deep red in autumn. There are white, yellow, purple, pink, red, even blue flowers — the annual *Sedum caeruleum*, to mention one gem, has cherry-red stems and leaves and sky-blue starry flowers in summer. There are 1″ dwarfs and 24″ giants.

Two fascinating uses are roof growing and rock planting. Sedums and sempervivums can be established on mossy shingled roofs, or, as the great English gardener Gertrude Jekyll suggests, they will even thrive in 4″ of peaty soil on the low-pitched roof of a galvanized iron shed (Horticulturist Edward P. Hume suggests a soaker hose along the ridge for easy watering in hot, dry climes). And Mrs. Bruce Crane of Dalton, Massachusetts, has created spectacular portable and hanging plantings on odd-shaped eroded rocks, manzanita roots or weatherbeaten branches, and in strawberry jars and other containers, producing marvelous "all-weather, all-year living sculptures."

A superb book is *"PLANT JEWELS OF THE HIGH COUNTRY — SEDUMS AND SEMPERVIVUMS,"* by Helen E. Payne ($15, autographed copies from the author), who with her husband owns *OAKHILL GARDENS (ROUTE 3, BOX 87, DALLAS OR 97338),* which offers a huge variety of these succulents.

PERENNIAL SOURCES

J. Herbert Alexander, Middleboro, MA 02346

Alpenglow Gardens, 13328 King George Highway, Surrey, B.C., Canada; catalog 25¢

Avalon Mountain Gardens, Dana, NC 28724

Carroll Gardens, Westminster, MD 21157

DeGiorgi Company, Council Bluffs, IA 51501; catalog 35¢

Garden Place, 6780 Heisley Road, Mentor, OH 44060

Gardens of the Blue Ridge, Ashford, NC 28603

Henderson's Botanical Gardens, Route 6, Greensburg, IN 47240

J. L. Hudson, Seedsman, Box 1058, Redwood City, CA 94064; catalog 50¢

International Growers Exchange, Box 397, Farmington, MI 48024; catalog $2

Lamb Nurseries, E. 101 Sharp Avenue, Spokane, WA 99202

Laura's Collectors' Garden, 5136 South Raymond Street, Seattle, WA 98118; catalog 50¢

Leslie's Wildflower Nursery, 30 Summer Street, Methuen, MA 01844; catalog 25¢

Lounsberry Gardens, Box 135, Oakford, IL 62673

Mincemoyer Nursery, Route 4, Box 482, Jackson, NJ 08527; catalog 25¢

Geo. W. Park Seed Co., Greenwood, SC 29647

Pellett Gardens, Atlantic, IA 50022

Putney Nursery, Putney, VT 05346

Rakestraw's Perennial Gardens, 3094 South Term Street, Flint, MI 48507; catalog 25¢

Clyde Robin, Box 2091, Castro Valley, CA 94546; catalog $1

Siskiyou Rare Plant Nursery, 522 Franquette Street, Medford, OR 97501; catalog 50¢

Sky-Cleft Gardens, Camp Street Extension, Barre, VT 05641; catalog 10¢

Sky Hook Farm, Johnson, VT 05656

Thompson & Morgan Ltd., Box 24, Somerdale, NJ 08083

Wayside Gardens, Mentor, OH 44060; catalog $2

White Flower Farm, Litchfield, CT 06759; catalog $3

The Wild Garden, 8243 N.E. 119th, Kirkland, WA 98033; catalog $1

Woodland Acres Nursery, Crivitz, WI 54114

PERENNIAL RESOURCES

"Color in the Flower Garden," by Gertrude Jekyll (London, 1908)

"The Complete Guide to Hardy Perennials," by Frances Perry (Branford, $5.75)

"Contemporary Perennials," by Cumming and Lee (Macmillan, $6.95)

"The English Flower Garden," by William Robinson (London, 1903)

"Gardening with Wild Flowers," by Frances Tenenbaum (Charles Scribner's Sons, $7.95)

"Garden Perennials" (Macmillan Plant Encyclopedia Series, $4.95)

"Growing Flowering Perennials," USDA Home and Garden Bulletin 114 (25¢ from Superintendent of Documents, Washington, DC 20402)

"Growing Wildflowers," by Marie Sperka (Harper & Row, $8.95)

"The Hardy Flower Book," by E. A. Jenkins (London, 1913)

"Have You Tried Perennials?" by C. H. Potter ($3.75 plus 15¢ from American Nurseryman, 343 S. Dearborn, Chicago, IL 60604)

"Herbaceous Flower Borders," by H. H. Thomas (London, 1928)

"The New Perennials Preferred," by Helen Van Pelt Wilson (Barrows, $4.95)

"Perennial Flowers for Small Gardens," Pan Piper Series ($1.50 plus 90¢ handling from Walter F. Nicke, Box 71, Hudson, NY 12534)

"Perennials for Your Garden," by Alan Bloom ($7.95 plus 50¢ postage from Garden Place, 6780 Heisley Road, Mentor, OH 44060)

Bulbs

Rhapsody in Blue

To the discriminating gardener, the rarer minor bulbs offer major rewards. One virtue is a rich range of blues, a color lacking in crocuses, tulips and daffodils.

For the best blues, a few suggestions from bulb expert Mrs. M. M. Graff: *Hyacinthus azureus,* most delightful miniature hyacinth, cobalt blue . . . *Scilla tubergeniana,* soft blue on silvery ground, a recent introduction from Persia that increases rapidly to make a broad mound of bloom . . . also new from Persia, *Muscari tubergenianum,* a brilliant clear blue; *Scilla siberica* 'Spring Beauty,' a blue so intense it must be planted alone . . . and *Chionodoxa gigantea,* blue-violet, boasting much stiffer, more weather-proof stems than others of its genus.

To these might be added the charming light-blue-belled *Puschkinia libanotica;* little-known *Triteleia uniflora,* with starry, fragrant lilac flowers on 6″ stems; *Iris histrioides major,* large-flowered, distinctive Oxford blue; and the new *Tecophilaea cyanocrocus* from Chile, gentian-blue, 2″ tall.

Good minor bulb sources: P. DE JAGER & SONS (SOUTH HAMILTON, MA 01982), FRENCH'S (BOX 87, RUTLAND, VT 05736) and INTERNATIONAL GROWERS EXCHANGE (BOX 397, FARMINGTON, MI 48024; CATALOG $2).

The Beautiful Onions

More than 100 species of *Allium* are recognized, the best known being the utilitarian garlic, onion, leek, shallot and chives. The decorative species, however, far outrank these in number — and in beauty. Many have extraordinarily showy blooms. Their airy spheres in soft to brilliant hues are equally dramatic in the garden or in arrangements.

Practically all are hardy, thrive in full sun in any well-drained soil and can be left undisturbed for several years. Seed is sown in spring, or bulbs planted in spring or fall.

A few of the finest: *A. giganteum,* jewel of Tibet, flower stems to 48″, with 8″ umbels of starry rose-violet blooms in late spring . . . *A. albopilosum,* star of Persia, 18″, glistening lilac flowers in 10″ heads, early summer . . . *A. schubertii,* recently introduced from Israel, 10″ high, rose-pink, with tiny "shooting star" flowers bursting from the center of the bloom on long stems . . . the snowflake allium, *A. neapolitanum,* white, sweet-scented stars in spring and summer, for the rock garden, naturalizing or pot culture indoors . . . *A. moly,* the golden garlic . . . *A. farreri,* plum-red . . . and three blues, *A. cyaneum,* 6″ stems, *A. caeruleum,* 24″, and *A. beesianum,* to 36″.

Many of these are available from INTERNATIONAL GROWERS EXCHANGE (BOX 397, FARMINGTON, MI 48024; CATALOG $2).

The Hardy Begonia

Just how hardy is *Begonia evansiana?* Most books say to 0°, but we've seen numerous reports of its thriving where winters go to − 10°, and a gardener tells us he has plantings that have survived frequent drops to − 20°.

B. evansiana is as delicate-appearing in leaf and stem as any tender begonia, and bears graceful tall spikes of bright pink single flowers in late summer and autumn. While in the North it generally grows to about 18″, in milder areas this begonia from the mountains of China can reach 30″, and makes an unusually attractive well-branched plant with large light green leaves which are reddish beneath. The numerous bulb-lets that form in the leaf axils can be planted for rapid increase.

Most important: very careful removal of winter mulch to avoid injuring the tubers, which are slow to start growth in the spring. *B. evansiana* needs

a humusy, rich soil, light to heavy shade and watering in drought. A source is WAYSIDE GARDENS (MENTOR, OH 44060; CATALOG $2).

Daffodils symbolize spring, but many minor bulbs can also be naturalized almost anywhere in the garden to give three seasons of beauty.

Top Tubers

For brilliant color and elegance in semi-shade, tuberous begonias are without peer. With each year there is dramatic improvement in their varieties and refinement of the cultural techniques necessary to grow them to perfection.

Charles A. Lewis, former Director of Horticulture at Sterling Forest Gardens, Tuxedo, New York, produced 7000 plants a year, for the largest outdoor display of tuberous begonias in the East, by this method:

In March, place dormant tubers, hollow side up, on a mixture of 1 part sand and 2 parts peat, at 65° to 70°. As soon as sprouts show, cover the tubers ½″ deep with the same mix and place the flat in full light. Transplant when 2 or 3 full leaves form, into 7″ or larger azalea pots containing equal parts of leafmold, peat and sandy soil, or outdoors into beds prepared 14″ deep with sand and leafmold — "good drainage is vital to prevent bud drop." Mix in ¼ cup of fish meal or Electra under each plant.

Correct light is essential: "Morning sun is ideal, as is the dappled sunlight under high trees. The more sun the better, short of the point where the leaves start to be damaged and the plants stunted." Always plant with the points of the leaves forward, as the flowers face this way. Stake early, water frequently and always early in the day, and fertilize twice a month through August, preferably with a slow-acting organic fertilizer. Any areas of rot should be cut out immediately and the wound painted with paste of Zerlate.

Sources of California and Belgian tubers are ANTONELLI BROTHERS (2545 CAPITOLA ROAD, SANTA CRUZ, CA 95060); and VAN BOURGONDIEN BROS. (BOX A, BABYLON, NY 11702).

Sterling Forest also grows tuberous begonias from seed, sown in October for early bloom (excellent directions are in the Antonelli catalog). The new heat-resistant Harlow Hybrids, developed by Prof. Gilbert H. Harlow, grow in nearly full sun. (For sources, contact KORAL GREENHOUSES, PATTERSONVILLE, NY 12137.)

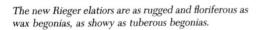
The new Rieger elatiors are as rugged and floriferous as wax begonias, as showy as tuberous begonias.

More hints for success: buy top-size tubers — those that develop two sprouts can be divided with a knife (dust the cut surfaces with fungicide) . . . tubers start well under two 40-watt fluorescents and two 25-watt incandescents, 10″ above them, lit 14 hours a day . . . if spring is late, harden off the plants in a shaded coldframe or porch for 2 to 4 weeks before planting . . . pinch young stems of hanging-basket types to induce branching, and remove flower buds from all types after planting to encourage vigor . . . a fast-drying fibrous mulch assures a cool root-run . . . controlled-release fertilizers like MagAmp or Osmocote plus frequent dilute liquid feeding gave best growth in tests in California . . . on hot nights, misting near but not on the plants helps . . . cut flowers last long floated in water, if the container is covered with plastic wrap and refrigerated the first night.

Elation Over Elatiors

The fabulous new Rieger elatior begonias, crosses of tuberous begonias with winter-flowering *B. socotrana* hybrids, can give bloom most of the year — as summer bedding, container and hanging-basket plants, and in the home and greenhouse in winter. The plants are vigorous, they have larger blooms than wax begonias and they are more resistant to adverse weather than tuberous begonias.

Developed by the German firm of Otto Rieger, the elatior begonia — which received 15 gold medals overseas — has been introduced here by the wholesale firm of PAUL MIKKELSEN, INC. (ASHTABULA, OH 44004). There are two types: the single-flowered Schwabenland, in red, orange, pink, yellow, ruffled red and other varieties; and the double-flowered Aphrodite series for growing in pots with staking or in hanging baskets, in pink, red, rose and bicolors.

The Lilies Called Tulips

The most neglected of all bulbous plants outside their natural range is the genus *Calochortus*. Despite / their often spectacular beauty, these western natives are seldom seen east of the Rockies. The number of species available has declined in recent years, mainly because their need for summer and winter aridity has not been stressed by dealers.

All three types — globe, star and mariposa tulips — must have very light, highly sandy, not very rich soil. Absolutely perfect drainage is essential, and a raised bed should be made if necessary to achieve this. Corms are planted in late autumn, and must be protected with a mulch of evergreen boughs or other light material to prevent heaving. Following flowering in May to July, they need a drying-off period, and in areas of wet summers should be dug and stored.

The charming globe tulips, which have 6″ to 12″ branched stems carrying nodding "fairy lantern" flowers, include the white *C. albus*, yellow *C. amabilis* and rose-lilac *C. amoenus*. They like light shade, as do the star tulips or "cat's-ears," of which *C. maweanus*, 6″, with white blooms fringed with lavender hairs, and the 8″ lavender *C. nudus*, are among the best. The flamboyant, sun-loving mariposa tulips have 12″ to 36″ stems, with large flowers varying from deepest crimson in *C. venustus* 'Red' to yellow in *C. luteus* and white blotched with red, yellow or purple in *C. venustus* 'Eldorado.'

These and others are offered by *EDGAR L. KLINE (17495 S.W. BRYANT ROAD, LAKE GROVE, OR 97034)*. All may be grown in pots, plunged without watering into the coldframe in late autumn and brought indoors in January.

Bright Bulbs

Two of the finest spring bulbs are camassia and fritillaria. Members of the lily family, they offer novelty and beauty for naturalizing, borders, rock garden, woodland edges and waterside planting, in light shade to full sun.

Camassias — Indian name, quamash — tolerate wet and heavy soils better than any other bulb. Their delicate racemes of starry flowers on tall spikes above grass-like leaves are unusually long-lasting. Plant them 4″ deep, 4″ to 6″ apart. Lowest growing is *Camassia esculenta*, 18″, with deepest blue flowers. *C. leichtlinii* grows to 24″, with lovely cream-and-white blooms; its variety *caerulea* is China blue. Tallest is *C. cusickii*, 36″ or more, lavender-blue. A source is *P. DE JAGER & SONS (SOUTH HAMILTON, MA 01982)*.

The European snakeshead lily or guinea-hen flower, *Fritillaria meleagris (DE JAGER)* is intriguing. Its pendent bells in checkered patterns of white, yellow, bronze, gray and purple on 9″ to 12″ stems resemble upside-down tulips. Plant 4″ deep in rich soil.

Even more charming are the fritillarias native to the western U.S.: *F. pudica*, 6″, clear yellow blooms; *F. pluriflora*, the adobe lily, 10″, with up to a dozen pink-purple flowers in each raceme; the chocolate lily, *F. biflora*, to about 9″; and the rare ricefoot fritillaria, *F. lanceolata*, 18″, with mottled green and brown blooms. These are offered by *CLYDE ROBIN (BOX 2091, CASTRO VALLEY, CA 94546; CATALOG $1)*.

Perhaps finest of all is *F. camschatcensis* from Alaska, Japan and Siberia. This "Eskimo potato" has fabulous gleaming black-bronze-mahogany 3″

bells on 12″ stems in late May. A source is *INTERNATIONAL GROWERS EXCHANGE (BOX 397, FARMINGTON, MI 48024; CATALOG $2)*.

Finally, there is *F. imperialis*, the spectacular crown imperial, introduced into Europe from Bokhara in 1576. Drooping in umbels crowned by whorls of leaves, its flowers are brilliant yellow, orange, burnt orange and red, on stately stems 3′ to 4′ high. Plant 6″ deep in rich but not heavy soil. A selection of varieties is offered by *INTERNATIONAL GROWERS EXCHANGE*.

Bengal Bulbs

Crinum or Bengal lilies — really members of the amaryllis family — are among the finest of summer bulbs and well worth the trouble of lifting and storing them where they are not hardy.

They have huge bulbs, like footballs with long necks, and long, shiny green strap leaves. The umbels of 3″ to 6″ flowers are borne on stout 2′ to 4′ stems. A warm sunny southern exposure, perfectly draining soil enriched to 2′ depth and regular watering until the plants have bloomed are essential. After flowering, water is withheld, and in the North the bulbs are lifted just before frost, dried for several days and then stored in a cool basement.

The very fine, deep pink *Crinum powellii* is considered hardy to −10° under a heavy mulch, and is especially lovely growing with blue agapanthus. Equally beautiful are var. *album*, rose-pink 'Krelagei' and shell-pink 'Harlemense.' In more tender types, 'Cecil Houdyshel' is a large-flowered, long-blooming rose-pink hybrid, and 'Ellen Bosanquet' is dark, almost wine-red. Rare *C. asiaticum*, white and sweetly scented, is almost everblooming in the South. The milk-and-wine lily, *C. bulbispermum*, has a deepest pink stripe on each palest pink petal.

These and others are available from *INTERNATIONAL GROWERS EXCHANGE (BOX 397 FARMINGTON, MI 48024; CATALOG $2)*.

European *Fritillaria meleagris* and our western native fritillarias are charming naturalized in grass and around rocks.

Discover Crocosmia

Two of England's finest gardeners have called attention to a superb summer-flowering South African bulbous plant which until recently was only rarely grown in England, and which now is becoming available here.

Crocosmia masonorum, awarded a First Class Certificate by the Royal Horticultural Society in 1963, is "a plant *I* would never like to be without," says Roy Hay. Alan Bloom states that "it is a relative of montbretia and grows from a corm, but is much finer and more reliable as a border subject. Its handsome sword-like foliage is over 2′ high, and the brilliant orange flowers come on arching, wiry stems, opening to face the sun and to show their beauty. This is a startling cut-flower subject, needing only a sunny place and perfect drainage."

C. masonorum is available for spring planting from CHAMPLAIN VIEW GARDENS (SOUTH HAMILTON, MA 01982), INTERNATIONAL GROWERS EXCHANGE (BOX 397, FARMINGTON, MI 48024; CATALOG $2) and VAN BOURGONDIEN BROS. (BOX A, BABYLON, NY 11702). The bulbs are hardy to slightly below 0° if given a winter mulch; farther north they are lifted and stored like gladioli.

Crocus "T"

"One of the best of all bulbs for naturalizing," says the Brooklyn Botanic Garden, is "Crocus 'T' " — *Crocus tomasinianus*, from Dalmatia and Serbia.

Blooming "several weeks before the big 'Dutch' crocus that all gardeners in cool climates recognize as a harbinger of spring," *C. tomasinianus* spreads very freely by seed and corm. The flower color has been described as bright lilac-mauve or sapphire-lavender. In England, says Patrick M. Synge, gardeners greatly prize "the little 'Tommies' shooting up all over the place in January or February," and several color selections have been made.

Two of the finest are 'Ruby Giant,' a deep ruby-purple (P. DE JAGER & SONS, SOUTH HAMILTON, MA 01982), and 'Whitewell Purple,' reddish-violet (FRENCH'S, BOX 87, RUTLAND, VT 05736).

Bedder Dahlias

The dwarf Dutch dahlias, now commonly planted in Holland to follow the tulips, bid fair to become one of America's most popular bedding plants. Low and neat, providing constant bloom from July through October if faded blooms are removed promptly, they're choice for cutting, and also make fine pot and tub plants. The single flowers are often 3″ or more across, and the plants grow no taller than 18″.

Some of the best are 'Snow White,' 'G. F. Hemerick' (coppery-orange), 'Irene Van Der Zwet' (bright yellow), 'Murillo' (brilliant pink), and 'Nelly Geerlings' (scarlet). For very early bloom, start the clumps in pots indoors about three weeks before frost-free planting time. A source is JOHN SCHEEPERS, INC. (63 WALL STREET, NEW YORK, NY 10005).

Daffo-Dillies

The new "collar" daffodils are exciting. These are sometimes called orchid-flowered daffodils, because the corona or trumpet covers most of the perianth. The Royal Horticultural Society has made a separate division for collars in its official daffodil classification.

Jack P. Gerritsen *(J. GERRITSEN & SON, VOORSCHOTEN, HOLLAND)* and *MR. AND MRS. A. N. KANOUSE (517 FLORAVISTA AVENUE, OLYMPIA, WA 98506)* are the leading hybridizers of collar daffodils. Mr. and Mrs. Kanouse, who have been growing and breeding daffodils since 1926, report that their latest accomplishment is blooming "some reverse-colored collars, seedlings from the reverse trumpet 'Daydream' — truly a break in this type."

Comely Corms

No fall bulb order should fail to include a selection of erythroniums, which provide delightful "turk's-cap-lily" flowers from early to late spring.

The trout lily or dogtooth violet is not difficult to grow if you can provide a woodland-type soil. Given a deep, slightly acid, peaty or leafmoldy pocket that drains well but never dries out, erythroniums will thrive almost anywhere, in nearly full sun to half shade. A 1″ leafmold, sawdust, or rough peat mulch is beneficial, plus a dressing of dried manure in early spring. Trout lily corms should be planted promptly upon receipt, 3″ to 6″ deep depending on size.

Outstanding early-flowering erythroniums are *E. mesochoreum*, lavender flowers on 4″ stems; *E. hendersonii*, lavender, 10″; the rare deep violet *E. japonicum*, 6″; and the many fine named varieties of the European *E. dens-canis*, in many colors, 3″ to 4″, with bronze-mottled leaves. Midseason types are *E. americanum*, yellow, 4″; *E. albidum*, white, 6″; *E. grandiflorum*, creamy, 8″; and *E. tuolumnensis*, yellow, 15″. Rose-lavender *E. revolutum* and two handsome hybrids, 'White Beauty' and yellow 'Pagoda,' all with 10″ to 15″ flower stems, give superb late bloom.

Two sources are *P. DE JAGER & SONS (SOUTH HAMILTON, MA 01982)* and *FRENCH'S (BOX 87, RUTLAND, VT 05736)*.

Heaven-Scented

More freesias can be seen in florists' shops than in many a year, and gardeners, too, are once again growing these enchantingly fragrant subjects for cool windows, porch or greenhouse. The new Tecolote Hybrids produce magnificent giant flowers in white, gold, orange, pink, scarlet,

bronze and blue — and breeding seems to have actually enhanced the fragrance. Two sources of these are *FRENCH'S (BOX 87, RUTLAND, VT 05736)* and *P. DE JAGER & SONS (SOUTH HAMILTON, MA 01982)*; de Jager also now stocks specially prepared freesias for outdoor planting in spring — these bloom from July to late autumn.

Freesia corms may be planted as late as December, 1″ deep in a porous soil mix, 6 corms to a 6″ bulb pan. Keep the pan in a cool dark place for about a month before placing it in a sunny location with 50° to 55° night temperature. Late-planted freesias will have shorter stems, but all will need to be staked with twine run around stakes set inside the pot rim. After flowering, watering is reduced until the foliage dries off, then the corms are stored in a cool place until replanting time. Freesias will bloom from seed in about 9 months.

Glad Tidings

Now there are gladioli that are hardy in much of the U.S. These Asian and European species — in contrast to the African, from which the great host of modern summer-blooming hybrids are derived — are also apparently free from thrips attack and disease.

Hardy gladioli are planted in autumn and bloom in May and June. Their charming flowers are more delicate in form than those of the tender types, the petals long, narrow and flaring rather than forming a tubular bloom. Three species are especially delightful: *G. byzantinus*, 2′, a rosy-purple, also available in a pure white variety; *G. communis*, rosy-pink, 1′ to 2′; and *G. segetum*, 2′, bright purple. Sources of these are *INTERNATIONAL GROWERS EXCHANGE (BOX 397,*

'Gravety Giant' is the finest summer snowflake, producing numerous heads of elegant green-tipped white bells.

FARMINGTON, MI 48024; CATALOG $2) and GEO. W. PARK SEED CO. (GREENWOOD, SC 29646). Plant them 4″ deep, give a light winter mulch in the coldest states, and lift and divide them every 3 to 4 years.

The even earlier blooming "baby" gladioli — the Nánus and Colvillei Hybrids, popular for forcing — are often rated as "semi-hardy." Planted 4″ deep in autumn (5″ in light soils) and given a winter mulch of straw or leaves several inches deep, they will come through 0°. They grow to 2′, with airy spikes in vivid colors. 'The Bride' is pure white, and there are fine blush white, orange, pink, salmon and scarlet varieties. Creamy *G. tristis*, a Colvillei parent, is fragrant. Sources are JOHN SCHEEPERS, INC. (63 WALL STREET, NEW YORK, NY 10005) and P. DE JAGER & SONS (SOUTH HAMILTON, MA 01982).

Oriental Roof Iris

The seldom-seen Oriental roof iris, *Iris tectorum* — so-called because it is widely grown on thatched roofs in Japan — is a connoisseur's iris, superlative for border, wall or rock garden, or clumping almost anywhere in sun or very light shade.

Very easy to grow in any well-drained soil, this rhizomatous crested iris has bold, sword-like 12″ leaves, and in May to June bears large flat flowers, soft lilac-blue with darker veins and crests. It is a prolific bloomer, with 2 or 3 flowers on each 15″ stem. They have an orchid-like quality, and *I. tectorum* is the iris most often called the poor man's orchid. There is also a pure white form with yellow crests, *I. tectorum album*, equally exquisite but smaller growing.

A source is LAMB NURSERIES (E. 101 SHARP AVENUE, SPOKANE, WA 99202).

Expanding Louisiana Iris Territory

Many gardeners believe Louisiana irises are suited only to Louisiana. Not so — they are flourishing in New England and Midwestern gardens, says

Charles W. Arny, Jr., of the University of Southwestern Louisiana.

High-organic soil and considerable moisture, especially in spring and fall, are keys to success. Mr. Arny recommends a soil mix of equal parts of peat or pine bark, leafmold, soil and manure. To each 100 square feet of bed or border he adds 8 to 10 pounds of a mixture of equal parts of a balanced fertilizer such as 12-12-12 and cottonseed meal. In alkaline soil areas, 10 pounds of agricultural sulfur is also incorporated to supply required acid conditions. Away from the Gulf Coast, early spring may be better for planting than the usual late summer. Rhizomes are set no deeper than 1½″, and a heavy mulch of pine bark, bagasse, rotted sawdust, oak leaves, rice hulls or cottonseed hulls should be maintained. Fertilizing before and after bloom is often desirable.

Louisiana irises today offer great variety in flower size, form, color and texture, and the recent creation of tetraploids promises new improvements. Some of the best new cultivars are white 'Queen of Queens,' orange-yellow 'Tressie Cook,' light blue 'Mr. Mac,' dark 'Blue Duke,' red 'Ira Nelson,' and bi-toned 'Katherine Cornay.' Two specialists in Louisiana irises are LAURIE'S GARDEN (17225 MCKENZIE HIGHWAY, ROUTE 2, SPRINGFIELD, OR 97477) and CHARJOY GARDENS (BOX 511, LA FAYETTE, LA 70501; CATALOG 10¢).

Spring and Summer Snowflakes

Though they are among the prettiest and most permanent flowering bulbs, snowflakes (*Leucojum*) are not often grown today, perhaps because new gardeners easily confuse them with snowdrops (*Galanthus*). Leucojums, however, have the advantage of being less demanding in their cultural needs, and they can be distinguished by their later bloom, heavier foliage and flowers having 6 equal petals rather than 3 prominent and 3 recessed (in Europe they are more aptly called "little snow bells").

Leucojum vernum, the spring snowflake, blooms a month or so after the snowdrops, which may be in flower as early as late January. Carrying a single dainty bell flower on each stalk, *L. vernum* grows only 6″ to 8″ high. More imposing is the so-called "summer" snowflake, *L. aestivum,* which actually flowers in April or May. It grows as tall as 24″ — an especially vigorous form is 'Gravety Giant' — and its long-lasting white, green-tipped bells are borne four or more to the stem. A very rapid multiplier, *L. aestivum* can form several dozen new bulbs from a single bulb in a few years, so should be divided about every fourth year.

The snowflakes require a leafmold-rich soil, light summer shade and watering in drought. Sources of leucojum are P. DE JAGER & SONS (SOUTH HAMILTON, MA 01982), and JOHN SCHEEPERS, INC. (63 WALL STREET, NEW YORK, NY 10005).

Remontant Irises

The "remontant" or reblooming irises are receiving much attention. Indeed, "remontant, before too long, will be the magic word for all iris growers," says Robert Paul Hubley of the Southern California Iris Society.

Mr. Hubley notes that "for an iris to bloom more than once in a year, it must have both the right hereditary characteristics and the right environment. According to most growers, remontant irises will be encouraged to rebloom if watered from March to September . . . This continuous watering program is necessary so that summer rebloomers and autumn rebloomers will have full opportunity to respond with the reblooming that is in their genetic make-up." Expert Edwin Rundlett reports that "in rainy summers there is more fall blooming than when summers are dry," and he also recommends heavy fertilizing after the spring blooming, and keeping weeds and aphids under control.

Lilies of the Field

The new hybrid lilies are superb — so superb they often make gardeners forget there are also improved species lilies that offer equally great garden value, says John E. Bryan in the "Garden Journal" of the New York Botanical Garden. He recommends several to the connoisseur:

The rare *Lilium nepalense,* flowering in July, bears up to 8 large, sweet-scented emerald-green flowers with eggplant-purple centers, on 4′ stems. Another rare treasure, only 2′ high, is *L. papilliferum,* deepest maroon-crimson, with 3 reflexed and 3 almost flat petals, blooming in August. Earlier species include the dainty, starry, brightest scarlet *L. concolor,* 2′, flowering in late May, and *L. monadelphum,* a deep yellow, to 3′, late

June. Most spectacular of all is the new 7′ *L. brownii australe*, the true Hong Kong lily, pure white and fragrant, blooming in August and September.

Three old-time species that have undeservedly been overshadowed by the hybrids are the pink *L. martagon* and its numerous fine forms such as the wine-purple *L. m. dalmaticum* and white *L. m. superbum album*, all very floriferous and so long-blooming . . . *L. speciosum rubrum*, the beautiful speckled lily of waxiest texture, marvelous as a cut flower . . . and *L. auratum virginale*, of which the improved Melridge Strain, with 8″ fragrant gold-striped white flowers on 6′ stems, is without peer as a border plant.

Some sources for these are REX BULB FARMS (NEWBURG, OR 97132), P. DE JAGER & SONS (SOUTH HAMILTON, MA 01982), and WAYSIDE GARDENS (MENTOR, OH 44060; CATALOG $2).

Fabulous for Forcing

Progressive commercial growers today force many lilies other than the traditional Easter lily. As foremost lily hybridizer Jan de Graaff has noted, gardeners who have been slow to follow suit are missing a very rewarding experience.

The American, Asiatic, Candidum, Martagon, Oriental and Trumpet Hybrids, as well as some species, all force easily. Mr. de Graaff particularly recommends Mid-Century Hybrids, such as 'Cinnabar,' 'Harmony,' 'Joan Evans' and the magnificent 'Enchantment.' Precooled bulbs may be purchased, or the necessary cold period can be supplied by 6 to 8 weeks' storage in plastic bags in the refrigerator.

Lilies can be forced for almost any day of the year — precooled Mid-Century Hybrids planted after November 15, when they became available, will flower in about 75 days. Planted later, as the days begin to lengthen, they force more rapidly. Pot in a porous soil mix, and place them in a sunny window with 55° minimum at night, about 70° during the day. When growth starts, give complete fertilizer every 10 days. Forced lilies planted outdoors after flowering bloom normally the following year.

The beautiful catalog ($1) of the wholesale OREGON BULB FARMS (BOX 529, GRESHAM, OR 97030) gives excellent descriptions and forcing instructions.

Made to Order for Autumn

Sternbergia lutea is an autumn-flowering member of the amaryllis family with daffodil-gold flowers in crocus form. For glowing ground-level color when little else is in bloom, it is peerless in border, nook or rockery, or naturalized on a south-facing slope.

Planted in August in full sun, each bulb first produces glossy, dark green 6″ to 9″ strap leaves, then several single-stemmed glistening flowers of heavy substance, long-lasting and weather resistant, opening to 4″ across. Sternbergias are hardy to at least − 20° if given a gritty soil with perfect drainage, and mulched for winter with a light covering of hay that will not mat over the foliage, which persists into spring. Set the bulbs 4″ deep and 4″ apart, and enrich the soil beneath with a handful of leafmold, plus a liberal sprinkling of bonemeal. In summer, the bulbs should almost literally bake in dry soil — as they do in their native Syria and Israel — and this is substantially aided if the gardener plants them on a southern exposure, with a heat-reflecting wall or rock behind them. Sternbergias will multiply readily and may be lifted and separated after the foliage dies away.

Bulbs are available from P. DE JAGER & SONS (SOUTH HAMILTON, MA 01982).

Garden Callas

Many a gardener who grows calla lilies in a winter window garden does not realize their value for summer planting outdoors. Set 4″ deep in sun or light shade after the soil has warmed, they provide unsurpassed tropical effects. Abundant moisture and soil enriched with 1 part manure to each 2 parts of soil, plus biweekly feeding with manure water or fish fertilizer, assures vigorous production of the handsome leaves and showy late-summer spathes. Where temperatures do not go below 0°, callas can be left in the ground under a mulch, but in colder climes they are lifted after the first frost, dried for a few weeks, then stored in sand or vermiculite at 50°.

Actually neither callas nor lilies, these South African members of the arum family are fine companions for ferns and other small-leaved moisture-loving plants. The giant white calla, *Zantedeschia aethiopica*, grows to 4′, with arrowhead leaves over 1′ long and creamy 10″ spathes. White 18″ *Z. albomaculata* has white-spotted foliage. Two golden varieties are *Z. elliottiana* and *Z. pentlandii*, both 3′, and a lovely pink is the 12″ *Z. rehmanii superba*. The black-throated 18″ *Z. melanoleuca (Z. tropicalis)* has a light yellow spathe with a large purple-black spot at its base.

Of special interest are *Z. aethiopica* 'Crowborough,' hardy to −20° with protection and producing several flower spikes per rootstock, available from GEO. W. PARK SEED CO. (GREENWOOD, SC 29647), and the new Sunset Hybrids (PARK) and dwarf Rancho Hybrids (INTERNATIONAL GROWERS EXCHANGE, BOX 397, FARMINGTON, MI 48024; CATALOG $2), in colors from white and cream through pink, orange, apricot, red and purple.

FOR BULBMANSHIP

"Bulbs for Summer Bloom," by John P. Baumgardt (Hawthorn, $8.95)

"The Complete Guide to Bulbs," by Patrick Synge (Dutton, $6.95)

"Dahlias for Everyone," by T. H. R. Lebar (St. Martin's, $3.95)

"Flowers in the Winter Garden," by M. M. Graff (Doubleday, $4.95)

"Hardy Garden Bulbs," by Gertrude S. Wister (Dutton, $4.50)

"The Iris Book," by Molly Price (Van Nostrand, $6.95)

"Lilies," by Jan de Graaff and Edward Hyams (Funk & Wagnalls, $6.95)

"The World of the Gladiolus," by the North American Gladiolus Council ($6.50 from Bob Ellis, Treasurer, NAGC, 6425 Adams Street, Lincoln, NB 68507)

ROSES

Dramatizing Roses

While breathtakingly beautiful close up, when viewed from a distance, roses are often disappointing as a feature of the landscape, noted Charles E. Maley in the "American Rose Magazine" (American Rose Society, Box 30,000, Shreveport, LA 71130). To use them as a landscaping tool, Mr. Maley suggests growing both the modern climbers and the old perpetuals "like a forsythia bush, encouraging canes to grow horizontally and to bend down. Then they will cover the entire length of every cane with blossoms.

Trained thus along walls, banks, fences, and invisible wire supports, they . . . provide both massive color and a variety of heights."

Another valuable but little-known technique is "fountaining" — growing climbers as superbushes with no supports at all. To achieve concentrated color density, Mr. Maley recommends "banking" — an extreme example would be planting climbers behind grandifloras behind hybrid teas behind floribundas behind miniatures.

Tree roses are striking grown alone or in combination with many low-growing plants, and also do well in containers.

Rose Complements

Good design of the rose bed enhances not only the roses but the entire garden. Although roses today are used as border plants, hedges, ground-covers, edgings, pillar and wall coverings, the bedding roses — hybrid teas and floribundas — are still often set in squared-off beds. But more than the shape of the bed is involved. To create a setting for the rose garden, a shrub background is ideal, especially one made up of feathery conifers such as dwarf hemlock or pyramidal arborvitae, or of broadleafs like holly, mahonia and rhodo-dendrons, perhaps accented with deciduous shrubs that bloom before or after the peak rose flowering.

Boxwood is an old-time favorite as an edging. Equally attractive are dwarf barberry, lavender cotton *(Santolina chamaecyparissus)*, or german-der *(Teucrium chamaedrys)*. Or try an edging of yellow marigolds or white alyssum with red roses, pink and white petunias to border red roses, pansies and violas around white roses, or blue lobelias edging yellow roses. Sky-blue delphini-ums marvelously complement red roses; hybrid lilies are a superb background for long rose beds.

Venerable Roses

The steady popular revival of the old shrub roses has many roots. Not the least of these is their historical value, which contributes much to the feeling of permanence that is the essence of a fine garden. The York and Lancaster roses, the dam-ask traceable to Babylonian gardens, the ancient everblooming China teas, the wonderful Pro-vence, Bourbon and moss roses all have associa-tions equaled by no other plants.

As landscaping plants, the old roses have specimen, border and hedging value — most modern hybrids are basically bedding plants. Even more appealing is their minimum-mainte-nance capability: the old roses are vigorous and thrive with little or no fertilizing, spraying, prun-ing and winter protection. With almost total neglect, they provide perfection of flower form and abundance of bloom equal to any modern rose, they are marvelously fragrant and many of them bloom far longer than almost any other flowering shrub.

We urge every gardener to become familiar with the great varieties offered by the dean of growers, TILLOTSON'S ROSES (BROWN'S VALLEY ROAD, WATSONVILLE, CA 95076; CATALOG $1). We would like to cite only one personal preference — *Rosa eglanteria*, the eglantine or sweetbrier rose of Elizabethan gardens. It grows 8' or more, is a good hedge plant, and its 2" single flowers are clear pink. Two of its finest attributes are the wonderfully potent apple scent of the foliage, and large brilliant orange hips that last through win-ter. It is long-lived; plants 1000 years old are reported in English castle gardens.

Modern Landscaping Roses

Some modern hybrids that do have excellent landscaping value were listed in *"THE ROSE BED," BULLETIN OF THE VANCOUVER ROSE SOCIETY.*

For specimen or border shrubs: 'Chinatown,' a vigorous, fragrant yellow floribunda; 'Fred Loads,' single, vermilion-orange, continuous-flowering; 'Gabrielle Noyelle,' a modern moss rose, orange-salmon; 'Sparrieshoop,' very large single pink blooms; and the superb 'Therese Bugnet,' hardy to Alaska, lilac-pink, with reddish stems. Fine for walls are the climbing form of 'Mrs. Sam McGredy,' copper-scarlet, blooming

Orange 'Sunfire' is one of Jackson & Perkins' new flora-tea roses, which combine the best characteristics of hybrid teas and floribundas.

A New Race of Roses

The flora-tea, a completely new type of rose, has been introduced by JACKSON & PERKINS CO. (MEDFORD, OR 97501).

Developed by J&P's director of plant research, William Warriner, flora-teas are described as "bouquet-branching hybrids, inheriting the best traits of both the hybrid tea (long-stemmed, beautifully formed, large flowers) and the floribunda (colorful masses of flowers on compact plants)." The flora-tea thus combines the show and arrangement value of the hybrid tea with the landscape usefulness of the floribunda. The new roses are 2½' to 4½' tall and broad, and the major canes terminate in clusters of 6 to 12 flowers, with each flower borne on strong 10" to 12" stems.

Patents have been applied for on the first three flora-teas — fragrant white 'Evening Star,' red 'Viva,' and deep orange 'Sunfire.' The American Rose Society is investigating the need for a new classification to cover judging of these roses.

To a Wild Rose

One of the loveliest roses of springtime, is *Rosa nitida*, which grows wild as far north as Newfoundland, usually along streams or on the borders of moist meadows.

About 10" to 13" tall, it is very shrubby, with abundant shiny foliage which turns brilliant red in autumn even in a mild climate. The single rose-pink flowers, 2" across, are delightfully fragrant. The earliness and charm of its flowers, plus diminutive size and unusual attractiveness as a plant, make *R. nitida* a fine subject for general garden use. A source is JOSEPH J. KERN ROSE NURSERY (BOX 33, MENTOR, OH 44060).

For Rosier Roses

"Several good rosarians in this alkaline belt," notes a report from the South Central District (Oklahoma, Arkansas, Texas) in the "American Rose Magazine," "have been having unusual success in using magnesium sulfate or what is commonly referred to as Epsom Salt. It has been used as a trace element applied in a solution,

continuously, red-leaved in spring; and of 'Sutter's Gold,' golden and intensely fragrant. Crimson 'Parkdirector Riggers,' and the June-blooming, very profuse flowering 'Paul's Lemon Pillar' will even do well on north walls. Climbing 'Cecile Brunner,' a long-blooming pink "sweetheart rose," is marvelous for training on that old dead apple tree, as is the late-flowering pink 'New Dawn.'

For tall formal hedges, "The Rose Bed" suggests 'Chinatown,' 'Heidelberg' (red) and 'Queen Elizabeth' (pink). 'Orangeade' (persimmon color, single) and 'Anna Wheatcroft' (gold-orange, single) are perfect for shorter hedges, and for an informal solid boundary hedge, 'Eddie's Crimson' is recommended.

Sources for many of these are ARMSTRONG NURSERIES (BOX 473, ONTARIO, CA 91764), ROSES BY FRED EDMUNDS (BOX 68, WILSONVILLE, OR 97070), and TILLOTSON'S ROSES (BROWN'S VALLEY ROAD, WATSONVILLE, CA 95076; CATALOG $1).

THE EXCELLENT *"GUIDE SHEETS"* by the Minnesota Rose Society, covering spring, summer and winter care, feeding, pruning, exhibiting and growing miniature and tree roses, are $1 for a set of 8, from Mrs. Charles R. Campbell (4128 Brunswick Avenue South, Minneapolis, MN 55416).

mixed with a spray, or incorporated in solid or liquid fertilizer mixes. A glossier, darker and healthier looking foliage results in just a few days . . .

"Why does this work? Plants require small amounts of magnesium to produce chlorophyll which is essential to photosynthesis. If a plant does not get enough magnesium, chlorosis occurs . . . Another reason given by one of the larger chemical companies manufacturing this product is that magnesium also helps plants to absorb phosphorus. This element helps in the production of flowers. Magnesium also increases plant resistance to disease."

Modern Moss Roses

The old-time moss roses, prized for their unusual fragrance and the pretty mosslike calyxes, are appearing in new everblooming bush and even miniature forms.

Recently SEQUOIA NURSERY (2519 EAST NOBLE AVENUE, VISALIA, CA 93277) introduced 'Fairy Moss,' the first miniature moss rose, with 2" bright pink semi-double flowers — a fascinating conversation piece. Also new is the pink 'Crested Jewel,' a crested moss type (having 3-cornered buds), growing as a shrub or pillar rose 4' to 6'.

SEQUOIA offers two everblooming bush moss roses — 'Goldmoss,' 3', bright yellow flowers, and 2½' to 3' 'Rougemoss,' bright red underlaid with red-orange. Both flower repeatedly all season and are highly fragrant. And a new miniature is 'Kara,' 10" high, with very mossy buds which open into 1" medium pink 5-petaled single flowers — a constant bloomer, charming for pots and planters, as well as in the garden.

Rose Protection Review

Winter protection for roses is a controversial subject. Every year there are reports of roses surviving −20° temperatures with minimal protection, while a few miles away heavily protected roses succumbed at 0°.

It is generally agreed that protection should be provided wherever temperatures go below 15°, and that it is best applied after several hard frosts. The most common method is to cut back hybrid teas, grandifloras and floribundas to 18", then mound up soil to a height of 12". Some gardeners prefer not to cut back their roses until spring, and others favor, instead of soil, mulch materials such as hay, straw, ground corncobs, leaves, wood chips, peatmoss, sawdust — or even snow.

In the Cornell Rose Gardens in central New York, there was no mortality in 1963's record cold winter of roses in covered roofing-paper cylinders, 12" in diameter and 18" deep, filled with dry soil, dry peatmoss, dry sawdust, fresh perlite and new terralite. Researcher A. M. S. Pridham recommends that "the depth of the insulation should probably be some 25% or more than the length of the cane which the rose grower feels necessary for building a good rose bush for the coming season."

An estate gardener in Maine reports an unusual method. He prunes, ties and digs his 500 roses after frost (a two-day job), plants them close together in another area and covers them with soil and an organic insulant after the ground is frozen well. He states that this is easier than applying and removing a soil cover in the rose bed, provides better protection, prunes the roots annually and allows easy soil improvement in the rose beds.

Newest emphasis among expert rose growers is on proper hardening before cold weather. Non-nitrogenous fertilizer such as 0-20-20 applied in late summer and early fall will aid hardening, as will slacking off on watering, and allowing late blooms to remain to set seed pods.

"The Minnesota Tip"

The "Tip," as the Minnesota Rose Society calls it, appears from all reports to be the best method for winter protection of roses devised to date. The canes are simply tied together and the soil loosened around the base of the plant, removing

Grass clippings are an excellent mulch for roses if applied no more than 2″ deep.

some from one side so that the canes can be bent over easily at root level. They are then pinned down with wire loops, either on the surface of the ground or in a shallow trench. Covering consists of 3″ of soil followed by about 18″ of dry leaves, marsh hay or similar material, all watered down well.

Many growers who bury their roses thus at full length with no cutting back report they have completely green canes with living buds all the way to the tips when they uncover them in the spring.

Twigs Sub Rosa

"The mulch for the rose bed," says horticulturist R. B. Farnham, "is always a problem and may do as much harm as help if it becomes soggy-wet, or too thin, at certain times of year. The perfect mulch starts in late fall by laying a well-aerated carpet of insulation over the soil surface, which will not become compacted and water-saturated from rain or snow, and can be adjusted to summer insulation needs, to avoid hot, dry soil.

"I have found an ideal answer. Using loppers, I cut woody prunings into 4″ to 6″ pieces and covered the bed surface 6″ deep with them. As the soil froze, I added a layer of maple leaves. These were removed, leaving the twig layer, as the warm days of April seemed likely to be permanent.

"Fertilizer applications easily reach the soil through the twig mulch, and rain or watering is easily dispersed to prevent compaction of the soil surface. As the sun gets hot, the twig layer

prevents extremes of either heat or cold or moisture. It also prevents bouncing of infection of last year's diseases to this year's foliage as rain or water hits the soil. And when the gardener has to step into the bed, foot pressure is no longer a packing force to reduce soil aeration and root health. Few other plants are as needful of loose, aerated soil for good roots as is the rose. My rose plants have never before been so healthy.

"If looks are objected to, pachysandra will spread through the twig mulch and mask future applications of twigs beneath its top foliage. I have also interplanted tall iris between the roses. These extend the period of bloom in the bed, and the foliage adds design and green beauty to the rose plants, whose lower plant structures are often less than beautiful."

Cut to Come Again

The way you cut off spent hybrid tea and grandiflora rose blooms will greatly affect succeeding flowers, says Harold H. Allen in the "American Rose Annual 1970."

Many gardeners snip spent flowers at the neck joint just beneath the bloom. However, this leaves a thin, weak stem and the shoot developing from this will be incapable of producing a quality flower. Mr. Allen recommends cutting much farther down, where the cane is pencil thick or thicker. He cuts approximately ¼″ above a good eye situated in a leaf-stem joint. The shoot that develops from that eye will become a stem of appreciable length and strength and will produce a fine bloom.

A SACRIFICIAL ROSE — a cultivar highly attractive to insects — keeps other nearby varieties uncommonly free of insects, says rosarian Ralph F. Gearson. His tests show 'Elsa Arnot' to be the best sacrificial rose, with 'American Heritage,' 'Ambossfunken,' 'Coup de Foudre,' 'Gail Borden,' 'Jack O'Lantern,' and 'Bishop Darlington' effective to a lesser degree.

Upstanding Roses

Northern gardeners are following the lead of Southerners who grow climbing roses not only on fences, trellises, arbors and pergolas, but also on poles, pipes and posts.

Pillar-rose practitioners favor lamp posts, or train their hardy climbers on wood posts or pipes about 8′ high, based in concrete. Several pipes set 3′ to 4′ apart can result in a stunning accent, or two pipes 6′ apart and connected at the top by a semicircular piece of scrap iron will make a beautiful rose arch. A reverse arch is formed by swinging a rope between the posts. Some fine roses for pillars are 'Don Juan,' 'Paul's Scarlet' and 'Blaze,' 'Coral Dawn,' 'City of York,' 'Golden Showers,' 'Dr. J. H. Nicolas' and 'Joseph's Coat.'

Incidentally, a source of 'Joseph's Coat,' ARMSTRONG NURSERIES (BOX 473, ONTARIO, CA 91764), recommends this rose for espalier. Probably quite a few climbers could be trained in this fashion, including 'Blaze.'

The dense-foliaged rugosa roses are carefree, stand dry soil, and bear fruit which is the best source of vitamin C known.

Rose Folios

The great increase in interest in hybridizing by amateurs is resulting in ideas useful beyond the field of plant breeding.

Very worthy, for example, is the concept of "folios," developed by the new and knowledgeable AMATEUR ROSE HYBRIDIZERS ASSOCIATION (MRS. BARBARA K. KRAM, SECRETARY, 5016 WILKINSON AVENUE, NORTH HOLLYWOOD, CA 91607). Each folio is a compilation of facts, figures and opinions supplied by the members on a subject related to rose breeding. "Handling Rose Seeds," is available and two more folios, "Handling Rose Seedlings," and "Roses for Hybridizers" are in progress. The idea could well be employed by other garden organizations as an investigative and educational tool.

A BUYING GUIDE for roses, entitled "HANDBOOK FOR SELECTING ROSES," is offered for 10¢ and a stamped return envelope by the American Rose Society, Box 30,000, Shreveport, LA 71130). More than 1000 cultivars are described and rated.

Locally adapted blends of the new "pedigreed" grasses give superb performance with minimum maintenance.

Lawns

Talented Turf

It's been a long time coming, but true high-quality, minimum-maintenance turf is fast becoming a reality. In fact, we are very close to the day when lawns equal to the great greenswards of England should be possible almost anywhere in America.

With the explosion in turf technology, says Dr. Robert W. Schery, Director of The Lawn Institute, Route 4, Marysville, Ohio, the newest practices and products, if utilized properly, assure such good performance of lawn grasses that it is now feasible to turn attention to the aesthetics of a lawn. The new "elite" grass cultivars vary in color, texture, height and density of growth, and the gardener should give the same serious thought to the landscape aspects of grass selection that he gives to choosing a specimen tree or shrub.

The remarkable improvement in lawn grasses is seen in varieties like 'Fylking' Kentucky bluegrass, which has been hailed as far and away the best of the blues. Introduced from Sweden, it thrives as far south as southern California. Its advantages include ability to stand mowing to an inch or less, a very tough, close-growing habit and less need for fertilizer. It is more resistant to diseases, weeds and wear than any previous bluegrass, and its rich, dark green color is maintained from early spring to late fall.

Other new bluegrass cultivars or blends show excellent regional superiority. 'Arboretum,' from the Missouri Botanical Garden, has proved the best for enduring beauty through the long hot summers in southern portions of the bluegrass belt. Mixtures of 'Fylking,' 'Pennstar' and 'Nugget' have scored highest of all in tests in the Northwest.

In the new fescues, 'Highlight' chewings fescue from Holland is unusually fine textured, produces a dense turf and is tolerant of acid soil, low fertility and some shade. It is a beautiful bright green, and stands extremely close mowing.

A breakthrough in ryegrasses is 'Pelo' perennial rye from Holland. In appearance and texture, it is equal to 'Merion' bluegrass. 'Pelo' has more drought, shade, disease and traffic resistance than any other ryegrass to date. On Long Island, test plots of 'Pelo' mowed ¾" high are still extremely attractive after eight years.

The bentgrasses, because of their high maintenance requirements, are usually not recommended for home lawns. However, 'Exeter' colonial bent and 'Kingstown' velvet bent, both recently released by the University of Rhode Island, need less careful attention to feeding and watering (but still require frequent, careful mowing). For steep slopes and water channels, 'Highland' and 'Penncross' make a virtually impervious erosion-preventing mat.

For the South, Clemson University's 'Pee Dee 102' bermudagrass is considered the best of the improved bermudas, although the U.S. Golf Association's 'U-3' bermuda has the advantage of being more cold-hardy.

Transition Area Turf

'Kentucky 31,' a variety of tall fescue, makes a fine lawn for the "transition area" from Washington, D.C., to northeastern Kansas, where neither northern grasses like Kentucky blue nor warm-season types such as bermuda will thrive. The U.S. Department of Agriculture reports that 9 years of tests show that pure stands of 'Kentucky 31,' seeded at 6 to 8 pounds per 1000 square feet and mowed to 2" height, do not develop the undesirable clumping common to bluegrass- and tall-fescue mixtures. The turf is attractive, has satisfactory winter color, is shade tolerant, grows well in heavy or acid or alkaline soils and stands wet or dry conditions.

The Magic Is in the Blend

A good lawn involves many variables, and success depends not only on culture but also on selecting a seed blend to "in effect establish a procession of grass plants that will succeed each other as conditions change, each 'doing his thing' for long or short periods of time." So says Howard Kaerwer, Chief Turf Agronomist of NORTHRUP, KING & CO. (1500 JACKSON STREET, MINNEAPOLIS, MN 55413).

"A formula weighted too heavily with competitive bluegrasses ('Merion' is one) can result in the bluegrass forcing out the fine fescues during the establishment years. Then when the bluegrasses begin to thin after the sod becomes mature, there are no fine fescues around to provide that much-desired continuity to the lawn. On the other hand, if you give an opportunity to some fine fescues (such as the chewing fescues), they will form a dense circle into which no bluegrasses can penetrate . . . Annual ryegrass is much too competitive, as is 'Lynn' perennial ryegrass. 'NK100' and 'Pelo' perennial ryegrasses are considerably less competitive and will form a compatible turf along with bluegrasses."

Color and texture should also be considered. In the bluegrasses, 'Prato' blends well in color with 'Fylking' and 'Pennstar,' but clashes a bit with 'Merion.' 'Ruby' red fescue goes well with 'Prato' too. Annual ryegrass mixed with bluegrass or fine fescues will stand out and look like weeds, and fine-leaved hard fescues form dense clusters that disfigure a bluegrass lawn. A more open fine fescue like 'Ruby' creeping red intermingles well with bluegrass.

There seems to be a trend toward deeper color in the new grass introductions. The Kentucky bluegrasses 'Baron' from Holland and 'Nassau' from Rutgers University, 'Jamestown' fine fescue from the University of Rhode Island and Rutgers' 'Manhattan,' a fine-leaved perennial ryegrass, all have dark green color, which can be valuable for cooling effect and contrast in landscape design.

Mr. Kaerwer also notes, " 'Newport' Kentucky bluegrass prefers the cool temperatures of spring and fall, 'Prato' or 'Merion' the warmth of a moderate summer. Your formula should combine these characteristics to give you 'a lawn for all seasons' that will green up early and stay pretty through the waning summer and into fall."

Undercover Work

Techniques in making new lawns haven't changed much. There is still unanimous agreement among turf experts that ample organic matter in the soil is the prime requirement for producing rapid deep rooting and sturdy growth of grass.

Peatmoss and compost incorporated liberally into the top 10″ of soil following grading and removal of rubble is the usual means of supplying this organic matter. Another method — slower but less costly — is growing a green manure crop for one or more seasons. Rye, vetch, crimson clover, alfalfa, cowpeas and others will greatly improve the tilth, fertility, aeration and drainage of soils when they are dug in. (Two useful publications, *"HOW TO DO WONDERS WITH GREEN MANURE CROPS,"* and *"CHART OF GREEN MANURES INFORMATION,"* are free from GARDEN WAY MFG. CO., 102ND STREET AND NINTH AVENUE, TROY, NY 12182).

Where the soil is so poor, poisoned or filled with rubble that improving it appears insurmountable, replacing at least a 6″ depth of it with clean topsoil may be the only road to a permanently successful lawn. The gardener might even consider a soilless lawn base, such as some greenskeepers now use to produce high-quality turf on tee and green areas. A golf course architect in California recommends sharp sand and fir bark "fines":

Following rough grading, a 14″ layer of sand topped by 4″ of ⅜″ fir bark is applied, then these are mixed thoroughly with a rotavator to a depth

Cheap "haygrass" seed mixtures (left) contrast startlingly with selected fine-leaved grasses given proper fertilization.

of 8″. The seedbed is graded, rolled and raked, and seed is sown mixed with 10 pounds of 10-10-10 fertilizer and 20 pounds of Milorganite per 1000 square feet. A final rolling is given, and the seedbed is kept moist until germination is complete. Several advantages are cited for this unique lawn-building method — the more uniform surface and excellent water retention by the bark insure highest germination; the bark is weed-free; less hand-raking is necessary; less compaction occurs; and less watering is needed.

One of the most critical problems, keeping grass seed moist until it germinates, is solved by applying a very thin mulch of rough peat, hay or straw immediately after sowing the seed, or by use of a cheesecloth netting. A new aid is Terra Tack (GRASS GROWERS INC., BOX 584, PLAINFIELD, NJ 07061), which may be mixed with the seed and applied by spreader, or sprayed on in solution after sowing to form a permeable crust that reduces evaporation and prevents erosion by wind and water.

Low-Cut Lawns

The new low-growing grasses make it easier to renovate a poor lawn or one of "dubious pedigree." By simply overseeding with the new grasses, then mowing at the height these prefer, the lawnsman soon eliminates the older grasses that require higher cutting.

Whether the overseeding is done in spring or fall, the lawn should first be scarified, scalping it by mowing very low and then raking vigorously with a metal rake to pull out the accumulated detritus called thatch. Spread the seed, at about

A GASOLINE-POWERED MOWER which exhausts under the hood can cause dead patches in the lawn if left running in one spot for even a few moments.

half the rate recommended for building new lawns, mixed with a slow-release fertilizer. Watering should be frequent and light until the new grass has rooted, then deep and less often in dry periods.

Some bluegrasses to use in an overseeding blend — all suitable to mowing as low as ¾" — are 'Nugget,' 'Fylking,' 'Sydsport,' 'Pennstar,' 'Baron,' 'Adelphi' and 'Prato.' The new fine fescues, such as 'Wintergreen,' 'Golfrood,' 'Highlight,' 'Jamestown' and 'Ruby' stand low mowing. Two of the newest colonial bentgrasses, 'Exeter' and 'Holfior,' also blend well with the low-cut bluegrasses.

Lean and Hungry Lawns

All lawn experts agree that fertilization is the biggest single maintenance determinant of lawn success. Dr. Robert W. Schery of The Lawn Institute says, "One is frequently able to keep his lawn robust and reasonably weed-free with little else than skillful fertilization . . . Nothing supports grass in its contest with weeds so well as does properly timed fertilization." Yet perhaps only one lawn in fifty is fed properly.

Southern grasses need feeding fairly evenly through the year. For northern grasses, autumn is the season for most generous feeding, with a small booster in early spring and another in late spring. Most grasses need a minimum of 3 to 4 pounds of actual nitrogen per 1000 square feet per year for acceptable performance. The improved Kentucky blues and bermudas require no less than 6 pounds, creeping bent no less than 8 pounds. (To calculate the actual nitrogen of a fertilizer, multiply the bag weight by the percent of nitrogen — e.g., a 25-pound bag of 10-6-4 = 25 × .10, or 2.5 pounds of nitrogen.) Where the gardener is willing to mow more often and water frequently, higher rates — to double or as much as triple the above — will give an even finer turf.

Slow-release fertilizers of the ureaform or IBDU type are preferable for steady sustained feeding and nonburning safety. Soluble inorganic fertilizers require more frequent lighter applications, but still spread within the schedules noted above for northern and southern grasses.

Northern Turf Tactics

Autumn is properly the beginning, not the end, of the lawn year. In the North it's time to build strength into the turf for next year.

Latest thinking on northern lawns emphasizes the great importance of fall fertilizing to promote "tillering" and build up food reserves. The lawn should receive a total of 2 pounds of actual nitrogen per 1000 square feet in autumn, ideally in two feedings six weeks apart. Phosphorus and potassium are currently regarded as vital to promote winter hardiness, disease resistance and "wearability" of grass. Borden's Nutro Winter Survival, a high-PK 7-22-15 formula with a wetting agent to speed penetration to the root zone, is used by many groundskeepers in late fall.

A review of autumn procedures followed by estate gardeners and other professionals suggests this program:

1. Mow as low as possible (in progressively lower cuttings if the grass has been high) and use a steel rake or thatching machine to remove accumulated litter.

2. Apply an herbicide such as 2,4-D + silvex or 2,4-D + dicamba to eliminate broad-leaved weeds if they are extensive.

3. Lime if need is indicated by soil test, and fertilize as noted above.

4. Topdress lightly with peat-humus (Michigan peat) or well-rotted compost, and rake in.

5. Overseed with high-quality seed at the rate of 1 to 4 pounds per 1000 square feet.

6. Water frequently but lightly until the seed sprouts. Mow as necessary, and give a second feeding as above.

Southern Lawn Strategy

Biggest trend in southern lawns: winter-seeding with northern cool-season grasses to give a beautiful-all-winter turf. This is analogous to "bolster" seeding in the North, except that the wintergrass is grown as an annual.

Ryegrass has long been used for this purpose, but has fallen into disfavor because it winterkills in severe weather, and does not fade away

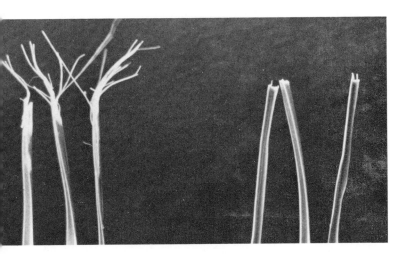

Bred for softer fibers, 'Pennfine' (right) perennial ryegrass cuts cleanly instead of shredding as most ryegrasses do when mowed.

gracefully as the southern grass revives in spring. Much better, says Dr. Robert W. Schery of The Lawn Institute, is a fine-textured blend containing fine fescues, the quickest to make an acceptable lawn; Kentucky bluegrass, to provide midwinter beauty; and 'Highland' bentgrass, which is at its best late in the season.

Timing is very important. Ideal time is just as the bermudagrass starts to go dormant, as shown by slowed growth and the beginning of loss of color. This ranges from early October in the Upper South to mid-November in Florida.

A winter-seeding program involves mowing close, to 1″; removal of thatch, if it is ½″ or thicker, with a rake or by machine; light topdressing with soil, compost or peat-humus; sowing the seed, usually at 5 to 10 pounds per 1000 square feet; and frequent watering until establishment. Feeding, which should continue through the winter, is best begun after the first mowing, as feeding at sowing time might encourage competitive new growth of the bermudagrass.

Toughest Turfs

Dr. Victor B. Youngner, of the University of California at Riverside, gives valuable tips for maintaining a good greensward on play or heavy traffic areas:

Fertilization is most important, neither too much nor too little. Play areas should receive ½ to ¾ pound of actual nitrogen per 1000 square feet per month of the growing season, plus an annual application of a 5-1-2 fertilizer to provide sufficient phosphorus and potassium. Secondly, aerification — as often as six times a year on heavily used areas — is essential to prevent soil compaction. Finally, bluegrass, perennial ryegrass, tall fescue and meadow fescue should be mowed no closer than 1½″, bermudagrass 1″.

In making a new play lawn, extra large amounts of organic matter should be incorporated to increase the soil's water absorption ability. Proper grading and leveling, plus the installation of tile drains where the subsoil is impervious, also aid in preventing wet spots where the turf will fail.

Shade Grass

Where shade is a problem, special seed mixtures and culture are the answer. A bluegrass that performs well in as much as 65% shade is 'Warren's A-34.' The turf can be improved annually by overseeding with fast-sprouting perennial ryegrasses such as 'Compas,' 'Manhattan,' 'NK100,' 'NK200,' 'Pelo' or 'Pennfine,' when the leaves fall. Grasses in shade should be mowed high and given double the fertilizer and much more frequent watering than grasses in sun, to compensate for nutrient and moisture losses to the shallow feeder roots of the shade trees.

Lawns 39

The roots of fine-leaved 'NK200' perennial ryegrass (left) go twice as deep as those of bluegrass (right), enabling it to thrive with minimal watering and fertilizing.

Reel-ly Good Mowing

The first lawn mower, invented in 1830 by Edwin Budding in England, was a reel type. Though rotary mowers are by far the most popular today, the reel mower still has important advantages for the gardener who wants a well-groomed lawn.

The JACOBSEN MFG. CO. (RACINE, WI 53403), which makes both reel and rotary mowers, states that the reel gives a smoother, more even cut. It is less apt to scalp high spots, and it shears the grass cleanly with no shredding of the tips which would cause browning and growth impairment. For fine-quality low-cut grasses like the new blues, bent or fine-leaf bermuda, the reel mower gives the neatest, velvet-surface cut, provided the turf is mowed frequently so that no too-high grass is present to be mashed under the bed knife.

While reel mowers generally cost more and are not quite as maneuverable in tight corners, they last longer, need sharpening less often and are available with conveniences such as handle-mounted controls and fingertip height adjustment. And as an organic gardener has noted, reel mowers do not have the high suction ability (to hold grass blades erect) of rotaries, so do not injure praying mantises, those invaluable destroyers of harmful insects.

To keep a reel mower sharp easily, spread carborundum valve-grinding paste on the fixed blade and work the cutting blades; wipe off the paste before mowing.

No-Mow Grass

The new 'No-Mow' shade-tolerant bermudagrass is exciting considerable attention throughout the South. The Mississippi Agricultural Experiment Station reports that 'No-Mow' does not grow taller than 3″, and so can be left uncut for long periods without looking like a hayfield. However, its growth is uneven and its appearance becomes "bumpy" at heights above ½″ in sun and 1″ in shade. Therefore, regular mowing is necessary to produce a superior lawn, with a professional mower that will cut this low. Also, its dense growth results in considerable thatch, and vertical mowing is recommended in late winter to remove this accumulation.

In heavy shade, 'No-Mow' showed elongated stems and leaves and did not become dense. But in full sun to 50% shade, it spread rapidly and produced excellent turf. In 50% shade, it grew more evenly than in full sun and lost its tendency to be patchy.

Thatch: Boon or Bane?

An easy way to control thatch — dead vegetation that accumulates on a lawn — is simply topdressing in spring with ⅛″ of good topsoil. The soil buries the thatch for rapid disintegration. Peat and similar organic materials do not have the same effect.

How much of a threat is thatch? Dr. Robert W. Schery of The Lawn Institute says it can definitely be a problem in mat-forming grasses like creeping bent, bermuda and St. Augustine. In looser-growing turfs like bluegrass-fine fescue, it may or may not build up sufficiently to be detrimental.

Heavy thatch harbors insects, provides a hospitable environment for disease organisms, creates acid soil, prevents the penetration of water and fertilizer and steals nitrogen for its decomposition, and of course is both unsightly and grass-smothering. Conversely, when not heavy, thatch provides nutrients and organic matter, releases soil fertility by increasing microbial activity, helps keep down weeds and may encourage organisms inimical to pests.

Probably a good general rule is to remove thatch if it builds up to ½″ or thicker. Besides topdressing, Dr. Schery recommends liming to aid decay, loosening with a rake or aerator, using a lawn sweeper to collect clippings when mowing and applying less nitrogen which stimulates grass production. Fungicides, which destroy bacteria responsible for decomposition, should be avoided as much as possible. A wooden rake will remove thatch with minimum bruising of the grass blades. Flexible-tine power rakes, which also de-thatch with little damage to the turf, may be rented at garden centers.

Casual Lawns

The trend to naturalistic landscaping is extending even to the "natural lawn." This can be predominantly grass with simply a few patches of veronica or bluets here and there, or it may be that fascinating conglomeration of numerous low-growing plants that is called an alpine lawn.

A natural lawn may evolve by itself from seed spread by wind and birds, with only obvious weeds such as plantain and dandelions removed when they appear. Or many plants may be artfully introduced, chosen for their flower or foliage colors, textures and patterns. Ajuga, wild strawberries, pussy-toes, cinquefoil, violets and scores of other wildflowers or rock garden plants or even "weeds" are suitable.

A natural lawn is easily kept in fine condition by mowing, less frequently than one would an all-grass lawn and with the mower set higher. It is, of course, best suited to an informal garden.

Scented Lawns

In the seventeenth century, notes the British "GARDENER'S CHRONICLE," lawns grown for fragrance were common in English and Irish gardens. Most frequently used were lavender (*Lavendula spica*), kept cut to 3″, or chamomile (*Anthemis nobilis*), which also stands close shearing. Peppermint (*Mentha piperita*) lawns were less popular, perhaps because their scent could be overpowering.

Only chamomile has been used to any extent here. It is not an ideal grass substitute everywhere, doing poorly in windy, dry or cold areas. A much better choice is creeping thyme. For a beautiful "thyme turf" in infertile, sun-baked, windy locations, use these varieties of *Thymus serpyllum*, all under 2″ and standing moderate traffic: *albus*, tiny-leaved white thyme; *aureus*, with gold-mottled leaves and purple flowers; *coccinea,* crimson-flowered; *lanuginosus,* woolly, with pink blooms; spice-scented purple 'Nutmeg'; and *splendens,* with showy red flowers.

Many of these are offered by NICHOLS GARDEN· NURSERY (1190 NORTH PACIFIC HIGHWAY, ALBANY, OR 97321; CATALOG 15¢).

Prairie Grass Lawns

Many native grasses deserve study for their value for lawns. Prairie-plant specialist Jim Wilson, of WILSON SEED FARMS (POLK, NB 68653), says:

"Some prairie grasses can make fine lawns, requiring only 2 or 3 cuttings a season. Buffalo grass grows in the 2″ to 4″ range and hardly needs mowing and no watering. The University of Kansas strain, F_2, competes effectively with weeds even in our area. This grass is adapted to the hardest, poorest, and exposed soil, and has no insect or disease problems like bluegrass. As with all dryland grasses, the new growth is largely root action the first year . . . one must wait until the second season before the lawn looks attractive. Then, however, you have a tough sage-green carpet that never needs watering. Seeding is done in mid-June, as this is a warm-season grass. This permits killing of the first weed crop mechanically by cultivation before seeding. Work up a shallow seedbed and roll it with no fertilizer. Cover the seed ½″ by harrow or rake."

Other species for prairie grass lawns include sideoats gramma and blue gramma, or these in combination with buffalo grass. Mr. Wilson states that prairie grasses "are well adapted on many sites as far east as central Iowa, but they're still experimental farther east. These are dryland grasses, and we don't know yet how successfully they will compete over a long period of time with weeds and aggressive cool-season grasses in a humid climate."

For more information on these and taller prairie grasses for background, foundation or "mini-prairie" plantings, contact Mr. Wilson, and read Jim and Alice Wilson's beautiful book, "GRASS LAND" (WIDE SKIES PRESS, POLK, NB 68654).

Sod Story

Sod is an easy — if expensive — way to an instant lawn. But even sodding can be less than satisfactory unless it is properly done.

An important factor is the difference between the soil on which the sod originally grew and the soil on which it is laid, says Thomas G. Byrne, of California's Alameda County Agricultural Extension Service. Most sod is grown on heavy muck soil. When it is laid on a lighter, coarse soil, the capillary or "wick" effect is not established, and gravity by itself may not be enough to pull moisture down. Heavy rains stand on the surface, and the sod fails.

The problem can be largely avoided by ordering sod cut as thin as possible, which will encourage root growth and rapid "knitting" into the base soil. If standing water does occur, the solution is aerification with a machine that lifts cores of soil, followed by topdressing and raking in coarse organic material. This will improve water penetration, and roots will grow quickly downward in the organic matter.

Lawns with Wet Feet

A wet spring means waterlogging of heavy clay soils, so that the deeper roots of turf die from lack of oxygen. In this situation, the usual rule of infrequent but heavy watering does not apply: heavy watering will only increase the drowning of lower roots, while the upper inch or so of soil will dry out between irrigations and so cannot support the surface roots upon which the grass is now dependent.

The answer is frequent — perhaps daily — light sprinkling. Occasional probing with a trowel or soil corer to a depth of 6″ to 8″ will show how well the excess moisture from spring rains is draining away. As drying is encountered to a greater depth, water applications can be less frequent but longer in duration. Mowing high will also help, as more top growth encourages deeper rooting. The same program will aid rebuilding of a good root system on grass damaged by grubs, chinch bugs and similar insects. To avoid fungus problems caused by frequent waterings, sprinkle early in the day, do not allow clippings to accumulate and apply a lawn fungicide weekly.

GROUNDCOVERS and Vines

Like an Oriental rug, groundcovers make subtle blendings of color, light and texture, and enhance the beauty of all that surround them.

Covering Ground

For far too long, groundcovers have been considered simply as substitutes for grass, plants to be used in places where grass won't grow or is too hard to mow. Thus they have become solutions for steep slopes, deep shade or dry, sandy, baked, moist, rough or rocky sites, rather than first choices on their own merits.

Granted, grass, where it can be grown successfully, is one of the finest groundcovers — but it is of definitely restricted landscape use and not exactly low in maintenance. A host of other carpeters, lacking only turf's fine texture and ability to be walked on, can provide landscape artistry of a higher order over a much wider range of situations.

The right groundcover or combination of groundcovers puts a finishing touch to a garden. These low-growing massed or self-spreading plants unify a design and enhance it through contrast and dramatic effect. They serve as settings for flowering plants and garden ornaments, soften the lines of walls, paths and steps,

and bring out-of-scale plantings and structures into proportion with other garden features. They help to define space, as well as to tie together disparate elements in the composition. And they offer tremendous visual variety, from smooth and neat to bold and rough, billowy to stark, and may be colorful all year or seasonally through bloom or fruit.

Practically speaking, groundcovers reduce maintenance, prevent erosion and act as "living mulch" to keep tree, shrub and wildflower roots cool. Groundcovers should also be a first consideration in planting new gardens, for they give an immediate finished effect even when very small specimens of shrubs and trees are planted, helping the gardener avoid the tendency to plant the latter too closely together, resulting in overcrowding at maturity.

Cover Design

What is a groundcover? The old definition of a low, fast-spreading, evergreen plant has been replaced by a much more liberal one: in modern garden parlance, a groundcover is any plant that covers the ground. It may be literally carpet-like, or several feet in height. Some of the finest are deciduous, some may be very slow to cover.

This opens the field to a vast number of woody and herbaceous plants. Shrubs, grasses, climbers, dwarf conifers and even annuals and herbs are part of the roster available to discriminating gardeners. The popular ivy, myrtle and pachysandra have their place — and often fulfill it admirably — but scores of less orthodox materials can give greater enjoyment. In the shade of large trees, for example, a mix of hostas and ferns with lily-of-the-valley and violets, or unusuals such as

Perennial candytuft circles a bed of epimediums for neat no-maintenance good looks from spring through fall.

foamflower *(Tiarella cordifolia)* or wintergreen *(Gaultheria procumbens)* bring special delight through diversity of form and color. On baking banks, the low junipers are always good choices, but certain cotoneasters, sweet fern *(Comptonia peregrina)*, thymes, sedums, snow-in-summer *(Cerastium tomentosum)* and many others can be more dramatic.

Some plants usually regarded as rock garden subjects or edgers make fine limited-area groundcovers — arabis, gold dust *(Alyssum saxatile)*, perennial dianthus, evergreen candytuft *(Iberis sempervirens)*. Self-sowing annuals like portulaca, cornflower and sweet alyssum can be considered as permanent groundcovers. Ornamental grasses such as blue fescue *(Festuca ovina glauca)* and blue oatgrass *(Avena sempervirens)* are handsome, especially when associated with purple-leaved plants like *Ajuga reptans* 'Atropurpurea.' Many low-growing annuals, of course, and even fall-planted cereal grains such as wheat, oats, rye and barley, can serve as temporary groundcovers.

A new trend is the use of native wildflowers and grasses. Gardeners with larger properties have found that almost anywhere except in the Deep South, wildflower meadows and prairie grass lawns are beautiful low-maintenance replacements for manicured turf and formal flower beds. Except for mowing once a year in late summer, a meadow, hillside or odd corner of butterfly weed, wild iris, black-eyed Susans, hawkweed and violets is work-free. A variation of this is free-style naturalizing of tough perennials like forget-me-not, monarda, iris, eupatorium or dianthus in small areas.

Combining groundcovers with each other and with plants of other types is truly an avant gardener's art. Evergreen candytuft and maidenhair ferns are superb around rocks, as are wild roses and thyme on a dry bank, periwinkle and Christmas ferns as an underplanting for trilliums and wild columbines, or tuberous begonias with maidenhair fern and meadow rue. One of the loveliest garden pictures we've seen is a dogwood underplanted with pipsissewa, bellwort, partridgeberry and white-flowered geraniums. More interesting banks and hillsides are created by combining carpeting plants with sprawlers, broad or mounded shrubs and even low trees.

Prof. Clarence E. Lewis of Michigan State University stresses that contrasting textures draw the attention. Large-leaved plants such as mahonias or rhododendrons are accented when underplanted with small-leaved cotoneasters, heaths, heathers, thymes, grasses like blue fescue, and some junipers. When plants more similar in texture and height are used, the attention is allowed to move easily to other features which the gardener wants to highlight. Combining light green or blue foliage with dark green attracts the eye — *Taxus baccata* 'Repandens' with Blue Rug juniper, for example — while a blend like Blue Rug and blue Pfitzer junipers is less eye-catching.

Where low and tall covers are used together, they should not be of the same width or mass, nor should one low plant be sited next to one tall one — grouping plants of each height gives a gradual gradation and avoids a "jumpy" effect. Neat-growing groundcovers, or ones which can easily be trimmed to make a neat edge, are important where emphasizing the line of a walk is desired. Finally, a flat-growing cover such as myrtle or periwinkle may be a better choice than pachysandra under dense-growing azaleas or yews, where the upright-growing pachysandra would give the effect of a tight collar around the base of the taller plants.

Criteria

In choosing groundcovers, the gardener should first decide what plants will give the desired effect, then select from these the one or several best culturally suited to the site. Observation in every season and on all manner of sites — in nature, in public and private gardens, shopping centers and industrial landscaping, on roadsides — will yield discoveries of exciting groundcover uses for a great variety of plants. Hardiness, of course, is a prime consideration, as is pest and disease resistance. In frequently viewed exposed areas, it may be important to select evergreens that do not need to be covered with leaves or boughs as a protection against winter browning. Salt-resistant plants are called for on roadsides subject to traffic splash.

In most cases, low plants of relatively fine texture are desirable, but taller groundcovers are often useful at a distance and in heavier shade. Coarse-textured vines and shrubs 2′ or more tall may be right for sizable open areas or slopes that are not in close proximity to the home. Vines that have a strong tendency to climb, such as Hall's honeysuckle, should never be used anywhere near trees or structures that can give them vertical support.

There are places where groundcovers may not be the wisest choice — for example, where a home has a wide overhang which keeps rain out from its sides. A bark or pebble mulch might be best here unless the gardener can water frequently. This can also be true for heavily shaded areas under very shallow rooted trees such as beech or sugar maple. Even pachysandra or myrtle will not flourish here without special attention (however, a gardener tells us she has had excellent success with maidenhair ferns in this situation).

Some of the best groundcovers can be invasive. Often this drawback can be overcome through either culture or curbing; many others are effectively contained by paving, paths or mowing strips, or by wood or metal edging, which may have to be 12″ or more deep for some offenders. If the top of an edging is allowed to extend about 1″ above ground, it will serve as a guide for shears, making annual trimming easy.

Cover Culture

How well a groundcover will spread, serve the purposes for which it was chosen and thrive with long life is determined by the care taken in planting it. Lack of soil preparation and aftercare until established will slow coverage of almost any groundcover. In the case of many of the most desirable but less tough covers, it can result in failure, or at least a less than satisfactory landscape effect.

Even plants suited to the poorest soils will benefit from some improvement of tilth and fertility — and over the entire area, not just in the planting holes. A minimum 2″ layer of peatmoss, compost or other organic matter, plus rotted manure, should be worked in 6″ to 10″ deep, deeper for shrub types. Acid peat or peat humus is used for acid-loving plants, with generous amounts of leafmold for woodland plants. A good general rule is to incorporate also about 3 pounds per 100 square feet of a fertilizer such as 5-10-5 or 10-6-4. Strongly alkaline soils may need to be treated with agricultural sulfur or ferrous sulfate to lower the pH; acid soils with limestone to raise it.

When the planting area is infested with perennial weeds such as quackgrass, bindweed or Canada thistle, fumigation is virtually essential. Vapam can be applied with a watering can and watered in, three weeks before planting. Treflan, which can be used at planting time, suppresses many broadleaf weeds and most grasses. In established plantings, Eptam gives excellent control of numerous weeds. Always check the label, of course, to be sure of the groundcover's tolerance to the herbicide. Usually a 1″ to 1½″ mulch of wood chips, bark, hulls, coarse compost, pine needles, chopped hay or straw, etc., is quite effective in holding down weeds, as well as in conserving moisture.

In planting, dig the holes wide and deep to avoid crowding the roots. Use a staggered row pattern. Spacing depends on the plant's habit, growth rate and the immediate effect desired. Small plants like ajuga are generally set 4″ to 6″ apart, and large ones such as cotoneaster or juniper as much as 48″ in all directions. Closer spacing gives faster coverage, but at higher cost. At 4″ spacing, 100 plants will cover approximately 10 square feet; at 8″, 45 square feet; 12″, 100; 18″, 225; 24″, 400; 36″, 900; 48″, 1600.

Soil improvement plus mulch or netting will aid establishment of groundcovers on clay or loam banks that are not steeper than 1′ of rise to 2′ of horizontal measurement. A sandy bank with much less slope may wash or slide easily in rains. For sandy or too steep conditions, cutting pockets or narrow level terraces and reinforcing these with edged stones may be sufficient. To give stronger stabilization, use 6″ planks partly buried on edge horizontally and held with vertical wood or metal stakes. On very gravelly slopes, soil-filled wooden produce baskets sunk to their rims will provide planting pockets. Or planting holes can be lined with plastic sheeting, with some holes punched in the bottom for drainage.

During the first year, deep watering weekly in dry weather is essential, especially for a groundcover in competition with tree roots in shade. Many plants will benefit greatly from weak liquid feedings in spring to early summer, or a pelleted balanced fertilizer can be applied at 2 to 3 pounds

per 100 square feet in spring. Use a suitable herbicide or hand-pull any weeds that come up through the mulch. For many evergreen groundcovers, an antitranspirant spray in the fall will reduce winter damage.

A set of large wheels that allow a rotary mower to cut 4″ to 6″ high will pay dividends in more beautiful groundcovers. All groundcovering euonymus are particularly handsome when sheared into an even-topped immaculate 5″ carpet. Many violets, creeping lilyturf, ivy, pachysandra, myrtle, evergreen candytuft, moss phlox, rock cress, snow-in-summer, lily-of-the-valley and mock strawberry are greatly improved by mowing when they get leggy or coarse. California gardeners often mow ajuga as low as 1¼″, sacrificing spring bloom but making this cover even neater and more turflike.

Tough Covers

A talk with a nurseryman has yielded some interesting facts on the "toughness" of groundcovers. If not exposed to drying winds, ivy — English ivy, *Hedera helix* 'Baltica,' in the North, and Algerian ivy, *H. cariensis*, in the South — are more durable than vinca or pachysandra . . . yarrow, *Achillea tomentosa*, stays green in the harshest winters when mowed . . . in shade, European ginger, *Asarum europaeum*, is outstanding for durability, rapid increase and evergreen beauty . . . *Euonymus fortunei* 'Coloratus' is the fastest-spreading euonymus and should be first choice where scale is no problem.

Of the creeping junipers, *Juniperus horizontalis* 'Blue Rug' has consistently proved the most satisfactory under extremely rigorous conditions . . . for the South and Pacific Coast, the lilyturfs, *Liriope* and *Ophiopogon*, in sun, and *Hypericum calycinum* in shade, are tops for poor soil and exposed situations . . . *Polygonum reynoutria* stands great heat and drought in poor soil (but is invasive in rich soil) . . . *Rosa wichuraiana* is still the best rose for covering banks . . . blue fescue, *Festuca ovina glauca*, is actually better in blazing sun and high wind than it is in less exposed conditions.

Plants for Paving

Creeping thyme (*Thymus serpyllum*) is often the first — sometimes the only — plant considered for the crevices of stone walks. Secondary

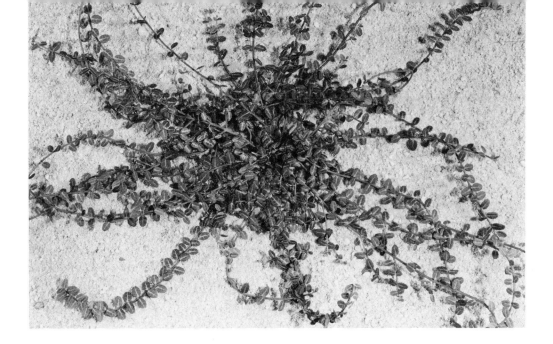

choices might be goldmoss (*Sedum acre*) where foot traffic is light, or, in the South, dichondra (*D. repens*) and lippia (*L. canescens*). But here are some unusuals, delightful and durable, that are fine stepping-stone "joiners":

Scotch moss or pearlwort, *Sagina subulata*, a tight 1″ evergreen mat smothered in tiny pearl-white flowers all summer . . . *Mazus reptans*, 1″, bronzy leaves, white flowers . . . *Herniaria glabra*, 1″, tiny-leaved, evergreen . . . the Corsican jewel mint, *Mentha requieni*, 1″ to 2″, peppermint-scented, with mauve flowers . . . New Zealand brass buttons, *Cotula squalida*, a 1″ ferny mat with yellow blooms . . . *Arenaria balearica*, Corsican sandwort, 2″ to 3″; *A. montana*, English moss, 4″; and other dwarf arenarias, all bearing white flowers.

Sources of these are SISKIYOU RARE PLANT NURSERY (522 FRANQUETTE STREET, MEDFORD, OR 97501; CATALOG 50¢), THE WILD GARDEN (8243 N.E. 119TH, KIRKLAND, WA 98033; CATALOG $1) and GEO. W. PARK SEED CO. (GREENWOOD, SC 29647).

Jewel Underfoot

"The prettiest, sturdiest, most reliable groundcover," it's been called, and yet it is rarely seen in gardens. Bearberry (*Arctostaphylos uva-ursi*), also known as hog cranberry in the East and kinnikinnick in the West, thrives on heat, neglect and the poorest soil — even pure sand.

An evergreen vine-like creeper with stems to 6′ long that root at the joints, it is adapted to sun or shade. The shiny, dark green oval leaves grow thickly all along the stem, and turn bronze in autumn. In May and June, bearberry is covered with urn-shaped blooms, white with pink tips,

A tiny-leaved wintercreeper, 'Kewensis' is equally useful as a groundcover or vine.

and in the fall and winter with bright scarlet berries favored by the birds.

One reason for its rarity in cultivation may be the difficulty of propagating it. The accepted method is to dig clumps when the temperature is well below freezing and plant them immediately. A Long Island gardener tells us that cuttings taken in winter will establish themselves equally well — but a pickax is still necessary to break the ground for planting.

A nurseryman who has had considerable success rooting cuttings in the greenhouse suggests the following method: Take 5″ to 6″ cuttings when the ground is frozen, dip them in a fungicide and treat with a rooting hormone. Set the lower 2″ in fine sand, water once and cover the pot or flat with polyethylene. Give bottom heat, good light but not sun, and 50° to 70° temperatures. Roots should form in about two months. Plant outdoors in early spring. Give a light acid mulch such as pine needles or oak leafmold, and water occasionally when rain is scarce. Bearberry should never be fertilized.

Once established, incidentally, this groundcover likes to be walked on. It will send out roots wherever the stems are forced into contact with the soil.

Plants are available from ALPENGLOW GARDENS (13328 KING GEORGE HIGHWAY, SURREY, B.C., CANADA; CATALOG 50¢).

Carefree Cover

Epimediums have been called the groundcover "with no faults at all." Their wiry-stemmed clumps completely choke weeds, they thrive in nearly full sun to deep shade and reportedly even grow well under maples where even pachysandra may fail. And the bishop's-hats or barrenworts are long-lived, free of pests and diseases and seldom need transplanting since the clumps never die out in the center.

Growing 6″ to 15″ tall and hardy to −30°, epimediums have deciduous to semi-evergreen heart-shaped leaves, rich bronze in spring, a beautiful fresh green in summer, then red-bronze in autumn. The flowers are equally delightful, with daffodil-like trumpets and often columbine-type spurs. Some very fine choices are *E. grandiflorum* 'Rose Queen,' 1½″ crimson-carmine flowers; *E. warlayense*, tangerine; *E. alpinum rubrum*, creamy, edged red; *E. versicolor sulphureum*, yellow — vigorous, very good as a groundcover under evergreens; and the dainty, slow-growing hybrid white *E. youngianum niveum*.

An excellent selection is offered by THE WILD GARDEN *(8243 N.E. 119TH, KIRKLAND, WA 98033; CATALOG $1)*. Epimediums are easily divided in early spring, or after blooming.

Splurge with Spurge

Recently an article in a major garden publication described a gardener's "discovery" of *Euphorbia cyparissias* as a beautiful groundcover for problem sites. Actually, horticulturists have long recognized this value of cypress spurge. Liberty Hyde Bailey recommended it as a "good, long-enduring groundcover" in his *"GARDENER'S HANDBOOK" (MACMILLAN, 1934)*.

This thickly tufted 8″ to 12″ hardy perennial with masses of soft, narrow light green leaves and dense umbels of green-yellow bracts in spring and early summer, is very definitely not for rich soils — fertility induces almost incredible rampancy. But for very poor, very arid spots in full sun to part shade, it has no equal. We once planted several divisions in a cinder bed beside our barn, where it thrived, spread to cover the bed and attracted so much attention that additional plantings were soon made on a dry bank and along a driveway. It was impervious to air pollution, road salt and total neglect, and was never troubled by pests or disease.

A source is THE WILD GARDEN *(8243 N.E. 119TH, KIRKLAND, WA 98033; CATALOG $1)*.

Many cultivars of Liriope muscari have handsomely variegated foliage and large clusters of bright lavender or violet flowers.

Box Huckleberry Boom

One of the choicest, rarest and most ancient of groundcover plants at last shows promise of becoming widely available to gardeners. The Department of Horticulture of the University of West Virginia has tested various methods of propagating box huckleberry, *Gaylussacia brachysera*, and found that cuttings of new wood root most readily in a 1:1 mix of perlite and peat, without rooting hormone. Thus this fabulous evergreen should soon be in good supply at better nurseries.

Hardy to at least −20°, box huckleberry stays as low as 3″ in full sun, but may grow 18″ to 24″ high in deep shade. It spreads slowly by underground runners, and a single plant covering more than a mile, found in 1919 in Pennsylvania, is believed to be over 10,000 years old. The 1″ boxwood-like leaves, rich green and leathery, turn a beautiful red-bronze in autumn. New growth is red, and in May white to pink bell flowers are lavishly produced, with blue berries in late summer. Box huckleberry needs acid soil high in organic matter.

New Coverage

Sometimes it is the gardener, rather than the professional horticulturist, who discovers the climatic range of a plant. This is certainly true with the lilyturfs, those grasslike, Oriental evergreen groundcover and edging plants of the genera *Liriope* and *Ophiopogon*. Long considered plants for the South and the Pacific Coast, many of them today are growing successfully where temperatures go as low as −20°.

Both *Ophiopogon japonicus*, the Mondo grass of the South, and the clump-forming *O. jaburan* are valued more for their 10″ to 12″ dark green leaves than for their lilac or white flowers and metallic blue-black berries. There are variegated cultivars, and also a new dwarf, *O. japonicus compactum*, which grows only 2″ high. The ophiopogons thrive in part to full shade, and will stand drought and poor soil but do best with adequate moisture and fertility. Plants set 6″ to 8″ apart will give full coverage in two years. A source is INTERNATIONAL GROWERS EXCHANGE (BOX 397, FARMINGTON, MI 48024; CATALOG $2).

Creeping lily-turf, *Liriope spicata*, makes a good turf, but its undistinguished flowers do not rise much above the foliage. Better choices are found in the numerous new cultivars of *L. muscari*, the blue lilyturf: 'Monroe's White,' best pure white; 'Majestic,' lilac-purple; 'Curly Twist,' with unusual yellow-green, curled leaves, low growing; 'Gold Banded,' foliage edged with gold; 'Christmas Tree,' with wide-based flower scapes in Christmas tree shape; and 'Lilac Beauty,' a rich violet. Most of these will stand full sun to much shade, and are divided easily in early spring in the North, late autumn in the South. They are available from GILBERT H. WILD & SON (SARCOXIE, MO 64862; CATALOG 50¢).

GROUNDCOVER PLANTS

In the following lists, groundcovers which will thrive in fully exposed areas are listed in the "sun" category. Many evergreens for shade will also do well in sun, but may need some protection from winter sun and wind to avoid poor appearance in spring. Some plants will do better with a higher degree of shade in the South where sunlight is more intense. The lists are by no means inclusive, and numerous other plants and cultivars are useful for groundcover in special situations or climes. Often it is wise to try small experimental plantings before committing a large area to a plant, to see its potential in the area's microclimate.

The textures and colors of blue fescue and 'Gold Banded' liriope are enhanced when they are grown in combination.

Evergreen Groundcovers for Sun

Juniperus — over much of the country, junipers are virtually the only evergreen groundcovers that will not brown in winter sun and wind. Some of the best are *J. chinensis sargentii*, in green, blue and gold forms, hardy to −20°; *J. communis* 'Depressa Aurea,' 'Hornibrookii,' 'Repanda' and others, −20°; *J. conferta*, shore juniper and the new improved 'Emerald Sea,' −10°; *J. horizontalis* and cultivars 'Bar Harbor,' 'Blue Rug' ('Wiltonii'), 'Douglasii,' 'Glomerata,' 'Marcellus,' 'Plumosa' and 'Plumosa Compacta' (Andorra juniper), all hardy to at least −20° — 'Blue Rug' is perhaps the best for extremely rigorous conditions, and several forms turn a fine plum-purple late in the year; *J. procumbens* and 'Nana,' slow growers with branches in tiered shelf effect, −10°; and *J. sabina* 'Tamariscifolia,' somewhat shrublike, to 24″, −20°.

Evergreen Groundcovers for Shade

Andromeda polifolia 'Nana,' dwarf bog rosemary — 12″ to 18″; fine-textured blue-gray leaves, red new growth, shell-pink flowers in spring; hardy to −50°, for very damp, very acid soil.

A shade plant with elegant rich green leaves, European ginger will also thrive in sun if given ample moisture.

Asarum europaeum, European ginger — 5″; very handsome, with shiny kidney-shaped dark leaves; hardy to −20°, stands dense shade. *A. canadense* and other native species are deciduous and not as beautiful.

Bergenia cordifolia, Siberian heartleaf — 12″; bold and tropical-looking, with thick shiny leaves and large rosy flower clusters in spring; hardy to −20°, tolerates sun, should have moist, fertile, humus-rich soil. *B. crassifolia* has lilac-purple flowers.

Cassiope lycopodioides — 3″ to 6″; a heather relative with scalelike foliage, white bell flowers in early spring; makes a neat mat in moist acid soil; very hardy.

Chimaphila umbellata, pipsissewa — 8″ to 10″; glossy leathery leaves, fragrant white flowers in summer; hardy to −40°, rapid limited-area cover in rich leafmold soil. *C. maculata* has white-spotted leaves.

Chiogenes hispidula, creeping snowberry — 3″; tiny leaves, nodding white flowers, aromatic white fruits; hardy to −35°, stands very wet soils.

Cotoneaster — evergreen groundcover types include *C. dammeri,* tiny-leaved *C. microphylla* 'Cochleata' and 'Thymifolia,' and *C. conspicua* 'Decora,' the necklace cotoneaster; these are hardy to −10°, stand part shade to full sun and bear white flowers and red berries. Many others are at least partially evergreen in mild climates.

Daphne cneorum, garland flowers — 12″; tiny leaves, fragrant pink flowers in spring; hardy to −35°, part shade to full sun, needs a cool root run. *D. blagayana,* 8″, is hardy to −5°, has creamy-white flowers and requires deep woodland soil and half shade.

Dryas octopetala, wood nymph — 2″; grows very dense, with oaklike foliage, showy 1½″ flowers; very hardy, but must have good drainage.

Epigaea repens, trailing arbutus — 3″; very fragrant white flowers in spring; a native treasure for acid woodland soils, but difficult to establish. Oriental *E. asiatica* has larger flowers, but is not adaptable to Eastern conditions.

Euonymus fortunei — 'Coloratus' is the most rapid spreader, and has red-purple foliage in winter; the new 'Longwood' is less apt to "pile up" than other varieties; 'Minimus' and 'Kewensis' have very tiny leaves; 'Vegetus,' the big-leaf wintercreeper, may grow to 4′, bears profuse long-persisting orange fruit, but is semi-evergreen in the North. *E. obovatus,* running strawberry bush, is semi-evergreen and slow to become established, but has fine scarlet fruit and red fall color. All are hardy to about −20°, and stand sun if given winter protection.

Ferns — evergreen ferns suitable for covering ground are found mainly in *Asplenium, Dryopteris* and *Polystichum.* It should be noted that in winter the fronds of many evergreen ferns tend to become prostrate or somewhat so. Moist but well-drained humusy soil, a shredded leaf mulch and avoidance of fertilizer are essential for all ferns.

Galax aphylla — 6″ to 8″; distinctive heart-shaped leaves turn bronze in autumn, fluffy white flower spikes in summer; hardy to −20°, moist leafmold-rich soil, colonizes beautifully in woodland.

Gaylusaccia brachysera, box huckleberry — a very handsome, very ancient creeper with 1″ boxwood leaves, pink spring flowers, light blue berries and rich bronze fall foliage; hardy to −20°, grows as low as 3″ in sun, to 24″ in deep shade, needs acid soil.

Heaths, Heathers — strictly, *Erica* is heath, *Calluna vulgaris* is heather. Both are suited to infertile acid soils and part shade to full sun, benefit from shearing in early spring, should not be fertilized, and need a straw or bough covering in colder areas. Hundreds of varieties, 4″ to 24″ high, are available, with white, pink, red or purple flowers, blooming spring through fall, plus gold-foliaged types. *Calluna vulgaris* is hardy to −20°, most ericas to −10°.

Hedera, ivy — 'Baltica' form of English ivy, *H. helix*, in the North, and Algerian ivy, *H. canariensis*, in the South, are often more durable than vinca and pachysandra. *H. helix* has great diversity of colors and forms, varying in hardiness; needs shade from winter sun and wind, rich humusy soil and ample moisture.

Leiophyllum buxifolium prostratum, sand myrtle — a neat, tiny-leaved shrub, bearing small white flowers in spring; hardy to −20°, needs moist peaty soil, part shade to full sun.

Leucothoë — 24″, but easily kept to 12″ to 15″; graceful mounds of arching stems, shiny dark leaves, racemes of white bell flowers in spring; hardy to −5°, moist peaty soil, part shade to full sun. *L. catesbaei*, 3′ to 4′, can also be cut back in spring; hardy to −10°.

Lycopodium clavatum, princess pine — 3″; looks like a miniature pine, creeps 8′ to 10′; hardy to −35°, needs dense shade, moist woodsy soil.

Mitchella repens, partridgeberry — 3″; shiny leathery leaves, fragrant pinkish flowers in spring, showy scarlet berries; fine under trees.

Pachistima canbyi — 6″ to 12″; boxwood-like leaves turn bronze in autumn; hardy to −20°, fine under small trees but will stand much sun.

Pachysandra terminalis, Japanese spurge — 6″ to 10″; dark green foliage, white flowers in spring; 'Silver Edge' is variegated; hardy to −30°. Native *P. procumbens* is hardy to −10° and truly evergreen only in the South, but has more attractive flowers.

Rhododendron — some azaleas, such as certain cultivars of *R. indicum* — 'Balsaminaeflorum,' 'Crispiflorum,' 'Flame Creeper,' hybrid 'Gumpo' — are low-growing, excellent massed, says horticulturist Harold Epstein. A new race of prostrate evergreen azaleas is the North Tisbury Hybrids, 10″ to 15″ high and 30″ to 40″ across, developed by MRS. JULIAN HILL (1106 GREENHILL AVE., WILMINGTON, DE 19805).

Rosmarinus officinalis prostratus, creeping rosemary — long, hairy and aromatic gray-green leaves, delicate blue flowers; hardy to 0°, good in light shade to hot, dry sites.

Sarcococca hookeriana humilis — 10″; shining dark green lanceolate foliage, small fragrant white flowers; hardy to −5°, should have moist high-organic soil.

Shortia galacifolia, oconee bells — 3″; very fine, slowly makes wide mats; dark green leaves, bronze and maroon in winter, and white or pinkish fringed bell flowers in spring; hardy to −10°. *S. uniflora grandiflora* is a Japanese species with larger flowers.

Taxus, yew — *T. canadensis*, ground hemlock, is semi-prostrate, with dark green foliage that turns reddish in winter, scarlet fruits; hardy to −40°, stands dense shade. Several English yews, such as *T. baccata* 'Cavendishii' and 'Repandens' and Japanese *T. cuspidata* 'Densa' are low and sweeping, good accents on shady slopes with lower covers.

Vinca minor, myrtle, periwinkle — 6″ to 8″; dark green leaves, lavender-blue flowers in spring; 'Bowlesii' has larger flowers, 'Miss Jekyll's White' is lower and finer-textured; also fine variegated, double-flowered and red- to red-purple-flowered forms; hardy to −30°, but avoid high-nitrogen fertilizers and poorly drained areas.

Groundcovers and Vines 51

Growing densely, Spiraea japonica alpina makes a tight mat under shrubs or in full sun.

Deciduous Groundcovers for Sun

Abelia prostrata nana — 6″ to 12″; a dwarf spreading shrub with small, glossy leaves, white flowers in summer; hardy to −5°.

Achillea tomentosa, woolly yarrow — 12″; feathery gray-green leaves, yellow flowers all summer; hardy to −40°, best in sandy soil on hot, dry sites. Other low achilleas are sometimes used, mainly in the West.

Antennaria, pussytoes — 6″; several species form vigorous mats, with white or rose furry cat's-paw flowers; some are hardy to −40°.

Arabis, rockcress — 4″ to 10″ *A. albida*, *A. alpina*, *A. caucasica* and *A. procurrens* form dense, broad mats with white flowers in spring.

Aronia melanocarpa, black chokeberry — 18″ to 36″; a creeping shrub with single white flowers in spring, blue-black berries, red autumn foliage; hardy to −30°. Highly recommended by Dr. Donald Wyman.

Campanula poscharskyana — 4″; a good small-area cover, producing many lavender-blue flowers all summer.

Cerastium tomentosum, snow-in-summer — 6″; white woolly leaves, white flowers in early summer; a rapid spreader, stands dryness, will grow in pure sand, excellent on slopes.

Comptonia peregrina, sweetfern — 2′ to 3′; fragrant ferny foliage; very useful for covering sandy or stony banks, hardy to −50°.

Cotoneaster — among the most useful are the rockspray cotoneaster, *C. horizontalis*, 12″ to 24″, and its variegated form, the fast-spreading *C. h. perpusilla* (sometimes offered as 'Little Gem'); *C. apiculata*, cranberry cotoneaster, 24″ to 30″, with very showy berries; mat-forming 12″ to 18″ *C.*

adpressa, mounded *C. a. praecox* and *C. a. praecox* 'Hessei'; and hybrid 'Herbstfeuer' ('Autumn Fire'), with willowy leaves, brilliant red in autumn. These are hardy to −20°, and some are evergreen or nearly so in mild climates.

Dianthus, pink — *D. alpinus*, *D. deltoides*, *D. gratianapolitanus* and *D. plumarius* make fine 2″-to-12″-high mats of blue-green grassy foliage with white, pink or red flowers; good for small areas and banks.

Festuca ovina glauca, blue fescue — 8″; a handsome tufted ornamental silver-blue grass; very good on dry, blazing, windy sites.

Forsythia 'Arnold Dwarf' — trimmed occasionally to 12″, this 3′ to 4′ dwarf with few flowers but good refined foliage makes a fine cover on banks and slopes; hardy to −10°.

Fragaria — *F. chiloensis* and *F. virginiana*, wild strawberries, make interesting carpets bearing white flowers, edible fruit; hardy to −20°.

Gypsophila repens, creeping baby's-breath — 3″ to 6″; an ideal carpeter for small bulbs or on small banks; white flowers, pink in *rosea* form.

Helianthemum nummularium, sunrose — 6″; masses of white, pink, yellow or red flowers in early summer; very popular in California, needs winter protection in the North.

Hemerocallis, daylily — 18″ to 60″; hundreds of varieties, all make a solid mass quickly; *H. fulva*, tawny daylily (the true species is hard to find), is one of the finest for difficult banks.

Hypericum, St. Johnswort — 6″ to 12″ *H. buck-leyi*, *H. calycinum*, *H. moserianum* and *H. patulum henryi* are hardy to − 10°, *H. coris* and *H. olympicum* to 0°; good in poor soil, exposed situations; yellow flowers in summer.

Nepeta — 3″ *N. hederacea*, ground ivy or gill-over-the-ground, is very hardy, has blue flowers in summer, and makes tight mats, but is so invasive it is risky even when surrounded by paving. 18″ *N. mussini*, blue-flowered and hardy to − 20°, is a fine cover, never weedy.

Phlox subulata, moss phlox — 6″; grassy foliage, almost evergreen, and white, pink, red or lavender flowers in spring; very useful for poor soil, banks, hardy to − 30°.

Polygonum, fleeceflower — 4″ *P. capitatum* ('Magic Carpet' — GEO. W. PARK SEED CO., GREENWOOD, SC 29647) has bronze leaves, pink flowers. *P. reynoutria* (*P. cuspidatum compactum*), 18″ to 24″, has pale green leaves, red in autumn, and deep pink flowers; it stands heat, drought and poor soil, but is definitely invasive in rich soil.

Ranunculus repens, creeping buttercup — 6″; double yellow flowers; a pretty cover, but very invasive.

Robinia hispida, rose acacia — 3′ to 4′; rosy-pink flowers in late spring; a stoloniferous locust, good for poor soils and banks, but can be a pest in rich soil.

Rosa — *R. wichuraiana*, memorial rose, is a semi-evergreen trailer with large single white flowers in summer, hardy to − 20°; pink-flowered hybrid 'Max Graf' is hardy to − 35°. Excellent covers for banks.

Spiraea japonica alpina — 10″; a neat mound, very good massed, bearing pink flowers in late spring; hardy to − 20°.

Veronica, speedwell — 2″ to 4″ blue-flowered *V. pectinata* (also pink *rosea* form), *V. officinalis*, *V. repens* and *V. rupestris* (*V. prostrata*, also *alba* form) are the best; will stand shade, poor soil. *V. filiformis* is considered invasive, but reportedly is good in quite dense shade, and can be eradicated easily where not wanted with the pre-emergence crabgrass killer Azak.

Deciduous Groundcovers for Shade

Aegopodium podagraria, goutweed — 12″; usually sold in silver-margined *variegatum* form; hardy to − 30°, but an invasive plant suitable only to poor soil, problem areas where nothing else will grow.

Ajuga reptans, carpet bugle — 6″ to 10″; nearly evergreen, a rapid spreader but easily controlled, with blue, white or pink flowers; many variegated forms with metallic, bronze, purplish-red or white-marked foliage; hardy to − 20°, good in sun if given winter mulch.

Asperula odorata, sweet woodruff — 6″; fine-textured, leaves in whorls of 8, bears fragrant white flowers in spring; hardy to − 20°, best in moist shady areas but also good in sun.

Aubrietia deltoides, purple rockcress — 3″ to 6″; a mat-forming perennial, excellent cover for bulbs, making white or pink to purple sheets in spring; part shade to full sun.

Campanula carpatica, Carpathian bellflower — 10″; white or blue flowers from June to September; small well-drained areas, part shade to sun.

Ceratostigma plumbaginoides (*Plumbago larpentae*) — 6″ to 10″; indigo-blue flowers in late summer; hardy to − 20°, half shade to full sun, slow to start growth in spring.

Convallaria majalis, lily-of-the-valley — 6″; long lance leaves, fragrant white or pink (*rosea*) flowers for a month or more in spring; stands poor soil and deep shade.

Groundcovers and Vines   53

The smallest dogwood, bunchberry is very hardy and flowers and fruits well in light to deep shade.

Cornus, dogwood — *C. canadensis*, bunchberry, is a stoloniferous plant with typical white bracts, red berries, for bright to dense shade; *C. stolonifera* 'Kelseyi,' to 30″, has red bark, stands wet soils. Both are hardy to at least −35°.

Coronilla varia, crownvetch — 24″; a dense cover with pink flowers all summer; a rapid spreader, best used on non-garden banks, roadsides.

Cymbalaria muralis, Kenilworth ivy — a dainty, ivy-like vine, finest over rocks; naturalized over eastern U.S. and widely used (as are *C. aequitiloba* and *C. hepaticaefolia*) as groundcovers in the West.

Duchesena indica, mock strawberry — 4″ to 6″; strawberry-like trailer with yellow flowers, inedible red fruit; −20°, sun or shade, is somewhat aggressive.

Ferns — 12″ to 36″; maidenhair (*Adiantum pedatum*), lady fern (*Athyrium filix-femina*), hay-scented fern (*Dennstaedtia punctilobula*), sensitive fern (*Onoclea sensibilis*), various osmunda ferns and Virginia chain fern (*Woodwardia virginica*) are very useful. Some can be invasive — ostrich fern (*Matteuccia pennsylvanica*) and bracken fern (*Pteridium aquilinum*).

Galium verum, yellow bedstraw — 24″; rather coarse, bears tiny yellow flowers in summer; −20°, useful on small banks in shade or sun.

Geranium, cranesbill — 6″ *G. dalmaticum* and *G. lancastriense* (*G. sanguineum prostratum*), and 12″ *G. endressii* make neat dense carpets, with pink to red-purple summer flowers; several rarer species are also good covers, for sun or shade.

Heuchera — 6″ *H. sanguinea*, coralbells, and several other species are good massed and bear white or coral bell flowers in panicles on 10″ to 18″ stems in summer; semi-evergreen, hardy to −30°, moist soil.

Hosta, plantain lily — numerous varieties with deeply veined, usually heart-shaped leaves in all shades of green and often beautifully variegated, and racemes of white to lilac flowers in summer or fall; hardy to −20°, very effective in any cool, moist area.

Houstonia serpyllifolia, creeping bluets — moss-like mats of tiny oval leaves blanketed with deep blue flowers in spring; good bulb cover.

Iberis sempervirens, perennial candytuft — 12″; white sheets of bloom in spring, leaves nearly evergreen; several fine named varieties are available; −30°, part shade to full sun.

Indigofera incarnata alba, white Chinese indigo — 18″; white flowers in July; a tenacious cover for banks; root-hardy to −20°, flowers on current year's growth.

Iris cristata, crested iris — 6″; pale blue flowers with yellow crest in late spring; forms large clumps quickly, hardy to −20°.

Lonicera, honeysuckle — *L. henryi* is hardier and less rampant than the commonly used *L. japonica* 'Halliana'; hardy to −30°, semi-evergreen far North, also good in full sun.

Lysimachia nummularia, creeping Charlie — 3″; makes a light green glossy carpet, with yellow flowers in summer; 'Aurea' is gold-leaved; hardy to −20°, good in wet soil, part shade to full sun.

Omphalodes verna, creeping forget-me-not — 8″; heart-shaped leaves, blue or white flowers; −20°, good in woodland.

Phlox — many useful species; two of the best are *P. diverticata* and *P. stolonifera*, 3″ to 4″, with white, blue or violet flowers in spring; hardy to −30°, good bulb covers.

Podophyllum peltatum, Mayapple — to 18″; huge leaves, waxy white spring flowers, big edible yellow fruit in autumn; hardy to −20°, multiplies rapidly, should have deep, rich, moist acid soil.

Polemonium reptans, Jacob's ladder — 10″; clusters of light blue flowers; hardy to −30°, a spreading wildflower for natural areas, under shrubs.

Polygonatum multiflorum, Solomon's seal — 30″; a creeping perennial with broad lance leaves, greenish-white spring flowers; hardy to −30°.

Potentilla, cinquefoil — 4″ *P. tridentata,* bearing white flowers in summer, and 2″ *P. verna,* yellow spring flowers, spread slowly, are good covers for bulbs; half shade to full sun; *P. reptans* can be invasive.

Salix, willow — *S. repens* is a prostrate shrub, hardy to −30°; *S. uva-ursi,* the Arctic bearberry willow, makes a dense 2″ to 3″ mat bearing large purple catkins in spring, is hardy to −50°.

Saxifraga stolonifera (S. sarmentosa), strawberry geranium — marbled round leaves, pink and white flowers on 10″ stems in summer; usually thought of as a house plant, but actually hardy to −20° and a fine cover for damp, shady places.

Sedum, stonecrop — dozens of dwarf creeping varieties of these succulents thrive in light shade to sunny dry areas, some are evergreen, most are hardy to at least −20°; foliage colors from light green to blue, gray, bronze, red, flowers mainly pink, red or yellow; *S. acre, S. album* and *S. sarmentosum* can be invasive.

Sempervivum, hen-and-chicks — succulents of myriad fascinating foliage forms and colors; slower spreaders and with less showy red, yellow or purple flowers than sedums; stand the poorest soil and drought, hardy almost everywhere, and especially good over rocks.

Stephanandra incisa 'Crispa' — 18″; gracefully arching branches, neat ferny foliage which turns red-purple in autumn; hardy to −10°, very useful on banks, irregular rocky sites.

Symphoricarpos chenaulti 'Hancock,' Chenault coralberry — 24″; small pink flowers in July, handsome clusters of red berries in the fall; hardy to −20°, good on banks.

Teucrium chamaedrys 'Prostratum,' creeping germander — 3″; sometimes offered as *T. canadense;* leathery scalloped foliage, rose-purple summer flowers; hardy to −5°, sun to part shade.

Tiarella cordifolia, foamflower — 6″; a wildflower that forms large mats of broad heart-shaped leaves, bronze-red in winter, and clusters of white flowers in late spring; one of the best for moist, rich acid soil, hardy to −20°.

Uvularia grandiflora, bellwort, wood daffodil — 12″ to 18″; bright green leaves, pendent yellow bell flowers in spring; stands dense shade, needs rich woodland soil, hardy to −40°.

Vancouveria hexandra — 12″ to 18″; a fast-creeping northwestern woodlander with glossy compound leaves, white flowers in early summer; hardy to −10°, acid humus-rich soil.

Viola, violet — 6″ to 15″; *V. odorata,* the common violet, is very invasive; better choices include *V. canadensis,* the Canada violet; *V. papilonacea albiflora* and *V. priceana,* Confederate violets; and *V. striata,* cream violet; all need some confinement, moist soil.

Groundcovers and Vines   55

Waldsteinia fragarioides, barren strawberry — 4″; strawberry-like foliage and habit, small yellow flowers; hardy to −30°, of easiest culture in shade.

Xanthorhiza simplicissima, yellowroot — 18″ to 24″; ferny foliage, little brown-purple star flowers in drooping racemes in spring; hardy to −20°, moist soil, medium to dense shade, good along streams, ponds; looks especially well combined with pachysandra; can be kept trimmed to 12″.

COVERING BOOKS

"Complete Book of Groundcovers," by Robert E. Atkinson (McKay, $7.95)

"Ground Cover Plants," by Donald Wyman (Macmillan, $5.95)

"Ground Covers for Easier Gardening," by Daniel J. Foley (Dover, $3)

"Growing Ground Covers," Home & Garden Bulletin 175 (15¢ from Superintendent of Documents (Washington, DC 20402)

"Lawns and Groundcovers," Time-Life Encyclopedia of Gardening (Little, Brown, $6.95)

"Plants for Ground-Cover," by Graham Stuart Thomas (J. M. Dent, $12)

"Sunset Lawn and Ground Cover Book" (Sunset Books, Menlo Park, CA 94025; $1.95)

SOURCES

J. Herbert Alexander, Middleboro, MA 02346

Avalon Mountain Gardens, Dana, NC 28724

Brimfield Gardens Nursery, 245 Brimfield Road, Wethersfield, CT 06109; catalog $1

Conley's Garden Center, Boothbay Harbor, ME 04538; catalog 25¢

Exeter Wild Flower Gardens, Box 510, Exeter, NH 03833

The Garden Spot, 4032 Rosewood Drive, Columbia, SC 29205; specialist in ivies, euonymus, liriope, ophiopogon and vinca

Lamb Nurseries, E. 101 Sharp Avenue, Spokane, WA 99202

Lounsberry Gardens, Box 135, Oakford, IL 62673; catalog 25¢

Oakhill Gardens, Route 3, Box 87, Dallas, OR 97338; sedum and sempervivum specialist

Putney Nursery, Putney, VT 05346

Clyde Robin, Box 2091, Castro Valley, CA 94546; catalog $1

The Shop in the Sierra, Box 1, Midpines, CA 95345; catalog $1

Sylvan Nursery, 1028 Horseneck Road, South Westport, MA 02790; heaths and heathers

Wayside Gardens, Mentor, OH 44060; catalog $2

The Wild Garden, 8243 N.E. 119th, Kirkland, WA 98033; catalog $1

VINES

Porcelain Berry Vine

A vine which is rarely grown today can provide one of autumn's finest garden highlights. *Ampelopsis brevipedunculata,* the porcelain berry, is a vigorous woody climber from Asia which bears unique multicolored, speckled fruit.

The leaves in the best form, var. *maximowiczii,* are beautiful, deeply lobed and toothed, about 5″ across and glossy dark green. Lush but not dense, they make a fine, delicate screen. Then, in late summer, the numerous clusters of fruits are stunning, each ¼″ berry turning from white or lilac to yellow, green and finally robin's-egg or bright blue, with all these colors present in a cluster at one time.

Porcelain berry grows rapidly to about 20′ in sun or semi-shade, and can be used as a groundcover or on banks. For upright growth a trellis is necessary, or twine or wire on a wall, as it climbs by tendrils. This ampelopsis is very tolerant of poor soil, drought and wind, and although generally rated hardy to −20°, has survived −35° at the Minnesota Landscape Arboretum. Seed, which is best sown in autumn, is available from *J. L. HUDSON SEEDSMAN (BOX 1058, REDWOOD CITY, CA 94064; CATALOG 50¢).*

The plumed fruit heads of the golden clematis make it an outstanding attraction in the fall garden.

Dutch Treat

It's more curious than showy in flower and foliage, yet Dutchman's pipe, *Aristolochia durior* (*A. macrophylla, A. sipho*) has been quietly popular since Colonial days.

This deciduous native twiner has few peers for shade or screening, for its large — up to 12" — bright green kidney-shaped leaves seem to grow in a single plane. It can quickly reach 30', making a flat mass of foliage that blankets a trellis or other sturdy support. The flowers, borne in June, are fascinating though not conspicuous, yellowish-green and brown-purple, U-shaped like a meerschaum pipe.

A. durior is hardy to −20°, free of diseases and pests and thrives in most soils. A source is GURNEY SEED & NURSERY CO. (YANKTON, SD 57078).

Celestial Vine

For fast growth, deep shade, handsome foliage and flowers of "pure celestial delight," as one gardener describes them, the moonflower vine is unsurpassed.

Calonyction aculeatum (often sold as *Ipomoea noctiflora* or *I. bona-nox*) will grow luxuriantly from seed to 30' in southern gardens, to 20' in the North. The big, glossy, bright green heart-shaped leaves make a dense screen on a pergola or trellis. In flower, this twiner has no equal for dramatic effect around porch or patio. Its huge — up to 6" — salver-shaped flowers have a luminous satiny sheen and are very sweetly scented. The long-tubed buds open in minutes at dusk, and in dull weather stay open until noon the next day. A lilac-pink variety is available, but of course is not as dramatic as the pure white at night (both from GEO. W. PARK SEED CO., GREENWOOD, SC 29647).

Seeds notched and soaked overnight before sowing outdoors in warm soil will give bloom from July to frost, or they can be started indoors in pots at 80°. Moonflowers should have full sun, a humusy but not rich soil, and abundant moisture. They do well even in city gardens, and will flower in sunny winter windows if started in pots in late August.

Top Twiners

America's most popular vine is clematis, particularly the large-flowered hybrids, with their flat, brightly colored dinner-plate blooms. But many of the species are equally rewarding.

A cultivar of *Clematis viticella* discovered in the garden of Mrs. Erastus Corning II in Albany, New York, is described by Agricultural Research Service botanist T. R. Dudley as "a dream ornamental: Summer-long bloomer with a profusion of large, fragrant flowers; a dense and graceful plant that is easy to cultivate, hardy in winter, and able to withstand drought."

The cultivar, which has been named 'Betty Corning,' is a vigorous climber with rich, dark green foliage in full sun, and trains well on trellises, fences and posts. It has withstood temperatures as low as −20°. The bell-shaped, violet-blue flowers appear in Albany from June through September, in Washington, D.C., from May through October.

The rarely seen golden clematis, *C. tangutica*, bears dainty but showy yellow bell-like flowers in early summer and again in autumn. The second blooming is often spectacular, for the flowers appear in conjunction with the silken, feathery bursts of the plumed fruit heads, making this

Groundcovers and Vines 57

An inverted, bottomless pot provides vital shade and coolness for the roots of a clematis.

hardy vine the most striking specimen in the garden at that season.

The golden clematis stands more rigorous exposure and less favorable soil conditions than the large-flowered types. However, like most clematis, it should have shaded and cool conditions for its roots and "neck." Specialist MARINUS VANDER POL *(776 WASHINGTON STREET, FAIRHAVEN, MA 02719;* descriptive-cultural booklet, *"CLEMATIS II," 35¢)* stresses that the foliage and flowers require sun, but a mulch, groundcover or some sort of "sun baffle" should shade the plant's lower 3″ and root area. A gardener recommends resting an inverted flower pot, with the bottom broken out, on the soil when planting clematis, letting the vine grow up through this.

"Shade at the roots, sun at the top," is by no means a hard-and-fast rule for all clematis. Deepshaded northern exposures are entirely suitable for many clematis species. These are fully as ornamental as the large-flowered hybrids, making up in sheer mass of bloom what they lack in size of flowers. And their billowing, clambering growth is wonderfully useful to cover fences, walls and banks, and to soften difficult spots in the landscape picture.

ARNOLD'S CLEMATIS NURSERY *(2005 S.E. PARK AVENUE, MILWAUKIE, OR 97222; CATALOG 25¢)* recommends these for shade: *C. alpina,* satiny blue; the evergreen, ferny-leaved, yellow *C. calycina (C. cirrhosa, C. balearica)* for mild climates or growing in pots; *C. chrysocoma,* soft pink; the popular and comparatively large-flowered *C. jackmani;* lavender-blue semi-double *C. macropetala;* the many fine white or pink varieties of *C. montana;* white *C. spooneri* and pink *C. s. rosea;* and shell-pink, vanilla-scented *C. vedrariensis rosea.* Also recommended is the large-flowered hybrid 'Nelly Moser.'

C. chrysocoma, incidentally, is a fascinating plant. It flowers profusely on old wood in spring, then on new wood in early summer through early autumn. Called the hairy clematis, it has yellow down covering its branches, leaves and flower stems. Another distinctive feature is the unusual length of the flower stems, which hold the blooms upward.

Late Dutch Honeysuckle

If only some nurseryman would specialize in honeysuckles! Practically all of the approximately 150 known species have ornamental value, yet only a dozen or so are widely offered.

One of the best that has recently become available (from WAYSIDE GARDENS, MENTOR, OH *44060; CATALOG $2)* is a selection of the English honeysuckle or woodbine, *Lonicera periclymenum serotina,* which in English catalogs is called the late Dutch honeysuckle. 'Winchester' has 2″ deep red-purple, yellow-lined flowers in dense terminal clusters, very sweet-scented and abundant from July to autumn. The leaves are rich dark green, blue-green beneath. A vigorous climber to 15′ to 20′, it can also be used as a groundcover. It is hardy to −35°, and makes a fine floriferous rambler for east, west or north walls, being especially welcome because it is in flower when most other climbers are past their best.

Hydrangea Vine

The climbing hydrangea, *H. petiolaris,* is equally suited to sun or shade and hardy to −20°, will grow to 60′, climbing fences, walls and trees, and won't harm trees as long as it does not cover the foliage.

The leaves are dense and lustrous, and the flat, fragrant white flower clusters, up to 12″ across, appear all summer. In winter the shredding reddish bark is highly attractive.

A source is WAYSIDE GARDENS *(MENTOR, OH 44060; CATALOG $2).*

Love That Lablab

Annual vines that grow rapidly from seed fill the need for colorful backdrops, shading, screening or covers for walls, too-stark fences or dead shrubs and trees. Many flower more lavishly and longer than woody vines.

One of the most interesting and ornamental is the almost-forgotten old-fashioned hyacinth bean, *Dolichos lablab*. Its large 3-leaflet leaves give cool shade to a height of 10′ or more, and it bears a profusion of dense flower clusters that resemble hyacinth spikes. The fragrant ¾″ to 1″ flowers — which last well cut — are a rich wine-purple in the variety 'Darkness,' white in 'Daylight.' Also highly attractive are the flat maroon seed pods, up to 3″ long, papery and beaked, and containing black or white seeds.

Hyacinth bean resents transplanting, so should be sown in place. Like most annual vines, it climbs by tight-curling tendrils, so give string, netting or thin stakes for support. A source is OLD'S SEEDS (MADISON, WI 53701).

Winter Jasmine

A "curtain plant," perfect for draping over retaining walls, is the delightful winter jasmine, *Jasminum nudiflorum*. This weeping shrub-vine, which bears its 1″ fragrant golden star flowers on bare green stems any time from November to March, does well as far north as southern Connecticut and, reports the Denver Botanic Gardens, thrives in Denver in sheltered spots.

Winter jasmine can be trained on walls or fences as well as planted along the tops of retaining walls to drape them. The tips of the arching stems often take root when they touch the ground. It is thus easily propagated by layering, and also by cuttings of nearly ripe wood. In colder climates it should not be pruned too drastically.

Two sources are WAYNESBORO NURSERIES (WAYNESBORO, VA 22980) and THE WILD GARDEN (8243 N.E. 119TH, KIRKLAND, WA 98033; CATALOG $1).

Virtuoso Vine

The matrimony vines or boxthorns are not generally recommended for garden cultivation, for with good fertility and moisture they sucker freely. But for dry, sandy soils, for covering banks, rockpiles, fences and walls, and as a wide informal and impenetrable hedge where they have plenty of room to spread, these sprawling, often spiny Eurasian shrub-vines are valuable.

Lycium halmifolium and the very similar *L. chinense* are unusually ornamental, with glossy gray-green leaves, red-purple flowers in early summer and orange-red berries through autumn into winter. The brilliance and profusion of the berries, produced all along the slender stems, prompt some horticulturists to suggest matrimony vines for espalier or arbors, or as "wall spillers" cascading down over retaining walls. In China, the sweet berries are sun-dried and used in many dishes, teas are made from the young leaves and the roots are used for tonics.

Both species are hardy to −20°, and grow rapidly to 6′ to 8′. They thrive in sun or shade, tolerate windy exposures and in England are prized seashore plants. A source is FIORE ENTERPRISES (PRAIRIE VIEW, IL 60069).

Forgotten Glory

A striking special-purpose vine is the Japanese crimson gloryvine or glory grape. Climbing by tendrils, *Vitis coignetiae* (*V. kaempferi*) will scramble rapidly over any trellis, porch, arbor or pergola, making 50′ growth in a season and producing dense screening and shade.

Both the flowers and inedible blue-black fruit are inconspicuous, but the foliage is truly magnificent. The light green leaves are rosy-tinted above and grayish beneath, and grow to 10″ or more across, heart-shaped at the base. In the fall, they turn a brilliant crimson-scarlet and stay on the vine for weeks before falling. Winter interest is added by the rope-like stems.

Gloryvine is hardy to −20°, and requires only a medium-rich, moist but well-drained soil, and sun to partial shade. Its growth can be restrained by frequent pruning when young. Seed is available from J. L. HUDSON, SEEDSMAN (BOX 1058, REDWOOD CITY, CA 94064; CATALOG 50¢).

Groundcovers and Vines   59

The pattern of branches and buds on a wisteria in winter is as impressive as its summer masses of bloom.

New Fashions in Wisteria

Few plants can match wisteria for spectacular bloom. It is also widely adapted, virtually trouble-free, and has the possibly unique capability of being grown as a vine, espalier, multi-stemmed shrub or tree. The tree form, either as a lawn specimen or in a tub, is returning to vogue — perhaps because gardeners have learned the vital requirement of heavy watering until a newly planted tree wisteria begins growth.

Tastes in varieties are changing, too. Chinese wisteria, *W. sinensis*, has long been the most commonly grown, both in its lavender-blue and white varieties, but the white silky wisteria, *W. venusta alba*, with the purest snowy flowers of all wisterias, is supplanting the white Chinese wisteria in many areas. Also more popular today is Japanese wisteria, *W. floribunda*, most preferable being *W. f. longissima*, with violet-blue clusters over 4′ long, the pink *W. f. rosea* and the dark violet, double-flowered *W. f. violacea plena* (these are offered by WAYSIDE GARDENS, MENTOR, OH 44060; CATALOG $2).

Reluctance of a wisteria to bloom abundantly is usually due to lack of one or more of these: full sun, perfect drainage, and proper feeding — feed sparingly in fall, never in spring. Another essential is annual pruning, shortening new shoots to 5 buds in summer. If a grafted or cutting-grown Chinese wisteria refuses to flower in 3 or 4 years after planting, or a Japanese in about 7 years, prune it heavily and feed with superphosphate only. If this fails, root-prune by driving a spade into the soil 24″ from the trunk all around the plant.

Gardeners in the northernmost states are often deprived of wisteria flowers because of winterkilling. However, "The Minnesota Horticulturist" tells of a St. Paul gardener who has fine bloom every year because "each fall he removes the vine from its trellis, places it on the ground, and covers it with marsh hay."

TREES

Getting the Best of Trees

Improved shade and flowering trees are the order of the day. America now surpasses Europe in the development of new ornamental trees, and superior cultivars not only of major but also many minor species are being introduced.

Four wholesale nurseries and a private horticultural organization are leaders in the discovery and introduction of these outstanding trees: COLE NURSERY CO. (R.D. 1, CIRCLEVILLE, OH 43113), PRINCETON NURSERIES (PRINCETON, NJ 08540), EDWARD H. SCANLON & ASSOCIATES (7621 LEWIS RD., OLMSTED FALLS, OH 44138), MONROVIA NURSERY (AZUSA, CA 91702) and the non-profit SARATOGA HORTICULTURAL FOUNDATION (BOX 108, SARATOGA, CA 95070).

Many other nurserymen, botanic gardens and arboretums are doing similar exciting work in finding and evaluating new woody plants. And the testing programs of many private and public horticultural institutions, such as the University of Minnesota Landscape Arboretum, are making it possible for the gardener to choose the best tree for any purpose, suited to his climate and the environment of his garden.

Finally, gardeners themselves are seeking out superior trees, and making their finds available to arboretums and nurseries for eventual distribution. A growing number of gardeners are patenting their discoveries, which assures both profitable and wide distribution through the

The 'Greenspire' little-leaf linden is a sturdy symmetrical tree with very fragrant flowers and resistance to drought and storm damage.

Trees 61

A solid, tightly burlaped ball of the proper size is essential to protect the roots and ensure survival of many trees.

states: "Most of the better nurseries and arborists and landscape professionals do not use the mechanical tree diggers due to root loss, root splitting by the blade as it 'pushes' through the soil, plus several other undesirable features for large trees."

On the Ball

A properly balled-and-burlapped tree or shrub, says "Arnoldia," the publication of the Arnold Arboretum, has "a completely intact ball of earth and roots, which is packaged so expertly it is unlikely to shift or come apart during transport and replanting." However, because of the increased costs of labor, many nurseries in recent years "have tended toward the 'soft' or 'homemade' ball for all but the largest or most difficult material."

"Arnoldia" warns that this is "really just a bare root tree wrapped in soil and burlap." When the root ball is not kept intact, many of the small feeding roots are damaged, which can severely jeopardize the plant's chance of recovery.

Also, any "B&B" stock which has not been properly stored — under heavy mulch, and watered regularly — can suffer severe root injury from drought and heat or cold. Plants showing defoliation or dieback should always be rejected. Another vital point is the size of the root ball: a 1½″ caliper shade tree should have a root ball no smaller than 18″ in diameter. The *"AMERICAN STANDARD FOR NURSERY STOCK," $2 FROM THE AMERICAN ASSOCIATION OF NURSERYMEN (230 SOUTHERN BUILDING, WASHINGTON, DC 20005)*, provides a wide range of criteria for selecting quality plants.

attention such registration attracts in the nursery industry.

Selection of a superior species or cultivar, of course, is only one factor in getting maximum value and pleasure from a garden or street tree. Purchasing a specimen of the proper size and in good health is another, and both early and continuing care are equally important.

Sizing Up Trees

Best choice for most gardeners, advises Dr. P. C. Kozel of Ohio State University, is a tree at least 8′ to 10′ tall, but not larger than 2½″ in trunk diameter for standard shade trees. Slower-growing ornamental trees should be a minimum of 6′ to 8′ tall, with a trunk diameter maximum of 1½″ to 2″.

For the homeowner seeking instant shade or immediate flowering beauty — and willing to pay the much greater cost — "full-grown" trees can be planted. However, this should be done only by a reputable and experienced firm. Unless properly dug, the trees may lose too great a proportion of roots and will decline over several years and eventually expire. As Mr. E. E. Irish of *CHARLES F. IRISH CO. (WARREN, MI 48089)* — a firm that often moves trees over 20″ in diameter successfully —

Maximizing Tree Growth

Reports from the University of Tennessee indicate that high-nitrogen feeding, beginning the second year after planting, will almost double the height, trunk diameter and canopy area of many trees. This accelerated growth results in broad, heavy-trunked trees, not spindly specimens as might be expected. Best is a 10-6-4 fertilizer, with the nitrogen partially from a slow-release organic or urea-formaldehyde source, applied on the soil surface in autumn to early winter in a circular area at least 2½ times the branch spread.

Experiments at the University of Florida show that mulch will accelerate growth. Mulch insulates the soil against solar heat — many tree roots cease growing at temperatures above 90° — and it eliminates competition from grass and weeds, which, tests have shown, can reduce root growth of young trees by 50%.

Root of Tree Troubles

Soil conditions are more often than not the "root cause" of poor growth, tree decline and other problems, say arborists. A great many trees die within a few to 10 years following home construction because the understory shrubs and herbaceous plants that shaded the soil, and the litter cover or "forest duff" that both fed and protected the fine upper-soil roots are removed. The damage is compounded by grade changes that pile heavy clay soil around the trees, by paving or a patio laid over part of their roots and even by people and mower traffic in the case of compaction-sensitive trees like many oaks, lindens, ash, hickory and tulip poplar.

The remedy is to establish a 12′ no-violation zone around each tree, allowing absolutely no soil disturbance in this area during or after construction. For trees already in lawns and showing symptoms of decline, a 3″ to 4″ mulch of leaves and other organic matter should be established in the 12′ zone. If the fine root system has not been severely injured, the conditions produced by the mulch should restore it. Regular feeding, plus watering in drought, will then maintain the tree in good vigor.

In planting trees, liberal additions of organic matter are essential for clay or sandy soils. For established trees, Dr. L. C. Chadwick of Ohio State University recommends adding organic material when fertilizing by the drill-hole method. He advises punching or augering holes — as deep as 24″ in very poorly structured soils — on 12″ to 15″ centers from 24″ from the trunk to beyond the drip-line (some trees have roots extending four to six times the tree's branch spread).

These should be filled with a complete fertilizer such as 10-6-4 at the rate of 3 pounds per inch of trunk diameter, mixed with peatmoss, compost, leafmold, peanut hulls or other organic matter. After the leaves fall in autumn is an excellent time to do this, as root growth continues until the soil temperature drops below 40°. Evergreens benefit from the same procedure, but it should be done in spring, using an acid fertilizer.

JOBE'S TREE FOOD SPIKES, compacted 16-8-8 fertilizer equipped with a rubber cap for pounding into the ground, are made by International Spike, Inc. (462 East High Street, Lexington, KY 40508).

Routes to Roots

Tree surgeon WAYNE SMITH (ROUTE 1, BOX 68, TAMPA, FL 33612) has patented an improved root-environment device to aid trees growing in paving.

The WANE — "water-air-nutrition-exchange" — system is a 4″ plastic tube, 18″ long, with an inner sleeve containing gravel and slow-release fertilizer pellets. This is sunk vertically into the ground, and capped with a perforated lid which extends ¼″ above the paving. Of very strong plastic, the tube and cap are undamaged by vehicle traffic. Water and air easily filter through the cap, and the fertilizer in the tube is easily replaced when necessary.

Curing Wood

New research at the Northeastern Forest Experiment Station in Upper Darby, Pennsylvania, shows there are more important measures to insure survival of injured trees and shrubs than applying wound dressing.

Dr. Alex L. Shigo says the plant will be much better served by cleaning and smoothing the wound, and then supplying water and nutrients to help it marshal its natural decay-resisting forces. Healthy trees, maintained in full vigor by deep watering in drought and annual feeding (in late autumn for deciduous trees, early in spring for evergreens), throw up strong chemical "barrier walls" against invasion of wound sites by infecting organisms. The more a tree has been weakened by lack of feeding, drought, competition from other plants, pollution or previous improperly tended wounds, the less able it is to produce these barriers effectively.

Where the bark is merely pulled away from the cambium, as in injury by a mower, regeneration of bark tissue will often occur rapidly if the wound is shaded by a heavy paper or cloth binding. And roots broken in planting can sometimes be healed by binding them together with cloth strips or twine.

EXTERIOR WHITE LATEX PAINT, at either full or half strength, proved superior to aluminum foil and other protective methods for preventing sunscald on the trunks of young trees, in tests at the Oregon Agricultural Experiment Station.

The new deep peat pots that force roots to grow downward improve survival and growth after transplanting.

SHADE TREES

Many-Splendored Maples

Choicest among the numerous Oriental maples so well suited to small gardens is the rare paperbark maple, *Acer griseum.* Growing to 20′ to 30′, it has a graceful form, open and round-topped. The leaves are compound, composed of three 2½″ leaflets, light to medium green and whitish beneath. In autumn, its foliage colors range from gold through brilliant orange and red. Its most spectacular feature, however, is its exfoliating bark. Throughout the year, the dark orange-red-cinnamon outer bark flakes off in papery strips, revealing younger bark in soft orange-red hues. A source is *WAYSIDE GARDENS (MENTOR, OH 44060; CATALOG $2).*

The coliseum maple, *A. cappadocicum,* from western Asia has been growing for decades in parks in Buffalo and Rochester, New York, where it is regarded as one of the very finest medium-size maples to be found anywhere. On dry, sandy soils in these locations it has grown slowly, reaching about 30′ in as many years (most references state that it will eventually attain 50′). It has a beautiful round head and light gray bark, and the foliage is light green, 5- to 7-lobed and heart-shaped at the base. In *A. cappadocicum rubrum,* the leaves are blood-red when they unfold, becoming light green as they mature, and shiny beneath. These stunning trees do well on poor soils, stand city conditions and are hardy to at least −20°. Both are available from *COLE*

Many of the stronger-growing Japanese maples take on beautiful character with age.

NURSERY CO. (R.D. 1, CIRCLEVILLE, OH 43113; WHOLESALE ONLY — have your nurseryman order).

The Tatarian maple, *A. tataricum*, is prized for its "red wings" in summer. This 20' to 30' Eurasian smooth-barked maple has a wide, dense, slightly rounded head. Although it can be trained to a single trunk, it is generally considered most interesting grown in multi-stemmed clump form. Hardy to at least −20°, it has dazzling bright green 3-lobed leaves which turn yellow with red tinges in autumn. The distinctive feature is the fruit: in late June, the wings of the samaras or seed capsules turn brilliant red, and they retain this color into mid or late August. The effect is spectacular. Two sources are DAUBER'S NURSERIES (BOX 1746, YORK, PA 17405), and VALLEY NURSERY (BOX 845, HELENA, MT 59601).

Although it can be grown as a single-stemmed round-headed tree with 6' to 8' of clear trunk, the English hedge or field maple, *A. campestre*, has long been favored in Europe for clipped hedges because of its extremely dense, low branching and small leaves. It makes a thick impenetrable screen when planted closely and tightly pruned. The dark, 3-lobed leaves turn yellow in autumn. Corky ridges on the twigs add to its winter interest. It is available from SILVER FALLS NURSERY (STAR ROUTE BOX 55, SILVERTON, OR 97381). Two unusual varieties are the purple-leaved 'Schwerinii' and white-variegated 'Pulveru-

lentum,' obtainable from HILLIER & SONS (WINCHESTER, ENGLAND). A very new form is 'Nana,' which grows to only about 5' (WAYSIDE GARDENS, MENTOR, OH 44060; CATALOG $2).

The Japanese maples offer marvelous variety for specimen, accent and container planting. *A. japonicum*, the less hardy (to −10°) of the two species, has two outstanding cultivars, 'Aconitifolium,' the half-moon or fernleaf Japanese maple, and 'Aureum,' the golden full-moon maple, both of which turn brilliant yellow and red in autumn. These can grow upright and round-headed to 25', but in the North are usually lower and shrubby.

The hardier (−20°) *A. palmatum* has perhaps 200 named forms, from the 20' purple-red 'Atropurpureum' and orange-red 'Oshio Beni,' to the laceleaf types that grow 7' to 8' high and twice as wide, such as bright green 'Dissectum,' bronze-red 'Dissectum Purpureum,' deep red 'Ever Red' and 'Palmatifidum,' pink-edged red 'Variegatum' and weeping 'Waterfall.' Sources of these and many other choice forms are BRIMFIELD GARDENS NURSERY (245 BRIMFIELD RD., WETHERSFIELD, CT 06109; CATALOG $1), ISLAND GARDENS (701 GOODPASTURE RD., EUGENE, OR 97401) AND JOEL W. SPINGARN (1535 FOREST AVE., BALDWIN, NY 11510; CATALOG 50¢).

Birch Build-Up

Birches admirably fill the need for small, fine-textured trees suited to low ranch-style homes; the multiple-stemmed types give an illusion of depth and distance, and grass grows well in their light shade.

The paper birch (*Betula papyrifera*) will thrive on new-house sites where the topsoil has been removed, and on sandy soils or poorly drained ones. The handsome fast-growing, pink-barked river birch (*B. nigra*) tolerates occasional flooding. European birch, *B. pendula*, offers the cutleaf weeping *gracilis*, vertically branched columnar *fastigiata* and the recently introduced red-leaved 'Scarlet Glory' and purple-leaved 'Purple Splendor.'

One of the most striking of all is the magnificent monarch birch, *B. maximowicziana*, hardy to −10° and growing to 100′ in southern California, although rarely over 50′ in lower Ohio and New England. It has flaky orange-brown bark that turns white, and brilliant yellow fall foliage. A source is COLE NURSERY CO. (R.D. 1, CIRCLEVILLE, OH 43113; WHOLESALE ONLY — have your nurseryman order).

The rarely seen 40′ fountain birch, *B. fontinalis*, reports South Dakota State University, "makes an attractive multi-trunked small tree useful for massing as well as individual accent. It is highly resistant to borer attack as well as being one of the most colorful birches with its reddish-brown bark and yellow fall color." Montana plantsman Clayton V. Berg notes that its foliage, which resembles that of the European white birch (*B. pendula*), is "very durable in heat, wind and drought," and that this Colorado-to-Alaska native "from its more northerly inland seed sources shows greater cold hardiness (to at least −30°) than any of the North American, European or Asian species known to have value in colder climates." A source is VALLEY NURSERY (BOX 845, HELENA, MT 59601).

The Blue Beech

An "understory" tree of great merit is the blue beech, *Carpinus caroliniana*, also known as the American hornbeam or ironwood. It has a beautifully rounded shape — a 30′ tall specimen may

DETAILS OF COLLECTING AND GERMINATING SEED O hundreds of woody plants are given in "Growing Trees in Small Nurseries," Cornell Extension Bulletin 1198, 10¢ from the College of Agriculture, Cornell University (Ithaca, NY 14850) "How to Grow Seedlings of Trees and Shrubs," 25¢ from F. W. Schumacher, Horticulturist (Sandwich, MA 02563), also a fine source of seed and "Woody Plant Seed Manual," USDA Miscellaneous Publication 654, $4 from Superintendent of Documents (Washington, DC 20402).

have a 30′ spread — outstanding yellow-orange autumn color, gray bark and sharply toothed bluish-green leaves. Young twigs are a light green, then become lustrous orange-brown. Both male and female flowers are borne on the same tree, the male catkins having green and red scales, the smaller female catkins hairy green scales. Blue beech likes rich soil, tolerates sun to dense shade and is hardy to −40°. A source is DUTCH MOUNTAIN NURSERY (AUGUSTA, MI 49012).

Turkish Tree Hazel

Turkish hazel, *Corylus colurna*, almost totally overlooked as an ornamental tree, is a shade tree of unusual merit, interesting in all seasons, with distinctive beige-colored corky bark and broadly oval, serrated leaves about 3″ across. Hardy to −20°, it grows slowly to 40′ to 50′ or more, very neatly conical in form, and stands strong sun and drought. Unlike most species of *Corylus*, it does not sucker. The heavy crop of catkins borne in late winter is a fascinating decorative asset. Beginning at about age 12, it produces small, thick-shelled but good-quality nuts. A source is DUTCH MOUNTAIN NURSERY (AUGUSTA, MI 49012).

The Hardy Rubber Tree

A handsome tree, hardy to −20° and yielding rubber — though low in content and difficult to extract commercially — is *Eucommia ulmoides*, from central China. In his evaluations of shade trees, Prof. Clarence E. Lewis of Michigan State University gives this 50′ tree a 100% rating. It thrives on the East Lansing campus, developing a fine round head, and the 3″ glossy alternate leaves are toothed and deeply veined — greatly resembling those of the American elm. In Cleveland and Cincinnati, *E. ulmoides* is growing as a street tree. Dr. R. W. Reisch, of the Ohio Agricultural Research and Development Center in Wooster, reports that it has high tolerance of "air pollution, reflected light and heat, salt runoff and spray, dry soil, and limited space for root growth." A source is EDWARD H. SCANLON & ASSOCIATES (7621 LEWIS RD., OLMSTED FALLS, OH 44138; WHOLESALE — have your nurseryman order).

Fraxinus oxycarpa 'Raywood' is a handsome round-headed new ash introduced by the Saratoga Horticultural Foundation.

New Ashes Liven the Landscape

The ash has become a standby for street and garden plantings. Flowering ash, *Fraxinus ornus*, is a beautiful small tree, to 35′ and hardy to −10°, bearing panicles of fragrant white blooms in May. In new introductions in "non-flowering" types, there is the outstanding *F. excelsior* 'Hessei,' a handsome round-headed tree to 50′, hardy to −35°, with lustrous dark green leathery leaves, single instead of compound as in other ashes.

In the seedless green ashes, oval-crowned *F. pennsylvanica lanceolata* 'Marshall Seedless,' hardy far into Canada, is very vigorous and tolerates drought and air pollution. A new seedless white ash, *F. americana* 'Autumn Purple,' grows to 70′ and is hardy to −35°, with deep purple or mahogany fall color. All these may be ordered through local nurserymen from the wholesale COLE NURSERY CO. (R.D. 1, CIRCLEVILLE, OH 43113).

Another new seedless white ash, 'Rosehill,' with bronze-red autumn color lasting up to 4 weeks, is available through the wholesale ROSEHILL GARDENS (9300 HOLMES ST., KANSAS CITY, MO 64131).

Two even newer ashes are 'Emerald' (MARSHALL NURSERIES, ARLINGTON, NB 68002), a slow-growing seedless red ash (*F. pennsylvanica*) with a compact crown, broad leaves and resilient bark which can be depressed by finger pressure

. . . and 'Honey Shade' (CHARLES KLEHM & SON NURSERY, 2 EAST ALGONQUIN RD., ARLINGTON HEIGHTS, IL 60005), a green ash hardy to −30° and distinguished for fast growth, horizontal branching and extremely glossy foliage.

Rugged Relic

One of the most ancient of trees, the ginkgo or maidenhair is also one of the most rugged. Hardy to −20°, it stands heat, air pollution, wind and ice storms, tolerates many soils, transplants easily and is virtually free of pests and diseases. Its most distinctive feature is the bright green fan-shaped leaves, which turn clear yellow in autumn and fall all on the same day, reportedly when the temperature drops to 22°.

The gardener can choose from many fine forms: 'Autumn Gold,' compact oval, finest fall foliage color (GIRARD NURSERIES, GENEVA, OH 44041), pyramidal 'Fairmount' (COLE NURSERY CO., R.D. 1, CIRCLEVILLE, OH 43113; WHOLESALE — have your nurseryman order), conical 'Lakeview' (COLE), weeping 'Pendula' (GIRARD) and the narrowly columnar 'Fastigiata' (GIRARD) or 'Princeton Sentry' (PRINCETON NURSERIES, PRINCETON, NJ 08540; WHOLESALE).

Massive gnarled branches and corky bark make the phellodendrons outstandingly picturesque.

Artful Tree

The all-too-uncommon Kentucky coffeetree has exceptional four-season value. *Gymnocladus dioica* is a tree for bold effects, at its most imposing in winter. The deeply furrowed gray bark of its trunk, the shaggy-barked branches with stubby twigs and its clusters of long — up to 12″ — brown pods which last through winter are outstanding against bleak sky and snow.

The doubly compound leaves, up to 36″ and with many leaflets, are pinkish as they open in spring, then become almost bronze, and finally turn dark green with lighter undersides. In May and June, purplish-white flowers are borne in bunches, and in autumn the foliage turns yellow. A slow grower, the Kentucky coffeetree may attain 50′ in as many years. It prefers moist, rich soil, but must have good drainage, and is hardy to −20°. Two sources are WAYNESBORO NURSERIES (WAYNESBORO, VA 22980) AND ZILKE BROTHERS NURSERY (BARODA, MI 49101).

Grand Larches

Deciduous conifers are very few in number, but they are unsurpassed for combining majesty and grace. The larches, for example, are lofty yet delicate, openly pyramidal in form, with irregularly spaced branches and long, pendulous branchlets which give a fountain effect, as picturesque when garlanded with cones in winter as when spring clothes them with bright apple-green needles. The short, narrow needles are borne singly and in brush-like terminal clusters of often 30 or more, and in autumn they turn brilliant golden-yellow.

There are larches for every region except Florida and the Gulf and Pacific Coasts. Best choices are the European larch, *Larix decidua*, hardy to −35°; Japanese larch, *L. leptolepis*, more widely branching, with bluish-green needles; and golden larch, *Pseudolarix amabilis* (*P. kaempferi*), also broad-branching, and with needles twice the length of the other species'. The Japanese larch tolerates poorer and wetter soils, is less susceptible to canker, and is very fast growing, averaging nearly 3′ a year when young. Japanese and golden larches are hardy to −20°, and all three species grow to 50′ to 70′ in deep, rich, moist sandy loam. All are available from BRIMFIELD GARDENS NURSERY (245 BRIMFIELD ROAD, WETHERSFIELD, CT 06109; CATALOG $1).

Corkers

Any gardener who has seen fine collections of cork trees, such as those at the Arnold Arboretum in Boston or the Morton Arboretum in Illinois, will agree that few deciduous trees offer more picturesque landscape character.

Massively round-headed at maturity, with gnarled trunks and branches and light gray, deeply ridged corky bark, phellodendrons are splendid ornamentals where their spread — which can exceed their height — can be accommodated. Fortunately, not all the species attain great proportions. The Amur cork tree, *Phellodendron amurense*, grows to near 50′, but *P. chinense*, the Chinese cork tree, rarely exceeds

Large wound cavities should be filled with asphalt or the new polyurethane foam, a job best entrusted to a professional arborist.

30'. Both are quite fast growing and hardy to −35°, thriving everywhere except on the extreme Gulf and West Coasts, with no particular soil requirements and complete freedom from pests and disease.

The handsome walnut-like compound leaves, glossy green and up to 15″ long, are dotted with glands containing aromatic oil. They turn bright yellow in autumn, and fall abruptly with the first hard frost. The yellowish-green flowers of *P. amurense* are not notable, but *P. chinense* bears decorative dense panicles of green flowers streaked with rose. Female cork trees, provided a male tree is in the vicinity, produce attractive clusters of strongly aromatic green fruit that turns lustrous black in the fall and persists most of the winter to provide food for the birds.

P. amurense is available from GURNEY SEED & NURSERY CO. (YANKTON, SD 57078), *P. chinense* from TINGLE NURSERY (PITTSVILLE, MD 21850).

Pistacia Pastiche

The Chinese pistache, *Pistacia chinensis*, a handsome spreading tree with compound leaves, is becoming popular in the South and California — and there is evidence that it should be a valuable ornamental much farther north.

P. chinensis is thriving in St. Louis and as a street tree in Wichita, Kansas, and has proved its worth at the Bartlett Arboretum in Stamford, Connecticut, and the Morris Arboretum in Philadelphia. Thus it is hardy to at least −10°, and

perhaps even lower: the related *P. vera*, which yields the delectable pistachio nut, has been observed to withstand −22° at a Maryland Plant Introduction Station.

A rounded, rapid-growing tree to 60', *P. chinensis* is most prized for its brilliant orange-red autumn color, which develops best in areas which have hot, dry weather in late summer and fall. 'Keith Davey,' a cultivar with intense red color, has been patented by the Saratoga Horticultural Foundation of California. A source of Chinese pistache is MONROVIA NURSERY (AZUSA, CA 91702; WHOLESALE — have your nurseryman order).

Options in Oaks

Sometimes transplantability is the biggest single factor determining the availability of plants. This is the reason for the predominance in the trade of the pin oak, *Quercus palustris*, over many more desirable oaks, says Dr. Benjamin Blackburn of New Jersey's Willowwood Arboretum. Pin oaks develop a branched root system rather than a deep taproot, and so are easier to move, but "as they quickly mature, shabby interiors and sagging low branches usually require costly treatment."

Although the superior 'Sovereign' pin oak has more evenly spaced, upright-tending branches, many other fine oaks should also be considered: the majestic, rapid-growing red (*Q. borealis*) and scarlet (*Q. coccinea*) oaks, both hardy in the far northern states, and Shumard oak (*Q. shumardi*), hardy to −10°, all with flaming autumn foliage . . . the stately English oak (*Q. robur*), with massive branches and round-lobed leaves that stay green through fall . . . narrow-leaved willow oak (*Q. phellos*), a rapid grower to 50', also hardy

Combined with sanitation and spraying, soil, trunk and root injection of Benlate is proving effective in controlling Dutch elm disease.

to −10° . . . and the highly ornamental shingle oak (*Q. imbricaria*), to 60', with laurel-like leaves that turn red and yellow in autumn (also useful as a clipped hedge). All these are listed by COLE NURSERY CO. (R.D. 1, CIRCLEVILLE, OH 43113; WHOLESALE — have your nurseryman order).

COLE is also offering the Asian sawtooth oak, *Q. acutissima*, one of the most promising new trees. It is hardy to −10° and grows as rapidly as a pin oak, reaching 40'. A shapely, round-headed tree, it has chestnut-like leaves, lustrous green, narrow and bristle-pointed.

One of the most dramatic columnar trees for screen or accent planting is the cypress oak, *Q. robur fastigiata*, usually mistakenly called the pyramidal English oak. Actually it originates in the western Pyrenees of France and Spain, and all its branches grow upright, rather than the lower ones being horizontal as in pyramidal forms. A cypress oak 50' tall will rarely have a branch spread of more than 8'.

Among its assets are moderately fast growth, dense branching, and neat leaves with rounded lobes. These are slightly smaller, and the branchlets are more delicate, than those of the English oak, *Q. robur*. The cypress oak is hardy to −20°, and where a beautiful columnar tree is desired it is certainly a finer choice than the much more commonly planted, but short-lived, Lombardy poplar. It is available from INTER-STATE NURSERIES (HAMBURG, IA 51640).

The Odd Willows

The willows are an extraordinarily varied family, abounding in oddities as well as numerous serviceable plants. In recent years, some of the more curious forms have been popular — the corkscrew willow, *Salix matsudana* 'Tortuosa,' a tree with contorted branches, hardy to −10° (GIRARD NURSERIES, GENEVA, OH 44041); the fascinating big-horn willow, *S. babylonica* 'Crispa,' its leaves spirally curved like a ram's horns, 30', hardy to −5° (INTER-STATE NURSERIES, HAMBURG, IA 51640); and the shrubby 15' *S. sachalinensis* 'Sekka,' the fan-tail willow, with red-yellow twisted and flattened twigs, hardy to −20° (GIRARD).

One of the finest of all willows is the 50' golden weeping willow, *S. chrysocoma* (often offered as *S. alba* 'Tristis,' 'Vitellina Pendula' or 'Niobe'). This gold-stemmed hybrid — its botanical name means "willow like a golden head of hair" — has crossed naturally with the corkscrew willow to make a contorted weeping willow with gold bark and curled leaves, named 'Golden Curls' by the discoverers of the chance seedling, Charles and Jack Beardslee of the wholesale BEARDSLEE NURSERY (PERRY, OH 44081). 'Golden Curls' should mature to a 40' or taller tree, hardy to at least −20°.

Elm Underststudy

The new 'Village Green' zelkova is becoming widely accepted as the best substitute for the American elm.

Japanese zelkova, *Zelkova serrata*, is related to the American elm, so there has been some concern as to its possible susceptibility to Dutch elm disease. 'Village Green,' however, is highly resistant. Among its other virtues are many qualities of the American elm: a vase shape, gray bark and arching branches. The leaves are handsome, sharply toothed and dark green, turning deep russet in autumn.

A moderately vigorous grower to 50' or so, this clone is hardier than the species, and does well to −20°. It is an introduction of PRINCETON NURSERIES (PRINCETON, NJ 08540; WHOLESALE — have your nurseryman order).

FLOWERING TREES

Choicest Horsechestnuts

More useful for modern gardens than the massive old-favorite horsechestnut, *Aesculus hippocastanum*, is the Ohio buckeye, *A. glabra*. It grows no taller than 40', is less dense and in May bears its 6″ clusters of white flowers on upturned twigs, giving the same striking candelabra effect as do those of the horsechestnut. The fall foliage is brilliant orange and gold. In winter, the large, sharp-pointed scaly buds are unusually attractive. The Ohio buckeye is also less subject to leaf scorch than the horsechestnut. Two sources are SPRING HILL NURSERIES (TIPP CITY, OH 45371) and GURNEY NURSERY (YANKTON, SD 57078).

Two other valuable species are the rare *A. carnea* 'Briotti,' bearing stunning red clusters in midsummer, and the handsome 8' to 10' *A. parviflora*, a wide-spreading shrub with white candelabra almost a foot long in July (both obtainable from BRIMFIELD GARDENS NURSERY (245 BRIMFIELD RD., WETHERSFIELD, CT 06109; CATALOG $1).

All About Amelanchiers

The amelanchiers — known as juneberry, serviceberry, sarvistree, shadbush and shadblow — are prized for their clouds of white bloom in early spring. They also offer graceful rounded form and small leaves, purple fruits, radiant yellow-orange-copper-red autumn tones, and spirally marked satiny gray-pink bark. Hardy to −20°, they thrive in sun or shade. Their only malady is a juniper rust, and amelanchiers should not be planted within 500 yards of junipers.

A. canadensis is usually a tall shrub but may grow as a tree to 45' on open sites. The more highly regarded *A. laevis* (RAYMOND NELSON NURSERY, DUBOIS, PA 15801) is a single- or multiple-trunked tree to 30', and has reddish-bronze young leaves. *A. grandiflora*, a hybrid of *A. canandensis* with *A. laevis*, has a form 'Rubescens,' with large flowers that open pink, then change to white (WAYSIDE GARDENS, MENTOR, OH 44060; CATALOG $2).

If the birds don't steal them, amelanchier's small apple-like fruits are delicious eaten from the tree or made into jelly. They have the highest vitamin C content of any tree fruit, even surpassing citrus. Especially sweet and juicy is the fruit of the shrubby saskatoon, *A. alnifolia*, native to Canada's prairies. A source of several fine varieties is JOHN WALLACE, BEAVERLODGE NURSERY (BEAVERLODGE, ALBERTA, CANADA).

Rosy Future for Redbud

It's hard to envision any tree challenging the popularity of the dogwood, crabapple and flowering cherry for spring bloom. But the new selections of redbud promise to do just that.

A clear pink form of *C. canadensis*, with no trace of purple in the flowers, is 'Wither's Pink Charm' (CARROLL GARDENS, E. MAIN ST. EXTENSION, WESTMINSTER, MD 21157). Recently registered is a clone of the white-flowered *C. canadensis alba*, 'Royal White,' which is more compact and earlier maturing, with larger flowers that open earlier in the season (LOUIS GERARDI NURSERY, R.F.D. 1, O'FALLON, IL 62269). Two with unusual foliage are 'Silver Cloud,' which flowers sparsely but has silvery-white margins and splashes on the leaves *(YELLOW-DELL NURSERY, CRESTWOOD, KY 40014)*, and the patented purple-leaved 'Forest Pansy' *(WARREN & SON NURSERY, 10901 N.E. 23RD, OKLAHOMA CITY, OK 73161)*. The latter nursery also lists the superb double-flowered 'Flame' with fully double ¾″ blooms. All are hardy to −20°.

Redbud will endure heat, drought and acidity or alkalinity, if the soil is light and well-aerated. It especially benefits from annual feeding with a 10-8-6 or similar high-nitrogen formula when the buds show color. In the North, it should not be planted on wind-exposed sites.

Top Dogwoods

The dogwoods are being re-evaluated. Mediocre *Cornus florida* cultivars like 'Prosser' and 'Springtime' are being replaced by such finer varieties as 'Cloud 9,' which begins to bloom heavily when only a few feet tall *(EMLONG NURSERIES, STEVENSVILLE, MI 49127)*, and the vigorous ruby-red 'Cherokee Chief' *(KELLY BROS. NURSERIES, DANSVILLE, NY 14457)*.

Other fine cultivars are 'White Cloud,' pink 'Apple Blossom' and rose-red 'Spring Song' *(WAYSIDE GARDENS, MENTOR, OH 44060; CATALOG $2)*; 'Royal Red' *(GIRARD NURSERIES, GENEVA, OH 44041)*; the very hardy 'New Hampshire' *(HEATHERFELLS NURSERY, ANDOVER, MA 01810)*; and a superior Chinese dogwood, *Cornus kousa chinensis* 'Milky Way' *(WAYSIDE)*.

Also worth noting are *C. florida* 'Welch's Junior Miss,' a red cultivar which blooms well in Florida and California *(INTRODUCED BY CLARENCE H. WELCH, WILMER, AL 36587)*; white 'Rainbow,' with yellow and green foliage turning scarlet in autumn *(WAYSIDE)*; and dwarf white-flowered 'Pygmy' *(BRIMFIELD GARDENS NURSERY, WETHERSFIELD, CT 06109; CATALOG $1)*.

MRS. MARY B. WAKEFIELD (MILTON, MA 02186) has been issued Plant Patent 3296 for a fastigiate dogwood, hardy to at least −20°, with distinctly ascending branches and branchlets, and "large white flowers, each having four broadly overlapping bracts . . . borne all along the numerous horizontal branches, which are so densely twigged that the flowers are quite close together and appear in vertical series as narrow white tiers, which is quite unusual and attractive . . ."

A dogwood that blooms all summer long has been patented by *PETER E. COSTICH* (patent assigned to *TREESEARCH, KINGSTON, NJ 08528)*. This variety of *C. kousa* offers a "prolonged and spectacular summer-flowering habit, with flowers retaining their white color and remaining unblemished from about mid-June to late August or mid-September . . ." The flowers are "about 25% more abundant and about 20% larger in comparison with flowers typical of *C. kousa*."

An unusual showpiece is the native *C. alternifolia*, which carries its branches in horizontal tiers or layers in pagoda or wedding cake style. It grows to 10′ to 15′, as a large shrub or small tree. Hardy to −35°, it tolerates shade, but should be used as a lawn specimen rather than in a border, so the wedding cake effect won't be obscured. The one drawback of this dogwood is susceptibility to twig blight, but Dr. P. P. Pirone of the New York Botanical Garden reports that this is controllable with Benlate. *C. alternifolia* is obtainable from *DUTCH MOUNTAIN NURSERY (AUGUSTA, MI 49012)*. *BRIMFIELD GARDENS NURSERY (245 BRIMFIELD ROAD, WETHERSFIELD, CT 06109; CATALOG $1)* has *C. alternifolia* 'variegata' ('Argentea') with green-white-pink leaves.

Horizons in Hawthorns

The new *Crataegus oxyacantha* 'Crimson Cloud' *(PRINCETON NURSERIES, PRINCETON, NJ 08540; WHOLESALE* — have your nurseryman order), which has very large, starry white-centered red single flowers, should be even more popular than the double-flowered scarlet 'Pauli,' double white 'Plena' and other cultivars of *C. oxyacantha*. The very hardy (to −35°) hybrid *C. toba*, with fragrant double pink flowers, is another fine flowering hawthorn, and for brilliant bronze-scarlet autumn foliage, there are the Washington thorn, *C. phaenopyrum,* and hybrid *C. lavallei. C viridis* 'Winter King' is perhaps the most profuse bearer of long-lasting red fruits.

Two species with very large fruit that is excellent for jellies have been introduced by *EDWARD H. SCANLON & ASSOCIATES (7621 LEWIS RD., OLMSTED FALLS, OH 44138; WHOLESALE* — have your nurseryman order). The handsome 20' Chinese big-leaf hawthorn, *C. pinnatifida major,* has dark, glossy, deeply lobed foliage. The native downy hawthorn or scarlet haw, *C. mollis,* is a strong grower to 25', with gray-green, leathery, slightly hairy leaves. It does well in poor soils and has great tolerance for air pollution.

Several dogwoods of unusually fine form, flower and floriferousness have been patented by Massachusetts gardener Mary B. Wakefield.

Divine Davidia

A fine ornamental from the Orient is *Davidia involucrata,* the dove or handkerchief tree, which grows to 20' or 30' in the North, to 50' or more in the South.

The dove tree is a slow grower and not easy to transplant, but its handsome linden-like form and foliage — the latter large and heart-shaped, turning soft yellow in autumn — and magnificent May bloom make it well worth growing. The beauty of the bloom is not in the flower itself, which is a tannish-yellow ball, but in the two drooping creamy-white dove-winged bracts that envelop it. One bract is about 6″ long, and the other half that.

Once well established — which usually takes several years — the dove tree blooms profusely and spectacularly. It is hardy to about −10°. A source is *BRIMFIELD GARDENS NURSERY (245 BRIMFIELD ROAD, WETHERSFIELD, CT 06109; CATALOG $1).*

Heritage Tree

Few choice plants have as exciting a history as *Franklinia alatamaha* — the genus named for Benjamin Franklin, friend of its discoverer, John Bartram, and the species for the river in Georgia near which he found it in the autumn of 1765. None of Bartram's discoveries on his prodigious travels through the Colonies could have thrilled him as much as his first sight of the small shrubby tree simultaneously garlanded with brilliant scarlet autumn foliage and snowy, gold-stamened blossoms. Bartram and his son William sent franklinia to England and also grew it in their botanical garden in Philadelphia — the first botanical garden in America. These are the source of all of today's plants, for the franklinia has not been seen in the wild since 1803.

Franklinia begins to bloom in mid-August, and its waxy, fragrant camellia-like 3″ to 4″ blooms appear until severe frost. It is handsome through most of the year, the foliage persisting long into

Trees   73

winter even at northern limits of its range. Hardy to −10°, it prefers full sun and a moist, peaty soil. A source is WAYSIDE GARDENS (MENTOR, OH 44060; CATALOG $2).

Carolina Silverbells

For a mixed woody border or miniature woodland planting — as well as lawn use if sheltered from strong winds — the snowdrop or Carolina silverbell, *Halesia carolina (H. tetraptera)*, is one of the most interesting spring-flowering trees. In April or May, the branches of this rounded, usually multi-stemmed 25′ to 30′ tree are draped from end to end with pendent white bell flowers in clusters of three to five, before the leaves open.

Like the similar but taller (to 60′) mountain silverbell, *H. monticola*, the Carolina silverbell has yellow-green 3″ to 5″ oval leaves that turn bright yellow in late autumn. Both have unusual scaly gray-brown bark and 4-winged golden-brown fruits that last well into winter. Native from West Virginia to Texas, both are hardy to −20°. *H. carolina* is available from WAYNESBORO NURSERIES (WAYNESBORO, VA 22980), *H. monticola* from WAYSIDE GARDENS (MENTOR, OH 44060; CATALOG $2).

Pollution-Proof Tree

Planted 3000 years ago in China on the tombs of scholars, the goldenrain tree, *Koelreuteria paniculata*, is being recommended today for urban streets and gardens as a small four-seasons-beautiful tree with unusual tolerance of polluted air, drought, heavy and even alkaline soils and hot winds.

Goldenrain meets all criteria for attractiveness of form, foliage, flower and fruit. Hardy to −20° and growing to 30′ or sometimes 40′, it develops a dense broad head, and curving, twisting branches that give it fine winter interest. The lacy pinnate or feather-form foliage is crowned in July to early August with showy, large, upright terminal pani-

cles of golden flowers with a touch of red-orange at the centers. These are followed by pale green, papery "Japanese lantern" fruit capsules which turn deep brown and often persist through the cold months, the hard seeds within rattling cheerily in winter winds. *K. paniculata* can be grown with a single trunk or multi-stemmed. A source is GIRARD NURSERIES (BOX 428, GENEVA, OH 44041).

A late-flowering, exceptionally floriferous cultivar is 'September Gold,' from EDWARD H. SCANLON & ASSOCIATES (7621 LEWIS ROAD, OLMSTEAD FALLS, OH 44138; WHOLESALE — have your nurseryman order). Mr. Scanlon also offers the extremely narrow growing 'Fastigiata,' but says it blooms very sparsely.

Lofty Liriodendron

Where there is room for it, the tulip tree or tulip poplar, *Liriodendron tulipifera*, is magnificent. One of the stateliest of our eastern natives, it thrives in every state where winters are no colder than −20°, growing rapidly to 60′ to 80′, straight-trunked and stoutly branched, with a fairly broad crown.

In late May to June, it bears a profusion of tulip-sized and -shaped greenish-yellow flowers, banded orange at the base. The unusual shiny bright green foliage, squarish and deeply lobed, turns bright gold in autumn. Both the woolly flower buds and the brown seed pods are cone-shaped, and the latter open in the fall, releasing winged seeds and leaving candle-like erect stalks with star-like outer rings that add unusual textural interest in winter. Two sources are EASTERN SHORE NURSERIES (BOX 743, EASTON, MD 21601), and KRIDER NURSERIES (MIDDLEBURY, IN 46540).

OSAGE ORANGE, *Maclura pomifera*, now being rediscovered as an ornamental, also has insect-repelling properties, reports the University of Alabama: a single green "orange" will rid an infested room of waterbugs and roaches in a few hours.

There are two columnar cultivars, 'Arnold' and 'Fastigiata,' and recently a form, 'Ardis,' described as miniature in leaf and growth, was registered (for information, contact PROF. J. C. MCDANIEL, UNIVERSITY OF ILLINOIS, URBANA, IL 61801).

Magnolia Boom

Many new magnolia species, cultivars and hybrids are appearing. This has been greatly stimulated by the formation of the American Magnolia Society (PHILIP J. SAVAGE, SECRETARY, 2150 WOODWARD AVENUE, BLOOMFIELD HILLS, MI 48013). Most of the finest introductions by individuals, nurseries and institutions like the Saratoga Horticultural Foundation are found in the catalog of the magnolia specialist, GOSSLER FARMS NURSERY (1200 WEAVER ROAD, SPRINGFIELD, OR 97477; CATALOG 25¢).

One of the best new ones is 'Centennial,' a cultivar of the charming shrubby star magnolia, M. stellata, with very large, open flowers. GOSSLER also lists fine M. soulangiana cultivars such as 'Brozzoni,' 10″ white flowers, and the shrubby 'Grace McDade,' lavender-pink, 11″ . . . M. loebneri 'Spring Snow,' pure white blooms, smaller in stature and more cold-resistant in bud than the popular 'Merrill' . . . the rare and exquisite Chinese magnolia, M. sinensis . . . M. wilsoni, the best of the Oyama magnolias, hardy to about −5°, with upside-down, dark-centered white flowers . . . and M. acuminata cordata, yellow-flowered, hardy to −10° and one of our rarest and loveliest native small trees.

The "Now" Crabapples

Horticulturists are taking a hard look at some widely accepted varieties of flowering crabapples and suggesting replacements. Dr. E. R. Hasselkus of the University of Illinois (Urbana, IL 61801) says that the popularity of 'Almey,' 'Eleyi' and 'Hopa' is not too well deserved. All three have flowers that fade rapidly, are susceptible to apple scab, and produce many water sprouts, suckers that spoil the appearance and sap the strength. To these might be added 'Van Eseltine,' which is susceptible to fireblight.

Dr. Hasselkus gives highest honors to disease-free 'Red Splendor' (developed by BERGESON NURSERY, FERTILE, MN 56540); new 'Radiant,' with deep red flowers (EARL FERRIS NURSERY, HAMPTON, IA 50441); 'Beverly,' a nonspreading cultivar good for limited space (KRIDER NURSERIES, MIDDLEBURY, IN 46540); and 'Bob White,' with yellow fruit that persists through late winter (introduced by the ARNOLD ARBORETUM, JAMAICA PLAIN, MA 02130).

Some other fine new crabapples are 'Snowdrift,' which has been called the finest white to date (COLE NURSERY CO., R.D. 1, CIRCLEVILLE, OH 43113; WHOLESALE — have your nurseryman order); the low-growing 'Sparkler' and upright 'Vanguard' (EARL FERRIS); late-blooming 'Silver Moon' (SIMPSON ORCHARD NURSERY, 1504 WHEATLAND ROAD, VINCENNES, IN 47591); and 'Pink Cascade,' a very narrow weeping crab (INTERSTATE NURSERIES, HAMBURG, IA 51640). SIMPSON has also introduced 'Indian Magic,' with rosy flowers and golden-orange fruit that persists all winter; and 'White Candle,' stocky, with heavy and glossy leaves and exceptionally large double white flowers.

Two new dwarf crabs are 'Kibele,' a compact grower to 8′, with purplish-red foliage, rose-pink flowers and deep burgundy fruits, and 'Coralburst,' growing to 8′ with upright branching and double rose-pink blooms. Both are available through COLE NURSERY CO., which produces 'Coralburst' in two forms: "Ground-budded plants will become neat little bushes suitable for foundation planting, 'front of the border' locations, or for dwarf hedges. Budded as half standards, 30″ to 36″ high, you have a pleasing compact little tree with the same landscape uses as tree roses." These top-budded 'Coralburst' will develop at near eye-level.

In the North, 25′ to 30′ is usual for a narrowly pyramidal single-trunk specimen, or it may be grown lower and wider with multiple stems. Sourwood is hardy to as low as −25° if protected from winter winds, and produces its best fall color when planted in full sun. An ericaceous tree, it requires acid, humusy soil with ample moisture. A source is GIRARD NURSERIES (GENEVA, OH 44041).

Picking Cherries

Oriental cherry trees are usually selected for quality of bloom. But veteran gardeners seek desirable features in all seasons.

On this basis, the very commonly planted 'Kwanzan' cherry (*Prunus serrulata* 'Sekiyama') should certainly yield to 'Daybreak' (*P. yedoensis* 'Akebono'), not only less blatantly aggressive in flower color but also a superbly formed tree with gracefully arching branches. 'Mt. Fuji' (*P. serrulata* 'Shirotae') is also magnificent in form, tending to a wide round head, with massive mahogany branches that set off its double white flowers beautifully. Another large grower, the Sargent cherry (*P. sargentii*), should be considered for the copper-red tones of its young foliage and fine crimson fall color.

One of the least known but finest of all for year-round interest is *P. serrula*, the Chinese birchbark cherry. The brilliant peeling bark has been described as having the texture and appearance of polished mahogany or burnished bronze. It grows quite rapidly to 25′, is somewhat columnar and has narrow willow-like leaves. The white flowers are small and starry. Birchbark cherry can be grown with a single or several trunks, and is hardy to about −10°. A source is BRIMFIELD GARDENS NURSERY (245 BRIMFIELD ROAD, WETHERSFIELD, CT 06109; CATALOG $1).

Low Callery Pear

Among the most highly acclaimed of all recent tree introductions have been the Callery ornamental pears. *Pyrus calleryana* 'Bradford,' 'Chanticleer' and 'Aristocrat' are beautiful 30′ to 50′ trees, hardy to −20°, with masses of white flowers in early spring, deep green glossy leaves that turn plum-red in autumn and russet fruits.

Now there is a dwarf Callery pear, 'Fauriei,' from COLE NURSERY CO. (R.D. 1, CIRCLEVILLE, OH 43113; WHOLESALE — have your nurseryman order). COLE says its attention was called to this fine tree by Roy Nordine of the Morton Arboretum.

'Royal Star' is one of the finest of the new cultivars of *Magnolia stellata*.

Singular Sourwood

In the past decade, no native flowering tree has been more widely praised than the sourwood, sorrel or lily-of-the-valley tree, *Oxydendrum arboreum*.

Especially spectacular clothed in its flaming autumn foliage and silvery-gray seed pods, the sourwood is equally showy in midsummer when its semi-drooping panicles of white bell flowers open at the branch tips. But it has much to offer in every season — long, light green leaves in spring, becoming dark green, leathery, lustrous and laurel-like as they mature, and in winter, thick fissured bark and the decorative seed capsules.

"Some of the Arboretum's glowing descriptions are 'unique round-headed variety — with profuse early white blossoms (late April–early May), picturesque branches and glossy summer foliage of deepest green. It colors orange-scarlet, crimson and purple in the late fall . . .' The tree is thornless like 'Bradford' and other grafted Callery selections. All the excellent qualities of Callery, but in a smaller package — to 15'."

Highly resistant to pollution, the 'Regent' scholar tree is being widely planted in European and American cities.

Oriental Wonder

The Chinese scholar tree, *Sophora japonica*, is one of the most versatile as well as handsomest of summer-flowering trees. This temperate-zone member of the pea family, hardy to −20°, rivals its many spectacular tropical relatives in floral beauty, and in addition thrives in hot, dry, infertile situations. It's also an exceptionally good city tree — fine specimens can be seen on the streets of Rome, Washington, Cleveland and Cincinnati.

S. japonica grows to 40' to 60', with a round head. An unusual feature is the shiny green color of young branches. The glossy, locust-like ferny foliage gives an open shade that does not deter lawn grass. The 15" creamy flower clusters are showy from August well into September, and pale green seed pods persist into winter.

The cultivar 'Regent' is extra vigorous, growing almost twice as rapidly as the species (COLE NURSERY CO., R.D. 1, CIRCLEVILLE, OH 43113; WHOLESALE — have your nurseryman order). 'Pendula,' a 15' weeping form, blooms sparsely but is wonderfully picturesque in large planters (BRIMFIELD GARDENS NURSERY, 245 BRIMFIELD ROAD, WETHERSFIELD, CT 06109; CATALOG $1).

The Other Snowbell

The Japanese snowbell tree, *Styrax japonica*, is valued for its graceful spreading form, attractive foliage and late spring clusters of glistening, deliciously fragrant bell-shaped white flowers.

But there is another snowbell from Japan that is much less well known — most undeservedly so. *S. obassia* is very different in character, columnar rather than spreading and with bold, broad leaves up to 8" long. It blooms slightly earlier, and has longer racemes of larger flowers. Where drama rather than delicacy is required, *S. obassia* is the perfect choice. It is hardy to −20°. A source is BRIMFIELD GARDENS NURSERY (245 BRIMFIELD ROAD, WETHERSFIELD, CT 06109; CATALOG $1).

Hardy to −50°, *Sorbus decora* is a small native mountain ash that bears large, showy bright red fruit.

Front-Line Lindens

The newest lindens, besides providing spicily fragrant flowers in early summer, are marvelously neat and tidy in form — they have a perpetually freshly pruned look.

Three fine new cultivars of the little-leaf linden, *Tilia cordata*, are 'Chancellor,' rapid-growing and narrowly upright, to 35′ (COLE NURSERY CO., R.D. 1, CIRCLEVILLE, OH 43113; WHOLESALE — have your nurseryman order); 70′ narrowly oval 'Greenspire' (WAYSIDE GARDENS, MENTOR, OH 44060; CATALOG $2); and 'June Bride,' a 40′ pyramidal tree so floriferous it resembles a flowering crab when in bloom (MANBECK NURSERIES, NEW KNOXVILLE, OH 45871; WHOLESALE). All are hardy to −35°.

A very desirable cultivar of the Crimean linden, *T. euchlora*, is 'Redmond,' a broadly oval tree to 40′, with striking cerise-red new growth and buds (INTER-STATE NURSERIES, HAMBURG, IA 51640).

SHADE TREE VALUE has been raised to $10 per square inch of trunk cross-section at 4½′ above the ground, in the basic formula used by the International Shade Tree Conference (Box 71, Urbana, IL 61801).

Sorbus Bonanza

European mountain ash, *Sorbus aucuparia*, is a spectacular performer — shapely, with handsome ferny foliage, spring clusters of white flowers and glowing red berries in autumn. The new Lombard Hybrids from Holland are named for their fruit colors: 'Carpet of Gold,' 'White Wax,' 'Red Copper Glow,' etc. (WAYSIDE GARDENS, MENTOR, OH 44060; CATALOG $2). There are also a fastigiate variety, and varieties with pendulous branches, light red branchlets ('Beissneri') and doubly serrate leaflets ('Asplenifolia'). All are hardy to −35°.

Another very worthy but less hardy species (to −10°) is the Korean mountain ash, *S. alnifolia*, which one horticulturist has called "the finest small tree one could possibly want." It grows dense and round-headed, with single instead of compound leaves, and the silvery-gray bark resembles that of European beech. A profuse bearer of pink flowers and orange-scarlet fruits, it has bronze-to-scarlet fall foliage and is notably borer-resistant. A source is BRIMFIELD GARDENS NURSERY (245 BRIMFIELD ROAD, WETHERSFIELD, CT 06109; CATALOG $1).

TOPS ON TREES

"The Guide to Garden Shrubs and Trees," by Norman Taylor (Houghton Mifflin, $6.95)

"Manual of Cultivated Trees and Shrubs," 2nd ed., by Alfred Rehder (Macmillan, $14.95)

"Manual of the Trees of North America," by Charles Sprague Sargent (Dover reprint, 2 vols., $2 each)

"Ornamental Trees for Home Grounds," by Harold O. Perkins (Dutton, $4.50)

"Tree Maintenance," by P. P. Pirone (Oxford University Press, $15)

"Trees for American Gardens," 2nd ed., by Donald Wyman (Macmillan, $14.95)

"Trees, Shrubs and Vines of the Northern United States," by Arthur T. Viertel (Syracuse University Press, $2.95)

Evergreens

First-Class Firs

Firs have neither the stiffness of pines nor the limpness of hemlocks, and their very glossy, soft, deep green needles with white bands beneath and often large, highly colorful erect cones make them outstanding in any conifer planting.

Silver fir, *Abies concolor,* is usually the choice in the North, and Himalayan fir, *A. spectabilis,* in the South. Best in the Midwest is the Nordmann fir, *A. nordmanniana,* not as dense and formal as most firs, but fast-growing and hardy to −20° (*DAUBER'S NURSERIES, BOX 1746, YORK, PA 17405*). Many magnificent species thrive in the Northwest, but do poorly outside of its cool, humid climate.

Several little-known firs, however, have proved worthy over wide ranges. The Nikko fir, *A. homolepis,* is a dense, narrow and fast-growing Japanese tree with large purple cones; it attains about 50′, is hardy to −20° and shows remarkable tolerance of heat and dryness (*GIRARD NURSERIES, GENEVA, OH 44041*). Also excellent under the same conditions, but hardy only to −10°, are the little-known Greek fir, *A. cephalonica* (*GIRARD*), which has sharply pointed needles, and the rare and unusual Cilician fir, *A. cilicica,* with short, notched needles that point up and out on the branches (*FRED W. BERGMAN, RARAFLORA, 1195 STUMP ROAD, FEASTERVILLE, PA 19047*).

A very hardy fir, to −35°, is *A. veitchii* from Japan, with striking white bands on the needle undersides, and blue-purple cones (*GIRARD*). The Korean fir, *A. koreana,* also has beautiful white-banded needles, grows somewhat smaller than other firs and thrives in almost any area that is not arid or below −10° in winter (*BRIMFIELD GARDENS NURSERY, 245 BRIMFIELD ROAD, WETHERSFIELD, CT 06109; CATALOG $1*).

An evergreen garden reaches its color peak in early spring with new foliage growth on the conifers and the flowering of many broadleafs.

Hardy to −5° is the very dense Spanish fir, *A. pinsapo,* which has a fine blue-needled form, 'Glauca' (*BRIMFIELD*). Finally, although the Fraser fir, *A. fraseri* (which greatly resembles the balsam fir, *A. balsamea,* used for Christmas trees) is hardy to −20°, it produces much handsomer specimens in southern areas (*BRIMFIELD*).

Cedars Short and Sweet

The true cedars have been called the world's most beautiful trees. Many gardeners, however, think they are precluded from growing them because of

The parent 'Monarch of Illinois' bald cypress, planted in 1866, is 85' high and 65' broad.

their massive size and/or their lack of hardiness.

Three majestic species do grow to 100' or more and very broad, but only after many years — 25' in 35 years is average for the famed cedar of Lebanon (*Cedrus libani*), Atlas cedar (*C. atlantica*) and deodar (*C. deodara*). Atlas cedar, hardy to 0°, is best known for its selected forms — columnar 'Fastigiata,' gold 'Aurea,' silver 'Argentea' and blue 'Glauca,' the last-named hardy in protected spots to −10°.

More diminutive cedars include the marvelous weeping blue Atlas cedar, *C. atlantica* 'Glauca Pendula,' which grows very slowly to about 15' high and 20' wide. Lebanon and deodar cedars also have weeping varieties, and the prostrate *C. deodara repandens* and very slow growing, dense and conical *C. libani* 'Nana' and 'Comte de Dijon' are other treasures. The rare *C. libani* 'Sargenti' grows only 15" high but cascades to four times as broad in 20 years. Finally, there is the fourth known species of cedar, *C. brevifolia* from Cyprus, closely related to the Lebanon cedar but growing only 15' high. Two sources of these are JOEL W. SPINGARN (1535 FOREST AVENUE, BALDWIN, NY 11510; CATALOG 50¢), and FRED W. BERGMAN, RARAFLORA, 1195 STUMP ROAD, FEASTERVILLE, PA 19047).

'Prairie Sentinel' (left of center) has a spire form, in contrast to the typical pond cypress growing on each side of it.

The deodar is generally rated hardy only to 5°, but the new 'Kashmir' is reported by its introducer, *J. FRANKLIN STYER (CONCORDVILLE, PA 19331)*, to survive −25°. And *C. libani*, considered hardy to −10°, is being grown in the McCrory Gardens at South Dakota State University, where temperatures can go to −30° — this may be the little-known hardier var. *stenocoma*.

Finest Weeping Conifer

Of all chamaecyparis, the weeping Nootka false cypress is the most striking. Dr. Leslie Laking of the Royal Botanical Gardens at Hamilton, Ontario, notes that it develops its exciting character when young, becoming "a handsome specimen when only 4′ or 5′ high." *Chamaecyparis nootkatensis* 'Pendula' is unique in form, basically conical, its somewhat sparse branches "giving ample room for its beautiful pendulous branchlets. These develop into flattish fans of foliage, hanging straight downwards like streamers from the branches, producing a strikingly distinctive silhouette."

Hardy to −20° and growing from sea level to the mountains of the northwestern U.S. and Canada, this conifer can reach over 100′ but grows slowly. Specimens at the Gardens have attained 15′ to 18′ in 19 years. Dr. Laking reports plants growing well on sunny, hot sites, in heavy to gravelly soils and in poorly drained areas.

The many dwarf golden forms of chamaecyparis, incidentally, give stunning four-season beauty grown with heaths and heathers, an English gardener suggests. The soft to brilliant golds of *C. lawsoniana* 'Minima Aurea,' *C. pisifera* 'Plumosa Rogersii,' *C. pisifera* 'Filifera Aurea' and *C. obtusa* 'Nana Aurea' are superb in association with *Erica carnea* 'Aurea,' *E. cinerea* 'Golden Drop' or *Calluna vulgaris* 'Spitfire' or 'Prostrata Orange.' *C. obtusa* 'Crippsii' and other large gold conifers consort well with the taller gold-to-bronze heather. A source is *JOEL W. SPINGARN (1535 FOREST AVE., BALDWIN, NY 11510; CATALOG 50¢).*

Mighty Midgets

Where it is hardy — to −5° if protected from winter winds, and where summers are not too hot and dry — *Cryptomeria japonica* is one of the most distinctive of all conifers. It grows narrowly pyramidal, to about 40′ in the U.S., but in Japan 350-year-old specimens towering 150′ are not uncommon. In foliage it resembles the giant sequoia, with deep green needles that turn bronzy in winter, and clumped branchlets. The bark is shaggy and red-brown, the cones small and round.

Most widely useful in modern gardens are the many dwarf shrub varieties of *C. japonica*. Forms from mound and globe to cone, pyramid and column are seen in the collections of specialists

like *JOEL W. SPINGARN (1535 FOREST AVENUE, BALDWIN, NY 11510; CATALOG 50¢).* All are slow-growing gems for the border, rock garden or foundation planting. Some of the most interesting: 'Globosa Nana,' a small-needled, very dense 3′ globe . . . 'Pygmaea,' wider than high, turning red-bronze in winter . . . taller 'Elegans,' with long, slender foliage, growing to 6′ or more, and the compact 'Elegans Nana' . . . the curious 'Monstrosa Nana,' of irregular growth and often having branchlets fasciated into "cockscomb" structures . . . and 'Vilmoriniana,' a beautiful dense globe, the slowest-growing cryptomeria — ¼″ to ½″ a year.

Serbian Spruce

Only the junipers and pines rank with the spruces for variety of form, from majestic trees to dwarf cushion, globe, weeping and prostrate types. Besides the great value of so many of them as specimen or border and foundation plants, there are quite a few, such as the sharp-needled Japanese tigertail spruce, *Picea polita*, that make excellent dense hedges.

A remarkably beautiful spruce, almost unknown — although it was introduced by the Arnold Arboretum in 1881 — is the Serbian spruce, *P. omorika.* A fairly fast grower, it tapers as it matures, becoming a striking spire. The lower branches sweep downward, while upper ones become horizontal until those at the top are nearly upright. Instead of being four-sided, as are those of most spruces, the needles of *P. omorika* are flat, glossy dark green above and blue-white beneath. Growing to 75′, it is hardy to −20° and also thrives farther south — almost to the Gulf Coast — than other species. Robert Hebb of the Arnold Arboretum calls it "a modern plant in every sense of the word," and reports that it stands considerable air pollution and grows on a wide range of soils, even near the sea.

One of the choicest spruces, Picea glauca 'Conica,' the dwarf Alberta spruce, forms a handsome dense 10′ cone.

Serbian spruce has produced two superb dwarf forms. *P. omorika* 'Expansa' is a semi-prostrate shrub which spreads widely — we have seen a 15-year-old specimen 30" tall and 14' across. For a beautiful dense spherical mound, there is *P. omorika* 'Nana,' about 3' high. The needles of these varieties point upward to expose both their green and their blue-white faces, giving the plants a stunning bicolor effect.

P. omorika is available from BRIMFIELD GARDENS NURSERY (245 BRIMFIELD ROAD, WETHERSFIELD, CT 06109; CATALOG $1), the dwarf forms from JOEL W. SPINGARN (1535 FOREST AVENUE, BALDWIN, NY 11510; CATALOG 50¢).

Prostrate Pines

Dwarfs and slow-growing pines are truly connoisseurs' plants. The soft, billowy blue-green globe that is *Pinus strobus* 'Nana,' dense spheres like *P. sylvestris* 'Pygmaea,' umbrella-crowned *P. densiflora* 'Umbraculifera' and the fabulous mounded, erect-branched *P. nigra* 'Hornibrookiana' — these never fail to draw attention.

For unusual landscaping effects, the very low, spreading, virtually flat-on-the-ground pines are especially fine. *P. mugo* 'Slavinii' is a low dense mat of lustrous dark blue-green. In 20 years, *P. densiflora* 'Prostrata' will be 5' across but only 12" high. A trailer with 5" needles is *P. strobus* 'Prostrata,' and *P. sylvestris* 'Saxatilis' is a dense short-needled spreader never more than 6" high but many times as wide.

Incidentally, that horticultural Methuselah, the bristlecone pine *(P. aristata)* — specimens 4600 years old have been found — can be made to spread laterally, "almost like a creeping juniper, if topped back when young." So says Andrew Sherwood, former owner of the wholesale SHERWOOD NURSERY COMPANY (13020 N.E. ROSE PARKWAY, PORTLAND, OR 97230), a leading propagator of bristlecone pine. This fantastic pine, he notes, can withstand a temperature range of 150°, thrives in 2% desert or 70% coastal humidity, will grow even in pure gravel and holds its needles for 20 years.

The Parasol Pine

A most impressive plant in the winter landscape is the little-known Japanese umbrella pine, *Sciadopitys verticillata.* Its 5" needles, which are pale green when young, take on a deeper hue with added bronzing in winter, so they appear almost black-green. The needles — really cladophylls, or flattened leaf-like branchlets — grow in groups of 15 to 30 or more, in whorls like the ribs of a parasol.

The umbrella pine is hardy to −10°, and grows densely pyramidal, with branches all the way to the ground. In Japan, it attains well over 100', but specimens at the Arnold Arboretum in Boston are 30' at 60 years of age. It has no serious pests or diseases, and dislikes only heat, wind and dryness. Thriving as far south as mid-Florida in loamy soil free from lime but well supplied with moisture, it asks only a pine needle or leafmold mulch to keep its roots cool when young.

A source is TINGLE NURSERY CO. (PITTSVILLE, MD 21850).

Ornamental Taxodiums

Earl Cully of the wholesale CULLY NURSERY (R.R. 5, JACKSONVILLE, IL 62650) is introducing superior forms of the pond cypress, *Taxodium ascendens,* and the bald cypress, *T. distichum,* two native deciduous conifers long regarded only as timber trees.

Mr. Cully is patenting *T. ascendens* 'Prairie Sentinel,' a rapid-growing columnar cultivar, *T. distichum* 'Shawnee Brave,' with an unusually full, densely pyramidal crown, and *T. distichum* 'Monarch of Illinois,' a magnificent tall, round-headed form. All are hardy to −20° and tolerant of air pollution, and thrive equally well in upland and very moist soils.

Prof. J. C. McDaniel of the University of Illinois says that *T. ascendens* and *T. distichum* have been grown as far north as Minnesota and Ottawa, and that *Taxodium* "excels the other deciduous conifers in winter interest. In particular, it does not have the dead tree look of a leafless *Larix.*" These "graceful, rugged trees with a combination of desirable features not quite matched by any other large-growing deciduous trees . . . should be very prominent among the really choice ornamental trees planted north . . ."

Royal Canadian Hemlocks

Dwarf Canadian hemlocks (*Tsuga canadensis*) have been called the "princesses" of conifers. Their unmatched soft, feathery gracefulness and diversity of form make them ideal for every sort of ornamental use in modern gardens.

Horticulturist Harold Epstein lists these among the finest varieties: 'Bennett,' like a miniature Sargent's weeping hemlock, to 2', broadly spreading, with pendulous branch tips . . . 'Jervis,' a dense 30" pyramid, branches arching, with "cockscomb" terminal growths . . . 'Minuta,' a true pygmy growing ¼" a year, and the weeping 'Minuta Pendula' . . . globular 'Ruggi,' with its top depressed in bird's-nest-fern form, and cinnamon-brown hairs on its terminal growths . . . 'Hussi,' upright to 3' but very irregular, with short twiggy branches . . . 'Cole's Prostrate,' a unique groundcover form, its twisted branches spreading flat in all directions . . . and the broadly conical 'Dwarf Whitetip,' with whitish new growth.

Three of the best sources are JOEL W. SPINGARN (1535 FOREST AVENUE, BALDWIN, NY 11510; CATALOG 50¢), FRED W. BERGMAN, RARAFLORA (1195 STUMP ROAD, FEASTERVILLE, PA 19047) and PALETTE GARDENS (26 WEST ZION HILL RD., QUAKERTOWN, PA 18951; CATALOG 50¢).

BROADLEAFS

New Northern Boxwood

William A. P. Pullman, a gardener near Chicago who has long experimented with plants of borderline hardiness, has registered a very hardy cultivar of *Buxus sempervirens*. 'Pullman' not only survived the exceptionally severe winter of 1963, but did not develop a single brown leaf.

THE AMERICAN BOXWOOD SOCIETY (BOX 85, BOYCE, VA 22620) reports that propagations of 'Pullman' show incredible vigor, and have several times withstood −20° with only a light mulch of bark or hay. Unlike *B. microphylla koreana*, which starts into growth as early as April — and so may be injured by a late freeze — 'Pullman' breaks dormancy around mid-May. It also grows much larger: Mr. Pullman's original plant is now 3' high and wide, and is expected to grow twice that size or more.

The President of the American Boxwood Society, Rear Admiral Neill Phillips, recently reported that proper feeding and drainage are his "secret formula" for the superb boxwood he grows at "Heronwood" in Virginia. No boxwood is ever planted where its roots will be damp. Feeding is

done with thoroughly rotted chicken manure, and with compost made from garden, orchard and nursery wastes plus wood ashes and household garbage, supplemented by bonemeal in the fall and bloodmeal in spring and early summer. Fertilizer is always watered in or scratched in very lightly so as not to injure boxwood's vital surface roots.

Holly Boom

Every type of holly is being improved today. No sooner, for example, does a fine low-growing Chinese holly like *Ilex cornuta* 'Rotunda' appear, than it is followed by a bud mutation, 'Carissa,' that is even more compact. 'Carissa' (MONROVIA NURSERY CO., AZUSA, CA 91702; WHOLESALE — have your nurseryman order) attains a height of 3' and a spread of 4' to 5' in about 8 years.

The first F_1 American-Chinese holly is 'Shin Nien.' Its breeder, Prof. J. C. McDaniel of the University of Illinois, says it combines the greater hardiness of *I. opaca* with the superior leaf qualities of *I. cornuta*. "Intermediate in leaf shape between *I. opaca* and *I. cornuta*, but with a leaf sheen comparable to the best in *I. cornuta*, 'Shin Nien' may indeed usher in a 'new year' for shiny-leaved, red-fruited evergreen hollies in much of the American Midwest."

The hybrid *I. meservae* resulted from a gardener's interest in developing hardier hollies with the beauty of English holly. Mrs. F. Leighton Meserve of St. James, New York, crossed the Japanese

26505). Gene Eisenbeiss of the U.S. National Arboretum (Washington, DC 20002) has registered 'Sparkleberry,' a selection of *I. serrata* x *verticillata,* hardy to −10°.

Euonymus Specialties

Among the worthiest of broadleafs for specimen, hedge or foundation plantings are the 'Emerald' varieties of wintercreeper, *Euonymus fortunei,* patented by CORLISS BROS. NURSERY (IPSWICH, MA 01938). Not least of their merits is great "sculpturability": they stand a great amount of shearing and shaping.

'Emerald Cushion' is 18″ to 24″, with a 3′ spread. 'Emerald 'n Gold,' 4′ to 5′ tall and 3′ wide, has gold-margined leaves. White-margined 'Emerald Gaiety' attains the same size, but 5′ 'Emerald Charm' spreads only 18″ and makes a very fine hedge. 'Emerald Beauty' grows 6′ tall and spreads 8′ to 10′, and bears abundant pink seed capsules with orange seeds in autumn, while 'Emerald Leader' is similarly fruitful but grows to 5′ with a 30″ spread. Most rounded in form is 'Emerald Pride,' 5′ and spreading 42″. All are hardy to at least −20°.

Another fine new *E. fortunei* cultivar is 'Golden Prince,' a low mounded form with strongly gold-variegated new growth, from MONROVIA NURSERY CO. (AZUSA, CA 91702; WHOLESALE — have your nurseryman order).

Winning Laurels

The native evergreen mountain laurel is a shrub desired by almost every gardener, but its many superb varieties have long been relegated to arboretum collections due to difficulty of propagation.

I. rugosa with *I. aquifolium,* and has released five handsome, vigorous cultivars — 'Blue Boy,' 'Blue Girl,' 'Blue Angel,' 'Blue Prince' and 'Blue Princess' (available from THE CONARD-PYLE CO., WEST GROVE, PA 19390).

In the rare yellow-berried hollies, 'Xanthocarpa' (CARROLL GARDENS, WESTMINSTER, MD 21157) is one of the best, and two yellow-fruited fertile Foster hybrids, one upright and one spreading, have just been registered by the GEDDES DOUGLAS NURSERY (3423 VALLEY BROOK ROAD, NASHVILLE, TN 37215).

An interesting "new" species is the 8′ *I. centrochinensis,* fastigiate, small-leaved and hardy to −10°. It bears when very young, and holds its red berries tightly along the twigs instead of in clusters. A source is EASTERN SHORE NURSERIES (BOX 743, EASTON, MD 21601).

The deciduous hollies are also receiving attention. The first yellow-berried possum-haw is *I. decidua* 'Byers Golden' (BYERS NURSERY, 7002 NORTH MEMORIAL PARKWAY, HUNTSVILLE, AL 35811). 'Fairfax,' 'Cacapon' and 'Shaver' are cultivars of the very hardy (−35°) winterberry, *I. verticillata,* developed by O. M. Neal of the University of West Virginia (Morgantown, WV

Evergreens 85

Now Dr. Richard A. Jaynes of the Connecticut Agricultural Experiment Station in New Haven has found it is possible to reproduce outstanding forms from seed by using bumblebees in cages to cross-pollinate selected plants. This results in the production of large quantities of seed.

Thus the dearth of fine *Kalmia latifolia* cultivars in nursery offerings is ending. Soon gardeners will be able to obtain not only the pure white 'Alba' and deep pink 'Rubra,' but also marvelous forms with red buds, "feather" petals ('Polypetala'), striking banded flowers ('Fuscata'), even silver-dollar-size flowers. And since *K. latifolia* requires pruning to keep it lower than its normal 6' or more, naturally dwarf forms such as 'Myrtifolia' and 'Obtusata' will be welcome.

Prime Privet

Not only are there better privets than the commonly planted California privet, *Ligustrum ovalifolium*, for hedges, but many are also eminently suited to use as specimen, border and foundation shrubs.

Regel privet, *L. obtusifolium* 'Regelianum' (WAYSIDE GARDENS, MENTOR, OH 44060; CATALOG $2), makes a handsome 4' to 5' mound when not sheared, distinctive for its arching horizontal branches which overlap each other, creating an unusual shingled effect. Its nodding clusters of fragrant creamy flowers are very freely produced in June or July, and the blue-black berries last quite long into winter. Hardy to −35°, it stands full sun to considerable shade.

For areas of winter temperatures no lower than 0°, 'Suwannee River' (MONROVIA NURSERY CO., AZUSA, CA 91702; WHOLESALE — have your nurseryman order) is an outstanding low and compact hybrid of the superb *L. japonicum* 'Rotundifolium,' a 4' shrub with very thick, leathery dark leaves, and the lustrous-leaved *L. lucidum*.

Equally attractive, and hardy to −20°, is a little-known variety of English privet, *L. vulgare* 'Nanum' ('Lodense'), which forms a very dense, tight mound to 4' (KROH NURSERIES, ROUTE 287, BOX 536, LOVELAND, CO 80537).

The Best Mahonias

To many gardeners, mahonias are the aristocrats of broadleaf evergreens. For many purposes, the dwarf *compactum* form of Oregon holly grape, *Mahonia aquifolium*, is the best choice. It has the species' lustrous holly-like foliage, yellow flower panicles in spring and bright blue-black berries, but rarely grows above 24". It is hardy to −10°, and its foliage, like that of the species, turns metallic bronze-red to plum-purple in winter. A source is CLYDE ROBIN (BOX 2091, CASTRO VALLEY, CA 94546; CATALOG $1).

Another excellent low grower is the Cascade or longleaf mahonia, *M. nervosa*, with even larger erect racemes of golden flowers (CLYDE ROBIN). In tall mahonias, the Japanese leatherleaf, *M. bealei*, is one of the handsomest large-leaved shrubs for light shade, hardy to −5°, and its flowers have a strong lily-of-the-valley fragrance (BRIMFIELD GARDENS NURSERY, 245 BRIMFIELD ROAD, WETHERSFIELD, CT 06109; CATALOG $1).

Especially interesting are the mahonia-barberry hybrids, of which *Mahoberberis aquicandidula*, a small-leaved 4' shrub with coppery-red new foliage in spring, is probably the finest (ROBIN). It is hardy to −10°, and can be kept very low and neat by pruning.

New Mahonia aquifolium 'Golden Abundance' is vigorous and dense, excellent for a hedge or screen.

N PLANTING EVERGREENS, never let the roots dry ut even slightly. A resin, impenetrable by water, orms over the roots when they dry, and only a mall number of sealed roots can cause serious etback.

Connoisseur's Rhododendrons

The American Rhododendron Society (Bernice J. Lamb, Secretary, 2232 N.E. 78th Ave., Portland, OR 97213) now has 35 chapters. Another indication of the universal popularity of rhododendrons and azaleas is the great number of top-rated species and hybrids that are described in *"RHODODENDRONS AND THEIR RELATIVES," HANDBOOK 66 OF THE BROOKLYN BOTANIC GARDEN (BROOKLYN, NY 11225; $1.50).*

The big trend is toward dwarf plants. Especially interesting are the new hybrids of 30″ *Rhododendron yakusimanum* with yellow, pink or blue flowers *(COMERFORD'S, BOX 100, MARION, OR 97359).* Others in the same height range rated as very fine by experts are 'Elizabeth,' with large deep red flowers *(ALPENGLOW GARDENS, 13328 KING GEORGE HIGHWAY, NORTH SURREY, B.C., CANADA; CATALOG 25¢),* and lavender-pink 'P.J.M.' and its hybrids *(WARREN BALDSIEFEN, BOX 88, BELLVALE, NY 10912; CATALOG $1.50).*

Tops in the 18″ to 24″ group are rosy 'Anne Baldsiefen' and violet 'Ramapo' *(BALDSIEFEN),* pink *R. racemosum (BALDSIEFEN)* and shell-pink *R. williamsianum* and its superb hybrid, 'Bow Bells' *(JOEL W. SPINGARN, 1535 FOREST AVENUE, BALDWIN, NY 11510; CATALOG 50¢).* In very low growers, there are 6″ purple *R. radicans (ALPENGLOW),* the new blue-purple *R. impeditum* 'Moorheim Beauty' *(GIRARD NURSERIES, GENEVA, OH 44041)* and the dwarf form of the yellow-flowered *R. keiskei (RAINIER MT. ALPINE GARDENS, 2007 SOUTH 126TH, SEATTLE, WA 98168).*

Evergreens 87

PRIVET is an excellent "nurse shrub" for tree and shrub seedlings, protecting them and creating an ideal microclimate for their development, and it is easily removed when the seedlings have become self-sufficient.

A fine background or specimen shrub, the staghorn sumac Rhus typhina, has crimson foliage and fruit in autumn.

SHRUBS

False Forsythia

The "white forsythia," *Abeliophyllum distichum,* has thrived and bloomed consistently for four years at South Dakota State University, where winter temperatures can drop to $-30°$. Thus this shrub is a good choice for early bloom where forsythia is not hardy, despite warnings in gardening books that its buds may be killed by severe winters.

Korean abelialeaf has glossy blue-green foliage and grows slowly and compactly to 5'. Like forsythia, it blooms before the leaves appear in spring. The bell-shaped flowers, however, are smaller and more numerous, white and fragrant, and they open slightly before those of forsythia. A source is WHITE FLOWER FARM (LITCHFIELD, CT 06759; CATALOG $3).

The Better Barberries

Japanese barberry, *Berberis thunbergii,* has long been highly regarded for its rugged, carefree virtues, and the number of cultivars that extend its usefulness is increasing. In tall types, the gardener can choose from the narrow truehedge columnberry ('Erecta'), the dense 'Thornless,' bronzy-red 'Atropurpurea' (all from STARK BRO'S

NURSERIES, LOUISIANA, MO 63353) and the new pink-crimson-scarlet 'Rosy Glow' (KELLY BROS. NURSERIES, DANSVILLE, NY 14437). Fine low-growers (to 30″) are the box-leaved 'Minor,' popular 'Crimson Pygmy,' the recently released golden 'Aurea' (KELLY) and the newest, the very bright green and rounded 'Kobold' (MONROVIA NURSERY CO., AZUSA, CA 91702; WHOLESALE — have your nurseryman order).

Other deciduous barberries are equally useful as specimens or barriers and equally tolerant of harsh conditions. B. koreana, an arching 5′ to 6′ shrub with deep red fall foliage and persistent red fruit, is even hardier (to −30°) than B. thunbergii (VALLEY NURSERY, BOX 845, HELENA, MT 59601). Hardy to −10° is the hybrid 7′ B. mentorensis, highly recommended for areas with hot dry summers (WAYSIDE GARDENS, MENTOR, OH 44060; CATALOG $2).

Some evergreen barberries are even more desirable. Warty barberry, B. verruculosa, has tiny glossy leaves, white beneath, which turn rich mahogany in winter, plus fine yellow flowers and blue-black berries; it grows to 3′ and is hardy to −10° (EASTERN SHORE NURSERIES, BOX 743, EASTON, MD 21601). Equally hardy are the graceful rosemary barberry, B. stenophylla (B. irwinii), up to 5′ and prolific flowering (CLYDE ROBIN, BOX 2091, CASTRO VALLEY, CA 94546; CATALOG $1); three-spine barberry, B. triacanthophora, to 4′ and excellent in shade (MEDFORD NURSERY, R.D. 1, MEDFORD, NJ 08055); B. gladwynensis 'William Penn,' a handsome, broad-spreading dwarf hybrid (MONROVIA); and the compact, refined 4′ hybrid B. chenaultii (MEDFORD).

Budding Buddleias

More and more named varieties of Buddleia davidii, the summer lilac or orange-eye butterfly bush, are becoming available, from 4′ to 10′ high and producing fragrant, glistening white, pink, violet or purple spires. Below about 0°, this buddleia dies back and should be cut almost to the ground in late winter, but new growth is remarkably rapid and the flower racemes — up to 18″ long — are produced abundantly. Two fine new varieties are 'Opera,' with vivid royal-red spires up to 24″ long (GULF STREAM NURSERY, WACHAPREAGUE, VA 23480; WHOLESALE — have your nurseryman order), and 'Sun Gold,' bearing pink-toned gold globes on 10″ spikes (WAYSIDE GARDENS, MENTOR, OH 44060; CATALOG $2).

Our own favorite is the hardier fountain buddleia, B. alternifolia (WAYSIDE), which does not die back above −10°. When Reginald Farrer introduced this Chinese species in 1914, he described it as "like a gracious, small-leaved weeping willow when it is not in flower, and a sheer waterfall of soft purple when it is." Left unpruned, it is an airy, almost umbrella-shaped shrub 8′ tall. In late spring, its arching branches are densely wreathed with clusters of fragrant lilac-purple flowers. This buddleia is especially magnificent grown in tree form, with only one stem allowed to develop and all side shoots pinched out to a height of 5′.

Shrubs   89

Late Summer Beauty

For bloom in late summer and berries in autumn, two little-known Asiatic shrubs are worth growing.

The Korean white-fruited beautyberry, *Callicarpa japonica* 'Leucocarpa' is a handsome 4' to 5' shrub with narrow toothed foliage that bears pink-toned white flowers in clusters in July and August. In early autumn, large clusters of long-persisting white berries adorn the slender arching branches. This beautyberry is hardy to −10°, and flowers and fruits heavily when quite young. A site with full sun is best, and perfect drainage is essential to prevent winterkill. A source is FIORE ENTERPRISES (ROUTE 22, PRAIRIE VIEW, IL 60069).

The Chinese beautyberry, *C. dichotoma* (*C. purpurea*), is slightly hardier and has lavender-pink flowers. The berries are a lovely lilac-violet, and this shrub should be planted against a white wall or near a window or walk where their unusual display can be enjoyed frequently. It is available from EASTERN SHORE NURSERIES (BOX 743, EASTON, MD 21601).

Contemporary Cotoneasters

More than 50 cotoneasters are currently offered by American nurserymen. Until recently, greatest emphasis has been on the low-growing types, useful as groundcovers and filler plants. The shrubby cotoneasters, however, are now almost equally in demand.

Some are unsurpassed where a dramatic accent is desired. The new 'Sealing Wax,' 4' to 5' and upright branching, bears pink flowers and profuse red berries, and its foliage is white-felty beneath. *C. dielsiana* is a very lovely arching-branched 5' to 6' shrub, heavily berried and boasting orange-red autumn foliage. Perhaps handsomest of all is the 6' *C. meyeri*, a recent introduction with slightly pendulous branches, gray-green to silvery leaves and coral-pink berries. These are obtainable from WAYSIDE GARDENS (MENTOR, OH 44060; CATALOG $2).

Quintessential Quinces

"As a flowering shrub," says Prof. J. C. McDaniel of the University of Illinois, "*Chaenomeles* now rivals azaleas for variety and beauty, besides being much less particular in soil and culture requirements." And the flowering quinces are useful not only as specimen, border and foundation shrubs, but also as hedges and espalier plants.

Greatest interest currently is in "limited space" types. These range from the neat 12" to 15" 'Knaphill Scarlet' to the 6' tall but only 2' wide 'Spitfire.' Really fine double-flowered quinces are appearing, too, such as the exquisite apricot-pink 'Cameo' and a number of bicolors — 'Toyo-Nishiki' has white, pinkish-white, pink and red flowers on the same branch.

An extended bloom season is also possible: Professor McDaniel notes two selections made by the late Dr. A. S. Colby at the University of Illinois — 'Echo,' "the latest-flowering of any I have seen," and "the as-yet-unintroduced Illini No. 11, with the most abundant off-season re-flowering (May through November) of any clone I know."

Two sources offering a wide variety are J. HERBERT ALEXANDER (MIDDLEBORO, MA 02346) and WAYSIDE GARDENS (MENTOR, OH 44060; CATALOG $2). Flowering quinces — still sometimes sold as *Cydonia* — are hardy to −20°, lower if protected.

Spring's Fringe Benefits

'Floyd,' a dense, upright-growing clone of the native fringetree or snow-flower, *Chionanthus virginicus*, has been introduced by Prof. J. C. McDaniel, University of Illinois. He reports it "has more branching on new growth, and branches emerge at an acute angle and grow straighter, producing a shrub taller than broad."

The usefulness of *C. virginicus* has been somewhat limited by its habit of growing a wide-spreading top, making it most suitable for specimen planting or as a background in shrub borders. The narrower 'Floyd' thus is valuable for more restricted areas.

Fringetree, hardy to −20° and thriving in moist soil and full sun, grows from 15' to 30' as a shrub or single- or multi-stemmed tree. Its big drooping clusters of feathery and fragrant white flowers in late May and June, just after the leaves open, are a welcome extension to the crabapple–flowering-cherry–dogwood bloom season.

New Shrub Tints

Long prized as a conversation piece for its summer clouds of silky fruiting panicles and brilliant autumn foliage, smoke-tree *(Cotinus coggygria)* is available in new colors.

EMLONG NURSERIES (STEVENSVILLE, MI 49127) offers 'Pink Fairy,' with plumes that are first chamois-colored, then a delicate pink. INTERSTATE NURSERIES (HAMBURG, IA 51640) lists 'Pink Champagne,' named for its striking plume color, and 'Nordine Red,' with new leaves a rich red-purple turning to green, and ruby-red plumes. 'Velvet Cloak' has uniformly colored dark purple foliage that retains its rich hue longer than other purple-leaved types, and its fruiting clusters are a contrasting fawn color (COLE NURSERY CO., R.D. 1, CIRCLEVILLE, OH 43113; WHOLESALE — have your nurseryman order).

Smoke-tree thrives in sun and well-drained, infertile soil, stands drought well and is hardy to about −20°. Often slow to establish, it benefits from pruning back at planting, and extra water, shade and winter protection the first year. It grows to about 8' but can be pruned lower, and is occasionally used as an unusual and impressive hedge.

Glory Bower

Few gardeners know there is a clerodendron hardy to as low as −10°. The Japanese harlequin glory bower, *C. trichotomum*, is a shrubby tree growing to 6' in the North and producing a marvelous display from August to October. The numerous clusters of fragrant, 5-petaled white flowers have conspicuous star-shaped calyces which become bright red to make a dramatic contrast to the blue fruits that soon follow. The calyces persist into winter, a rich red-brown.

C. trichotomum blooms on the current year's growth, so it will flower even if it dies back in the northernmost areas of its range. A hay mulch will protect its roots in winter. It grows easily from seed (F. W. SCHUMACHER, SANDWICH, MA 02563).

The charming Rhododendron yakusimanum is being used to produce dwarf mounded hybrids with blue, pink or yellow flowers.

Warminster broom is one of the most spectacular May-blooming shrubs, making a solid mound of golden flowers.

Southern Leatherwood

A delightful southern shrub-tree which is even more delightful in its northern range is the little-known leatherwood, *Cyrilla racemiflora*. Semi-evergreen and growing to 30′ in the South, in colder climes it rarely exceeds 15′ and produces a marvelous medley of autumn colors: the glossy leaves turn blazing crimson gradually and erratically, giving an extended, extraordinary display of simultaneous green and red.

Native from Virginia to Florida and Louisiana, *C. racemiflora* is hardy to −10° and needs an acid, moist soil. In June and July, it bears slender 4″ to 6″ racemes of white flowers. These are very attractive to bees, and leatherwood honey is famed among connoisseurs. The hanging clusters of seed heads add to its autumn beauty.

A source is TINGLE NURSERY CO. (PITTSVILLE, MD 21850).

New Sweep to Brooms

In flower, brooms have been likened to "a burst of sunshine," and the best species are densely twiggy, with green bark that provides winter beauty. Best known is *Cytisus praecox*, Warminster broom, 6′, hardy to −20°. Some hybrids of *C. scoparius*, such as 'Burkwoodi,' 'Windesham Ruby' and 'Zeelandia,' are also popular for their yellow, red or bronze blooms.

But certainly others deserve greater use: *C. kewensis*, the charming 8″ Kew broom that forms dense mats 6′ across . . . 12″ *C. albus*, the white-flowered Portuguese broom . . . purple-flowered, 18″ *C. purpureus* . . . and *C. procumbens*, which makes a 30″ mound several feet broad for the front of the shrub border. Summer-blooming brooms are appearing, too, such as 15″ crimson-flowered 'Peter Pan.'

Of the genistas, the 3′ very hardy *Genista tinctoria*, bearing double yellow flowers in early summer, is superb. Also worthy are the showy 2′ *G. lydia*, and several fine mounding or matting ground-huggers such as spiny *G. germanica prostrata*, in flower for many weeks, and *G. pilosa*, silvery-green leaves and rich yellow flowers. These and many others are hardy to −10°.

A source of the less common brooms is SISKIYOU RARE PLANT NURSERY (522 FRANQUETTE STREET, MEDFORD, OR 97501; CATALOG 50¢). F. W. SCHUMACHER (SANDWICH, MA 02563) has seeds of many unusuals such as *C. multiflorus* 'White Gem' and *C. scoparius andreanus* hybrids with flowers in pastel shades of yellow, rose and white. Mr. Schumacher especially recommends the weaversbroom, *Spartium junceum:* "When in bloom here in June and July, it is a joy to behold with its intensely fragrant golden yellow flowers displayed in profusion over a vase-shaped bush about 4′ high."

Elaeagnus Everywhere

'Cardinal,' the cultivar of autumn olive, *Elaeagnus umbellata*, that yields up to 40 pounds of berries — excellent for jelly or attracting birds — has become even more popular than the Russian olive, *E. angustifolia*. This wide-spreading 10' to 15' silvery-leaved shrub, hardy to −25°, is excellent where a wide hedge or windbreak is needed, as well as handsome as a single specimen. A source is EARL FERRIS NURSERY (HAMPTON, IA 50441).

Two handsome new evergreen elaeagnus for milder climes (to 0°) are the large-leaved *E. macrophylla* 'Ebbingi' and compact dense 'Clemsoni' (MONROVIA NURSERY CO., AZUSA, CA 91702; WHOLESALE — have your nurseryman order).

An elaeagnus that bears clusters of very fragrant frosty flowers in October is *E. pungens* 'Fruitland' (WAYNESBORO NURSERIES, WAYNESBORO, VA 22980). Reportedly hardy with protection to −10°, this 12' evergreen has wavy-margined round leaves with white and brown scales beneath.

Nipponese Knockouts

A deciduous, ericaceous Japanese shrub of upright habit to 10' or more, redvein enkianthus, *E. campanulatus*, is prized for its profuse nodding clusters of waxy bell-shaped flowers in spring, yellow-orange with red veining, and its brilliant scarlet and orange autumn foliage.

More unusual and widely valuable, however, is the rare *E. cernuus rubens*, a very slow grower that reaches 4' to 5' only after many years. Both flowers and fall foliage are deep red. Few shrubs are as distinguished for foundation and border planting, particularly in combination with azaleas and rhododendrons. A source is BRIMFIELD GARDENS NURSERY (245 BRIMFIELD ROAD, WETHERSFIELD, CT 06109; CATALOG $1). Both are hardy to −20°.

Everblooming Althea

The new triploid rose of Sharon, *Hibiscus syriacus* 'Diana,' is so outstanding it is being called a breakthrough.

This introduction of the U.S. National Arboretum (Washington, DC 20002) is a tremendous improvement in form, growing densely and compactly branched from its base to 8', with none of the stiff branching habit common to *H. syriacus*. Its foliage is dark green, heavy and glossy, and stays on the plant far longer after frost than do the leaves of any other cultivar. Most remarkable, however, is its bloom, which is outstanding in beauty, size and season. Instead of a short burst of bloom in summer, 'Diana' produces its purest white, waxy and ruffled flowers — up to 6" across — in great profusion from late June until frost.

Being a triploid, 'Diana' produces no seed, so the gardener is not plagued with a constant crop of seedlings. Once established, it is hardy to −20°.

Hardier Hydrangeas

Hydrangea macrophylla, the florist's hydrangea or hortensia, is now obtainable in cultivars hardy to −20°.

Three are 'Blue Giant,' 'All Summer Beauty' and semi-double-flowered 'Domotoi,' all growing to 3' to 4'. These cultivars flower on new wood, which eliminates the problem of most hortensias — lack of bloom due to winterkilling of the flower buds produced on the previous season's growth. The globular flower heads range up to 12" across. Their color is dependent on the degree of soil acidity — the more acid, the deeper the blue, the more nearly neutral to alkaline, the pinker the hue. A source of these is WAYSIDE GARDENS (MENTOR, OH 44060; CATALOG $2).

Prof. J. C. McDaniel of the University of Illinois reports three new and very showy-flowered cultivars of oak leaf hydrangea, *H. quercifolia*.

To the handsome leaves, crimson fall foliage and flaking tan bark of the species, 'Harmony,' 'Roanoke' and 'Snowflake' add a much higher proportion of showy-sepaled sterile flowers than of non-showy smaller fertile flowers in each cluster. Also, the positions of these two types of flowers are reversed in the cluster so that the non-showy blooms are hidden by the showy ones.

Professor McDaniel has grown all three culti-vars at Urbana, and they should be hardy to at least −10° in protected locations. All grow about 6′ high, and give long bloom: in Birming-ham, Alabama, 'Snowflake' flowers profusely from April to August.

Crape Myrtlettes

The new dwarf forms of *Lagerstroemia indica*, the South's showiest shrub, are an exciting develop-ment. Japan's prestigious seed house, T. Sakata & Company of Yokohama, states that "seed sown in April or May will start flowering July to August from a height of 1′ or so. Colors range from bright red, rose, pink, lavender to white. Dwarf in habit and will come to flower in a small pot if desired . . . Warm temperature is needed for good germination of the seed."

Probably hardy to about 0°, in northern areas the dwarf crape myrtles require mulching or mounding up with soil for winter protection. The tops die back, but the new growth will bloom profusely. In warmer areas, they will eventually reach about 4′. Seed is available from GEO. W. PARK SEED CO. (GREENWOOD, SC 29647).

Potentilla Potentials

The potentillas or cinquefoils are probably the most varied, useful and accommodating group of summer-blooming perennials and low shrubs American gardeners have. Their virtues include hardiness to −50°, drought resistance, freedom from pests, long and profuse bloom and ability to thrive in any soil and full sun to part shade.

In the shrubby types, many outstanding culti-vars of *Potentilla fruticosa* are available, with white, yellow or orange flowers. Most of these grow 3′ to 4′ tall. However, there are several low growers that can be useful in many situations — 'Sutter's Gold,' for example, 12″ high and 36″ across, and the Washington Cascades form, 8″ high and 24″ across in 10 years (both from THE WILD GARDEN, 8243 N.E. 119TH, KIRKLAND, WA 98033; CATALOG $1). The WILD GARDEN and LAMB NURSERIES (E. 101 SHARP AVENUE, SPOKANE, WA 99202) also list many unusual perennial potentillas.

Berry Good

Where a tall, fast-growing screen is desired, the many white-, pink- or red-flower cultivars of the 8′ Tartarian honeysuckle (*Lonicera tatarica*) have long been almost an automatic choice. But its red berries are usually consumed by birds by late August, so many gardeners have come to prefer *L. maacki*, the fall-fruiting Amur or Manchurian honeysuckle. It grows taller than *L. tatarica* — up to 15′ — but its creamy spring flowers are sweeter scented, and its brighter berries last into winter.

An improved Amur honeysuckle is 'Rem-Red,' which is a selection from REMINGTON FARMS (CHESTERTOWN, MD 21620). It is outstanding for its yield and retention of fruit, which "raisins" well, drying and remaining on the plant as a source of wildlife food long after most other sources are exhausted. Its dense, multi-stemmed growth also provides wildlife shelter. *L. maacki* 'Rem-Red' is hardy to −20°, and does best on well-drained, fertile soils, with full sun desirable for maximum berry production.

Mock-Orange in Transition

Mock-oranges (*Philadelphus*) are invaluable "transition" plants, bridging the gap from spring to summer, and making fine back-of-the-border companions for iris, peonies and early hemerocal-lis. Recently both their size and hardiness ranges have been expanded.

Two of the best dwarfs, 'Frosty Morn' (FARMER SEED & NURSERY CO., FARIBAULT, MN 55021) and 'Dwarf Miniature Snowflake' (EARL MAY SEED & NURSERY CO., SHENANDOAH, IA 51601), grow no taller than 3′, are hardy to −35° and have double fragrant flowers. In medium-height mock-or-anges, our first choice would be 'Innocence' (WAYSIDE GARDENS, MENTOR, OH 44060; CATALOG $2), a graceful slender 5′ to 6′ shrub, hardy to −20°, bearing an almost incredible profusion of scented white blooms.

Of the many fine selections and hybrids in the 6′ to 10′ class, the old-time favorite *P. virginalis* 'Virginal,' hardy to −20°, has impressive 2″ semi-double flowers near spring's end and less abundantly all summer (KELLY BROS. NURSERIES, DANSVILLE, NY 14437). And in the same height and hardiness group is the most fragrant of all mock-oranges, 'Belle Etoile' (WAYSIDE GARDENS), prob-ably the finest of the Lemoine hybrids from France.

Fabulous Firethorns

'Mohave,' a selection of the new hybrid pyracantha, *Pyracantha koidzumi* x *coccinea*, bred by the U.S. National Arboretum, is unsurpassed for specimen, hedge and espalier use. Hardy to −10°, it grows upright and is densely branched, with glossy foliage, abundant 2″ creamy flower panicles in midspring and great numbers of spectacular ⅜″ orange-red berries that begin to color in August and remain brilliant through midwinter. The fruit is produced heavily even in part shade, and birds do not find it attractive. This cultivar is resistant to both scab and fireblight. It is evergreen to about 0°, and an eight-year-old specimen at the National Arboretum is 13′ high and 16′ wide.

Two new low-growing pyracanthas, hardy to 0°, are 'Red Elf,' a fine small hedge or container shrub, and 'Ruby Mound,' which has long graceful intertwining branches and flowers and berries very heavily. All three of these are obtainable from MONROVIA NURSERIES (AZUSA, CA 91702; WHOLESALE — have your nurseryman order).

Special Spireas

One of the most interesting new summer-blooming spireas is 'Goldflame,' a cultivar of *Spiraea bumalda* with golden new leaves and copper-orange fall foliage (GULF STREAM NURSERIES, WACHAPREAGUE, VA 23480; WHOLESALE — have your nurseryman order).

Another outstanding summer spirea is the 5′ hybrid S. *macrothyrsa*, which produces lilac-like rose-pink flower spikes from late July into September (KELLY BROS. NURSERIES, DANSVILLE, NY

Amur honeysuckle has later, brighter, and longer-lasting fruits than popular Tatarian honeysuckle.

Shrubs 95

14437). The new 10″ pink S. *japonica alpina* (*WAYSIDE GARDENS, MENTOR, OH 44060; CATALOG $2*) and 4′ red S. *j.* 'Atrosanguinea' (*KELLY*) are also well worth growing.

In spring-blooming spireas, the 3′ to 4′ S. *nipponica* 'Snowmound' is valued almost as highly as the much taller S. *vanhouttei*, and it has blue-green boxwood-like foliage (*WAYSIDE*).

Autumn Sapphires

One sight of the Asiatic sweetleaf, *Symplocos paniculata*, garlanded in October with its lustrous, brilliant blue berries confirmed a gardener's description of "gorgeous, a knockout!"

Hardy to −20°, S. *paniculata* grows to about 15′ (to 25′ or more in the South), and may be trained as a small tree. It is rounded in form, grows vigorously in full sun and fertile soil, and early in spring is densely clothed in 2″ rich green leaves. In midspring it bears a multitude of fragrant white flowers in 3″ panicles. The bead-like fruits which make it so stunning in autumn have given it the well-merited common name, sapphireberry.

A source is *DUTCH MOUNTAIN NURSERY* (*AUGUSTA, MI 49012*).

Invincible Viburnums

Several dozen viburnums are available today, practically all desirable for one or more attributes. V. *carlcephalum* will likely always be a standby for large and fragrant flowers, V. *opulus* 'Aureum' for golden foliage, V. *tomentosum* 'Mariesi' for form and showy flower heads and V. *juddii* for

Intermediate in size between Persian lilacs and the French Hybrids, Chinese lilacs make a 9' to 10' hedge.

handsome foliage and shade and pollution tolerance.

Two less well known viburnums deserve more attention. The tea viburnum, *V. theiferum*, is a graceful, narrowly upright shrub to 10', producing great clusters of brilliant red fruits in autumn (*WAYSIDE GARDENS, MENTOR, OH 44060; CATALOG $2*). The nannyberry, *V. lentago*, thrives on swampy sites to barren windswept hillsides, has blazing scarlet autumn foliage and bears sweet edible berries that change from red to blue and finally black. Hardy to −35°, it can be grown as a single-stemmed tree to 15' or more, pruned into a narrow hedge, or allowed to grow naturally as a soft, billowy fountain plant. A source is *GIRARD NURSERIES (GENEVA, OH 44041)*.

The Korean Stewartia

The choicest stewartia — and one of the finest large shrubs or small trees — is *Stewartia koreana*, says Gordon P. DeWolf, Jr., of the Arnold Arboretum.

In 1929, the great plant collector, Ernest H. "Chinese" Wilson wrote: "The flower is fringed, pure white, from 3½" to 4" in diameter, flat and saucer-like with the ovary and stamens rich yellow. The leaves are oval-elliptic, shining bright green with impressed veins and rounded base. It is a more cheery looking plant than its close relative, *Stewartia pseudocamellia*, which has dull green leaves, longer and narrower at the base, less prominently impressed veins and flowers more cupped."

Growing perhaps 15' tall, Korean stewartia blooms for four weeks in early summer, and has orange-red autumn color. The mottled light and

dark brown peeling bark is an attraction in winter. As Mr. DeWolf says, *S. koreana* "is worth cultivating for almost any excuse." A source is *BRIMFIELD GARDENS NURSERY (245 BRIMFIELD ROAD, WETHERSFIELD, CT 06109; CATALOG $1)*.

Lilacs Out of Limbo

Three trends in lilacs, according to the new International Lilac Society (Walter Oaks, Secretary, Box 315, Rumford, ME 04276), are toward new flower forms, hardier lilacs and smaller lilacs.

The new Rochester Hybrids, hailed as a breakthrough, have 5-petaled flowers that resemble phlox or primroses. For hardiness to −40°, the Preston Hybrids are unexcelled, and they bear enormous clusters of flowers in exquisite colors on 8' to 9' plants.

Of special value as barrier plants are the 6' Persian lilacs, which lilac authority John C. Wister has said make hedges "more magnificent and more graceful than almost any deciduous shrub"; and the Hungarian lilac, *Syringa josikaea*, described by Dr. A. R. Buckley of the Canadian Plant Research Institute as a very useful 10' screen plant, "surpassing all other large shrubs in density and rapidity of growth."

In diminutive lilacs, 'Kim' is a 3' cultivar of the Korean lilac, *S. palibiniana*. Hardy to −20°, it is outstanding for very late bloom, has long dark green waxy leaves which turn a brilliant burgundy-red in autumn, and very fragrant single flowers which are deep purple in bud and open to ice-blue. Seldom growing over 5' tall, the distinctive littleleaf or daphne lilac, *S. microphylla* 'Superba,' grows densely to the ground, has leaves only 1½" long and lavishly bears branched panicles of red buds that open to intensely fragrant lilac-pink blooms. It dependably blooms twice a year, and is considered the most graceful of all lilacs in habit.

Many of these are available from lilac specialist *J. HERBERT ALEXANDER (MIDDLEBORO, MA 02346)*. Mr. Alexander's list of over 100 species and hybrids of all types of lilacs includes several of his own crosses, of interest for unusually ornamental foliage, dwarf habit or extremely late bloom.

Worthier Weigelas

Much hardier weigelas are coming. The MORDEN EXPERIMENTAL FARM (MORDEN, MANITOBA, CANADA) has released 'Centennial,' a deep pink hardy to −35°, and the UNIVERSITY OF MINNESOTA LANDSCAPE ARBORETUM (ROUTE 1, BOX 132-1, CHASKA, MN 55318) is introducing equally hardy hybrids. These are crosses of fine varieties such as 'Bristol Ruby' with the very hardy *Weigela florida mandshurica* recently brought from Manchuria.

The low-growing weigelas with variegated or colored foliage are used for border and foundation plantings. *W. florida* 'Nana Variegata,' 3' to 4', has leaves edged cream-white, and pink flowers (EARL MAY SEED & NURSERY CO., SHENANDOAH, IA 51601). 'Variegata Rosea' is 4', with golden-edged foliage and rose blooms (GIRARD NURSERIES, GENEVA, OH 44041), while 4' 'Java Red' ('Purpurea') has purplish leaves and deep pink flowers (EARL MAY). These are hardy to −10°.

The Gray Lady

A delightful native plant, more appreciated in England than here, is *Zenobia pulverulenta.*

Its 3″ oval leaves are covered with glaucous bloom, making them appear an unusual gray-blue and earning it the name "gray lady." The glistening white bell flowers, each ½″ across, borne in terminal clusters in May and June, stand out beautifully against this background. Zenobia makes a decorative 4' to 6' mound, and is evergreen in its native Southeast, deciduous in the North.

Horticulturist Harold Epstein notes that this species appears to be variable in hardiness: it has not proved hardy in his garden near New York City, but has grown well for years at the Arnold Arboretum in Massachusetts, where similar winter lows of −10° are encountered. A member of the heath family, zenobia should be given peaty soil, a leaf mulch and full sun to part shade. A source is DAUBER'S NURSERIES (BOX 1746, YORK, PA 17405).

HEDGES

Hedging Around

Fashions in hedge plants and purposes are changing. Hedges are no longer regarded as merely screens or barriers, nor are they limited to privet, yew, barberry and boxwood.

Prof. Clarence E. Lewis of Michigan State University says that hedges offer many possibilities for enhancing garden beauty through design. A hedge, for example, can guide the eye and emphasize certain areas or garden highlights. A special feature can be accented by a short line of trimmed hedge behind it, while nearby shrubs are allowed to grow informally. Lightly or closely clipped hedges also accentuate trees or shrubs with graceful flowing lines. And they can be used, in varying lengths and heights, as dividers to separate areas of garden interest or create gardens within gardens.

To emphasize perspective, Professor Lewis suggests a slight — perhaps 1″ in 10' — rise or fall in hedge height, and also a slight bending in or out in the length of the hedge. These increase or decrease the effect of distance, as does using progressively larger- or smaller-leaved plants.

Tapestry Hedges

"THE GARDEN BOOK," the catalog of WHITE FLOWER FARM (LITCHFIELD, CT 06759; $3), features a beautiful tapestry hedge. Popular in England, these multi-hued hedges are made with plants of similar size and habit but different colors, carefully arranged to give a tapestry effect.

Five dwarf conifers are used in White Flower Farm's hedge: soft green and gray-green *Thuja occidentalis ericoides nana;* yellow and gold *Chamaecyparis pisifera filifera aurea* and *C. p. plu-*

Weave a Living Fence

A "flowering shrub fence" less than 2′ wide, fast-growing but needing much less trimming than a hedge, is easily constructed by setting posts 6′ apart and stringing wires, 8″ apart, between them, says horticulturist R. B. Farnham.

"At regular intervals in between, plant your favorite flowering shrub. Remove all main branches which cannot be woven in and out (basket weave) between the horizontal wires. As new growth appears, weave each stem in a similar way to fill open areas. Once in May, July and September, use the hedge shears to cut off twigs not contributing to a dense wall of leaves.

"In four years, using *Forsythia suspensa*, my shrub fence reached a dense height of 8′. At the soil level it used less than 2′ of precious space in depth."

A variation on this is the "apple fence" developed by Dr. H. A. Rollins of Virginia Polytechnic Institute. His method of training dwarf apple trees on wire trellising to make a fruitful screen or garden divider is described in EXTENSION CIRCULAR 1000, FROM THE AGRICULTURAL EXTENSION SERVICE, VIRGINIA POLYTECHNIC INSTITUTE (BLACKSBURG, VA 24060).

---

mosa lutescens; blue-green and silver *C. p. squarrosa;* and gold-in-spring, green-in-summer *C. p. plumosa aurea.* These do not exhaust the possibilities — other varieties of *Thuja* and *Chamaecyparis,* and of *Euonymus, Juniperus, Picea, Pinus, Taxus* and others lend themselves admirably to this purpose.

Many deciduous plants suitable for hedging also offer a tremendous variety of not only greens, from light to dark to yellow-, blue-, gray- and bronze-green, but also more striking colors. The green, gold and purple forms of European beech, *Fagus sylvatica,* are much used for tapestry hedges in England.

Some unusual choices might be the silvery sea-buckthorn, *Hippophae rhamnoides;* the fine-textured blue-green purple osier, *Salix purpurea* 'Gracilis'; creamedge dogwood, *Cornus alba* 'Argenteo-Marginata'; gray-green *Lonicera xylosteum* 'Clavey's Dwarf'; golden privets, *Ligustrum vulgare* 'Aureum' and *L. vicaryi;* golden ninebark, *Physocarpus opulifolius* 'Luteus'; golden mock-orange, *Philadelphus coronarius* 'Aureus'; red barberries, *Berberis thunbergii* 'Atropurpurea' and 'Sheridan's Red'; purpleleaf hazel, *Corylus avellana fuscorubra;* purpleleaf sand cherry, *Prunus cistena;* and the black myrobalan plum, *Prunus cerasifera* 'Nigra.' The bolder colors, of course, need restraint, and in many cases may be better suited to use for occasional accents than the soft tapestry blend.

VIEWS ON SHRUBS

"Flowering Shrubs," Handbook 44 of the Brooklyn Botanic Garden (Brooklyn, NY 11225; $1.50)

"Flowering Shrubs," by Isabel Zucker (Van Nostrand, $17.50)

"Ornamental Shrubs for Temperate Zone Gardens," by Edward Hyams (Barnes, $20)

"The Shrub Identification Book," by George W. D. Symonds (Barrows, $15)

"Shrubs and Vines for American Gardens," 2nd ed., by Donald Wyman (Macmillan, $14.95)

vegetables and herbs

Vogue for Vegetables

For the first time in 50 years, according to a national survey by Union Fork and Hoe Company of Columbus, Ohio, more garden acreage is devoted to food crops than to flowers.

The fact that every $1 spent on fertilizer, seed, etc., will return at least $4 in crops is a powerful incentive today. But the new vegetable gardeners also say that today the connoisseur of quality, variety and flavor must grow his own. Production and marketing economics compel the commercial grower to stress uniformity, high yield and keeping quality. Thus the number of varieties, fresh, frozen or canned, available in markets is steadily decreasing. Many fresh vegetables must be harvested for shipping when either green or oversize, and in long travel all suffer loss of flavor and food value.

Cultured Vitamins

"Food value" is perhaps even more important than superior taste as we become more health conscious, more concerned about pesticide residues, chemical additives and overconsumption of overprocessed foods.

Sprouted seeds have very high food values, and can be used in soups to salads to home-baked bread.

In the names of housewife convenience and longer shelf life, many of our foods are hydrolized, emulsified, dehydrogenated, homogenized, dehydrated, bleached, pre-cooked and pre-digested. They are treated with some 2500 additives — stabilizers, preservatives, synthetic sweeteners, surfactants, sequestrants, artificial colorings and flavorings — all nutritionally useless and some possibly harmful. Nutritionists warn that we consume too many sugars and starches today, and that overprocessing causes "a sorrowful degeneration of food values" — empty calories, altered proteins and extreme loss of vitamins and minerals. The latest Federal diet survey shows that only 50% of Americans can be considered to have a good diet.

Many a vegetable gardener, it seems, realizes the merit of replacing empty calories and artificial additives with home-grown produce, rich in health values and of unquestioned purity.

Spacemanship

Lack of space has become an almost totally invalid reason for forgoing a "kitchen garden." We see them today even on city terraces and rooftops, in every imaginable type of container, spurred by the development of midget vegetables and by such aids as the new HOME AND GARDEN BULLETIN 163, "MINIGARDENS FOR VEGETABLES" (15¢ FROM THE SUPERINTENDENT OF DOCUMENTS, WASHINGTON, DC 20402).

Some more limited-space ideas:

Train vining crops — peas, tomatoes, pole beans, squash, limas, cucumbers, small melons — on trellises, fences, walls. Given full sun, a one-foot strip of these trained vertically will yield as lavishly as the ten-times-larger area needed if they are allowed to sprawl.

Take advantage of the ornamental attributes of vegetables — the texture, color, foliage pattern, flower and fruit interest the artistic eye will discern in many of the most prosaic crops. Landscape architect Alice Upham Smith has often lauded the merits of mixed flower and vegetable plantings — parsley, chives, Bibb or Oak Leaf lettuce, and red-and-green-topped beets for border use . . . feathery dill or ferny asparagus as a background for flowers . . . New Zealand spinach as a groundcover . . . the accent value of large dark rhubarb leaves . . . red-flowered scarlet runner beans or red or green Malabar spinach trained upright for dramatic screening . . . flowering kale for autumn beauty . . . these and others lend themselves remarkably to a beauty-with-utility scheme of gardening.

The design of a vegetable plot too, can make it a decorative asset. A "wagon wheel" of almost any diameter can be both aesthetically pleasing and highly productive. Triangular, semicircular or more intricate formal or informal shapes are often practical. Design possibilities may be enhanced if the gardener remembers that quite a few vegetables, most notably salad and leafy crops, will stand some shade.

Vegetable Plotting

Whether space is limited or not, intensive cropping is vital for maximum harvest. Basic to this are the time-honored techniques of companion and succession cropping.

Companion cropping, or interplanting quick- and slow-maturing crops so that the latter fills in the row after harvest of the former, offers myriad possibilities: lettuce, spinach, radishes and early beans interplanted among eggplant, melons and tomatoes, or early corn with tomatoes, okra, peanuts or bush sweet potatoes. A variation is intercropping short and tall vegetables that mature at the same time, such as squash or pumpkins around hills of corn. Rapid-maturing crops like radishes can utilize between-row space while other crops are starting.

Succession cropping means either replacing a crop as soon as it is harvested with another crop, or sowing the same vegetable at intervals to lengthen the harvest period. A long harvest may also be achieved by planting early, midseason and late varieties simultaneously. Two oft-forgotten rules: root crops should succeed top crops and vice versa, and cabbage family members should not follow each other because of the soil-borne diseases common to all of them.

Many vegetable gardening books give detailed charts that simplify the calculations necessary for full utilization of these techniques. To really speed production, maintain a little "nursery" to supply husky seedlings of many succession-crop vegetables, ready to transplant as needed. Peat pots, Jiffy-7's, BR-8 blocks and similar "no-shock" planters are useful aids.

Beyond these, there are several exciting new techniques which give promise of phenomenal yield increases.

Togetherness Pays

One idea which appears simple but has many ramifications, is close planting. Less distance between plants and rows, so that by maturity many plants form a "closed canopy" over the soil, is advocated for both farms and gardens. The Mississippi Agricultural Experiment Station has found that higher plant populations of corn and sugarcane, besides giving higher per-acre yields, do not reduce per-plant yields and often actually increase them. Suppression of weeds by shading was noted as a bonus benefit on non-mulched plots.

The Organic Experimental Farm maintained by "Organic Gardening" recently recommended these spacings: celery, 18″ rows; Bibb lettuce, 8″ bed spacing; bush beans, 18″ rows; broccoli and cauliflower, 12″ bed spacing; beets and carrots, 10″ rows.

Another close-cropping tip: lay out each row so that the plants in it alternate with those in the

A summer organic mulch that feeds the soil, keeps roots cool and prevents weed competition is an important factor in vegetable yields.

biodynamic techniques — which emphasize organic fertilizing, companion planting for growth stimulation and the use of certain plants for insect control — a vegetable plot of as little as ⅕ acre should produce $6000 worth of crops a year, depending on the crops grown and season length. So says *"HOW TO GROW MORE VEGETABLES THAN YOU EVER THOUGHT POSSIBLE ON LESS LAND THAN YOU CAN IMAGINE"* ($4 FROM ECOLOGY ACTION OF THE MIDPENINSULA, 2225 EL CAMINO REAL, PALO ALTO, CA 94306).

Rich Diet

Close-planting experimenters emphasize that the more plants you grow in a given area, the more you must increase the supply of growth-promoting factors — nutrients, water, light, carbon dioxide.

An ample and constant supply of nutrients, tailored to the needs of the crop at each stage of growth, is essential. This is best achieved by building a reserve of fertility in the soil — through copious additions of organic matter and long-lasting fertilizers — supplemented by frequent applications of fast-acting fertilizers during the growing season.

The better the fertilizer reserves and tilth of a soil and the greater its depth, the more nutrients, water and oxygen it can supply to root crops. This condition can be attained in building a new vegetable garden by turning the soil to 18″ depth in autumn and thoroughly mixing in compost material and slow-release organic fertilizers, followed by sowing a deep-rooted leguminous green manure crop such as clover, alfalfa or vetch to be

next row, in a diamond pattern. This results in better "filling in" of the between-row space as the plants grow.

The new French Intensive Method combines close planting and mounded beds to give higher yields of superior crops. Raising the beds results in improved aeration and drainage and faster warming of the soil. Beds should be 3′ to 5′ wide for leaf and root crops, 1½′ wide for vertical crops like tomatoes, peas and beans. The bed is dug 12″ deep, and equal volumes of the soil, sand and compost are mixed and mounded in it. Then 1″ to 2″ of rotted manure and a thin dusting of bonemeal and wood ashes are worked into the upper 3″ to 6″ of the mound. The soil should be soaked the day before planting, then the vegetables are sown or set just far enough apart so their outer leaves will touch as they near maturity. Sow or transplant in staggered rows to give full coverage of the bed.

By teaming the French Intensive Method with

turned under in spring. For established gardens, turning the soil spade-deep and adding organic matter and fertilizer every three years should be adequate.

Longest-lasting phosphorus and potash fertilizers are phosphate rock or colloidal phosphate, and granite dust or greensand (for sources, write *"ORGANIC GARDENING," EMMAUS, PA 18049*). These also supply essential trace elements, which are lacking in many soils to a greater degree than is commonly recognized. Dolomitic limestone corrects acidity (vegetables require pH 6 to 7) and also provides calcium and magnesium.

Before spring planting, dig in a fertilizer with a 1:2:1 ratio, such as 5-10-5. Use a half-strength "starter" solution of this immediately after transplanting seedlings, too. Thereafter, at 10-day intervals — longer when the weather is overcast — apply a half-strength solution of a formula with equal proportions of the major nutrients, such as 20-20-20, or apply the same formula dry as a side-dressing at 3- to 4-week intervals. This should be continued through the season for leafy vegetables. For root and fruiting crops like carrots, broccoli and tomatoes, switch over when they are about half grown to a low-nitrogen fertilizer to deter excessive vegetative growth.

New Emphasis on Watering

It is a rare vegetable garden that receives sufficient moisture to enable its plants to reach their full growth potential. Mulching to conserve water is therefore vital, as is an adequate watering system. Deep, long-lasting waterings can be easily furnished with any inexpensive sprinkler, soaker or ooze hose, or perforated pipe system. Given good drainage and topsoil with a structure close to the ideal of 50% solid matter and 50% pore space, it is difficult to overwater most crops — as long as nutrients, light and other growth factors are at correspondingly high levels.

The Light Fantastic

Other than growing low crops to the south and taller to the north, gardeners give little thought to the possibilities of increasing light on their plants. But it has been shown that aluminum foil or white plastic reflective mulches can boost yields re-

Homemade cloches of wire hoops and clear plastic give a "greenhouse start" to tender row crops.

markably. The avid vegetable gardener unconcerned about aesthetics might try aluminum foil vertically on simple racks or wooden horses. In tests by Dr. J. W. Pendleton of the University of Illinois, this raised corn yields from 100 bushels per acre to 377 bushels.

Carbon dioxide, which has proved so stimulating to flower and vegetable crops under glass, is also being studied for use outdoors. It is produced naturally by decomposing vegetation — a potent reason for organic mulching — and some is also released through the planting holes in plastic mulch over biologically active soil.

Mulching by Degrees

Finally, by controlling soil temperature, the gardener can do much to hasten maturity and raise yields. If you use a year-round mulch, pull it back from the rows at least 10 days before planting to let the soil warm up. For fastest warming, lay a strip of heat-transmitting green plastic on the row — or use water-filled plastic bags, a technique which has proved very successful in promoting early, highly productive growth in tests at the Huntley Branch Experiment Station in Montana.

Then maintain a black plastic, aluminum foil or organic mulch between the rows to keep roots cool in summer; temperatures above 85° cause virtual cessation of root growth in many crops. A caution: go easy with organic mulches in a wet year, particularly on heavy soils. A constantly soggy deep mulch restricts oxygen in the soil and also encourages root fungus diseases.

Foiling the Blighters

All-around good culture that provides the proper balance of all growth factors is, without question, a major aid in preventing many pest and disease problems. They are also minimized by growing resistant varieties (state extension service offices issue lists of these), by faithfully rotating crops or fumigating the soil before planting with chemicals such as Vapam and by growing repellent plants and employing natural pesticides and cultural and biological controls. Infected or infested crop residues should always be burned or relegated to the refuse pail.

When serious problems threaten, maneb is generally considered the safest fungicide for vegetables, and Sevin or a combination of malathion and methoxychlor are recommended for insect control — but follow all directions meticulously.

Season-Stretching

Practice extra-early direct seeding. Ohio State University recommends planting corn at least 3 days before the average date of last killing frost, sowing as deep as $1\frac{1}{2}''$ so the growing point is deep enough to avoid freezing. Risk later-than-usual summer sowings, too, and remember that catalog notations of days to maturity refer to spring-planted crops, and summer plantings generally mature more rapidly.

Cloches, hotcaps, bottomless glass jugs and similar devices are used by vegetable gardeners seeking extra-early harvests. Commercial growers of tender vegetables and bedding plants use a simple method easily transferred to the home garden: wide-mesh wire fencing, such as cattle fence, is bent into a Quonset-like semicircle over the rows and covered with inexpensive polyethylene film.

Frost protection in autumn can be provided with covers of loose mulch material, baskets, etc., or by sprinkling: Cornell University recommends applying $\frac{1}{10}''$ of water per hour, beginning when the temperature falls near 32°, and wetting plants at least once a minute until no ice remains on them.

"Self-storing" crops — beets, carrots, parsley, Brussels sprouts, kale and others — give harvests under a mulch long into winter. Many late crops also store well in a cool cellar, pit or buried barrel, or laid outdoors on plastic and covered with plastic and several inches of soil. Every vegetable gardener should have *"HOME AND GARDEN" BULLETINS No. 119, "STORING VEGETABLES AND FRUIT"; No. 8, "HOME CANNING"; AND No. 10, "HOME FREEZING" (FREE FROM THE OFFICE OF INFORMATION, U.S. DEPARTMENT OF AGRICULTURE, WASHINGTON, DC 20250).*

Most vital to full enjoyment of a vegetable plot is proper preparation of its bounty. Eat more vegetables raw, or rapid-cooked only to the "tender-crisp" stage, for maximum preservation of flavor and nutrients.

SPECIAL TACTICS

Underground Duplex

An interesting combination of soil and soilless culture is described in *"RING CULTURE," BY FRANK ALLERTON (FABER & FABER, 24 RUSSELL SQUARE, LONDON W.C. 1, ENGLAND; $1.75).* Gardening in rings — actually in bottomless pots or cylinders of soil over an inert aggregate such as vermiculite — is attracting considerable attention in England.

The method was developed at Tilgate Horticultural Research Station about 20 years ago. Tomatoes growing in bottomless cylinders placed over boiler ash gave almost double the yield of toma-

Summer-sown 'Salad Bowl' lettuce gives an excellent harvest until very late in the fall.

toes in the same type of container set on a tile floor. The plants growing over the ash, it seems, developed an enormous secondary root system in the ash, with roots much thicker and less branching than the fibrous ones in the soil above. These thick roots drew up great amounts of water, while the upper roots mainly absorbed nutrients.

In early stages after planting, little water is given the soil, while the aggregate is watered well to encourage roots to extend down into it. The soil is given liquid fertilizer frequently, beginning several weeks after planting, but the aggregate always receives only water.

The method seems adaptable to containers with bottoms if a tube by which water can be supplied is extended down to the aggregate. Outdoors a layer of aggregate at the bottom of the planting hole could be similarly watered with a tube.

Stalk Talk

A new technique — and a very old one — can give extra-early harvests of those two delightful perennial spring vegetables, asparagus and rhubarb.

Green plastic spread over an asparagus bed will warm the soil rapidly and stimulate growth (sun heat is transmitted even better by clear plastic, but weeds will sprout under it). As the shoots push up the plastic, simply cut holes in it to let them through. The asparagus season can be

lengthened at the other end, too: mulch a portion of the bed with black plastic, which transmits almost no heat, so keeps the soil cool and delays growth of the shoots under it.

The green plastic can be used to spur early rhubarb production, but with this addition: as soon as a clump begins to sprout, put a drain tile, basket, small barrel or deep box, with the bottom removed, over it, and cover the top with a sheet of clear plastic or glass. This will trap warmth, and the light coming in from above will draw up the stalks. The cover may need to be removed on warm days to prevent too much heat build-up. A sprinkling of fertilizer, plus watering if rain is lacking, will help speed growth. When the stalks grow up near the top of the "vertical coldframe," remove it to let them redden before harvesting.

Keeping a Cool Head

"Tobacco shading" plus evaporative cooling, a vegetable gardener tells us, produce fine head-type lettuce through severe summer heat and drought, even when the best slow-bolting kinds rapidly go to seed.

This gardener uses a simple inverted-V wire frame covered with cheesecloth over the row. Then he provides further cooling with a sprinkler set to apply just enough water to match the evaporation rate but not to wet the soil. A 3″ straw mulch also helps to keep the roots cool. Finally, like commercial growers, he applies a high-nitrogen soluble fertilizer when the plants reach the "soft-head" stage.

The Last Sows of Summer

Boston gardener Ruth Tirrell supplies tips on best vegetables for the last summer sowings. In tender crops, she recommends 'Topcrop' and similar quick-maturing bush beans, and 'Seneca Zucchini' summer squash, maturing in 47 days (SEEDWAY, INC., HALL, NY 14463). She extends the

An All-America Selections winner, 'Goldcrop' is one of the first high-quality long-pod straight wax beans.

true spinach but delicious (widely available); and 'Full Heart Batavian' endive (BURNETT BROS., 92 CHAMBERS STREET, NEW YORK, NY 10007).

To give midsummer sowings a good start, Mrs. Tirrell soaks large seeds overnight, and covers all rows with hay. Watering is done through this, at least daily until the seeds have sprouted, then every other day if rains are scarce.

harvest by covering with hay or burlap bags during first frost.

Kale is another good fall crop, and loose-leaf lettuces such as 'Salad Bowl' and 'Oak Leaf' are the easiest and most dependable for long harvests, covered and mulched with leaves or hay on cold nights. Peas are possible, using the 'Wando' heat-resistant variety. In root crops, beets and carrots last well into winter under mulch; the short, blunt carrot types are easiest to dig. 'Purple Top White Globe' turnip is sweet-flavored and lasts under mulch for Mrs. Tirrell until Thanksgiving. For superior greens as well as roots, the 'Japanese Foliage' or 'Shogoin' turnip (NICHOLS GARDEN NURSERY, 1190 NORTH PACIFIC HIGHWAY, ALBANY, OR 97321; CATALOG 15¢) is excellent. Rutabagas make small but finer-flavored roots when sown in midsummer. Fine winter radishes, good raw or cooked like carrots, are 'Chinese Rose,' 'Long Black Spanish' and 'Chinese White' (LANDRETH SEEDS, BOX 4404, BALTIMORE, MD 21223).

Some recommendations by other gardeners: "cold-resistant" 'Explorer' sweet corn (OTIS S. TWILLEY, SALISBURY, MD 21801); 'Italian Green Sprouting' broccoli (GURNEY SEED & NURSERY CO., YANKTON, SD 57078); 'Stokes Extra Early Snowball' cauliflower (STOKES SEEDS, BOX 548, BUFFALO, NY 14205); 'Green Wave' mustard (FARMER SEED & NURSERY CO., FARIBAULT, MN 55021); 'Cocozelle' squash (JOSEPH HARRIS CO., MORETON FARM, ROCHESTER, NY 14624); New Zealand spinach, not a

Vitamin Seeds

The Chinese have been sprouting seeds for food for at least 5000 years. A seed has been called the "concentrated vital force" of a plant, and when it sprouts, one of nature's most valuable phenomena, nutritionally speaking, occurs: its food value increases amazingly. Sprouting oats, for example, increases their vitamin C content 4 times, vitamin B_2, 13 times. In addition to up to 2000% rises in some vitamins (according to Dr. Paul Burkholder of Yale University), complete protein forms in many grains and legumes when they are sprouted, and the sprouts are also rich in minerals.

Almost any seeds can be sprouted — corn, barley, alfalfa, lentils, soybeans, rye, peas, millet, limas, garbanzos, fenugreek, sunflowers, etc. Use any wide-mouthed container such as a Mason jar, or bulb pan or clay saucer. Soak the seeds overnight, then drain and place them in the container, and cover with a double cheesecloth layer held with rubber bands. Set the container in a consistently warm spot, and rinse and drain the seeds 3 times daily. In 3 to 5 days, sprouts will be 1″ to 3″ long and ready for harvesting. Use them in salads, sandwich fillings, soups, stews, casseroles, Oriental recipes, with eggs, rice — even in baking bread.

Seed treated with chemicals should not, of course, be used for sprouting. Many health food stores have suitable seed.

Vegetables and Herbs 107

SPECIAL VEGETABLES

Artichokes Up North

Globe artichokes, raised commercially in central California's coastal region, can actually be grown in home gardens even in the Midwest and north to Quebec. Given very rich soil, frequent misting to increase humidity, and protection in winter, they will produce a reasonable crop — and the grower can harvest delectable baby artichokes, only 1½″ thick, which have no thistly centers and so are totally edible.

Artichokes (*Cynara scolymus*) are grown from seed (*R. H. SHUMWAY, ROCKFORD, IL 61101*) or roots (*CALIFORNIA NURSERY CO., NILES, CA 94536; STRIBLING'S NURSERIES, BOX 793, MERCED, CA 95340*). They are planted 4′ apart, with roots set 5″ to 6″ deep, in spring after frosts, in a well-drained soil heavily enriched with compost, manure and 5-10-5 fertilizer. The 3′ to 4′ high and 4′ to 6′ broad plants are quite handsome. A deep mulch and occasional feedings of liquid manure or fertilizer through the season are beneficial, plus mist-spraying in warm, dry weather. Young buds may be harvested the first year if the plants are grown from roots.

In the fall, the plant is cut off a few inches above the ground and covered with an inverted box filled with dry straw or leaves, then soil is mounded 2′ deep over this. Replace the plants every third year with suckers from their own roots. Globe artichoke is also a fine ornamental for flower or shrub borders, especially if the buds are allowed to develop into the spectacular purple flowers.

Beans-Talk

A short note on some unusual beans we wouldn't be without:

'Dixie Butterpea,' a 75-day lima that really rates its catalog description of "the finest, meatiest, most delicious bush lima bean ever offered" (*GEO. W. PARK SEED CO., GREENWOOD, SC 29647*) . . . flageolet 'Vert Suma,' a delightfully mellow flavored little French kidney bean (*NICHOLS*

GARDEN NURSERY, 1190 NORTH PACIFIC HIGHWAY, ALBANY, OR 97321; CATALOG 15¢) . . . 'Royalty,' the purple-podded snapbean shunned by beetles (*NICHOLS*) . . . the ornamental scarlet runner bean, a high-climber with brilliant red blooms, long green pods (*STOKES SEEDS, BOX 548, BUFFALO, NY 14240*) . . . 'Romano 14,' bush form of the Italian wide-podded pole bean of distinctive flavor (*W. ATLEE BURPEE CO., PHILADELPHIA, PA 19132*) . . . 'Long Pod' English fava or broad bean, shelled and used like limas but with pea flavor (*NICHOLS*) . . . and asparagus pea, a fascinating edible ornamental, with red-brown flowers and squarish, flanged pods which are cooked whole (*PARK*).

Cultivate Cardoon

The ancient cardoon, popular in France and Italy but virtually unknown to Americans, offers unequaled garden and culinary pleasure. Cardoon (*Cynara cardunculus*) looks like a cross between a thistle and celery, grows 3′ to 4′ tall and bears large blue flower heads. It is easily grown in fertile, well-drained soil, as a perennial in the South and from seed sown in early spring in northern states.

The edible stalks and leaf midribs, which may be blanched by wrapping in the fall, are excellent sautéed, deep-fried or boiled, and in soups, salads and stews — see French and Italian cookbooks for a variety of recipes. Seed is obtainable from *J. L. HUDSON, SEEDSMAN (BOX 1058, REDWOOD CITY, CA 94064; CATALOG 50¢).*

A fine hot-weather substitute for spinach, climbing Malabar spinach is excellent cooked or in salads.

Heat-resistant tampala is another good spinach substitute.

Chichi Chicory

The forcing strain of chicory *(Cichorium intybus)* known as Belgian endive or witloof is the gourmet's first choice for winter salads and unusual dishes (for fine recipes, see *"THE HOME GARDEN COOKBOOK," BY KEN & PAT KRAFT (DOUBLEDAY, $6.95)*.

Seed *(W. ATLEE BURPEE CO., PHILADELPHIA, PA 19132)* is sown in late spring in a light, stone-free soil enriched with organic matter and low-nitrogen fertilizer. Thin the seedlings to 6″ apart. The tender early leaves can be used in salads or as a pot herb. Then in late fall after several frosts, the parsnip-like roots are dug and the tops trimmed to 1″ of the crown, the roots to a uniform length of about 8″. Store them in any cool place.

Whenever the forced heads or "chicons" are desired, stand some of the roots 1″ apart in soil up to their tops in large pots, tubs or boxes. Water well, then cover with 6″ of dry sand, light soil or sawdust. In 3 to 4 weeks at 55° to 60°, the tips of the blanched oval heads will be seen, and they can be uncovered and snipped or twisted off. In mild climates, forcing is done in boxed-in beds in the garden.

Incomparable Comfrey

According to many reports, the new Quaker or Russian broadleaf comfrey *(Symphytum peregrinum)* is a truly extraordinary perennial vegetable.

It's decorative, with handsome, deep green, broadly sword-shaped leaves and, when permit-ted to bloom, long clusters of lavender-blue bell flowers . . . it's rich in food value — very high in protein and vitamins, plus minerals brought up from deep in the soil by 10′ roots . . . it's versatile, the younger leaves delightful as salad greens or cooked like spinach, in blender drinks or brewed fresh or dried for a healthful tea, and as a last-minute seasoning addition to soups or stews . . . and it is a fantastic producer of mulch and compost material — in England, Africa and New Zealand, where comfrey is grown for livestock feed, harvests of over 100 tons per acre have been reported.

In the garden, comfrey requires full sun and ample room. Space plants 3′ apart each way, and fertilize often for top production. Root cuttings are available from *NICHOLS GARDEN NURSERY (1190 NORTH PACIFIC HIGHWAY, ALBANY, OR 97321; CATALOG 15¢)*.

Quick Corn

Here are some ways to have sweet corn by July 4th, even way up north:

Use the very fastest maturing varieties (60 days or less), such as 'Polar Vee,' 'Earlivee' *(STOKES SEEDS, BOX 548, BUFFALO, NY 14240)* or 'Hybrid 4th of July' *(EARL MAY SEED & NURSERY CO., SHENANDOAH, IA 51601)* . . . start seeds indoors 3 weeks early in peat pots, or in milk cartons from which they are transplanted outdoors with minimum root disturbance . . . or sow very early in the garden — 5 weeks before the usually recommended planting time has been successful in Connecticut — first warming the soil with a green plastic mulch applied a week or so before planting, then replace this with organic mulch after the plants are well up, or, better yet, with aluminum foil to bounce light onto the plants . . . use some type of cloche until frost danger is past, of bent clear plastic corrugated panels or clear film over wire hoops.

Health Food

The Jerusalem artichoke, *Helianthus tuberosus*, is attracting special attention these days. Weight watchers have learned that its knobby, white-fleshed underground tubers are high in vitamins and minerals but low in calories — only 75 per pound contrasted to potato's 300. Totally starch free, they contain carbohydrate in the form of insulin and sugar as levulose, so are recommended for diabetics and others on restricted carbohydrate diets. An additional benefit is almost complete freedom from fat and sodium.

Jerusalem artichokes can be served raw, or boiled, baked, sautéed or creamed. The texture is crisp, the flavor delicate and nut-like, sweeter than potatoes. The seed pieces can be planted in either fall or spring, 18″ apart in 3′ rows. Growing 6′ to 8′ tall, the plants are excellent for screening, and the yellow flowers are bright and pleasing.

No pests or diseases attack the plants, and the yield of tubers is high, several times that of potatoes. They can be dug in autumn and stored, or left in the ground all winter, covered with a loose mulch, and harvested during thaws.

A source is NICHOLS GARDEN NURSERY (1190 NORTH PACIFIC HIGHWAY, ALBANY, OR 97321; CATALOG 15¢).

Gourmet Onion

Leeks (*Allium porrum*), those bulbless "overgrown scallions" esteemed since the days of the ancient Egyptians, give an extremely long harvest. The sweet stalks serve as a fine subtle substitute for onions in soups and stews, or rival asparagus when boiled and buttered. They can be harvested as young as 8 weeks, or allowed to mature for a fall or winter vegetable — leeks frozen under a mulch thaw perfectly when cut off and brought indoors.

Seed may be started indoors, or sown directly in the garden. Commercial growers transplant into 8″ by 8″ trenches, gradually filling these with soil as the stalks grow and hilling up more soil to blanch the stems. But gardeners use a shallower trench, or surface-plant and simply draw soil up around the stems, and flavor is as good as any fully blanched stalks. This also makes them easier to dig or cut in winter. Leeks should be thinned when 3″ high to stand 6″ apart, and the soil hilled gradually to about 4″ high. Several varieties are offered by STOKES SEEDS (BOX 548, BUFFALO, NY 14240).

Piquant Cresses

Vegetable growers are growing more salad plants than ever before. The cresses especially are desired. For the gardener with no brook, garden cress or peppergrass (*Lepidium sativum*) and upland cress (*Barbarea vulgaris*) are fine substitutes for watercress.

Upland cress tastes most like watercress, while peppergrass is somewhat "hotter." Peppergrass is the more decorative, its bright green, lacy foliage making an attractive edging. Fast growing, it allows cutting to begin 3 weeks after sowing. It also thrives in winter in pots, in a cool, sunny window. Upland cress has larger leaves than watercress, and grows 18″ high. A hardy biennial, its special advantage is ability to live over winter under a loose mulch, providing salad greens in thaws and in the spring.

Both are available from LANDRETH'S SEEDS (BOX 4404, BALTIMORE, MD 21223), which also lists the infrequently seen corn salad, *Valerianella locusta olitoria*, a favorite in Europe. Its 5″ oval leaves, which grow in pretty rosettes, are ready for harvest in 6 weeks for use in salads or cooked like spinach. It will winter over under a straw covering.

Melon Mastery

"A gardener is as good as the melons he grows," an old saying goes. But good harvests of watermelons and cantaloupes are becoming easier even for northern gardeners, with new varieties and new techniques. High-quality midget and seedless watermelons maturing in 65 to 80 days, and 75-day cantaloupes are widely available. With "early start" methods and succession planting, these allow an extended harvest even in the North.

Seed should be sown in peat pots 3 to 4 weeks before outdoor planting, and the seedlings hardened off. A clear or green plastic mulch will warm the soil in the planting area, and the area

Planting a new crop as soon as one is harvested keeps the entire vegetable plot producing all season long.

where the vines will spread should also have a mulch: tests in Iowa and North Carolina showed that clear or black plastic, paper, or aluminum foil all increased yields and hastened maturity by as much as 10 days — besides giving freedom from soil-borne diseases, since the fruit never touches the soil. A gardener reports that melons set out extra early under "tepees" made of wire-mesh translucent plastic grew considerably faster than those protected by hotcaps or glass jugs.

Melons must have absolutely full sun, and a rich porous soil, pH 6 to 6.5 . . . fertilizer should

be high in phosphorus and potash, low in nitrogen
. . . melons can stand drought better than most
crops, and it is especially important to hold back
water when they begin to ripen, to develop
sweetness . . . radishes planted among the vines
are said to repel beetles that attack melons.

Easier to grow than muskmelons — and far
more delicious — is the little-known banana
melon. Maturing in 96 days, it grows long and
tapering to about 18″, with a green skin ripening
to lemon-yellow. The flesh is salmon-pink, thick,
fragrant and sweet. Recommended is a rich,
well-drained soil, supplemental feeding at planting time and topdressing later with 5-10-10, and
mulching with black plastic or 4″ of old hay or
grass clippings. Most important is ample water
until the melons start to ripen, when dry soil
increases the sweetness. Seed is available from
R. H. SHUMWAY SEEDSMAN (ROCKFORD, IL 61101).

Mushrooming

The urge to grow one's own food has brought new
popularity for that most flavorful indoor crop,
mushrooms. *Agaricus campestris (A. bisporus)* is
not only delicious but low in calories and very
high in protein, minerals and vitamins — especially the B vitamins.

Mushrooms are fascinating as well as easy to
grow. The mycelium or network of "roots" is

*'Burpee White' radish develops best texture and flavor
when grown in cool weather.*

actually the body of the plant, while the above-
ground edible part is the fruit. Spawn, a culture
of the microscopic spores of the fungus, is sown
on special compost. The basis of this compost
used to be strawy horse manure, but now most
growers use corn cobs, hay and poultry manure or
dried brewers' grains, composted for two weeks
with nutrients added, then pasteurized. Two
weeks after the spawn is planted, the bed is
"cased" or covered with 1″ of loam.

Home growers usually prefer the simple pre-
planted mushroom kits (a source is EDMUND
SCIENTIFIC CO., 555 EDSCORP BUILDING,
BARRINGTON, NJ 08007). Only watering is necessary
to produce a crop, which will be ready in about 4
weeks, with successive "flushes" appearing for
several weeks thereafter. Any shaded area at 50°
to 70°, with high humidity but good ventilation, is
suitable. At the lower temperature, the crop will
be produced over a longer period. More adven-
turous gardeners, or those seeking larger crops at
lower cost, may want to prepare their own
compost and casing, and plant pure-culture
spawn *(W. ATLEE BURPEE CO., PHILADELPHIA, PA
19132).*

Mushrooms are best harvested just as the cap starts to expand to expose the gills, and should be picked by twisting slightly so the soil is disturbed as little as possible. Mushrooms are truly no-waste products — they need no peeling, and after cropping the compost is ideal for garden soil building. Mushrooms are easily home-dried by stringing them chain-fashion with a needle and thread and hanging for two weeks in a warm, dry place.

Two good books are *"MUSHROOM GROWING TODAY," BY FRED C. ATKINS (MACMILLAN, $5.95),* and *"MUSHROOM GROWING," BY ARTHUR J. SIMONS (95¢ PLUS 50¢ SHIPPING FROM GARDEN WAY PUBLISHING, CHARLOTTE, VT 05445).*

Southern Accent

That valuable southern staple okra or gumbo (*Hibiscus esculentus*) bids to become a favorite in northern gardens. Tender home-grown okra can be boiled, broiled, fried, deep-fried or roasted, used in soups, stews and relishes, and preserved as pickles or frozen and dried. Okra is mineral-rich and also contains a substance, mucin, said to be an aid in digestive disturbances.

Seed is sown when the soil is definitely warm, $\frac{1}{2}''$ deep in rows 4' apart, and thinned to 15" for dwarf varieties, to 24" for larger types. The sturdy upright plants produce extremely showy flowers, like morning glories. Top yields of the pods, which should be harvested while immature when the stems are easily cut with a knife, are achieved with ample water but moderate fertility.

Best varieties: 'Emerald Green,' 3', with pods which stay tender even when large (*OTIS S. TWILLEY SEEDS, SALISBURY, MD 21801*); fast-growing, high-yielding 'Perkins Long Pod,' to 3' with 9" pods (*NATURAL DEVELOPMENT CO., BAINBRIDGE, PA 17502*); white-podded 'White Velvet,' 4'; and the All-America Winner, 'Clemson Spineless' (*LANDRETH SEED CO., BOX 4404, BALTIMORE, MD 21223*). *NICHOLS GARDEN NURSERY (1190 NORTH PACIFIC HIGHWAY, ALBANY, OR 97321; CATALOG 15¢)* offers an unusual red-podded okra.

Super Spud

The potato can be a gourmet garden crop. For flavor and special uses, for example, the German 'Fingerling' is "a quality potato that has no peer," reports William R. Block in "Organic Gardening."

The best potato for salad and German-fried potatoes, the 'Fingerling,' has yellow skin and flesh. It produces vast numbers of 2" to 4" long potatoes, only 1" or so in diameter. Mr. Block advises planting 12" apart, in rows 18" apart, in loose or sandy soil. He adds 2" of compost, 4 pounds of bonemeal per 10 square feet and several handfuls of soybean meal, mixed in well to 10" depth. The seed pieces, which should have at least two eyes each, are planted 6" deep with the eyes up. The bed is then covered with 6" of organic mulch, which is never allowed to dry out. For extra nitrogen, 2 pounds of soybean meal per 100 square feet is broadcast monthly.

A thin-skinned potato, 'Fingerling' should be gently washed, rather than scrubbed, for storage. They mature in 90 to 115 days. A source is *OLDS SEED CO. (MADISON, WI 53701).*

High-Borne Onions

One of the most intriguing but least known crops is the Egyptian, top or tree onion, *Allium cepa viviparum.* An agricultural staple in ancient times — Herodotus reports that it took 9 tons of gold to pay for the onions fed to workers constructing the Great Pyramid — these unusual onions are hardy perennials and very easy to grow.

They are top-multipliers, so-called because they produce their little onions on top of their fat hollow stalks. The onions are delicious in salads or pickled, or used in stews, soups and meat dishes. Their flavor is distinctive, somewhat stronger than chives but certainly milder than garlic. The hollow stems can be sliced for salads, or split and stuffed with cream cheese, and the bases of the stems are cooked like leeks. Finally, when the stalk bends over, the little bulbs take root to increase the planting and provide scallions in early spring.

Vegetables and Herbs   113

THE AVERAGE YIELD OF 3 OR 4 PEAS per pod can b‹ doubled if ample nutrients are supplied, wit‹ special emphasis on magnesium, which make‹ more phosphorus available to the plant, report‹ the University of Wisconsin.

Seed of Egyptian onions is planted in spring, or sets in spring or fall. Like all onions, they should have a moist, rich soil. A source is GREENE HERB GARDENS (GREENE, RI 02827).

Garden Goobers

Peanuts can be a fascinating garden crop as far north as Ontario, Canada. The secret is early planting in warm soil — a sandy soil, mulched with green plastic early in spring. A south-facing slope plus cloches over the seedlings are also recommended in northern areas.

Home-grown peanuts, freshly roasted, are much more flavorful than any from the store. Nutritionists say peanuts are high in protein, niacin, thiamine and phosphorus, and enhance soups to desserts ("PEANUTS AS YOU LIKE THEM," a recipe booklet, is offered by GROWERS' PEANUT FOOD PROMOTIONS, BOX 1709, ROCKY MOUNT, NC 27834). A legume, peanuts enrich the soil, and the 18″ plants with light green foliage and showy yellow blossoms are quite ornamental — a peanuts-and-petunias combination makes a fine border for the vegetable plot.

Best varieties are the small-kerneled, 110-day Spanish and larger 120-day Virginia (DEGIORGI COMPANY, COUNCIL BLUFFS, IA 51501; CATALOG 35¢), plus the new 112-day Virginia-type NC-17 (GURNEY SEED & NURSERY CO., YANKTON, SD 57078). Plant shelled nuts no deeper than 2″ in the North, in a light soil enriched with organic matter. When the plants start to flower and produce the shoots that go down and make the "goober peas" underground, hill up the soil and mulch with hay, straw or grass clippings. Harvest before frost by lifting the vines with a fork, and either hang them or remove the peanuts and put them in shallow trays to cure in a dry spot indoors for a month or so. Roast them shelled or unshelled, 20 minutes at 350°.

Haute Cuisine Onion

Considering the price of fine specialty vegetables in today's markets, every gourmet should certainly be a gardener. Very easy to grow, for example, is that indispensable of French cookery, the shallot, Allium ascalonicum.

This onion-like native of Asia has been prized since the time of the early Greeks for its cloves or little brownish pointed bulblets. These impart a subtle flavor, considerably milder than onions, with the slightest overtone of garlic. The leaves are sometimes chopped to add pungency to salads.

Shallots are grown like onions, and the bulbs are pulled up when the leaves turn brown, then dried and separated into cloves. ALEX D. HAWKES, IN "A WORLD OF VEGETABLE COOKERY" (SIMON & SCHUSTER, $8.95), says his shallots thrive in pots in a rather sandy soil, and the bulbs keep in perfect condition in a cool dry place for 8 to 12 months.

Shallots are available from LE JARDIN DU GOURMET (CAMPGAW ROAD, RAMSEY, NJ 07446).

Off-Beat Beans

Soybeans are not often thought of as a garden vegetable. But the 2′ rich green plants are very easy to grow, they actually build soil and they produce a highly nutritious crop of many uses. Soybeans can be shelled green and prepared like peas, used like navy beans when mature, ground into flour or meal or sprouted for increased flavor and food value.

Robert Rodale, editor of "Organic Gardening," reports that soybeans rival meat in protein content, and supply valuable minerals, oils and carbohydrates. When sprouted, the vitamin content is increased dramatically. Sprout by soaking overnight, then storing for several days in a Mason jar, kept dark at 70° and moistened by occasional sprinkling.

Soybeans thrive wherever garden beans do. Being a legume, the plants "fix" atmospheric nitrogen — as much as 100 pounds per acre per year — through symbiotic root-nodule bacteria. For maximum nodulation and yield, an inoculant such as Nitragin *(EARL MAY SEED & NURSERY CO., SHENANDOAH, IA 51601)* should be dusted on the seed. The Ohio Agricultural Research and Development Center recommends planting in rows as close as 10″, and the University of Illinois has improved yields by increasing light with reflective mulches such as aluminum foil or white polyethylene. Fertilizer high in phosphorus and potassium is beneficial.

Best garden varieties: 'Bansei' *(NICHOLS GARDEN NURSERY, 1190 NORTH PACIFIC HIGHWAY, ALBANY, OR 97321; CATALOG 15¢)*; new 'Disoy' *(SEEDWAY, INC., HALL, NY 14463)*; 'Giant Green' *(FARMER SEED & NURSERY CO., FARIBAULT, MN 55021)*; and 'Kanrich' *(W. ATLEE BURPEE, PHILADELPHIA, PA 19132)*.

Sweet Talk

Sweet potatoes are tricky. The one essential is a warm, sandy soil, low in nitrogen — commercial growers use a 1:4:5 ratio fertilizer. Since the soil temperature must be above 65° for good growth, it's wise in the North to mulch the sweet potato area with green plastic in spring to hasten warming. Another aid is a cloche-type wire-supported plastic enclosure set over the young vines after planting. These make it feasible to set out the plants earlier than the usually recommended 3 weeks after the average date of last frost.

Good varieties are 'Centennial' *(BURGESS SEED & PLANT CO., GALESBURG, MI 49053)*, the semi-upright, fast-maturing 'Bunch Porto Rico' *(FARMER SEED & NURSERY CO., FARIBAULT, MN 55021)* and 'Allgold,' which contains three times the vitamin A and 50% more vitamin C than other sweet potatoes *(FARMER)*. The gardener can also

'Michihli' Chinese cabbage is sown in summer for fall harvests of 18″ heads.

Vegetables and Herbs 115

grow his own, sprouting the potatoes in water or sand at 75° four to five weeks before planting time, then carefully pulling off the rooted sprouts and transplanting to the garden about 15″ apart in the row.

Sweet potatoes are harvested before or immediately after frost, digging very carefully to avoid bruising. If they are "cured" in the sun for a couple of hours, then for two weeks in an airy room at 80°, they will last for months stored at 55°.

Tomato Tactics

Gardeners are following the lead of commercial tomato growers, who have found that wire "cages" give higher yields for less work. A piece of concrete reinforcing wire, 48″ long and 30″ high or higher, is formed into a circle and set over the young plant. This cage supports the plant, keeping the fruit well off the ground, and eliminates staking and pruning. Besides increased yields, growers report considerable reduction of sunscald and cracking of the fruit because the plants spread out and give the ripening fruit ample shade. Some growers theorize that the plants also get the benefit of electroculture, the metal cage setting up a growth-stimulating electromagnetic field.

More tips for top tomato production:

Deep planting — removing all except the top 4 or 5 leaves and planting with only these above the soil surface — encourages heavier rooting which promotes bigger crops . . . so does mound planting, growing on enriched mounds of soil 10″ high and 3′ in diameter . . . sucker growth can be layered to produce more plants, by bending the sucker over when about 12″ to 15″ long, covering all but 3″ of the end with soil, then severing it from the main stem when good roots have developed in about two weeks . . . give tomatoes tremendous amounts of food, by liberally using

leafmold, compost, rotted manure and long-lasting fertilizers such as bonemeal and greensand (a potassium source, vital to good fruiting) in the planting hole, then feeding frequently with dilute liquid fertilizer through the season . . . mulch heavily, to conserve moisture, eliminate weed competition and stabilize soil temperatures.

A 1″ to 1½″ deep mulch of black gravel has increased tomato yields up to 10 pounds per plant without supplementary watering in the semi-arid Great Plains. The Colorado Agricultural Experiment Station found that plants mulched with black gravel yielded 10.27 tons per acre of tomatoes, against 8.8 tons for white-gravel-mulched plants, and 2.86 tons for bare-soil plants. Also, the tomatoes grown on black gravel were more uniform, freer of end rot and larger. If black gravel is unavailable, the darkest color gravel common to the local area will do a good job of conserving soil moisture and improving yields.

Tomatoes planted in shallow trenches matured much earlier and gave more than ⅓ greater yields in tests by the Agricultural Research Service at Weslaco, Texas. ARS soil scientists planted single rows of tomatoes in the bottom of a trench 6″ deep and 4″ to 7″ wide. These tomatoes not only matured 3 weeks earlier than tomatoes planted conventionally, but also yielded 102 pounds per 50′ row as compared to 65 pounds for those grown in conventional beds. These advantages were attributed to the higher nighttime soil temperatures in the trenches, plus increased soil moisture content due to less evaporation and reduced wind stress on the young seedlings.

A double row of tomatoes, mulched with black plastic, is trained on a tepee made of old window frames nailed to posts.

HERBS

New Outlook

Knot gardens are a means to much beauty in little space — and these sixteenth-century formal ornaments of interlaced herb "ropes" have a place in informal modern gardens, according to *"HERBS AND THEIR ORNAMENTAL USES," HANDBOOK 68 OF THE BROOKLYN BOTANIC GARDEN (BROOKLYN, NY 11225; $1.50).*

A knot garden can be a fine decorative feature, particularly in association with a patio or terrace. The only environmental essential is full sun. "The design may be traditional," says Bernard Currid, "or as original as one's artistic imagination can create." He advises drawing a plan to scale, then using sand or lime to mark the planting lines on the soil. Numerous herbs of compact habit and varied textures and colors are suggested, both for the strands and for specimen planting between them. Mr. Currid notes that shearing the plants sharply in very early spring, then giving light clippings every two weeks from late spring through early summer, is the best way to maintain uniform height.

The Handbook's 36 articles give an amazing array of ways to make more than 250 common and unusual herbs serve as ornamental assets everywhere in the garden. This is a valuable innovative work, taking herbs out of their traditional culinary-medicinal niche and focusing attention on their important contemporary values for beautification.

Another valuable compendium is the *BROOKLYN BOTANIC GARDEN'S HANDBOOK 58, "JAPANESE HERBS AND THEIR USES."*

Sweet basil stands harsh environments and is a handsome plant for bold edging effects.

HOME-GROWN TOMATOES, because they are ripened on the vine, have one-third more vitamin C than commercial artificially ripened tomatoes, says Michigan State University's Department of Food Science.

Urban Herbs

A conversation with a city gardener has yielded several decorative yet iron-hardy herbs of value for city gardens — or for shady, acid, poorly drained situations anywhere.

For a 2′ to 3′ specimen shrub or hedge, rue (*Ruta graveolens*) is superb with its unusual

Old bricks, gravel and a few dozen herb plants combine to make an exquisite kitchen herb garden.

compound blue-green leaves, evergreen and garnished with yellow-green flowers and brown-red seed pods. Many of the mints are suitable, but two of the best for border use are the woolly apple mint, *Mentha rotundifolia,* and curly spearmint, *M. spicata crispa.* Sweet basil, *Ocimum basilicum,* is useful in both its small-leaved and large-leaved forms, but the compact purple basil, *O. minimum purpureum* ('Dark Opal') is unexcelled as an edging plant under city rigors. Rosemary, *Rosmarinus officinalis,* will stand smog and soot if lime is added to counteract soil acidity, and its gray-green needle foliage gives needed textural interest.

In any small garden, herbs can be supremely useful container plants for all sorts of decorative effects. And for indoor gardens, one of the finest ornamental-culinary windowsill plantings is a strawberry jar filled with little plants of basil, camomile, chives, lavender, marjoram, parsley, thyme and winter savory.

Sweet and Sour Herbs

Many are the methods of preserving herbs. After harvesting at the peak of flavor — just as the flower buds are about to open — they can be frozen in small heat-sealed envelopes following a 1-minute blanching and cooling, but color and flavor are not retained too well. Much better is drying, either on wire screens or hung in loose bunches in a warm, shaded, airy place, or on a rack in an oven under very low heat. When the leaves are crisp, they are stripped from the stems and packed in tightly closed glass or china containers.

"Salting down," by alternating thin layers of salt with ½" layers of the leaves of one or several herbs in a jar stored in the refrigerator, will keep them for months and also supply intriguingly flavored salt. Then there are herb butters, made by creaming lightly salted butter, mixing in finely cut herbs, and creaming again. And a delightful confection is created by "sugaring," brushing single leaves or small clusters with egg white,

then dipping them in sugar and drying for two days before storing in tight containers.

To make epicurean herb vinegars, stuff a large jar with one or more herbs, fill it with cider or white wine vinegar, agitate occasionally over a period of 1 to 3 weeks, then pour off the vinegar through cheesecloth and rebottle it. Chive bulbs, incidentally, can be pickled like little onions, and pickled nasturtium buds substitute admirably for capers.

Modern Herbal

In ancient times, knowledge of the medicinal values of plants was essential to life. Egyptian temple gardens were the first medical schools, and it was not until the fourteenth century that the earliest botanic gardens were formed for the study of the economic and ornamental uses of plants in addition to the medicinal. Then, in the last 250 years, the art of healing with plants was all but forgotten.

The pendulum may now be swinging back. A book which has been the top best seller in France is now available here: *"OF MEN AND PLANTS," BY MAURICE MESSEGUE (MACMILLAN, $6.95).* For 30 years, the author has been known as the world's most famous natural healer. He achieved fame when he cured the rheumatism of the legendary Mistinguett, and his patients have included Churchill, Adenauer and Farouk.

M. Messegue's book is fascinating, not only for the extraordinary story of his career, but also for its detailing of his use of flowers, vegetables and herbs in potions, gargles, baths and poultices to treat simple to complex ailments. He tells how to grow all types of beneficial cultivated and weed plants and, best of all, he gives much valuable nutritional advice, stressing healthful foods for each season of the year.

The variety in parsleys, from 'Plain' to 'Extra Triple Curled,' makes them ornamental as well as flavorful.

KEYS TO THE VEGETABLE KINGDOM

"All About Vegetables," edited by Walter L. Doty (Ortho Division, Chevron Chemical Co., Box 3744, San Francisco, CA 94119; $2.95 — specify West, South or Midwest-Northeast edition)

"Betty Crocker's Kitchen Gardens," by Mary Mason Campbell (Charles Scribner's Sons, $6.95)

"The Complete Book of Home Winemaking," by H. E. Bravery (Collier-Macmillan, paperback $1.50)

"The Food-Lover's Garden," by Angelo M. Pellegrini (Knopf, $6.95)

"The Green Thumb Book of Fruit and Vegetable Gardening," by George Abraham (Prentice-Hall, $7.95)

"Herb Gardening in Five Seasons," by Adelma Grenier Simmons (Hawthorn, $7.95)

"The How to Grow and Cook It Book of Vegetables, Herbs, Fruits, and Nuts," by Jacqueline Heriteau (Hawthorn, $7.95)

"Preserving the Fruits of the Earth," by Stanley Schuler and Elizabeth Meriwether Schuler (Dial, $6.95)

"A World of Vegetable Cookery," by Alex D. Hawkes (Simon & Schuster, $8.95)

SOURCES

Burnett Brothers, Inc., 92 Chambers Street, New York, NY 10007

W. Atlee Burpee Co., Philadelphia, PA 19132

Farmer Seed & Nursery Co., Faribault, MN 55021

Henry Field Seed & Nursery Co., Shenandoah, IA 51602

Glecklers Seedman, Metamora, OH 43540 — unusual vegetables

Gurney Seed & Nursery Co., Yankton, SD 57078

Johnny's Selected Seeds, North Dixmont, MA 04932; catalog 25¢ — many unusuals

Joseph Harris Co., Moreton Farm, Rochester, NY 14624

J. W. Jung Seed Co., Randolph, WI 53956

Landreth Seed Co., Box 4404, Baltimore, MD 21223

Earl May Seed & Nursery Co., Shenandoah, IA 51603

Natural Development Co., Bainbridge, PA 17502 — untreated seed

Nichols Garden Nursery, 1190 North Pacific Highway, Albany, OR 97321; catalog 15¢ — unusuals

Olds Seeds, Madison, WI 53701

Seedway, Inc., Hall, NY 14463

R. H. Shumway, Rockford, IL 61101

Stokes Seeds, Inc., Box 548, Buffalo, NY 14240

Otis S. Twilley, Salisbury, MD 21801

FRUITS AND NUTS

Dwarfs of Giant Interest

The biggest news in fruits is smaller and smaller plants. More fruits are being dwarfed, and the dwarfs are getting dwarfer. England's East Malling Research Station, for example, recently developed a new dwarfing rootstock, EM 27, which reduces standard apple trees to less than one-quarter their normal size.

The ultimate appears to have been reached in the single-shoot apple trees originated at Long Ashton Research Station in England. The plants are grown as single unbranched shoots for a year, then the growth retardant B-9 (UNIROYAL CHEMICAL CO., NAUGATUCK, CT 06770) is applied to induce budding all along this 3′ to 4′ shoot. These buds will flower and fruit the following year, and in commercial practice a combine harvester is used to simultaneously pick the fruit and "mow" the orchard, chopping up the shoots and returning them to the soil as mulch. When the stump begins to grow again, the growth is chemically pruned back to one shoot, and the cycle is repeated. Fruit thus is harvested in alternate years. With the shoots spaced 12″ apart to give about 45,000 per acre, the "meadow orchard" can produce as much as 75 tons of apples an acre.

With hand work replacing the chemical pruning and irrigation application of growth retardant, the system could be adapted to the garden, making it possible to grow fruit in the smallest nook or corner.

Soilless Culture Bears Fruit

Many gardeners grow dwarf fruit trees in soil in big tubs or planter boxes. But California gardener Dr. A. W. Sears uses a soilless medium, plastic pots and bonsai techniques to raise fine crops of fruits and nuts.

Dr. Sears grows apples, pears, peaches, nectarines, apricots, cherries, grapes and citrus, plus almonds and walnuts, in plastic pots 10″ to 16″ wide and 8″ to 10″ deep. He uses the University of California mix (sand and peatmoss), which has "several advantages: no saline accumulation (our water is very alkaline); does not dry out; clean and easy to maintain; easy to sterilize; doesn't break down, puddle, or pack; gives great fibrous root structure to trees."

Seedling rootstocks, he states, work best, rather than dwarfing rootstocks. "For size control I like heavy root pruning, usually performed in the fall; and summer pruning of the tops (the trees are kept to 4′ to 5′) . . . Natural fertilizers work best for me: hoof and horn meal, and horse manure . . . chemicals washed out too fast and left a crust on the soil."

The Fruit Clamp

When a fruiting plant refuses to fruit, try this simplified method of "ringing the vine," developed by fruit hobbyist Rudolph A. Leide:

Wrap a protective strip of kraft paper around the trunk or limb, then a 1″ to 3″ strip of sheet metal (which can be cut from a tin can), long enough to overlap slightly. Over this put a circular clamp of the type used to tighten plastic pipe or auto radiator hose. This clamp can be screwed as tight as desired to slow the downward flow of nutrients from the leaves to the roots. It does not damage the bark or cambium, and can be removed at any time.

Mr. Leide used his fruit clamp, applied in early fall, on one arm of a four-arm espalier apple tree which was making excessive vegetative growth. The following spring this arm was loaded with fruit buds, while the other arms had vegetative growth as usual.

Flawless Fruit

Mr. I. B. Lucas of Markdale, Ontario, grows perfect apples without insecticides or fungicides — and with one-tenth the labor of protecting with pesticides. When his apples are the size of small walnuts, he simply encloses each one in a 4″ x 4½″ bag (actually a sleeve) of 1 mil polyethylene, fastening it with a stapler.

Mr. Lucas reports that in the six years he has been using the sleeves his fruits have been totally free of apple maggot, scab and other injury. He notes that the sleeves "are pleated and can be readily slipped around the apple. As the apple grows it first fills and then expands the tissue which eventually forms a cobweb-thin skin over the entire apple except for the open ends, the uncovered areas being sufficient to allow the apple to breathe." The only insect the sleeves do not foil is the codling moth.

Mr. Lucas says the sleeves are obtainable from the KEYSTONE CO. (555 WARREN STREET, PHILLIPSBURG, NJ 08865). The method is applicable, of course, to many other fruits.

TREE FRUITS

Antique Apples

One of the most exciting recent developments is a renaissance of the old-time apples. Sparked by the best gardeners in several areas, it's bringing back remarkable varieties that are vastly superior in "eating quality" to today's standard apples. Commercial orchardists must choose their apples for good looks, shipping qualities and the like — a russet-skinned apple, for example, is considered unsalable, and many other fine varieties are unsuited to machine harvesting. But none of these requirements are deterrents in the garden.

What are the best "old" apples? Some 5000 to 6000 cultivars have been named over the centuries, and over 1000 are said to be currently available. The NORTH AMERICAN FRUIT EXPLORERS (ROBERT KURLE, SECRETARY, 87TH AND MADISON, HINSDALE, IL 60521) is making efforts to evaluate and save the finest apples through its members' collections, and NAFEX is hoping eventually to spearhead "National Fruit Trials" such as those sponsored by the Royal Horticultural Society.

Here are some of the very best "antique" apples, by consensus of connoisseurs: 'Cox's Orange Pippin,' 'Ashmead's Kernel,' 'Macoun,' 'Twenty Ounce,' 'Tompkins King,' 'Vandevere,' 'Sops of Wine,' 'Winter Banana,' 'Golden Sweet,' 'Roxbury Russet,' 'Summer Pearmain,' 'Chenango Strawberry,' 'Fameuse' and 'Duchess of Oldenburg.' These and many others are described and offered as budwood or scionwood by BAUM'S NURSERY (R.D. 4, NEW FAIRFIELD, CT 06815); NEW YORK STATE FRUIT TESTING CO-OP ASSN. (GENEVA, NY 14456); WORCESTER COUNTY HORTICULTURAL SOCIETY (30 ELM STREET, WORCESTER, MA 01608); SOUTHMEADOW FRUIT GARDENS (2363 TILBURY PLACE, BIRMINGHAM, MI 48009; CATALOG $1); and HENRY LEUTHARDT (EAST MORICHES, NY 11940; CATALOG 25¢). Also very helpful in locating sources is MILO T. ROBERTS (ROUTE 2, VILLISCA, IA 50864), APPLE VARIETY SOURCES CHAIRMAN OF THE NORTH AMERICAN FRUIT EXPLORERS.

Chinese Che

A fascinating new fruit is under study by Dr. George M. Darrow (OLALLIE FARM, GLENN DALE, MD 20769), retired head of the USDA Small Fruits Division.

The che, *Cudrania tricuspidata*, is a small Oriental tree to 30′, with a spreading top and short spines on many of its branches. It is probably hardy to −20°, and grows readily from root cuttings taken in late fall. In China, where it is called the wild mulberry, the leaves are used to feed silkworms. The 1″ to 1½″ fruits, which ripen through October in Maryland, are dull maroon and soft when fully ripe, and have a unique delightful flavor and rich red flesh. The seeds are very few and less than half the size of apple seed.

The che seems to bear heavily at an early age, and a mature female tree at the BLANDY EXPERIMENTAL FARM (BOYCE, VA 22620) bears hundreds of pounds of fruit in loose clusters of 4 to 8 over the entire tree. Dr. Darrow says, "The sexes are said to be borne on separate trees, but the one tree I have has set well with 3 to 6 seeds per fruit. My tree seems to have no pollen — no male flowers — yet it has again set fruit but the heaviest on the east side where there is a thornless branch. It has set heavily on the thornless part."

Canned Figs

Gardeners seeking unusual plants for tub culture should consider the fig tree. Both as a producer of luscious fruit and as a decorative asset, figs have garden value equaled by few other plants.

Container gardening is the answer where temperatures go below about 15°, to avoid the "bundling" required for winter protection of fig trees planted outdoors. The dwarf everbearing variety is especially suited to growing in large pots or tubs. It bears from early in the season to late autumn, and is similar in compact habit, high production and fruit quality to the popular 'Brown Turkey.' Full sun, rich soil, ample moisture and a deep mulch guarantee good crops. Fertilize in spring only, and winter the plants in a cool, dry basement or similar structure. A source is BOUNTIFUL RIDGE NURSERIES (PRINCESS ANNE, MD 21853).

Where a bold tropical effect is desired, the large, striking leaves, pungently scented in hot weather, make figs a choice ornamental — to say nothing, of course, of providing an emergency source of both food and clothing.

Chinese Confection

The Chinese date or jujube, *Zizyphus jujuba,* deserves more use as a garden fruit. It is hardy to −20°, and although long hot summers are supposedly necessary to mature the fruit, it bears excellent crops in the arboretum of Bernheim Forest, 20 miles south of Louisville, Kentucky. And Clifford H. Dabb of Ogden, Utah, reports that in his garden "they have borne well after cold winters followed by late spring frosts . . . in years when the apples froze.

"The fruit is easily dried if laid in single layers, and may be kept for years. They taste like dried apples. They may be cooked in a sugar syrup, and taste much like a date, as well as look like one." The Chinese jujube is a deciduous shrub or small tree to 20′ or 25′ that begins bearing the first or second year after planting and produces great quantities of 1″ to 2″ round, sweet brown fruit. It has slender prickly branches and small, shiny light-green leaves, and is considered quite ornamental. It is pest-free and tolerates strongly alkaline soil and drought, but yields most abundantly with ample water. Several references state that the fruit is excellent eaten fresh when fully ripe.

The only mail-order source we know is the TENNESSEE NURSERY COMPANY (CLEVELAND, TN 37311).

Peachy Fruits

'Bonanza,' the first true dwarf peach, was introduced a few years ago by ARMSTRONG NURSERIES (BOX 473, ONTARIO, CA 91764). A genetic or natural dwarf, rather than dwarfed by being grafted on stunting rootstock, 'Bonanza' grows only to 6′ and can be pruned much lower, so proves ideal for special effects, limited space and growing in containers. Its double pink spring bloom is as showy as an azalea's, the foliage is highly ornamental and the yellow freestone fruit is slightly larger than that borne by standard trees. Unlike a grafted dwarf peach, 'Bonanza' is as long-lived as a standard peach — 12 to 15 years.

These desirable traits have spurred the breeding of more genetic dwarf fruits. ARMSTRONG has also introduced 'Golden Treasure,' another peach, and 'Nectarina,' the first true dwarf nectarine. Very recently, 'Garden Sun' peach and 'Garden Delight' nectarine made their appearance, through SPRING HILL NURSERIES (TIPP CITY, OH 45371). Another new introduction is 'Stark Starlet' peach, by STARK BRO'S NURSERIES (LOUISIANA, MO 63353). Several others are now listed by wholesale growers.

All these true dwarfs are hardy to −20°, but the fruiting buds can be killed at −10°. In cold climes, therefore, they should be container-grown so they can be moved into a cellar, cool greenhouse or other structure — they must have a minimum of two months at a maximum of 55° for proper functioning.

However, hardier genetic dwarf peaches may be in the offing, through crossing 'Bonanza' or one of the others with the new 'Reliance,' developed by the University of New Hampshire and impressive for its ability to produce excellent crops after −25° winter temperatures. ('Reliance' in standard size is available from J. E. MILLER NURSERIES, CANANDAIGUA, NY 14424, and on dwarfing rootstock from STARK BRO'S.)

There is also a genetic dwarf pie cherry, 'North Star,' which grows 6' to 9' tall. Developed in Minnesota, it is as hardy as the 'Reliance' peach, and also thrives better in the South than other tart cherries. 'North Star' is a heavy bearer, and its dwarfness makes it easy to cover with netting to protect the crop from birds. A source is J. E. MILLER NURSERIES.

Banana of the North

The "hardy banana" or pawpaw has long been due for upgrading, and the efforts of an amateur fruit grower to this end are beginning to bear valuable fruit.

Asimina triloba is a native American fruit, nicknamed the northern banana because of the banana-like texture and flavor of its golden fruit. The only hardy member of the largely tropical custard apple family, the pawpaw is a handsome landscape plant, attaining 10' to 15' when grown with multiple trunks, up to 25' with a single trunk. Its lustrous tropical-looking leaves, 8" to 10" long, turn brilliant yellow in autumn. The fragrant 2" flowers, which appear in midspring, are green when they open, then turn a beautiful maroon-purple. Pawpaws are pest-free, and thrive in moist, deep, rich soils.

The pawpaw's fruit is too perishable for marketing, but is easily grown at home — and the tree is a showy ornamental.

The only named variety now on the market is 'Davis,' hardy to −25° and bearing clusters of 3" to 5" fruits, shaped like very fat bananas and brown-skinned and soft when ripe (available from ZILKE BROTHERS NURSERY, BARODA, MI 49101). But its originator, CORWIN DAVIS (ROUTE 1, BELLEVUE, MI 49021), has since found several superior clones which he is now propagating. One bears fruits weighing 12 ounces each, as compared to the average of less than 6 ounces for other clones.

Peerless Pears

Among garden fruit connoisseurs, pears perhaps rate a notch higher than apples and peaches. The finest pears have meltingly delicious flavor, and the trees have fewer pest problems. Many new varieties are resistant to fireblight, while in nonresistant pears its incidence can be reduced by avoiding excessive pruning and heavy nitrogen fertilization.

Numerous fine pears are becoming available in dwarf sizes, which can be set only 10' apart and are also often ideal for espalier. The USDA-developed early, blight-resistant 'Magness' and 'Moonglow' are highly recommended for the North, and resistant 'Orient' for the South. 'Duchess d'Angouleme' and 'Starkrimson' (STARK BRO'S NURSERIES, LOUISIANA, MO 63353) have been acclaimed for size and excellence of fruit. There is even a coreless pear, 'Cope's Seedless' (BOATMAN'S NURSERY, BAINBRIDGE, OH 45612), but it is not yet obtainable as a dwarf.

These and the ever-popular 'Bartlett,' 'Clapp's Favorite' and 'Seckel' are the most widely offered.

Fruits and Nuts   123

But gardeners seeking truly superb pears should consider such outstanding unusuals as everbearing 'Colette' (J. E. MILLER NURSERIES, CANANDAIGUA, NY 14424), 'Dana Hovey,' 'Marguerite Marillat,' 'Flemish Beauty,' 'Vermont Beauty' and the 'Beurre' series — particularly 'Buerre Bosc,' 'Beurre d'Anjou' and 'Beurre Giffard.' Two sources are HENRY LEUTHARDT NURSERIES (EAST MORICHES, NY 11940; CATALOG 25¢) and SOUTHMEADOW FRUIT GARDENS (2363 TILBURY PLACE, BIRMINGHAM, MI 48009; CATALOG $1).

At least two varieties should always be planted, as even self-fruitful types produce better if cross-pollinated. A sunny, open but not windy site, and a hay, gravel or stone mulch are important for best growth.

Puckerless Persimmons

"99% of Americans," says Robert Rodale in "Organic Gardening," "know persimmons only for their faults." Certainly the wild fruit, unless eaten when dead ripe in winter, is as astringent as a lemon and full of seeds. But the named varieties of American persimmon (Diospyros virginiana) which have become available in recent years have fine flavor and fewer seeds, and ripen much earlier than the wild type. While their fruits are not as large as those of the oriental persimmon (D. kaki), which is hardy to 0°, many consider them more flavorful — and they thrive as far north as the Great Lakes.

They also make fine ornamentals. Growing slowly to about 50', with glossy leaves, somewhat pendulous branches and interesting bark deeply marked in rectangles, they have inconspicuous flowers, but the beautiful red-orange fruit is a highlight of the autumn garden. Unripe fruit can be ripened by putting it in a plastic bag with ripe apples, which give off ethylene gas, for several days. A selection of varieties will yield fruit from September until Christmas.

Oriental persimmon trees are available from BOUNTIFUL RIDGE NURSERIES (PRINCESS ANNE, MD 21853). TALBOTT NURSERY (LINTON, IN 47441) offers several fine varieties of American persimmon, including 'Early Golden' and 'Ennis Seedless.'

Plumdingers

Numerous fine dwarf and standard-size fruiting plums are currently available. Even more popular are the flowering plums such as the purple-leaved cherry plum or myrobalan, Prunus cerasifera pissardi, a dense 20' tree with single pink flowers in spring and edible cherry-like fruit — 'Thundercloud' is a fine cultivar, hardy to −20° and useful for hedges (JACKSON & PERKINS CO., MEDFORD, OR 97501).

Newly popular is P. martima, the beach plum of the Atlantic Coast, a vigorous and handsome shrub to 5'. It is treasured for its profuse white flowers and the deep red fruits which make superb jelly. Hardy to −35°, it has been found to thrive as beautifully inland as on the shore (COLE NURSERY CO., R.D. 1, CIRCLEVILLE, OH 43113; WHOLESALE ONLY — have your nurseryman order).

Quaint Quince

Once a very popular home fruit, the quince, Cydonia oblonga, has been overshadowed by the great number of modern apples, pears, cherries and so on. Yet as an ornamental — especially in flower — it outranks every one of these. Its big pink-blushed blossoms rival those of almost any spring-flowering tree, and its dense furry foliage and many gnarled branches are unusually picturesque.

Standard-size quince trees will grow to 25', but a dwarf quince reaches only 10' to 15'. The best choice for the home garden is the dwarf 'Orange' (KELLY BROS. NURSERIES, DANSVILLE, NY 14437), which bears large golden fruit relatively free of grit. It can be grown in bush or tree form, espaliered or used for hedging, is hardy to −25° and produces a bushel of fruit per mature tree. Most important for a high yield and long life are a fairly heavy, moist soil and minimal use of fertilizer — light soils and high fertility spur rapid growth that is susceptible to fireblight. A permanent mulch of rough compost or hay, and an annual scattering of phosphate rock and wood ashes will adequately feed and protect the shallow roots.

Quinces can be picked just slightly under-ripe and stored in a cool place for 2 to 3 months. They are too astringent to eat raw but may be made into sauce or baked like apples. They also make marvelous jelly, or can be grated and cooked with water and sugar for "quince honey."

BUSH FRUITS

Blueberry Bonanza

Blueberries are very popular garden fruits, due partly to the fantastic yields of grape-size fruit produced by the newest hybrids. But perhaps just as important is their all-year ornamental value. The striking pinkish bell-shaped flowers, crisp green foliage that turns coppery-red in autumn and red-toned twigs in winter are encouraging wider use of cultivated blueberries as hedges and lawn specimens and in foundation plantings and shrub borders.

There are three essentials for maximum beauty and harvest:

Culture — full sun, an open, water-retentive, acid soil (easily provided by liberal additions of acid peat) and a 4″ to 6″ mulch of pine needles, oak leaves, sawdust or similar material. Especially important are applications in early and late spring of complete fertilizer, and liberal watering.

Harvesting — some varieties, such as 'Berkeley' and 'Earliblue,' "sweeten up" as soon as they turn blue, but others need up to a week to develop sweetness. Little ripening occurs after picking, which is why store-bought blueberries, picked by the grower as soon as they become blue, rarely compare in flavor to home-grown. Experts advise picking early in the day.

Pruning — to maintain berry size and quality, prune annually in the dormant season after the plant is about 5 years old. Head back less vigorous canes to strong laterals, eliminate shoots less than 3″ long and prune out the older canes at the crown so that no more than 6 to 8 strong canes remain.

Because cross-pollination gives more, larger and earlier berries, several varieties should be planted. Specialists such as J. HERBERT ALEXANDER (MIDDLEBORO, MA 02346) and RAYNER BROTHERS (SALISBURY, MD 21801) offer the widest selection of hardy early-to-late varieties for months-long harvest. TENNESSEE NURSERY CO. (CLEVELAND, TN 37311) lists 'Homebell,' 'Menditoo' and 'Tifblue,' the new southern "rabbiteye" blueberries successful in North Florida and along the Gulf Coast.

Beach plum's cherry-like fruits, which are easily harvested by shaking them onto a canvas, make marvelous jelly.

Incidentally, Mr. Alexander — whose variety 'Herbert' is regarded as the largest (up to 1″ diameter) and most flavorful blueberry to date — says blueberries are rich in vitamin C, calcium, iron and magnesium, and contain neo-mertylin, a natural sugar desirable for diabetics.

More Cultured Blackberries

With the development of thornless varieties, high-yielding virus-free stock and novelty types, blackberries are becoming an important garden fruit. Some new introductions are unusually decorative: thornless 'Smoothstem' bears huge clusters of pinkish flowers and is nearly evergreen. Blackberries are valued also because they ripen after raspberries and before most tree and vine fruits, thus extending the fruit harvest.

Highly rated among current varieties are 'Darrow,' generally considered the all-around best blackberry for the North and East. Originated by the New York Agricultural Experiment Station, it is hardy to −20°, highly productive, and very flavorful when picked dead ripe. The new self-fertile 'Ebony King' is equally hardy and dependable (both available from BOATMAN'S NURSERY, BAINBRIDGE, OH 45612). 'Snyder' (HENRY FIELD

SEED & NURSERY CO., SHENANDOAH, IA 51602), like the old favorite 'Eldorado,' is virtually coreless.

Less hardy and ripening later than most others are the new USDA-originated thornless, nonsuckering, long-bearing 'Smoothstem' and 'Thornfree' (FIELD). 'Smoothstem' is hardy to 0°, the somewhat more vigorous 'Thornfree' to −10°. Several thornless varieties (though not genetically thornless — new canes coming from the roots have thorns) have been developed for the South and Pacific states, such as 'Thornless Boysen' (IN LOCAL NURSERIES). For Florida, thorny 'Flordagard' and 'Oklawaha' are superior in quality and yields. Finally, two unusuals are the "everbearing tree" blackberry, growing 6′ to 8′ high, and the "white" blackberry, which bears creamy-white mild-flavored berries (both from ZILKE BROTHERS NURSERY, BARODA, MI 49101).

Blackberries should have deep, well-drained soil, an organic mulch and considerable moisture in the 2 or 3 weeks before ripening. They are trained to a trellis, fence or pergola, and each year after fruiting, all suckers, weak canes and canes that have borne fruit are pruned out. Leave no more than 12 to 16 strong new canes. In spring, before growth starts, side branches are pruned back to 12″ to 18″.

Better Raspberries

The first red raspberry for warm, humid areas is now available. 'Southland' has thrived in tests from North Carolina to Arkansas, thus extending much further south the range of the red raspberry, northern America's second most popular fruit (after the strawberry). 'Southland' ripens its spring crop at about the same time as the very early 'Sunrise' and also produces a good fall crop beginning in mid-August.

Best of the new northern varieties, according to many reports, are 'Fallred,' which ripens its heavy fall crop much earlier than other everbearers; 'Clyde,' a summer-bearing purple raspberry superior in vigor and yield to all previous purples; 'Allen,' a fine one-crop black raspberry for jam; and 'Fallgold,' an everbearing yellow many gardeners hail as the most delicious of all raspberries. A source for these is J. E. MILLER NURSERY (CANANDAIGUA, NY 14424).

'Darrow' is one of the finest of the new high-yielding varieties which are making blackberries a valuable garden fruit.

Much recent research on raspberry culture emphasizes the value of mulch — a deep mulch, of leaves, hay, sawdust, wood chips, etc. For everbearers, a new idea is cutting back all canes to the ground after harvest, which will result in the new canes yielding a heavy crop for 3 months from late summer through fall, rather than for several weeks in summer followed by a light fall crop.

Cherry Bushes

The better bush cherries have a fine reputation in the Great Plains states, and gardeners elsewhere are beginning to discern their virtues. Very hardy and productive, they are excellent ornamentals, with lustrous foliage, white flowers in abundance and red to purple fruits good for pies and jams.

Best known is the Western sandcherry, *Prunus besseyi*, 4′ to 6′. The top varieties — 'Black Beauty,' 'Brooks,' 'Sioux' and 'Hansen' — bear early and heavily. Nanking cherry, *P. tomentosa*, grows 6′ to 8′ and is often used for hedges. An improved, large-fruiting Nanking, 'Drilea,' is listed by GURNEY SEED & NURSERY CO. (YANKTON, SD 57078), which also offers the best sandcherries. BURGESS SEED & PLANT CO. (BOX 218, GALESBURG, MI 49053) offers its exclusive Himalayan bush cherry (*P. jacquemontii*), a 3′ shrub that produces bright red cherries which can be eaten fresh, and which last in good condition on the bush for a month.

Even better bush cherries may be in the offing, for there are several of ornamental and edible merit that have as yet only been cursorily investigated, such as the Korean (*P. japonica*) and Mongolian (*P. fruticosa*) cherries. The cherry-plums also offer great possibilities. 'Oka' and 'Compass' (available from GURNEY) are two that grow 6′ to 8′ and bear over 1″ fruit. MR. PERCY H. WRIGHT (409 109TH STREET, SASKATOON, SASKATCHEWAN) has a selection, 'Wessex,' from a cross between an improved sandcherry and a Manchurian plum, about which he says, "I am happy enough about 'Wessex' that I feel my life would have been worth living had I originated nothing else." 'Wessex' is hardy to −60°, grows as an erect tree to 8′ or 9′ and its reddish freestone fruit "hangs on and dries up like a prune, so that it can be eaten with relish up to 3 weeks after fully ripe."

Elderberry Bounty

Though the wild elderberry (*Sambucus canadensis*) is falling prey in many areas to urbanization and herbicides, improved cultivated varieties are appearing increasingly.

They have much to recommend them. Growing only 5′ to 6′ tall — instead of 10′ — and less sprawling than the wild type, they have great ornamental value in the shrub border, groupings or hedges. All are heavy bearers of flowers, fragrant and ivory-white in early summer, and of the purple-black fruits so attractive to birds and prized for jams, jellies, juice and pie. The fruits, incidentally, are excelled in vitamin C content only by black currants and rose hips.

Highly rated varieties such as 'Adams,' 'Johns' and 'York' are obtainable from ZILKE BROTHERS NURSERY (BARODA, MI 49101).

A Gander at Gooseberries

In England, more than 1000 gooseberry varieties are commonly grown. Gardeners prize them both for the delicious fruit — best picked when dead ripe for eating "out of hand" — and for their ornamental value. Gooseberries are regarded as handsome shrubs for fencerow, border and foundation plantings. And in the finest gardens they can be seen trained to single stems and grown as standards.

Only now are gooseberries beginning to attract American gardeners. The European type (*Ribes grossularia*) has been considered difficult to grow, and the American (*R. hirtellum*) was small-fruited, thorny and rarely achieved its potential because it was usually relegated to poor soils. Our native gooseberry, however, is rapidly being improved. 'Pixwell,' a North Dakota Experiment Station selection, bears heavily, with the berries "underslung" on the branches for easy picking. The University of Minnesota's 'Welcome' has few thorns but large berries (available from HENRY FIELD SEED & NURSERY CO., SHENANDOAH, IA 51601).

Both European and American gooseberries do best on rich, heavy, moist but well-drained soil. This is vital for the European type, as is some shade from midday sun, particularly in the southern part (USDA Zone 7) of their range. All gooseberries respond magnificently to a deep mulch, plus high-nitrogen fertilizer every spring.

Pruning consists of removing weak canes and all canes over three years old in the fall. With European gooseberries, maintaining an open head helps to discourage powdery mildew, but this can also be prevented easily by regular use of a fungicide such as Karathane.

A source of European varieties — some with berries almost as big as eggs — is SOUTHMEADOW FRUIT GARDENS (2363 TILBURY PLACE, BIRMINGHAM, MI 48009; CATALOG $1). A special note: the number of areas where gooseberries are prohibited (because they are host to a stage of white pine blister rust) has greatly decreased, but check with the dealer before ordering.

VINE FRUITS

Viticultural Revival

Grapes are first-class dual-purpose plants, trainable on a great variety of structures, and giving dense, compact growth. The fruit, of course, is a superb decorative asset — the new 'Aurora,' for example, adds glowing pink to the white, amber, green, red and blue grapes already available. And no other fruit provides such an amazing range of flavors and uses.

Two decades of concentrated research are yielding superior garden grapes of every type. Many are available from KELLY BROS. NURSERIES (DANSVILLE, NY 14437) — northern bunch grapes, hardy to −15°; and OWEN'S NURSERY (GAY, GA 30218) — southern muscadines, hardy to near 0°. Muscadine bunch grape hybrids, by the way, combining the best characteristics of each type, may soon be available, reports breeder Robert T. Dunstan (Route 1, Alachua, FL 32615).

A unique enterprise, begun as a hobby, now offers the country's largest selection of vines of American-type dessert grapes. James W. Humphreys' "vitisetum" — a word he coined for his "collection of grapevines established for the edification of the public" — is known as SHILOH NURSERY (BOX 221, SHILOH, OH 44878).

Mr. Humphreys has assembled 200 varieties of grapes, concentrating on very fine old and new grapes which are ignored by commercial growers because of marketing difficulties. His lists include, for example, 'Worden,' a seedling of 'Concord' and superior to it for both table and wine; 'Captivator,' one of the superb hybrids by T. V. Munson and "among the top ten for dessert"; the very early ripening 'Portland,' of incomparable flavor; and 'Diamond,' a "sprightly, sweet, melting champagne grape." He provides cultural directions with every order, and can supply pamphlets on all aspects of viticulture, fruit growing and gardening.

Strawberry Shortcut

Although strawberries are America's favorite home-grown fruit, few gardeners achieve the maximum yields of top-size fruit — and most of them work far too hard at it, to boot.

Some valuable tips can be gleaned from commercial growers' practices. In addition to full sun and adequate drainage, the main factors in high production are very high fertility and humus levels, mulch and proper utilization of runners. A strawberry bed should have liberal amounts of fertilizer and organic matter, such as peat, leafmold, compost or rotted manure, incorporated in the initial building of the bed, and additional fertilizer applied every spring. A 2″ mulch of wood chips, sawdust, straw, grass clippings, etc., will conserve moisture, reduce weeds and keep the berries clean.

California growers are producing up to 50,000 quarts per acre of everbearing strawberries on raised 2- and 3-row beds, never allowing the plants to set runners. Best work-saving system for the gardener is planting in a 3-row bed, with rows 1′ apart and plants set 3′ apart in the row, and allowing two of the earliest runners from each plant to remain, one up and one down the row. These will replace the original plants the second year, and thereafter only single runners from occasional plants will be needed to maintain the bed. This eliminates replanting, and gives spring-through-fall production because little if any strength is taken away from the leaves to make runners.

"The Apple Kitchen Cookbook," $1.50 from New York and New England Apple Institute (Box 320, Westfield, MA 01085)

"Dwarfed Fruit Trees," by Harold B. Tukey (Macmillan, $15)

"Fruits for the Home Garden," by Ken and Pat Kraft (Morrow, $6.95)

"Growing Unusual Fruit," by Alan E. Simmons (Walker, $10)

"Small Fruits for the Home Garden," by J. H. Clarke (Doubleday, $4.95)

FRIENDLY FRUITIERS

The American Pomological Society, America's oldest fruit organization, publishes a quarterly journal and provides other useful services to its members; details from Dr. L. D. Tukey, Secretary-Treasurer (103 Tyson Building, University Park, PA 16802). California Rare Fruit Growers (c/o Paul H. Thomson, Star Route, Bonsall, CA 92003) is a new organization for hobbyists, with special emphasis on subtropical fruits.

The catalog of the New York State Fruit Testing Cooperative Association (Geneva, NY 14456), a non-profit 5000-member organization that tests new fruits recommended for trial by the New York State Agricultural Experiment Station and others, describes a great many superior fruits of all types for home gardens. Those available at very reasonable prices range from some especially worthy old varieties to the newest introductions, and include many hard to find elsewhere.

The North American Fruit Explorers (Robert Kurle, Secretary, 87th and Madison, Hinsdale, IL 60521) serves as a clearinghouse for information on all types of fruits, publishes an invaluable quarterly, "North American Pomona," and has an excellent book exchange.

The Southern Fruit Council (R.R. 3, Box 40, Summit, MS 39666) aids gardeners interested in growing fruit in the somewhat difficult conditions of the Deep South.

NUTS

Hazels, Filberts . . . and Filazels

Several ornamental species of hazel or filbert are deservedly popular — Corylus columa, Turkish tree hazel; 'Harry Lauder's Walking Stick,' C. avellana contorta; and the purple-leaved filbert, C. maxima purpurea. But the shrubby edible-nut types are rarely seen in gardens.

The American hazelnut, C. americana, 5' to 7', reliably produces small but delicious nuts where temperatures go down to − 30°. European hazel or filbert, C. avellana, to 15', is hardy to about − 20°, but even its best varieties such as 'Barcelona' and 'Royal' produce scant crops in cold areas where spring frosts kill the catkins. However, where hardy these are valuable as specimens, backgrounds in the shrub border, hedges and screens, as well as for the occasional crops they supply for the gardener and wildlife. All the hazels should be maintained at 5 or 6 trunks, and two varieties are needed for cross-pollination. The above are available from EMLONG NURSERIES (STEVENSVILLE, MI 49127).

Breeders are beginning to improve both cropping and landscape values. THE NEW YORK AGRICULTURAL EXPERIMENT STATION (GENEVA, NY 14456) has crossed American and European hazels to produce larger nuts and greater hardiness — 'Bixby,' 'Buchanan,' 'Potomac' and 'Reed' are the most promising under test. Even more interesting are the hybrids developed by J. U. Gellatly of GELLATLY BROS. (WESTBANK, BRITISH COLUMBIA), who crossed European filberts with the beaked hazel, which is hardy to − 50°. Some of his "filazels" have borne heavy crops of large nuts despite − 25° winter temperatures. Mr. Gellatly has also interbred Turkish, Chinese (C. chinensis) and Indian (C. jacquemontii) tree hazels to achieve handsome high-yielding trees.

Valentine to the Heartnut

One of the most ornamentally valuable of all nut trees is the heartnut, Juglans sieboldiana cordifor-

mis, writes Consulting Arborist Homer L. Jacobs in "Arboretum Leaves," published by the Holden Arboretum, Mentor, Ohio.

This variety of the Siebold or Japanese walnut grows to 50′ or 60′, wide-branching so that it is almost as broad as tall. The abundant compound leaves, up to 2′ long with more than a dozen leaflets, give the tree a fascinating tropical look, as do the long strings of nuts. Mr. Jacobs notes two other attractions: the delicately colored male catkins, often 12″ in length, borne just back of the new spring shoots, and tiny, two-plumed pink-tipped female flowers at the shoot ends.

Hardy to −20°, the heartnut is a rapid grower which bears while quite young — "grafted trees often producing a few nuts in the third or fourth year after being planted out from the nursery." Unlike the Japanese walnut, the heartnut has a smooth, easy-to-crack shell and few kernel cavities, so that the tasty kernels often can be extracted in halves or even whole. A source is ZILKE BROTHERS NURSERY (BARODA, MI 49101).

A leading breeder and supplier of heartnut trees is J. U. Gellatly of GELLATLY BROS. (WESTBANK, BRITISH COLUMBIA). Especially promising are some of his new crosses between the larger selected heartnuts and the best cracking butternuts (*Juglans cinerea*) such as 'Dunoka' and 'Fioka.'

New Pecans and Hicans

The pecan (*Carya illinoensis*) has become a very popular dual-purpose tree throughout the South. Superior cultivars such as 'Hastings,' 'Stuart,' 'Mahan' and the new 'Desirable' and 'Harris Super' (H. G. HASTINGS CO., BOX 4088, ATLANTA, GA 30302) are widely planted in home landscapes for their fine ornamental value and delicious nuts. Incidentally, though pecans have a very high oil content, most of the oil is unsaturated.

Pecans are large trees — at least 50′ — but the USDA Pecan Field Station (Brownwood, TX 76801) is working toward dwarf varieties. Most current research, however, is aimed at developing "northern" pecans. While many pecan trees are hardy to −20°, nuts are produced only with a long growing season and sustained summer heat. Some new varieties which will mature nuts with as few as 160 frost-free days are 'Colby' (BOATMAN'S NURSERY, BAINBRIDGE, OH 45612), 'Peruque' (BOATMAN'S), 'Starking Hardy Giant' and 'Major' (STARK BRO'S NURSERIES, LOUISIANA, MO 63353).

Hicans, crosses of pecan with shellbark (*C. laciniosa*) or shagbark (*C. ovata*) hickories, are equally handsome trees and bear very flavorful nuts — and some varieties mature even earlier than northern pecans. Two readily available hicans are 'Clarksville' and 'Gerardi' (BOUNTIFUL RIDGE NURSERIES, PRINCESS ANNE, MD 21853).

Pecans and hicans require rich moist soils and good air circulation. Since they have long tap-roots, the planting hole should be dug at least 3′ to 4′ deep, and the soil enriched with organic matter for improved aeration and drainage. Two varieties are needed for cross-pollination.

Big, Bountiful Nut Tree

The many excellent varieties of Carpathian walnut — a hardy strain of the English or Persian walnut, *Juglans regia* — are bringing this relatively new tree much deserved attention. A superb round-headed lawn or street specimen growing to 40′ to 60′, it has large, glossy, pleasingly fragrant foliage, gray-white bark and strong branching. Since it is tap-rooted, it will neither clog sewer lines nor hamper grass growth beneath it.

Originating in Poland, Russia and Germany, Carpathian walnut has many cultivars hardy to at least −25°. The nuts of the best varieties are as flavorful as those of the Spanish and French cultivars grown in California. The best clones also have been selected for late blooming to escape spring frosts, and for high production of thin-shelled, well-filled kernels in climates with short, cool summers. Some are self-pollinating, and all will produce up to 6 bushels of nuts per tree when mature. Grafted trees generally begin to bear within 2 years. Harvesting is easy, as the nuts fall free of the husks, which wither and cause no litter problems.

Carpathians stand poor soil but will benefit from spring feeding and a mulch. They are best planted on slight slopes for cold air drainage. Some sources are BOUNTIFUL RIDGE NURSERIES (PRINCESS ANNE, MD 21853), ZILKE BROTHERS NURSERY (BARODA, MI 49101), EARL FERRIS NURSERY (HAMPTON, IA 50441), and H. G. HASTINGS CO. (BOX 4088, ATLANTA, GA 30302).

Nut Tree Guide

"THE HANDBOOK OF NORTH AMERICAN NUT TREES," PUBLISHED BY THE NORTHERN NUT GROWERS ASSOCIATION (4518 HOLSTON MILLS ROAD, KNOXVILLE, TN 37914; $7.50), contains 32 chapters of information on varieties, culture, propagation, breeding, landscape uses and wildlife plantings.

GROUNDWORK
-soil, water, fertilizer

SOIL

Remodeling Clay

Improving tight, sticky clay soil requires the arduous addition of copious organic matter — or does it? Actually, the transformation to mellow granulated soil can be accomplished without turning a spade. Gypsum is the answer.

Clay soil is packed, airless and "puddly" because of an excess of sodium. Adsorbed on the clay particles, this sodium makes each particle strongly attract water. As the water drains away, the particles are left tightly packed like thin plates, with very little pore space for air.

The adsorbed sodium can only be removed from the soil particles by chemical exchange with hydrogen, magnesium or calcium ions. It is impractical to supply hydrogen by making the soil strongly acid. Providing magnesium by adding Epsom salts (magnesium sulfate) won't work because the magnesium quickly leaches away or becomes insoluble. Limestone (calcium carbonate) is slow acting and can raise soil pH undesirably.

Gypsum (calcium sulfate), however, is ideal, providing ample calcium without altering the pH. It exchanges its calcium ions for the sodium ions, and the clay particles soon separate into aggregates or popcorn-like "crumbs" that leave large pore spaces in the soil. The gypsum is simply spread on the soil surface, mulch or lawn at any time of year, at the rate of 50 pounds per 1000 square feet. Its rate of penetration is about 6″ a year, and annual applications for 3 years are generally recommended. It should also be mixed in liberally with the soil in planting holes. Incidentally, the calcium it supplies is an important nutrient, often lacking in modern "pure" fertilizers.

Gypsum for garden use is available at garden supply outlets.

Two other new cures for hardpan or claypan: one or more applications of a wetting agent, such as Water-In (WATER-IN, INC., BOX 421, ALTADENA, CA 91001); and augering holes throughout the area and filling these with organic matter such as rough peat or compost. Useful for the latter method is the 24″ Jisco Jumbo Professional Auger, which fits a ⅜″ or ½″ electric drill and makes holes 2″ in diameter (JOHNSON'S INDUSTRIAL SUPPLY COMPANY, 1941 KARLIN DRIVE, ST. LOUIS, MO 63131).

Sand Stratagem

Here's a way to build soil quickly from pure sand: Dig out the bed 24″ deep, lay a sheet of roofing paper on the bottom, then put in a 12″ layer of organic matter such as peat, compost, leafmold or straw mixed with some soil and fertilizer. Replace the sand, and plant. The paper will hold the soil-building materials until the plants make sufficient fibrous roots to bind the mass, then it will disintegrate.

Salty Wisdom

A heavy concentration of soluble salts in the soil results from over-fertilization or too frequent fertilization; from "hard" water; from poor drainage; or from frequent light waterings that draw the salts to the surface, then evaporate, leaving them to accumulate. Often "mystery" ailments of plants, both indoor and outdoor, can be traced to this concentration of salts.

Where soluble salt levels are too high, seeds may fail to germinate or plants fail to grow properly or be killed by the accumulation of salt in the soil. To leach out or wash the salts downward, flood the area with about 5″ of water or apply water slowly so that the water will move downward to a depth of 18″ to 24″. Soils that are heavy-textured or high in clay content will be difficult to leach, and in some cases it may be desirable to apply gypsum to facilitate the movement of the salts downward.

Tiller Buyers' Guidelines

For easy tilling, for mixing in organic matter, fertilizer, green manure and cover crops, for rebuilding lawns and reclaiming wild land, a properly chosen rotary tiller can do the work of 7 or 8 strong men.

Sufficient horsepower is most important. For light soils, 3 hp can be adequate, but for heavy clays a minimum of 5 hp and close to 300 pounds of machine weight are considered necessary. Most tillers have front-mounted tines, but greater stability and ease of handling is conferred by tillers with rear tines. A reverse gear adds to maneuverability and allows quick removal of wedged objects. Easy adjustment of the tilling depth, and of tilling width if narrow areas must be worked, is also important. Some tillers offer a choice of tines for various uses, furrowers, snow plow attachments, and even electric starting.

Before buying, study the capabilities of every tiller available in light of the soil and layout situation of your garden. Some dealers and manufacturers: GARDEN WAY MFG. CO. (102ND STREET & NINTH AVENUE, TROY, NY 12180); JOHN DEERE (MOLINE, IL 61265); MERRY MFG. CO. (EDMONDS, WA 98020); MONTGOMERY WARD (ALBANY, NY 12201 — ask for Lawn, Garden & Farm catalog); and ROTO-HOE COMPANY (NEWBURY, OH 44065).

Soil Problems with Canned Plants

Container production of nursery stock, generally in soilless media, has made trees and shrubs available and plantable all through the growing season. But many gardeners have had disappointing results with "canned plants." Indeed, the plants often desiccate and rapidly die — all because of the little-understood interface problem.

A heavy green manure crop is quickly turned under by a rotary tiller to improve soil tilth and fertility.

WATER

According to Dr. John J. McGuire, in an article in "Rhode Island Resources," the lightweight medium becomes dry much more rapidly than the surrounding soil in which it is planted. When this occurs, the root ball shrinks away from the soil, leaving an air space between the root ball and the soil.

Several cultural practices will minimize this hazardous condition, says Dr. McGuire. The lightweight ball should be gently disturbed before it is planted, so that the larger roots are spread out into the soil. The lightweight ball also should be watered much more often than the surrounding soil, and a mulch is useful to reduce the rate of drying. It is also helpful if the soil immediately surrounding the container ball is modified to include the ingredients in the ball, such as peatmoss and perlite.

Water Ways

Watering, it has been said, is the most complex but least understood of all gardening processes. Fallacies abound, such as the one that lawns and gardens should not be watered when the sun is brightest and hottest. Horticulturist Andre Viette says that midday watering is actually beneficial, since it increases humidity around the plants and cools the leaves, decreasing transpiration.

This eliminates "incipient wilting," the temporary midday wilting from which plants recover in evening. And — contrary to another common belief — this transient wilting does harm plants: any stress affects growth, and a plant checked in any way, even for a very short period, will never achieve its potential.

An octogenarian gardener once told us he believed half the secret of a green thumb is the gardener's "environmental eye" — his observance of sun, wind and humidity conditions, and his tailoring of watering to them. The other half is management of his soil's moisture-holding and transmitting ability. This involves insuring ample organic matter to at least a 15″ to 18″ depth, and mulching.

Groundwork — Soil, Water, Fertilizer   133

New Soaker System

Newest technique for achieving the much-desired "optimum environment" for plants is drip irrigation. Developed in Israel, it is being hailed here as a tremendous breakthrough, as important as the discovery of mulching. It saves water and work, and increases both the growth rate and the quality of plants.

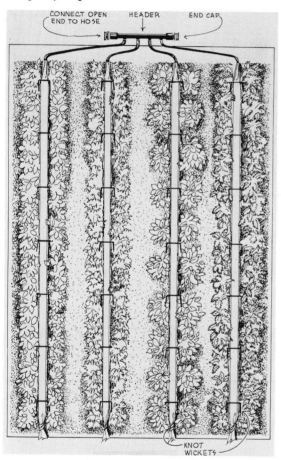

Viaflo ooze hose is easily installed to water a garden area completely and uniformly.

Drip irrigation is a system of maintaining root zone moisture between saturation and field capacity through the growing season. The moisture stress that occurs with natural cycles of rain or irrigation is eliminated — the plant has sufficient moisture constantly, instead of being alternately too wet or too dry. The result is faster growth of ornamentals, and yield increases of 30% to 100% for fruits and vegetables.

Actually, drip irrigation is a much more efficient version of the "soil soaker" hoses gardeners use, and the "spaghetti tube" container-watering systems used in nurseries and greenhouses. It employs emitters or "droppers," set in rigid or flexible pipe, to supply water very slowly to the root zone. No runoff can occur, and no water is wasted outside the root zone. The system can be installed on the soil surface or underground and on slopes. A fertilizer injector is usually incorporated to provide constant feeding and allow the application of systemic pesticides. Soluble salts rarely are a problem because they are diluted by the high soil moisture.

Additional information is found in *"PROCEEDINGS OF DRIP-IRRIGATION SEMINAR" (AGRICULTURAL EXTENSION SERVICE, UNIVERSITY OF CALIFORNIA, BUILDING 4, 5555 OVERLAND AVENUE, SAN DIEGO, CA 92123)* and also in literature by the equipment manufacturers CHAPIN WATERMATICS (BOX 298, WATERTOWN, NY 13601); SPEARS MFG. CO. (2840 NORTH MIAMI, BURBANK, CA 91504); SUB'TERRAIN IRRIGATION CO. (1740 SOUTH ZEYN STREET, ANAHEIM, CA 92802); and WATERSAVER SYSTEMS (BOX 2037, POMONA, CA 91766).

Totally automated operation of drip equipment, as well as of conventional sprinkler systems, is attainable with a line of electronic moisture-sensing controllers made by AGTRONICS MFG. CO. (BOX 1248, BARSTOW, CA 92311). Aquastat is a specialized computer, utilizing solid state circuitry, that monitors soil moisture by remote buried sensors. These continually feed back information to the control unit, which is programmed to open the proper control valves. Models — some under $100 — are available for single-station to 26-station controllers.

Micro-Por Hose, by BORG-WARNER COMPANY (200 SOUTH MICHIGAN AVENUE, CHICAGO, IL 60604), is made from acrylonitrile butadiene styrene, a porous plastic which has about 1000 microscopic holes in each foot of its length. Under low pressure, water oozes through these holes, seeping at a steady rate into the soil. The hose is buried from a few inches to 18″ deep, depending on the plants grown and soil character, which also determine the distance between lines of hose. A "grid" in any pattern is easily set up with couplings, tees and end caps, and a filter installed in the connection to the garden hose supplying the water will prevent clogging by impurities.

Du Pont's new Viaflow Irrigation Tubing, an ooze hose which can be installed above or below ground, is available from BRIGHTON BY-PRODUCTS CO. (BOX 23, NEW BRIGHTON, PA 15066), or as a Garden Watering Kit to cover 625 square feet, $14.95 from DU PONT COMPANY (WILMINGTON, DE 19898).

Pinpoint Watering

Soaker hoses, since they emit water over their entire length, can be wasteful when it is necessary to run them over paths, lawns and other areas where water is not wanted. A better solution might be the new Sprinkler Spikes (SIMPLER COMPANY, BOX 868, SARATOGA, CA 95070). These are simply hammered into garden hose near the plants to be watered, and are adjustable for direction and amount of spray.

Chapin's Spray Stakes and Spin Stakes (CHAPIN WATERMATICS, BOX 298, WATERTOWN, NY 13601) also provide an easily set-up and semi-permanent system for placing water where it is wanted. The 360° Spray Stakes, in 10" to 36" lengths, will water areas up to 8' wide, and models covering 180° are available. They may also be used for mist propagation. Spin Stakes, in 16" to 30" sizes, cover beds from 3' to 12' wide.

Water Beds

The ultimate in watering systems for beds, borders, lawns, planters, golf courses, etc., appears to have arrived. Developed by Dr. W. H. Daniel of Purdue University, the Purr-Wick Rootzone System aims for optimum soil moisture at all times through a reservoir maintained in the subsoil.

The Purr-Wick concept involves excavating the area to a depth of 12" or more, enclosing this with a wooden border or berm, and lining it with polyethylene sheeting. Perforated pipe is laid across this, the perforations covered by screening and gravel to prevent their becoming plugged. The pipe extends through the border frame to a drain pit which supplies or removes moisture as needed.

A 6" layer of sand is then laid over the pipe, to provide a "subsoil" through which the water is distributed to roots by capillary action. This is topped with a growing mix — in tests of the system for lawns by California State Polytechnic College, the "topsoil" is a 3-1-1 mix of sand-shredded bark-digested sewage sludge.

The Purr-Wick Rootzone System has also been tested by the Kansas City Department of Parks and Recreation. Flower beds were dug 18" deep and lined with 4 mil polyethylene sheeting with all overlaps carefully sealed. Perforated drain-pipe was laid on this and extended through the plastic to a standpipe in a bottomless concrete box. This controls the height of the water in the bed. The bed was then filled with washed sand, compacted by watering, and 2" of peat with slow-release fertilizer was mixed into the top 2" of bed.

The researchers report that three months after planting, the plants in the Purr-Wick beds were twice the size and had four times as many roots as plants in conventional soil beds. Weed growth was far less, and the Purr-Wick beds required far less watering. Water was given only when the level in the standpipe fell below its top, which occurred only in droughts.

Tempering Water

Water temperature is useful in controlling growth. The principle is simple: cold water slows growth, warm speeds it. In winter, serious checks in growth result from direct application of main or well water, which is usually between 32° and 50°. But when it is warmed to the optimum temperature of 90°, says the Danbury School of Horticulture of the Federal Correctional Institution in Danbury, Connecticut, "the cell characteristics are speeded above normal growth until the soil's cooling effect slows reaction to the norm . . . If 5 hours within any 24 hours is lost growing time, and it can be gained with the use of 90° water, then 150 hours each month in active do, and so does not reduce growth. In fact, the manufacturer states, the reduction of transpiration, plus an additive which screens out harmful sun rays, actually promote growth: Plantgard-treated gloxinias were 150% larger than untreated ones.

Plantgard is also reported to serve as a protective shield against salt spray, air pollutants and chewing insects, to extend the active life of insecticides and to protect against frost damage — Plantgard-coated begonias held at 27° for six hours were unharmed.

growing time is added to each 30 days with daily watering." The School reports that stock *(Mathiola incana)* given 90° water matured 5 weeks earlier than plants that were given water at ordinary greenhouse temperatures.

Similar dramatic speeding of seed germination by warm water has been noted by Dr. W. H. Carlson of Michigan State University. Horticulturists also suggest that warm water could speed root regeneration in transplants. And in tests in Oregon and Washington, 90° irrigation water from power plants hastened growth of beans, strawberries, asparagus and melons, enabling growers to bring them to market earlier.

Controlling water temperatures should be a useful tool for exhibitors, too — cold water will slow down a plant maturing too rapidly for a show, while warm can be employed to speed up a behind-schedule plant.

Wilt-Proofing

Antitranspirants — "wilt-proofing" compounds — reduce moisture loss by transpiration from leaves. They prevent winter drying injury, and aid in transplanting by decreasing transpiration until roots are established. Wilt-Pruf *(NURSERY SPECIALTY PRODUCTS, 410 GREENWICH AVENUE, GREENWICH, CT 06830)* is probably the best-known and most widely available antitranspirant.

An antitranspirant product that also helps in stimulating growth is Plantgard *(POLYMETRICS INTERNATIONAL, 919 THIRD AVENUE, NEW YORK, NY 10022)*. Described as a "breathable polymer with unique additives," it forms a long-lasting clear film which decreases the rate of moisture loss from indoor and outdoor plants by more than 50%. However, it does not block the normal exchange of carbon dioxide and oxygen through the leaves, as other film-forming antitranspirants

Evaporative Cooling

Every gardener knows how plants "perk up" after a shower or sprinkling on a hot day. But the actual plant growth benefits of evaporative cooling — long a useful greenhouse technique — are revealed by research by Dr. C. R. Unrath of the Department of Horticultural Science at North Carolina State University.

Working in an apple orchard, Dr. Unrath used an overtree sprinkling system, set to operate whenever the temperature rose above 87° and supplying just sufficient water to match the evaporation rate so as to avoid excessive soil watering. The results were increased size and weight of fruit, earlier coloring and one week earlier harvest, and a 50% reduction in cork spot and bitter pit disorders. Dr. Unrath found that on a 95° day, apples may register 120°, and the cooling lowered the fruit temperature by an average 12°.

How Well Is Your Water?

Both amateur and commercial gardeners' publications have been warning that water quality is as important as quantity. Where otherwise unexplainable ailments plague garden or indoor plants, an analysis from your local Water Department may be in order (where a home well is the source, or a pond or creek is used for irrigation, a water analysis can be obtained from a commercial testing laboratory, or sometimes from the soil testing laboratory at a college of agriculture).

Sprinkler spikes, which can be hammered into any plastic hose, save water by directing it where it is needed.

Too high acidity or alkalinity and excess of one or more mineral salts can cause many problems. High or low pH, for example, reduces availability of certain trace elements, and excess sodium causes deficiency of calcium and potassium and also breaks down the soil structure. A change in fertilizing practice may be necessary, or even a new source of water — the old rain barrel is still a valuable tool, or in extreme cases the indoor gardener can use distilled water. Incidentally, water softeners should be avoided, except those which work on the ion-exchange principle.

FERTILIZER

New Feeding Philosophy

"Feed the soil in the fall, the plant in the spring," is the new rule. There is much evidence that late fall — after frost — application of fertilizer greatly improves the growth of ornamentals the following year.

Dr. Harold B. Tukey of New York State College of Agriculture at Cornell University has found that in spring the air may be warm enough to stimulate growth but the soil is still cold, and roots are unable to take up nutrients applied then. This hampers growth. But if fertilizer is applied in the fall, nutrients will have been carried up in the plant during the winter, all the way to the apical buds where they can be immediately utilized when air temperatures rise. Roots are able to absorb nutrients in winter whenever temperatures in the soil around them exceed about 35°.

For plants such as forsythia that require a rapid spring flush of growth, Dr. Tukey states, fall fertilization plus a foliar feeding just as growth starts results in extremely vigorous growth. Foliar feeding in late fall, incidentally, has been shown in other experiments to reduce winter injury in broad-leaved evergreens, and also helps them maintain good color.

For flower beds and the vegetable garden, follow the farmer's practice of applying phosphorus, potash and lime in the fall, but holding off nitrogen — which is easily leached out — until spring.

Three-Season Booster Feeding

Commercial growers are finding valuable new applications for foliar feeding. The practice of feeding plants through their leaves, of course, is an old one — estate gardeners long ago sprayed their finest plants regularly with dilute manure and coal soot solutions. More recently, foliar feeding has been proved to have these benefits:

It gives quick results in correcting obvious nutrient deficiency problems, such as chlorosis due to insufficient iron or nitrogen . . . it is advantageous where getting fertilizer to the roots is difficult, as with trees growing in paved areas . . . early spring foliar feeding spurs growth, which otherwise would be restricted because the soil is too cold for the absorption of nutrients by the roots . . . it similarly compensates in summer for decreased nutrient uptake in excessively wet or dry spells . . . and foliar feeding in late summer through autumn keeps plants green and sturdy without the stimulation of soft, easily winterkilled growth that nitrogen applied to the soil then can cause.

Now nurserymen have found that foliar feeding in combination with the new slow-release soil fertilizers gives amazing results. The foliar sprays enable newly planted stock to continue undiminished growth until new roots form, and the phosphorus they supply speeds formation of new roots. Then continued foliar applications serve as a "booster," supplementing the slow-release fertilizers to maintain a high rate of healthy growth. This booster effect has been demonstrated with young to mature plants of all types, from trees to tomatoes to bedding plants.

Since foliar nutrients can be absorbed only when the plant surface is moist, they should be applied frequently in weak solutions, preferably when humidity is high, and early in the day. Use the finest spray possible for even wetting of the entire plant. Use only fertilizers specified on the label for foliar use; many may be combined with pesticides.

Fertility Pills

The trend definitely is to controlled-release fertilizers. Combining the slow action of organics with the concentrated content of chemical fertilizers, they "meter" nutrients depending on temperature and moisture, are not lost by rapid leaching, and do not easily burn roots if overapplied.

These useful products are now available in small quantities and numerous formulations. Some of the most useful forms of Osmocote and Agriform (SIERRA CHEMICAL CO., BOX 275, NEWARK, CA 94560) include Osmocote 18-6-12, which feeds boxes, beds, and hanging baskets for 8 months . . . "The Pill," Agriform 20-10-5, for trees and shrubs, feeding up to 2 years . . . and "The Mini-Pill," Agriform 14-4-6, feeding 3 to 4 months, for house and patio plants in 4″ to 8″ pots.

Magamp (GEO. J. BALL, INC., WEST CHICAGO, IL 60185) is a 7-40-6 formula for soil incorporation to feed all types of plants for a full year. Eeesy Grow (S & D PRODUCTS, BOX 66, PRAIRIE DU CHIEN, WI 53821), developed at the University of Wisconsin, is available in packets that feed for one, three, five or eight years.

Two points should be noted for best results with these fertilizers. Some of them do not supply any trace elements (check the analysis on the package), so it is advisable to add these — particularly when a soilless mix is used — in the form of soluble or fritted trace elements, or by supplementary feeding with a fertilizer rich in the minor elements (we like Sea-Born, a liquefied seaweed, obtainable from WAYSIDE GARDENS, MENTOR, OH 44060). Secondly, improved growth will often be achieved at certain seasons if light "booster" foliar or soil feedings of soluble fertilizer are given.

A caution: on several occasions, we have heard that some slow-release fertilizers may contribute to winter injury. This appears likely where a long-term fertilizer such as Osmocote 18-6-12, which feeds for 8 months, is applied in spring in the North where the growing season is short. It will still be supplying nitrogen in the fall, inducing soft, easily cold-injured growth. So a wiser choice would be a fertilizer with a shorter release period.

Acid Remarks

Soil alkalinity spells failure for ericaceous plants such as rhododendrons. Incorporating large amounts of acid peat, oak leafmold or rotted pine needles helps where the pH is not too far above the ideal 5.5. But for a higher pH, a chemical corrective is needed. A safe one is agricultural or elemental sulfur (flowers of sulfur, from drugstores). Spread or mix in 3.5 pounds per 100 feet where the soil tests neutral, 5.5 pounds if it is strongly alkaline.

Sulfur may take several months to be effective, but ferrous sulfate works immediately, says Ted Van Veen, author of *"RHODODENDRONS IN AMERICA"* (*$20 FROM VAN VEEN NURSERY, 4201 S.E. FRANKLIN, PORTLAND, OR 97206*). He suggests 16.5 pounds per 100 square feet to bring pH 7 down to 5.5, 11.8 pounds for pH 6.5, 7.1 pounds for pH 6. The often recommended aluminum sulfate, Mr. Van Veen states, is toxic to rhododendrons and should never be used.

Used as a germination medium, fertilizer and mulch, seaweed is an unusually valuable growth promoter and health builder.

Iron-Poor Plants

"Subclinical" deficiencies of minor elements — particularly iron — may affect a great many ornamentals, fruits and vegetables. Although the deficiency is not severe enough to produce the typical interveinal chlorosis iron "hunger sign," the plants' growth is reduced.

The problem is most common in sandy soils low in organic matter — indoor growers report it occurs, too, with soilless media when they use fertilizers lacking in minor elements. High phosphorus content of the soil also makes iron unavailable, as does high pH: excess liming can cause iron deficiency symptoms that are confused with nitrogen hunger signs, especially when they are seen on grass or conifers.

Iron deficiency usually occurs in spring, when the rapid rate of growth makes the plant unable to get sufficient micronutrients to balance the large amounts of macronutrients it is taking up. Low soil temperatures, or a compacted or waterlogged condition, can also reduce iron intake by roots.

Containing 15% nitrogen, bloodmeal is valuable as a top or side dressing, and will also stimulate bacterial action when used in composting.

Solutions are: more organic matter in the soil — organic matter contains chelating compounds that free otherwise unavailable iron . . . regular use of fertilizer formulations that include trace elements . . . supplementary applications of fritted or chelated (sequestered) iron, or, reportedly better yet, micronized iron (Green Garde), said to be more rapidly effective, non-toxic, less expensive and easier to use, indoors and in the garden.

Egging Them On

Horticulturist R. B. Farnham calls attention to the necessity of supplying calcium to plants. Soluble fertilizers contain little if any of this element, because it tends to reduce the solubility of the other nutrients in the container. Calcium is not only a soil "sweetener" and an aid to soil granulation, but also an important nutrient even for acid-loving plants.

Lime, bonemeal and superphosphate are sources. Or, suggests Mr. Farnham, you can crush eggshells and spread them over plant beds, one eggshell to four square feet. One crushed eggshell will also rejuvenate a calcium-starved house plant (general symptoms: yellowing and drying of tips and margins of leaves, and death of roots).

Bee Line for Boron

In many areas, a deficiency of boron is a limiting factor in plant growth. It causes poor root growth and reduced vigor, manifested by abnormally small foliage and by dead brown leaf vein areas in many plants in severe cases.

Often, however, the deficiency is not so pronounced as to cause noticeable symptoms or growth suppression. But there is a way to tell if plants are suffering from a lack of boron. Experiments with clover and raspberry bushes show that this trace element is vital to nectar secretion. Any plant in flower that is neglected by honeybees may be in need of boron. A very light dusting on the soil of ordinary household powdered borax, or 1 ounce in 25 gallons of water, will quickly correct the deficiency.

Seafood

Seaweed was used for mulching and livestock feed by the ancient Greeks, Vikings and Chinese. Its horticultural values are now under study at Clemson University in South Carolina, reports Tracy Childers of the Horticulture Department.

Seaweed extract used as a soak and germinating medium for seeds increased the percentage of germination. Even in the lowest concentrations used, respiratory activity was improved. Seaweed was shown to be an efficient source of boron, magnesium, manganese and zinc for citrus trees. On geranium plants, it produced more flowers, and flower weight increased up to 27%. Very small amounts of seaweed in a soil mix for poinsettias resulted in darker green foliage, plants more uniform in size and flowering, and longer bloom life.

The author asserts that seaweed "produces or stimulates plant hormones that respond as regulators of growth and development. It is believed that the usual crystalline compound decomposition product of proteins, an organic substance able in low concentrations to promote elongation of plant shoots, is present. In addition, perhaps some new growth regulator substances, which may be found only in marine organisms, are also present."

Formulating Your Own Fertilizer

Economy- and ecological-minded gardeners often build their entire indoor-outdoor feeding programs around organic wastes, many of which may be available for the hauling from local industries. To aid gardeners who want to utilize these slow-release materials singly or blended, here are approximate average nitrogen-phosphorus-potash percentages for some of these residues and commercial organics:

Activated sludge, 5-3-0; alfalfa meal, 2.5-.5-2; animal tankage, 7-12-0; antibiotic wastes, 3-3-1; apple pomace, 2-0-0; bloodmeal, 15-1-1; bonemeal, 3-16-0; cannery wastes, 3-1-2; castor pomace, 5-1.5-1; cocoa shell dust, 2-1-3; coffee grounds, 2-.5-.5; cottonseed meal, 7-2.5-1.5; cattle manure, 2.5-5-1.5; dried blood, 12-3-0; fish meal, 8-13-4; greensand, 0-1.5-5; hoof-and-horn, 12.5-1.5-0; incinerator ash, 0-5-2; poultry manure, 3.5-3-1.5; seaweed, 3-1-5; sewage sludge, 2-1.5-2; spent hops, 2-.5-.5; tea leaves, 4.5-.5-0; tobacco stems, 2-.5-8; wood ashes, 0-1.5-7; wool wastes, 5.5-1.5-1.

Some of these — cottonseed meal, dried blood and fish meal — acidify the soil, while others, such as bonemeal, tankage and tobacco stems, are alkaline in effect. Many contain appreciable amounts of trace elements which can result in improved growth, as well as having a beneficial effect on soil texture. Numerous other organic materials, of course, have lower nutrient content but still are valuable for composting and mulching.

Vitamin Therapy

Interior-exterior landscape designer Ron-Dean Taffel of THE MANHATTAN GARDENER (201 EAST 74TH STREET, NEW YORK, NY 10021) has given a most enthusiastic report on SUPERthrive, the "original vitamin-hormone solution" (VITAMIN INSTITUTE, 5409 SATSUMA AVENUE, NORTH HOLLYWOOD, CA 91603).

The use of vitamins for plants has long been controversial. To our knowledge, certain of the B vitamins are recognized to be needed for root growth, and are synthesized in plant tissue and translocated to the roots. The stimulation of root and top growth from soil applications of SUPERthrive — a formulation containing over 50 hormones and vitamins, including B_1 — is remarkable, according to reports from growers, nurserymen, landscapers and others. Recommended solutions: 1 drop per gallon of water for weekly feeding, 10 drops per gallon in planting. SUPERthrive is not a fertilizer, but rather a fertilizer adjunct.

MULCHING

Mighty Mulch

"To mulch or not to mulch" is not the question these days to any gardener worth his soil. He who has mastered this recently discovered but actually most ancient of natural practices knows well its nigh incomparable value as a plant protector, soil builder and labor saver.

The word mulch derives from the Anglo-Saxon *melsc* or German *molsch*, meaning mellow. Wherever climate permits, nature mulches with fallen leaves, grasses and other litter, softening and mellowing the soil, and recycling the raw materials the plants took from it to build their own structures. The deep sod mulch of the plains and the rich duff of the forest floor are nature's means to plant survival, for soil long uncovered becomes barren and lifeless.

Few gardeners today have any passion for the "neatness" of bare soil, for they know that such "clean cultivation" works against the welfare of their plants. But not every gardener is aware of more than the readily apparent virtues of mulching — or of all its possible disadvantages in some situations. The why of mulching is perhaps better understood than the when and what and how . . .

The Better Earth

The often remarkable plant growth results of mulching are due, of course, to its unequaled efficiency in providing and maintaining an optimum environment for roots. Mulch beneficially

Hay and straw work well when heavily applied, but pose a danger of fire in dry seasons.

affects the texture, fertility, moisture content and temperature of the soil:

1. An organic mulch adds organic matter, producing humus compounds — technically, the humate fraction of organic colloids — as it decomposes. These filter down and improve texture by binding soil particles into aggregates or "crumbs." Thus a sandy soil is given body, while a packed clay is dispersed, increasing its aeration and moisture permeability.

It has been shown many times that the best plant growth is achieved on a coarsely aggregated soil having the ideal "pore ratio" of 50% capillary pores (water spaces) and 50% non-capillary pores (air spaces). In this respect, mulch can actually be superior to digging organic matter into the soil. A frequently replenished mulch provides a constant supply of humus. Digging in organic material, on the other hand, makes large amounts available for short periods, promoting aggregation only temporarily until decomposition is complete and no more soil-building substances are produced.

An inorganic mulch, such as plastic or stones, supplies no organic matter, but it does help to conserve that already present by preventing its loss to high temperatures or moisture extremes.

2. Organic mulch nourishes plants. It does this both directly by supplying its own nutrients to the soil, and indirectly by releasing — through its stimulation of soil organisms and production of acids — soil nutrients held in unavailable forms.

Myriad types of micro-organisms multiply fantastically to carry on the decomposition of the mulch, and these mobilize not only minerals but also growth-stimulating hormones, plus substances that protect the health of the plant. Earthworms, too, increase under the cool, moist, food-rich conditions of a mulch, and their soil-enriching abilities should not be underestimated: an earthworm "digests" its own weight in soil daily, and its castings contain 5 times the nitrogen, 7 times the phosphorus and 11 times the potash found in the material it consumed.

To a certain extent, some of these benefits are afforded by an inorganic mulch, for soil organisms are stimulated to greater activity by the more uniform moisture and temperature conditions the mulch provides in contrast to bare soil.

3. Mulch conserves moisture. It has been reliably estimated that three quarters of the rain falling on bare soil is lost to plants through evaporation and runoff. Both of these are reduced up to 90% by an adequate mulch.

Moisture and the nutrients that can be conveyed only in solution are therefore available over longer periods, so the plants do not suffer the temporary checks to growth that occur with sporadic rains or waterings. And of course, erosion by water and wind is prevented, as is the compacting by hard rains that causes a poreless crust to form over the surface. Finally, on soils suffering from excess salinity, mulch keeps the surface moist so the salt is not concentrated by evaporation to plant-damaging amounts.

4. Mulches smooth out temperature fluctuations. On a hot summer day, mulched soil can be 10° to 25° cooler than bare soil, a vital benefit, considering that most plants' roots become inactive when soil temperatures reach about 90°. On cool nights, mulched soil is very slow to lose its growth-pushing warmth. In winter, mulch similarly maintains comparatively even soil temperatures, retarding the freezing-thawing cycles that heave shallow-rooted plants. Also, cold penetration is reduced so that roots can continue to take up moisture and nutrients, which are stored in stems and foliage for immediate use when dormancy ends.

The color and conductivity of a mulch, as we shall discuss later, can be important when we wish to warm the soil quickly in spring to give plants a fast start.

Mulches also (5) suppress weeds, which compete with plants for moisture and nutrients . . . (6) prevent "splash inoculation" of plants' lower leaves with disease spores in heavy rains, and muddying of plants, walls, low windows . . . (7) cushion the soil against compaction by traffic . . . (8) encourage extensive feeder roots in the rich, well-aerated upper layers of soil . . . (9) if organic, have organic matter's capacity to buffer excess fertilizers and herbicide residues . . . and (10) reduce pollution caused by vaporization or dust-carrying of soil-applied pesticides.

Finally, (11) organic mulches produce carbon dioxide as they decay, adding to the air's supply of this compound vital to plants' food-making process . . . and (12) reflective mulches can be used to stimulate growth remarkably by increasing the light reaching the lower portions of a plant.

Cover with Care

A few general cautions are in order to avoid problems with mulch (specific disadvantages of certain mulches are noted where the materials are listed).

There is danger of damping-off if a mulch that holds much moisture is placed around seedlings on a wet soil. Rots and cankers can occur when mulch is laid closer than a few inches from the crown, stem or trunk of many plants. In a wet year, loose materials are to be preferred over those that tend to become soggy and add to the soil's waterlogging. Conversely, dry soil should always be watered deeply before mulching.

In cold climates, mulch must not be renewed too early in spring or the soil will stay cool and inhibit growth. If a heavy year-round mulch is used on vegetable and flower beds, pull it back from planting areas to let the soil warm up and dry out. Where a soil is packed clay, mulching alone will take years to produce aggregation to appreciable depths, so in this situation it is best to improve the soil first by incorporating gypsum or organic matter, or green-manuring.

When a highly carbonaceous (low in nitrogen) mulch such as sawdust, straw or shredded sugarcane is used, decomposition organisms will steal this element from the soil unless a fertilizer that supplies 1 pound of nitrogen for each 100 pounds of mulch is applied.

For mice and moles which may become a problem, mothballs seem to be the most frequently recommended deterrent — but we question eliminating moles, valuable for their consumption of grubs and other pests. Wood products and gravel are less attractive to mice than grassy mulches.

Ground Rules

With due regard to the cautions noted above, mulches can be applied at any time of the year. For trees, shrubs and evergreens, a permanent mulch, maintained at 3″ to 4″ depth when settled, is invaluable. Fall-planted material especially requires promptly applied mulch, to keep frost out of the soil as long as possible so new roots can grow. Remember to keep mulch away from woody stems, which mice can girdle, and

particularly from the stems of broad-leaved evergreens so these can harden before winter. Give groundcovers a mulch to hold down weeds until the plants cover the soil. Mulch all annual plants after germination or transplanting, renewing the mulch frequently through the growing season.

For winter protection of herbaceous perennials, biennials, and bulbs, mulch 2″ to 3″ deep with a loose, non-packing, non-waterlogging material following several frosts. Mulch the soil around herbaceous plants which retain foliage in winter, but cover the foliage only lightly with hay or needled evergreen boughs to prevent winter burn. Plants in containers need a mulch in the fall; in addition, they usually need extra insulating material packed around the sides of the container.

Mulches should be checked often during winter, and pulled back or removed from evergreen or emerging plants only when spring has truly come.

Selecting and Stretching Materials

Theoretically, almost any material that insulates well yet permits gaseous exchange and moisture penetration will make a satisfactory mulch.

But each material must be evaluated for additional practical considerations. The ideal mulch does not need frequent renewing, is non-toxic to plants, easy to apply, free from disease and weed seed, and not so absorbent that it can take moisture the plants need . . . and it does not pack, blow, wash, ferment or burn easily. Special factors may also be important, such as the need for a coarse, heavy mulch on a windy hillside site. And appearance is often a prime factor, the earth-colored materials of fine texture being most desirable for areas on display — but often these can be used thinly to cover other less attractive

Applied no thicker than 3″, grass clippings are fine moisture conservers and fertility builders — and they also reduce nematodes.

materials if the latter are easily procurable at low cost.

By these standards, few materials are ideal, but many of those commercially available fulfill most of these criteria. So do quite a few that are free or obtainable at just the cost of hauling. Sources are lumberyards and woodworking plants, farms, mills, breweries, street and highway departments, utility companies, stables, dairies, quarries and many types of food- and fiber-processing plants. The classified telephone directory is a great aid to the confirmed mulcher.

And his most indispensable tool may be a shredder-grinder. Numerous inexpensive models reduce all manner of crop residues, prunings, trimmings and other wastes to far less obtrusive, more manageable and much more mulch-worthy substances. Like compost, shredded material should be screened and the "fines" spread on the soil surface, with the "rough" on top of this, as in nature.

ORGANIC COVERALLS

BAGASSE (CHOPPED SUGARCANE — STAZDRI, ZORBIT) — clean, effective, long-lasting; somewhat light-colored for show areas.

BARK — outstanding for effectiveness and appearance; high in lignin, so adds much humus; medium to coarse grades best for mulch, fine grades for soil incorporation.

BUCKWHEAT HULLS — rich dark brown color, comparatively expensive but quite long-lasting; 2″ depth is usually adequate.

COCOA BEAN HULLS — attractive, but tend to pack and mold, so may be best mixed with or topdressing other materials; also very high in potash, may be toxic to azaleas and rhododendrons if used heavily and long.

COCONUT FIBER — good color, long-lasting, very good anywhere if procurable.

COFFEE GROUNDS — rich color, also high in nitrogen and some trace elements.

COMPOST — excellent in half-rotted form; put finished compost under other mulches.

CORNCOBS — best chopped to walnut size; have 6% to 8% sugar content which stimulates aggregating organisms; nitrogen fertilizer may be necessary.

CORNSTALKS — very good shredded, or lay whole stalks over other mulches in the vegetable garden.

COTTONSEED, PEANUT, PECAN, RICE HULLS — all good where available, but smaller ones may blow or wash.

EXCELSIOR — non-packing, but highly flammable.

GRASS CLIPPINGS — will mat and ferment if used fresh, deeply and alone — use dried, thinly or mixed with dry mulches.

GREEN MANURES — any crop (preferably leguminous) which can be grown on spare land and cut for mulch.

HAY AND FIELD GRASS — should be mowed before going to seed; legume hays are richest in nitrogen.

LEAFMOLD — especially good for wildflower plantings.

LEAVES — best spread around shrubs and on bare plots as they fall, or shredded or composted; avoid maple and other soft leaves which mat, or mix with coarser material; oak leaves do not pack, are excellent for ericaceous plants (dust with limestone for others).

LICORICE ROOT — good-looking and long-lasting, will not pack or blow, but can be a fire hazard.

MANURE — best well-rotted and strawy, for liberal use on vegetable garden and roses, lightly on other plants.

PEATMOSS — fine-textured types dry out and crust badly; use chunky peat, such as "poultry litter" grade.

PINE NEEDLES — very good, especially for acid-loving plants, but can be a fire hazard.

SALT MARSH HAY — one of the best for all uses, light and airy, weed-free, but generally obtainable only near coasts.

SAND — can be useful mixed with peat or sawdust for bulbs.

SAWDUST — use 2″ deep, and add nitrogen; weathers to brown color; avoid sour sawdust that has fermented in deep piles.

SEAWEED — superb shredded and mixed with materials of similar texture; rich in many minerals and aggregating and growth-promoting substances.

SNOW — nature's finest, free mulch; shovel from walks, etc., to root areas.

SPANISH MOSS — fluffy, excellent where available.

SPENT HOPS — effective, but light in color; fire-resistant.

SPENT MUSHROOM SOIL — earthy color; supplies some nutrients.

STRAW — good general mulch, but more flammable than hay.

TOBACCO STEMS — attractive, effective; have some insecticidal and repellent properties; do not use on bulbs or tomatoes because of danger of mosaic disease.

WOOD CHIPS — long-lasting, contribute much humus; use 4″ deep or more.

WOOD SHAVINGS — intriguing appearance; add extra nitrogen.

MANUFACTURED MULCHES

ALUMINUM FOIL — repels aphids, thrips, other insects; reflected light also gives large yield increases of many crops.

ASPHALT (BUILDING) PAPER — effective, long-lasting and not too unattractive used alone.

CLOTH — burlap, even old rugs are sometimes used between the rows in the vegetable garden.

EROSION CONTROL NETTING AND BLANKETS — for holding mulch and grass seedlings on steep slopes (BEMIS CO., BOX 178, MINNEAPOLIS, MN 55402; CONWED CORP., 332 MINNESOTA STREET, ST. PAUL, MN 55101).

FIBERGLASS MATTING (WEED-CHEK) — very effective, permeable to air and water; glass fibers repel pests (BRIGHTON BY-PRODUCTS CO., BOX 23, NEW BRIGHTON, PA 15066).

GRAVEL, MARBLE CHIPS, MINERAL CLAY CHIPS (TERRA-GREEN, TURFACE), CRUSHED STONE — decorative, especially good for rock plants; often used over paper or plastic; avoid marble on acid-loving plants; use dark-colored types for less heat reflection on ornamentals.

NEWSPAPER — basically wood fiber, plus harmless and fertilizing substances; use 3 to 6 sheets thick, and cover with organic mulches for appearance and to speed decomposition.

PERLITE, VERMICULITE — horticultural grades are useful around tiny seedlings or on plants in containers; can blow badly.

PLASTIC FILM — unattractive alone; should be well perforated to allow aeration and moisture penetration; clear plastic permits weed growth — green and black do not and can also be used for soil temperature regulation.

ROCKS AND STONES — decorative, very effective except for weed growth between them; hold sun heat in spring and fall to warm soil; can be placed in interesting patterns, and the gardener can make "stones" of concrete in desired shapes.

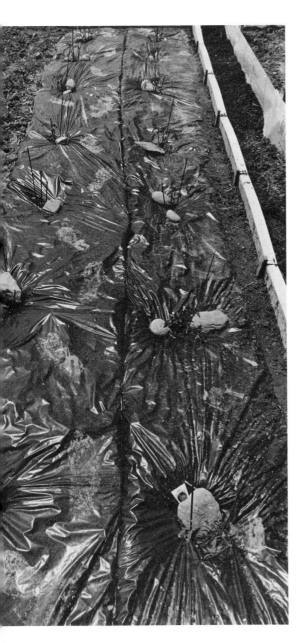

Because it keeps the soil warmer than other mulches and also totally eliminates weeds, black plastic is favored for increasing growth of both herbaceous and woody plants.

Grass Wins Mulch Test

The benefits of mulch have been strikingly demonstrated at the Connecticut Agricultural Experiment Station, at New Haven.

Plots of petunias were mulched with manila bags, roofing paper, double sheets of newspaper, 3″ of grass clippings or 3″ of salt hay. Dry weather following planting showed the water-conserving value of mulch: two months later, the plants in the paper- and hay-mulched plots were up to one-third larger than unmulched plants, and those mulched with grass clippings were almost twice as large. Also, 50% to 80% more flowers were produced in the paper and hay plots, while the grass-mulched plot yielded almost 200% more.

With the exception of roofing paper, the mulches reduced meadow nematode populations. There were 25% fewer nematodes under the manila bags, 50% fewer under the salt hay, 63% fewer under newspaper and 75% fewer in the grass-mulched plot.

Bloom Booster

Mulches hasten blooming, at least of bearded iris, according to "Mississippi Farm Research" of the Mississippi Agricultural Experiment Station. Bloom dates of the variety 'Pinnacle' were advanced as much as 11 days when the plants were mulched with pine straw, gin trash, leaves, perlite, plastic, sawdust or peatmoss. Better plant survival, taller flower stalks and more flowers per stalk were also noted. Sawdust, peatmoss and gin trash, however, retained excessive moisture and caused increased weed growth and incidence of soft rot and leaf spot. Best in all respects were pine straw and gravel-covered black plastic.

The Chips Are Down

Hardwood bark is very nearly the perfect mulch, according to studies at Northeastern Forest Ex-

MULCHERS' AIDS

"Handbook on Mulches," $1 from Brooklyn Botanic Garden (1000 Washington Avenue, Brooklyn, NY 11225).

"How to Have a Green Thumb Without an Aching Back," by Ruth Stout (Cornerstone Library, Simon & Schuster, $1.45).

"Mulches for Your Garden," U.S.D.A. Home and Garden Bulletin, 10¢ from Superintendent of Documents (Washington, DC 20402).

periment Station at Princeton, West Virginia. Widely available in many sizes and types, bark is certainly one of the most decorative mulches. More important, notes the Station's Research Forester, Charles H. Wolf, a 2″ to 3″ bark mulch reduces evaporation, prevents water and wind erosion, suppresses weeds, insulates roots from rapid temperature variations and adds vital humus to the soil.

Unlike peatmoss and sawdust, bark mulch does not tend to seal over and thus require cultivating after rain or watering. Also, plant roots do not grow up into it, as they do into a peat or sawdust mulch, making them subject to winter injury and summer desiccation.

Two new ideas in bark mulches have been quickly developed into readily available products.

Fibrex (MASONITE CORP., 29 NORTH WACKER DRIVE, CHICAGO, IL 60606) is bark impregnated with the pre-emergence herbicide Dacthal. Applied early in spring, it suppresses weeds all season, then biodegrades. Only a 1″ depth is necessary.

Terra-Tex (TERRA-TEX CORP., PINE STREET EXTENSION, NASHUA, NH 03060) is "a continuous web of pressed natural bark, bonded with resin and backed by impregnated bark fines." A "mulch carpet" ⅓″ thick, it is made in rolls and rings for indoor and outdoor use. Terra-Tex is readily permeable by water and fertilizer, and stays effective up to 5 years in the garden.

Fibrex and Terra-Tex are available at most garden supply outlets.

Leaves Are Not for Burning

Do you want neatness — or miracles? Leaves heaped 2′ deep may not be neat, but they can bring about miraculous recovery of declining plants, says horticulturist R. B. Farnham. He reports two such recoveries in his garden, of a 30-year-old globe arborvitae hedge and an old asparagus bed.

Mr. Farnham states that leaves can be piled "deeply around any plants large or woody enough not to be smothered by such a layer when wet and packed. A pile of almost any leaves except oak, 2′ high after compaction by walking on them, will almost disappear by the end of the next

Bark is a long-lasting and decorative mulch which never packs, mats or encourages plant roots to grow into it.

148   The Avant Gardener

summer, in the meantime controlling all weeds and revitalizing many a declining evergreen or shrub and raspberry or asparagus bed . . .

"Why does it work? As always there are probably many reasons, but certainly it is a desirably lazy, low-cost way to provide a continuous source of rotting organic matter to the soil surface. Earthworms flourish beneath it, moving the resulting humus down into rooting areas. From many related observations, it seems certain to me that both leafmold and the fast-rotting sedge peats (Michigan Peat, Sterling Forest Peat, etc. — not peatmoss) release enough of various things as they rot to adequately nourish many garden plants growing in a decent soil."

In a remarkable article, *"THE COUNTRY IN THE CITY," REPUBLISHED IN THE "MORTON ARBORETUM QUARTERLY" (LISLE, IL 60532)*, the late great Dr. Edgar Anderson reinforces these points through an examination of "forest duff." The thick blanket of rich leafmold resulting from layer after layer of fallen leaves is one of the main feeding zones of upland forest trees and is essential to their vigor and very survival. To grow these trees well in city or country, he notes, this blanket or its equivalent — mulch and fertilizer — must be provided.

Municipalities, incidentally, are learning to use leaves. Amityville, New York, has spread 11,000 large bags of them, collected from homeowners, on a new beach park. Ground limestone was added, and sand will be mixed in when the leaves have decomposed, to make an excellent seedbed for lawns.

Bed Rock

Besides their decorative value and elimination of the need for periodic renewal, stone and similar materials provide all the benefits — weed reduction, soil temperature stabilization, moisture retention — of organic mulches, except humus production. Also, stones can be placed right up to the trunks of plants, where organic mulches used thus would encourage attack by mice, borers and the like.

A sampling of the materials available: Vermont Marble Chips *(VERMONT MARBLE CO., PROCTOR, VT 05765)*; Campbell Decorative Natural Stone *(HARRY T. CAMPBELL SONS CO., TOWSON, MD 21204)*; Decra Chips — kiln-fired clay, in earth tones *(GENERAL CLAY PRODUCTS, 1445 GOODALE BOULEVARD, COLUMBUS, OH 43212)*; Leisure Lawn Stone — vinyl-coated crushed rock in 12 colors *(BOX 296, URBANA, IL 61801)*; Terra-Green Jumbos — porous mineral chips *(TERRA-GREEN, 520 NORTH MICHIGAN AVENUE, CHICAGO, IL 60611)*; Turface Mulch — calcined clay *(WYANDOTTE CHEMICALS CORPORATION, WYANDOTTE, MI 48192)*.

Selective Chopper Shopping

A relatively new tool is the "garden waste reduction unit" — which may be a shredder, grinder or chipper, or all three. Manufacturers are producing an ever-increasing multitude of machines that employ knives, flails, rotary blades or hammermills to make compost and mulch material of any wastes from leaves and twigs to metal cans and even stones and bones. Many models have bags to catch the chopped material, others have sweep-in leaf pick-up attachments, and there are electric-, gasoline-, mower- and tractor-powered types.

A few points to look for, in addition to sufficient power and capacity for the volume of wastes available or collectible, are ability to handle both wet and dry material, size of prunings handled, easy and safe means of freeing jams and clogs, and protection against flying materials. The following manufacturers provide detailed literature that will help in selecting the right model:

Amerind-MacKissic Inc. (Box 111, Parker Ford, PA 19457) . . . Atlas Tool & Mfg. Co. (1515 Natural Bridge Avenue, St. Louis, MO 63115) . . . Billy Goat Industries, Inc. (Box 229, Grandview, MO 64030) . . . Gilson Brothers Co. (Box 152, Plymouth, WI 53073) . . . Hahn Eclipse

(1625 North Garvin, Evansville, IN 47717) . . . M. A. Johnson Co. (Route 5, Box 447, Taylorsville, NC 28681) . . . Kemp Shredder Co. (Box 6275, Erie, PA 16512) . . . Lindig Mfg. (1875 West Country Road C, St. Paul, MN 55113) . . . Magna American Corp. (Raymond, MS 39154) . . . MTD Products Inc. (5389 West 130th Street, Cleveland, OH 44111) . . . Omark Industries Inc. (9701 S.E. McLaughlin Boulevard, Portland, OR 97222) . . . Osborne Mfg. Co. (Box 29, Osborne, KS 67473) . . . Red Cross Mfg. Co. (Box 50042, Indianapolis, IN 46250) . . . Roto-Hoe Co. (100 Auburn Road, Newbury, OH 44065) . . . Sunbeam Outdoor Co. (Kingstree Highway East, Manning, SC 29102) . . . The Toro Co. (Bloomington, MN 55420) . . . Vandermolen Corp. (119 Dorsa Avenue, Livingston, NJ 07039) . . . Winona Attrition Mill (1009 West 5th Street, Winona, MN 55987) . . . W-W Grinder Corp. (2957 North Market Street, Wichita, KS 67219).

ORGANIC GARDENING

Perspective on Organic Gardening

Once vilified as "muck and mysticism," organic gardening has become a subject worthy of reasoned, balanced examination — indeed, a subject of great concern to gardener and non-gardener alike.

In part, this is due to evolution of the concept of organic gardening itself. In its early days, much of its basic tenets were confused, and the idea of "gardening and farming without chemicals" questioned the very fundamentals of a new and burgeoning technology. In recent years, however, the value of many of its principles has been convincingly demonstrated by practicing gardeners.

More important, organic gardening has become "relevant." Its practitioners, it seems, may well hold a major key to the ecological crisis that threatens the survival of mankind.

From Fad to Good

The origins of organiculture in America lie with one man, a layman who 30 years ago began to be concerned about practices that "mine" the soil, the decline in food quality and early signs of pesticide problems. The late J. I. Rodale's first issue of "Organic Gardening" appeared in May, 1942. He based his condemnation of reliance on synthetic chemicals on the work of Sir Albert Howard, an English agricultural advisor in India, whose *"AN AGRICULTURAL TESTAMENT" (OXFORD UNIVERSITY PRESS, $4)* proposed that the soil's ability to grow healthy crops is best preserved by returning plant and animal wastes to it.

Many gardeners will recall how Mr. Rodale's thesis earned him such titles as "fanatic" and "faddist." Both supporters and detractors leaned to extremist positions. Indeed, there are still remnants of a cult faction in organiculture, and an extremist fringe on the other side of the fence, whose attitudes tend to obscure the values of an approach that is now achieving considerable scientific confirmation.

Recently, however, J. I. Rodale has been awarded the status of a prophet with honor, and organic gardeners and organic ideas are everywhere. There are hundreds of organic gardening clubs and thousands of markets that feature organically grown foods. For the first time in the long history of horticulture, organics appears to be making gardening an important force in the lives of the young. Organic gardening courses have been instituted in schools from Vermont to California, from kindergarten to university levels.

Qualifying Organics

The pendulum thus has swung far in the opposite direction, and, in the minds of many, the organic concept is vindicated. But several questions arise:

Is the pendulum overswinging? Should chemical fertilizers and pesticides be rejected totally? Are all the principles of organiculture valid — and just how effective are they in actual practice?

In attempting to answer these questions, it is essential to examine what organic gardening is and what it is not, for few aspects of horticulture have been so bound with misconceptions. Too many critics of the organic method have based their condemnation of it on just such misconceptions — and conversely, in many instances the enthusiasm of organiculturists has led them to wildly far-fetched conclusions.

The Dynamic Component

Without question, the greatest debt horticulture owes organiculture is for its promotion of a greater awareness of the importance of organic matter.

Replenishment of organic matter to maintain soil structure is recognized today to be as essential as maintaining the mineral content of the soil — a function also performed, incidentally, by additions of organic matter if made in sufficient quantity and variety to compensate for the minerals removed by crops. This is nature's system of perpetual renewal, as it occurs in virgin fields and forests where no "net biological product" — a crop — is taken.

It's been said that organic matter — called humus in its more advanced stages of decomposition — is the life of the soil. It is the dynamic component, the support of a tremendous microbiological population. One of the primary results of the activity of these organisms is the production of humic substances which bind soil particles into relatively stable aggregates or "crumbs." Both clay and sandy soils are thus given a desirable spongy, granular structure, well aerated, draining easily but capable of storing vast amounts of moisture in its pore spaces, and non-crusting and non-compacting.

The microorganisms also release the nutrients in organic matter added to the soil, and make available minerals already present or added as fertilizer, both by producing acids that dissolve them and by compounding substances active in ion exchange. These nutrients are held in forms not easily leached away, and are released to roots as needed.

Organic matter serves many other functions, some of which we are only beginning to detect. Canada's Department of Agriculture recently found that fulvic acid, a humic compound, greatly stimulates root production. Nematodes are reduced by the build-up of parasitic fungi resulting from continual applications of organic matter. Mycorrhizal fungi, which live symbiotically on roots and aid their absorption of nutrients, are maintained by organic matter. And humus is an effective buffer against excess acidity or alkalinity, overdoses of fertilizer and toxic amounts of pesticides.

Dozens of communities have begun to compost leaves and garbage to produce a useful — and profitable — garden product.

Earth Making

Organiculture has developed or rediscovered many ways to supply this vital material. Organic wastes can be buried in trenches, or "sheet-composted" — spread on the soil surface and tilled in. Or the gardener can produce organic material in quantity right where it is needed by green manuring: one or more green manure crops, sown in spring, summer or fall, then tilled in while immature to insure rapid decomposition and maximum nutrient availability, will quickly build up any poor soil (best text on green manuring, with plant recommendations and sources: *"HOW TO DO WONDERS WITH GREEN MANURES,"* free from GARDEN WAY MFG., 102ND STREET AND NINTH AVENUE, TROY, NY 12180).

Robust Refuse

Compost made in heaps, however, will always be the gardener's prime source of organic matter. A heap, when screened, will provide both half-rotted, fibrous material for working into the soil or mulching, and fine, "finished" compost ideal for sowing seeds, making potting mixes, top- and side-dressing lawns and plants, and mixing with soil in planting holes.

But many a gardener has been discouraged from composting by over-elaborate directions, the length of time required, fear of odors or the fact that a compost heap may be unattractive. Actually, none of these objections are valid.

The basic method involves alternating 4″ to 6″ layers of vegetable and animal material with 1″ layers of soil, then waiting several months to a year or longer for this to be reduced to compost. But the process can be greatly speeded up by 1) shredding the materials to expose more surfaces to attack by the bacteria and fungi; 2) adding a high-nitrogen fertilizer (nitrogen is the primary food of the organisms); 3) aerating the pile by making holes from top to bottom, or by turning it occasionally; and 4) especially in winter, covering the pile with black plastic to hold in the heat (this anaerobic or airless technique also prevents loss of valuable elements through oxidation).

A recipe for real "speed composting": grind up everything with a shredder or rotary mower, liberally sprinkle in nitrogen fertilizer, then turn the heap every 3 days and keep it moist. This will produce dark, crumbly, sweet-smelling compost in 2 weeks.

To clear up some misconceptions: unless large quantities of acid leaves or other acid material are used, lime is not necessary . . . neither are "inoculants," because soil, fresh green matter and nitrogenous fertilizers will amply activate decay organisms . . . nor are additions of earthworms, those most efficient of all soil-making organisms, as they will enter the heap naturally if it is made on the ground. Kitchen wastes are perfectly satisfactory for composting, if buried in the pile to prevent odor and flies; even greasy scraps decompose well, reports the excellent *"RECLAMATION OF MUNICIPAL REFUSE BY COMPOSTING"* (TECHNICAL BULLETIN 9, $1 FROM SANITARY ENGINEERING RESEARCH PROJECT, UNIVERSITY OF CALIFORNIA, BERKELEY, CA 94720).

Finally, "container composting" solves the problem of aesthetics. We've seen attractive compost bins made of picket fence, snow fence, lumber, bricks, stone, concrete, wire or plastic mesh and metal drums. Compost can be made anaerobically in covered pits, or indoors in large plastic bags. The 32-gallon garbage can liners are especially useful in the fall when garden debris and leaves are so plentiful. A couple of shovelfuls of plant wastes are put in the bag and sprinkled with fertilizer and lime (omit the lime if making compost for acid-loving plants). This is repeated until the bag is full, then about a quart of water is added and the bag is tied tightly. Fast decomposition, space saving and no need to turn the "heap" are advantages of this method — and the bags can be stored in the cellar or heated garage where cold will not slow the composting action.

Municipal Material-ism

To those gardeners who prefer to purchase organic matter — and to answer the frequent comment that there can never be enough organic material to meet all garden and farm needs — we note this:

Supplies are substantially increasing, as industries find their wastes often have horticultural and agricultural uses — witness bark, formerly burned, now widely sold for soil amendment — and municipalities discover that composting relieves the pressure for landfill and dump sites, and eliminates air and water pollution from incineration and dumping.

Pilot garbage-composting projects are under way in many states. For example, HORTICULTURE SERIES NO. 16, *"UTILIZATION OF PROCESSED GARBAGE IN THE PRODUCTION OF FLORIST CROPS"* (AGRICULTURAL EXPERIMENT STATION, AUBURN UNIVERSITY, AUBURN, AL 36830), details experiments with two products of the Mobile, Alabama, Municipal Compost Plant — one a coarse-ground compost, the other a more finely ground compost marketed as Mobile Aid. Also tested were garbage composts from St. Petersburg, Florida, and Houston, Texas, and a humic and biological fertilizer, Cofuna, made by Natural Humus Company, Paris, France, from vegetable wastes.

Processed sewage and many industrial effluents are being utilized for soil improvement in dozens of cities. Some 20 years ago, we saw a pioneering project by New York City's Parks Department. Sewage sludge brought by tankers was pumped through irrigation pipe and sprayed by fire engine deckpipes set in the pipe onto Brooklyn's Marine Park, at that time an 868-acre dump containing every kind of rubble from garbage and incinerator fill to old taxis. Sixteen sprayings of a gallon per square foot at 3-day intervals, followed by disking, produced rich, mellow topsoil that soon supported trees, flowers and golf greens. And the city saved $1600 a week over the cost of dumping the sludge at sea.

More recently, Dr. William Sopper at Pennsylvania State University has shown that sewage effluent and sludge sprayed on barren strip-mine spoilbanks makes possible successful revegetation almost overnight. He has also demonstrated that effluent sprayed on cropland increases crop yields, while the soil acts as a "living filter" so the waste water becomes potable in the water table. Since sewage treatment destroys all disease organisms, there is no health hazard in using effluent and sludge.

An alternative method is drying the sludge and selling it to gardeners, as Milwaukee does. Its Milorganite is a fine organic soil amendment, beneficial to all plants. The average sludge contains over 2% nitrogen and 1.5% phosphorus and potash, plus colloidal material that builds soil structure.

Not surprisingly, organiculturists are leading the trend to large-scale composting. The publishers of *"ORGANIC GARDENING" (RODALE PRESS, EMMAUS, PA 18049)* also publish a technical journal, *"COMPOST SCIENCE,"* and *"GARBAGE AS YOU LIKE IT" ($4.95)*, a book we recommend to everyone interested in seeing America's 350 million tons of garbage a year recycled as it should be.

~~~~~~~~~~~~~~~~~~~~~~~~

"A CITIZEN'S GUIDE TO PROPER DISPOSAL OF LEAVES AND OTHER ORGANIC MATERIALS" is a useful brochure on garden and community composting, free from Larry Menchofer, Ohio Environmental Protection Agency (Box 1049, 450 E. Town St., Columbus, OH 43216).

~~~~~~~~~~~~~~~~~~~~~~~~

Confronting Fertilizers

Supplying organic matter is one facet of the organic concept. Much more controversial is the subject of fertilizer.

Organic gardening came into being as a reaction to overemphasis on fertilizers. Deterioration of cultivated soils, organiculturists rightly observed, is inevitable when crops are constantly taken and little organic matter is returned. Fertilizer cannot be totally substituted for organic matter without eventual loss of soil structure and the many other benefits associated with microbiological activities.

Organic gardeners, however, carried this thesis further, asserting that "artificial" fertilizers *per se* are harmful to soil life, destructive of soil structure, productive of increased plant susceptibility to disease and even capable of altering the food values of some crops.

We submit that it is not the fertilizer that causes any adverse effects, but rather misuse and overuse of that fertilizer. It is true, for example, that overdoses of rapidly available nitrogen cause weak, succulent growth more subject to disease, insect attack and winter injury. It's also true that too much fast-acting soluble fertilizer can burn roots, and if long continued can injure the soil and plants through a build-up of soluble salts. And it is true that applying excess amounts of one nutrient may result in the plant's being unable to take up sufficient amounts of other nutrients, so that it suffers deficiencies.

Organic Gardening   153

Barren strip-mine spoilbanks, where even weeds would not grow, are able to support lush vegetation after being sprayed with sewage effluent and sludge.

Applying quickly soluble fertilizer too generously is undoubtedly the average gardener's prevailing sin. Good judgment in selection, rate and timing is essential. The more soluble and high-analysis a fertilizer is, the more important is the rule, "use half as much twice as often."

For the gardener who nevertheless has a "heavy hand," it is probably sensible to choose the slow-acting all-organic fertilizers — manures, dried blood, cottonseed meal, etc. — for nitrogen; bonemeal and phosphate rock for phosphorus; and greensand, granite dust, wood ashes and the like for potassium. However, it should be noted that more and more mixed organic and chemical formulations that give the advantages of both are being marketed, and more strictly chemical fertilizers are appearing in slow-release form.

Controlling Pesticides

The one factor most responsible for the new spotlight on organics is the current great furor over the dangers of persistent pesticides. The organic movement must be credited with raising its voice in warning long before Rachel Carson, the Audubon Society and other great ecologists and conservation organizations.

While few horticulturists can share organiculturists' almost total indictment of pesticides, most will unhesitatingly agree that minimum usage with extreme caution is mandatory for human and environmental safety. Pesticides should not be employed routinely, but only as a part of integrated control, in combination with proper soil and plant management, and with biological, cultural and mechanical controls. Much is being accomplished — and much more is promised — in the development of safer insecticides and such techniques as sterilization, attractants, repellents, hormones, even sound waves.

Converging Conclusions

Since its inception, the organic movement has had healthful food as its main goal. Its warnings of declining food quality — recently reinforced by the Federal diet survey showing only 50% of Americans are adequately nourished — have included a long-needed indictment of the vast amount of nutrition-destroying processing to which food is subjected, the perils of pesticide residues and the possible dangers of the 2500-odd additives with which foods are treated today.

These very valid points have sometimes been obscured by a claim that organic fertilizers produce crops nutritionally superior to those grown with chemical fertilizers. There is no scientific evidence of this. Both chemical and organic fertilizers will produce equally nutritious crops — provided both are used in proper amounts and balance, and provided ample organic matter is maintained in the soil (these criteria, we must admit, are all too often ignored by farmers, compelled by economics to "push" crops for maximum yields).

Except for some unsupportable prohibitions of "synthetics," organiculture has made tremendous contributions in calling attention to wasted sources of fertility and excessive use of techniques best reserved for emergency situations. It has brought a new perspective to gardening, and reminded horticulture that recycling gardening's waste products is vital to its continued health.

And now that we are, ecologically speaking, only inches from Armageddon, we need to heed the organic movement's call to control the "toxic technology" that is contaminating soil, plants, air, water, and man himself. Organics is helping to bring back the deep respect due nature as the source of life and natural cycles as its guiding principles.

For avant gardeners, of course, we realize this discussion of organic vs. chemical methods is somewhat academic. The best gardeners have long used a combination of the two. The values of both are apparent in such combined practice . . . their disadvantages become obvious when either is practiced to the exclusion of the other.

ORGANIC ROOTS AND REFERENCES

"The Encyclopedia of Organic Gardening" (Rodale Press, Emmaus, PA 18049; $11.95)

"Three Hundred Most Asked Questions About Organic Gardening" (Rodale Press, $6.95)

"Gardening With Nature," by Leonard Wickenden (Fawcett, 95¢)

"Sunset Guide to Organic Gardening" (Sunset Books, $1.95)

"Grow Your Own," by Jeannie Darlington (The Bookworks, 1611 San Pablo Avenue, Berkeley, CA 94702; $1.75)

"Gardening Without Poisons," by Beatrice Trum Hunter (Houghton Mifflin, $5)

"The Pfeiffer Garden Book" (Bio-Dynamic Farming and Gardening Association, R.D. 1, Stroudsburg, PA 18360; $2.75)

Pest Control

The Great Pesticide Revolution

From being hailed as miracle weapons against plant pests and diseases, many pesticides in recent years have come to be indicted as "biological villains," and the current restrictions on their sale and use are considered a victory in the war to save the environment.

While it is true that evidence against, for example, DDT, is inconclusive and that its use has undeniably saved millions of lives and untold crops, it is also true that DDT is found in the soil, the oceans and throughout the food chain, and the possible hazards of its universal presence

imply a risk to present and future generations. As the report of the Department of Health, Education and Welfare's Commission on Pesticides said, "The field of pesticide toxicology exemplifies the absurdity of a situation in which 200 million Americans are undergoing life-long exposure, yet our knowledge of what is happening to them is at best fragmentary and for the most part indirect and inferential."

There are other important reasons for more careful selection and use of pesticides. Insects often develop resistance to them, making it necessary to switch to other and perhaps stronger chemicals. The pesticides destroy predators and parasites that aid in holding down noxious pests — almost any gardener or farmer can cite at least one instance where a pesticide applied to control one pest caused a population explosion of another pest whose natural enemies were destroyed by the chemical. This leads to more and more pesticides being necessary.

Safer pesticides are being developed, and more reliance is being placed on biological, mechanical and cultural controls. Scores of governmental and private research facilities are concentrating on combining these methods into integrated control systems. Many of the non-chemical methods, of course, are more adaptable to garden than to farm use, so the gardener can more easily reduce his reliance on hazardous pesticides.

The New Chemical Arsenal

For all-around use, the gardener has several relatively non-persistent insecticides. Since all have some degree of toxicity to man, wildlife, and/or beneficial organisms, label directions for these should be followed as carefully as for the extremely toxic products formerly used.

Malathion, carbaryl (Sevin), diazinon (Spectracide), and the old-time nicotine sulphate (Black Leaf 40) are basic weapons against flower, vegetable, lawn and woody plant pests. For use on ornamentals only, the systemic insecticides are effective up to 6 weeks. They make the plant itself toxic, are selective and pose no residual problems or threat to beneficial insects. Di-Syston, Meta-Systox R and Cygon are the safest. The new Dasanit is also nematocidal.

Commercial pesticides offering high degrees of human and environmental safety include such old standbys as the dormant "superior" oil sprays for scale, whitefly, mites, mealybugs, leafrollers and others; and the plant derivatives, rotenone, pyrethrins, and ryania (Ryatox), effective against a great many chewing and sucking insects — but toxic to fish, and often containing additives such as piperonyl butoxide, a possible carcinogen, so use only pure formulations such as Tri-Excel DS, from the NATURAL DEVELOPMENT COMPANY (BOX 215, BAINBRIDGE, PA 17502).

One of the newest, totally safe products is a household cleaner derived from soybeans, Basic H, which gardeners report is a near-perfect annihilator of thrips, aphids and red spider. It is available in many health food stores. Also completely safe is the biological insecticide *Bacillus thuringiensis* (Dipel, Biotrol, Thuricide), which is highly effective against many worm and caterpillar pests.

Two new weapons against slugs and snails are mesurol (Slug-Geta, by CHEVRON CHEMICAL COMPANY, 200 BUSH STREET, SAN FRANCISCO, CA 94120), reportedly more effective than the old-time metaldehyde, and Snail Snare (NATIONAL CHELATING CORP., BOX 352, WEST COVINA, CA 91790), which dehydrates the pests rather than poisons them.

In fungicides, best current recommendations are captan, ferbam, folpet, Karathane, maneb and zineb. Excellent for mildew control are Acti-Dione PM, Consan No. 20 and Parnon. Daconil 2787 is good for lawn diseases and botrytis. Most wide ranging in effectiveness, however, are the new systemic fungicides. The first to be released, benomyl (Benlate) has been highly praised for its control of everything from blackspot and powdery mildew on roses to various blossom blights, root and crown rots, verticillium and fusarium wilts, and anthracnose on many plants. It is, however, not a cure-all: fungi tolerant to Benlate have appeared, and normally harmless fungi have reportedly become pathogenic after Benlate eliminated competing fungi. The manufacturer, E. I. DU PONT DE NEMOURS & CO. (WILMINGTON, DE 19898), suggests that "other effective non-benzimidazole fungicides should be used in combination with Benlate or in intermittent spray schedules with Benlate" to avoid these problems.

Best selective herbicides include Betasan, Casoran, Chloro-IPC, Dacthal and trifluralin, and the new Eptam. Less selective and requiring very careful use are aminotriazole, diuron, monuron, silvex, 2,4-D (use only the amine form) and simazine. Best literature: "CREATING NEW LANDSCAPES WITH HERBICIDES" ($1 FROM CONNECTICUT ARBORETUM, NEW LONDON, CT 06320), and "CHEMICAL WEED CONTROL." (BULLETIN 516 from the KANSAS AGRICULTURAL EXPERIMENT STATION, MANHATTAN, KS 66502).

Minimize Use, Maximize Kill

How you use a pesticide is as important as your choice of it. The first consideration, of course, is correct identification of the pest. State and county extension services will aid in difficult cases, but often the gardener can rely on the illustrated literature supplied by many pesticide manufacturers (a good example is the *"LAWN AND GARDEN INSECT CONTROL MANUAL" BY GEIGY CHEMICAL CORPORATION, ARDSLEY, NY 10502*).

Secondly, restrict and localize pesticide applications as much as possible, and use equipment that does the best job with the least amount of chemical. Without going into the merits of the many types of sprayers and dusters, we note the great enthusiasm accorded the first portable mist blower, the Root-Lowell Airblast Atomist by *ROOT-LOWELL CORP. (LOWELL, MI 49331)*. It is lightweight, uses up to 80% less spray material than other types and gives far better coverage with a clinging mist that does not drip.

Always apply pesticides from the ground up, hitting the undersides of the leaves — where most sucking insects work, and many diseases enter — as well as the upper surfaces, and keep your wrist moving from side to side for best coverage.

Safety First and Last

From buying a pesticide to disposing of the empty container, safety should be the most vital consideration — safety to people, plants and the environment. Never forgo protective clothing, for example, if the label on the pesticide container directs its use. A mask or respirator is often required — those by eight manufacturers are evaluated in *"RESPIRATORY DEVICES FOR PROTECTION AGAINST CERTAIN PESTICIDES," BULLETIN ARS 33-76-2*, free from the *AGRICULTURAL RESEARCH SERVICE (BELTSVILLE, MD 20705)*. Always use natural rubber gloves, as synthetic rubber gives little protection against many chemicals.

Proper pesticide dosages are often important to prevent plant damage. Measuring powders with a regular teaspoon can give hazardous inaccuracies. Use a measuring spoon, do not press down the powder, and level it off with a straight edge — or, better yet, weigh the dosage with a postal scale.

Home Brews

Homemade pest controls are a new trend. In Germany, smoke from oak leaves is widely used to control aphids and mites in greenhouses. Purdue University reports that a spray of 5 pounds of wheat flour and 1 pint of buttermilk in 25 gallons of water destroys spider mites by immobilizing them on foliage. The University of Wisconsin has used a spray made with mashed turnips and corn oil against flies, mites, aphids and bean beetles.

M. C. Goldman, managing editor of "Organic Gardening," supplies this round-up of home remedies:

Tomato stems and leaves boiled in water and sprayed on many plants destroy aphids and other pests, and also act as a repellent . . . a "whitewash" solution of water and lime painted on tree trunks deters boring and climbing pests . . . lime mixed with wood ashes prevents damage by maggots and others if sprinkled around onions, cabbage and beets, and kills squash bugs when applied to them . . . a paper cup containing a solution of 1 part blackstrap molasses to 9 parts of water and hung in apple trees traps codling moths . . . Japanese beetles flock to traps containing geranium oil . . .

A tea made by boiling wormwood (artemisia) leaves is useful against many soft-bodied insects . . . all flying pests can be combatted with a quassia spray — soak 2 ounces of quassia chips in 1 gallon of water for 2 to 3 days, then simmer 2 to 3 hours, strain and mix thoroughly with 2 ounces of soft soap . . . grind up hot peppers, green onions, garlic, mint, geranium leaves and other strong-flavored plants and make a spray; the more ingredients, the more bugs it is likely to repel . . . trap larvae of mosquitoes by floating cabbage or mustard seeds, which exude a sticky "glue," in pans of water.

Saucers or jar tops filled with beer, sunk flush into the soil and covered with a slightly raised shingle, are very efficient slug traps. Wood ashes sprinkled on the ground or foliage deter cutworms, bean beetles, squash bugs, many borers and others, and slugs and snails will literally dry up when they encounter a line of wood ashes. Coffee grounds mixed into the soil controlled fusarium-root rot of beans in experiments by the Agricultural Research Service.

Nematodes are killed by asparagus juice — pour the cooking water, with some asparagus ends mashed up in it, around plants. Garlic is one of the most potent repellents of insects, and even kills some: the University of California found that only 12 ppm of an extract of garlic gives 100% kill of mosquito larvae when sprayed on breeding ponds.

Dr. John E. Bier of the University of British Columbia uses a "saprophyte solution" to control fungus diseases of trees. Saprophytes are beneficial bacteria, yeasts and fungi that live in and on tree bark and are inimical to pathogenic fungi. Dr. Bier soaks about ½ ounce of healthy bark in a quart of distilled or rain water for 5 days at 70° minimum, aerating the solution several times a day by pouring it from one container to another, then applies it with a hand sprayer. Results reported include reduction or disappearance of scab and cankers on apple trees, vigorous new growth on an apparently dying dwarf pear and exceptionally healthy, strong growth of all trees even in severe drought.

Mechanical Controls

Much damage can be prevented by hand-picking larger insects as soon as the first ones appear . . . covering plants with netting and enclosing fruit in plastic bags . . . knocking smaller bugs off plants with a strong hose stream . . . banding trunks of trees with tanglefoot to prevent borers, caterpillars and cankerworms from climbing them, or replacing the soil around the root crowns with large stones . . . trapping earwigs with towel strips hung in shrubs, or apple maggot flies with yellow rectangles coated like flypaper . . . and deterring cutworms with paper collars around seedlings.

Aphids, thrips and Mexican bean beetles are repelled by an aluminum foil mulch. Dramatic increases in vegetable yields have been achieved by reduction of insect damage and of aphid-transmitted virus diseases. A foil mulch reduces thrips on roses more effectively than systemic insecticides. Gladiolus protected by foil produces taller flower spikes with flowers showing much less virus discoloration. The Connecticut Agricultural Experiment Station reports that oxidized or used aluminum surfaces, because they reflect more shortwave light, are better than shiny new aluminum. Since the foil's reflectivity is not effective above about 24″, foil attached to cross-pieces on stakes is suggested to protect the upper parts of tall plants.

Cultural Controls

Quite simple cultural techniques can be very effective in eliminating pests or at least reducing their damage to an acceptable minimum.

Some are excellent preventives, such as choosing disease- and insect-resistant varieties — your state experiment station will recommend these for your area. Sanitation is most useful: prompt burying, burning or composting of plant refuse, and removal of weeds that serve as hosts, will cut off sources of infection and infestation. From autumn to late winter, prune out and burn the shiny tan-brown to blue-black egg cases of the

The marigolds not only protect the cabbage from many above-ground insects, but also kill nematodes in the soil.

tent caterpillar and the brown egg cases of bagworms. Be sure, however, to save the valuable foamy egg cases of the praying mantis; for best survival, bury them in a straw bed covered with evergreen boughs.

Crop rotation is important in annual beds and the vegetable garden. Nematodes that attack cabbage and beets, for example, are foiled by rotating these with corn or onions — but never alternate potatoes and tomatoes, as this causes a build-up of nematodes. Timing of planting can also prevent damage: squash planted very early suffers negligible damage from midsummer borers, and radishes and cabbages planted after mid-May usually escape maggots. Timing of other chores also helps — at Colonial Williamsburg, boxwood is given an over-all clipping 2″ to 3″ deep in late winter to eliminate boxwood miner, which at that season is concentrated in the outer leaves of the plant.

Spading or rototilling in early spring will expose grasshopper and slug eggs to drying, and give effective control of pests such as the western cutworm and grape berry moth. Tilling in a green manure crop helps kill nematodes by stimulating inimical organisms.

Biological Controls

Biological weapons available to gardeners are many and multiplying. Encouragement of birds, of course, by providing nesting boxes, hedgerows and winter feeding, is highly effective. Also helpful are snakes, lizards, toads. Even moles, which eat grubs, wireworms and cutworms, and wasps, destroyers of caterpillars and flies, deserve protection when possible.

Lesser-known predators which should be conserved by minimal use of poisons include robber, syrphid and tachinid flies, the tiny braconid wasps, spiders, ground beetles and a great many others: the wise gardener never forgets that 99% of the perhaps 1,600,000 known insect species are beneficial.

The "big three" biological controls gardeners can introduce as preventive or emergency measures are ladybugs, trichogramma wasps and praying mantises. All are incredibly voracious eaters of many of our worst pests — aphids, mealybugs, scales, mites, many moths and worms. A leaflet giving sources of these biological controls is available from *READERS SERVICE, ORGANIC*

GARDENING (EMMAUS, PA 18049).

Two bacterial insecticides are highly praised by gardeners. Milky spore disease, sold as Doom by *FAIRFAX BIOLOGICAL LABORATORY (CLINTON CORNERS, NY 12514)*, destroys grubs of the Japanese beetle and European chafer. Very effective against the larvae of lepidopterous insects such as cabbage looper, gypsy moth, cankerworm, tent caterpillar, corn earworm and tomato hornworm, is *Bacillus thuringiensis* (Dipel, Biotrol, Thuricide).

Many new biological controls are in the offing. England's Glasshouse Crops Research Institute (Littlehampton, Sussex) has found a wasp-like parasite that destroys whiteflies, several parasites and predators of aphids, and a predator which completely eliminates red spider in greenhouses at one-tenth the cost of sprays. The University of California has discovered a virus that gives 98% control of codling moth. In the Midwest, a braconid wasp which saved Europe's elms by parasitizing the eggs of the elm bark beetle is being released by the millions. A new multimillion-dollar firm, *ZOECON CORPORATION (975 CALIFORNIA AVENUE, PALO ALTO, CA 94304)* has developed several insect hormones, which it calls Entocons, that control mealybugs, scale, aphids and other pests by disrupting their growth or reproductive processes.

Strange Bedfellows

Companion planting, which generally refers to interplanting fast- and slow-maturing crops so the latter fill in after the former are harvested, has taken on a new meaning. Some plants help others when grown in close proximity to them, either by repelling pests or acting as "trap crops," or by actually stimulating the growth of the associated plant.

Garlic is a top crop protector, repelling aphids, Japanese beetles and several other pests. Mint, sage and mustard will guard members of the cabbage family, and savory, cosmos and asters repel bean beetles. Basil is a great protector of tomatoes, nasturtiums lure aphids from other plants, radishes attract onion maggots, and chamomile, catnip, chives, feverfew (*Chrysanthe-*

mum parthenium), shallots, dill and tansy repel a great variety of pests. A few plants of the blue-flowered annual Peruvian ground cherry or "shoofly" *(Nicandra physalodes)* spotted around the garden, some gardeners say, will keep it totally free of flies while in bloom.

The Connecticut Agricultural Experiment Station at New Haven has shown that marigolds produce a chemical which kills nematodes — improved growth of many flowers, vegetables, fruits and ornamentals results from interplanting with marigolds (the marigolds must be grown for at least a year to achieve control of the nematodes). Carrots thrive when interplanted with shallots or chives. Roses reportedly grow more vigorously if garlic is grown among them, and their fragrance is actually said to improve. Rosarians also say that if you plant tomatoes among your roses, you'll have no blackspot.

The more varied a garden's plantings, the less pest damage is likely, says Prof. R. B. Root of Cornell University: "The confusion of chemical stimuli offered by a mixture of plants can cause the breakdown of an insect's orientation, feeding habits, and population numbers."

An excellent list of herbs and the plants they aid is given in the *"HANDBOOK OF HERBS,"* $1 from MERRY GARDENS (CAMDEN, ME 04843).

Bug Lures and Snares

Traps baited with sex pheromones or other attractants are rapidly becoming important biological pest-control tools. Many orchardists, for example, are cutting pesticide usage by as much as 50% through the use of two traps, Sectar and Pherocon, produced by the Zoecon Corporation.

The traps are generally employed for early detection of rising pest populations to determine the most effective time to spray or employ natural controls such as the release of sterilized males. Traps are available to monitor oriental fruit moth, codling moth, several leafrollers and other nut and fruit pests. The most effective trap has proved to be a fluorescent yellow baited with an attractant and coated inside with a sticky substance. An added benefit from reduced insecticide applications has been an accompanying 50% cut in miticide use, as the smaller amounts of pesticides eliminated less of the mites' natural enemies.

Direct control with the traps is also possible. The New York State Agricultural Experiment Station at Geneva reports that mass trapping of male red-banded leafrollers before mating reduced larval populations below damaging levels. An organic gardener, Eugene Carpovich, reports excellent control of fruit pests with a combination of traps, spraying with the natural insecticide ryania (Ryatox, by BONIDE CHEMICAL CO., UTICA, NY 13502), and plastic oranges (from the five-and-dime) coated with Tanglefoot *(TANGLEFOOT CO., 314 STRAIGHT AVENUE, S.W., GRAND RAPIDS, MI 49504)*.

Bio-Control Success Stories

Nurserymen, horticulturists and even park departments are proving the efficacy of biological controls. In 1968, at Stonegate Farm Nursery (Algonquin, IL 60102), owner George Schuman, Jr., released a half-gallon of ladybugs in a block of 1000 yews infested with mealybugs. In a few weeks, the mealybugs were totally gone. Since then, he has converted to biological controls exclusively. He "employs" ladybugs to control aphids and mealybugs, and notes that since using them he has never been troubled by red spider.

Trichogramma wasps control moth and butterfly larvae, green lacewings (aphid lions) destroy aphids, thrips, mites, leafhoppers and caterpillars. On the rare occasions that Mr. Schuman finds a tree infested with insects not controllable by his biological agents, he destroys the plant. His program costs about $100 a month for his 140 acres through the growing season.

At Daytona Beach Community College in Florida, ornamental–horticulture students found that avoidance of widespread use of powerful poisons allowed beneficial organisms to increase so well that they almost annihilated whiteflies and aphids. Torymid wasps decimated the whiteflies, and the few aphids that were not destroyed by lacewings and ladybugs were easily controlled by nicotine sulphate and soap. A viburnum hedge which previously required frequent spraying with malathion or Diazinon is now protected by ladybugs and aphid lions.

In the flower garden, nicotine sulphate controlled sucking insects, while the bacterial insecti-

A combination of chemical, biological and mechanical methods is proving as effective as DDT in controlling the gypsy moth.

cide *Bacillus thuringiensis* proved potent against caterpillars. For pill bugs, the more toxic Kepone was necessary, but was used in bait form so as not to harm beneficial organisms. Non-toxic Oilicide controlled most scales, except tea scale on Chinese hollies, which was treated with DiSyston applied to the soil — being restricted to the plants' tissues, this systemic causes little if any harm to helpful organisms.

In a 70-acre section of New York City's Riverside Park, the release in late spring of 1,000,000 ladybugs, 40,000 praying mantises and 5000 trichogramma wasps gave as good control of insects as a spraying program did in the rest of the park — and at far lower cost. The Department of Recreation and Parks in Berkeley, California, found that control of pests on its 35,000 street trees can be achieved totally without chemical insecticides. Of the two main pests, aphids are controlled by an introduced parasite or by simply hitting the trees with a strong stream of water, and oakworms are destroyed by spraying with *Bacillus thuringiensis.*

Gypsy Mothproofing

The banning of DDT raised dire predictions that the gypsy moth — the most publicized tree-defoliating insect in American history — would increase its rate of spread west and south and decimate many more millions of trees.

However, integrated control promises an effective solution. Sevin and *Bacillus thuringiensis* are toxic to gypsy moth caterpillars. Disparlure, the sex attractant emitted by the female gypsy moth, is being tested in traps to catch the males, and also used as a "confusion technique," being sprayed over infested areas to confuse the males so they cannot locate females. At least 11 parasites of the gypsy moth have adapted to conditions in the Northeast, and the Agricultural Research Service is testing nearly 100 other predators and parasites. Also under study are the release of sterile gypsy moths, and a nucleopolyhedrosis virus that infects gypsy moth larvae.

The gardener can do much to reduce gypsy moth damage: spray with Sevin or *Bacillus thuringiensis* when the caterpillars are feeding in May to June . . . hand-pick the caterpillars, which will congregate on burlap strips tied around the tree trunks, or trap them with a band of Tanglefoot . . . in summer, scrape off and burn the pupa cases or cocoons, and do the same with the 1″ to 2″ tan oval egg cases, found on rocks and wood surfaces, in fall and winter — these can also be destroyed by painting them with a mixture of creosote and fuel oil. Encourage birds, too, which find the eggs fine winter food. Fall and spring fertilizing, and deep watering in drought, will restore vigor to injured trees.

Gypsy moth attack, it should be noted, is not the disaster it has often been called. Massachusetts is anything but denuded of trees after over 100 years of playing host to the pest. And Virginia Viney Smiley, of the famed nature resort,

Lake Mohonk, in New Paltz, New York, reports that Mohonk's 7500 acres of forest had a severe gypsy moth infestation at the height of a 5-year drought, yet — without spraying — the loss of trees was only 2%. She notes that most trees can survive two or more years of total defoliation, and disease and predators rapidly reduce the moth population so that such repeated attack on a tree is uncommon.

Repelling Boarders

Four-footed marauders can wreak havoc in gardens. The surest deterrent to deer which attack suburban gardens in severe winters is an 8' woven wire fence, but several "taste" repellents are also effective: Improved Z.I.P. (PANOGEN CO., RINGWOOD, IL 60072); Magic Circle (STATE COLLEGE LABORATORIES, UNIVERSITY PARK, PA 16802); and Penco Thiram (PENNSALT CHEMICALS CORP., BOX 1297, TACOMA, WA 98401). These should be applied carefully, observing all cautions on the label. An intriguing natural repellent that emits the scent of mountain lion is offered by the NATIONAL SCENT CO. (BOX 7, GARDEN GROVE, CA 92640).

Scent-off, made by JOHNSON NURSERIES (BOX 411, DEXTER, NY 13634) harmlessly repels dogs and cats. Red pepper is a powerful deterrent to squirrels, and Squell (PENNYFEATHER CORP., BOX 3681, GREENVILLE, DE 19807) or Vaseline lathered on the pole of a pole bird feeder will keep squirrels from climbing it. A gardener reports that a solution made by soaking a chunk of liver in a bucket of hot water for 30 minutes is an excellent rabbit repellent spray.

The field mice and moles which are often a problem when deep mulching is practiced can be ousted with mothballs or moth flakes (gardeners say these are also effective in controlling ants, earwigs and taxus weevil, and in ridding pachysandra of armyworms). The mole plant, *Euphorbia lathyris*, has high mole repellency, according to reports from South Africa.

For pest birds, No-Pidge (MIDDLE STATES OIL CO., 14812 DETROIT AVENUE, CLEVELAND, OH 44107) is non-toxic but discourages nesting and roosting. Volck oil sprayed on berried shrubs such as holly, cotoneaster and pyracantha harmlessly repels berry-eating birds, but must be re-applied after each rain as long as one wishes to preserve the berry display. Woodpeckers whose drumming in the fall can drive the homeowner to distraction can be induced to seek other feeding sites by temporarily emptying birdfeeders and removing all deadwood from trees near the house. Yellow-bellied sapsuckers, which drill holes that can harm or kill young trees, will vacate any area where several small mirrors are hung on a string.

OF PESTS AND PESTICIDES

"Gardening Without Poisons," by Beatrice Trum Hunter (Houghton Mifflin, $5)

"The Organic Way to Plant Protection," by the editors of "Organic Gardening" (Emmaus, PA 18049; $4.95)

"Diseases and Pests of Ornamental Plants," 4th ed., by Dr. Pascal P. Pirone (Ronald Press, $12)

"Safe Use of Pesticides," by the American Public Health Association (1740 Broadway, New York, NY 10019; $3 plus 35¢ postage)

"Health Hazards in Farming and Gardening," by the American Medical Association (Order Handling Department, 535 North Dearborn Street, Chicago, IL 60610; $1)

"Destructive and Useful Insects — Their Habits and Control," 4th ed., by C. L. Metcalf and W. P. Flint (McGraw-Hill, $17.50)

A parasitic wasp deposits its eggs in a gypsy moth pupa, which will die when the eggs hatch.

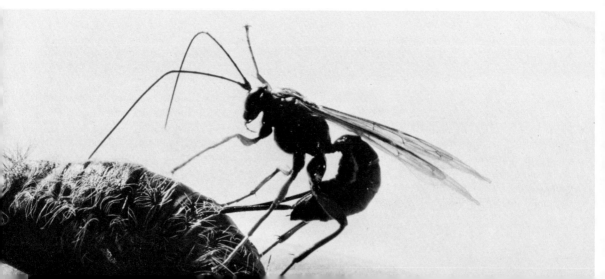

PROPAGATION

Cubism

The newest school in the art of plant propagation is definitely cubism. From peat pots, gardeners have graduated to cubes or "growing blocks" of inert or organic material, impregnated with fertilizers. Seeds or cuttings are simply set in a hole in the cube and grow until rooted, then cube and all is planted. A sterile medium, great ease of handling and no transplanting shock are very worthwhile advantages.

Some widely available cubes are Jiffy-7 Peat Pellets (*JIFFY-POT COMPANY OF AMERICA, BOX 338, WEST CHICAGO, IL 60185*); Solo-Gro Cubes (*PLANT PRODUCTS CO., PORT CREDIT, ONTARIO, CANADA*); Quickee Sure-Start Cubes (*FLORALIFE, INC., 4420 SOUTH TRIPP AVENUE, CHICAGO, IL 60632*); BR-8 Blocks (*AMERICAN CAN CO., GREENWICH, CT 06830*); 0-903 Foam Blocks (*SMITHERS-OASIS, BOX 118, KENT, OH 44240*); and Kys-Kube Blocks (*PULLEN MOLDED PRODUCTS, INC., NEW IBERIA, LA 70560*).

For best results, commercial growers recommend thoroughly soaking the cubes with warm water before sowing . . . using cubes with the right-sized hole, or dibbling and pressing the medium around the seed or cutting to insure firm contact . . . watering well both before and after transplanting, and covering the cube when planting it with $\frac{1}{4}''$ of soil so it cannot act as a wick and dry out quickly.

Sowing Styles

Some useful ideas on sowing seed outdoors and transplanting seedlings:

All but the tiniest seed, say commercial growers, germinates more quickly and more surely if pre-soaked in water, a few hours for fine seed to 24 hours for hard-shelled types. Some European gardeners say germination is even better when the seed is soaked in weak "manure tea."

How deep should seed be planted? Prof. Richard Clemence reports he has excellent results following nature's method of sowing seed on top of the ground. He simply spaces his seeds on the surface, shakes fine peatmoss over them, presses it down with a board, roller or his feet and uses a sprinkler to insure sufficient moisture until germination occurs.

Another method, by horticulturist R. B. Farnham: seed is sown $1''$ deep, in a trench $5''$ wide with gently sloping sides. Small seeds are then covered with $\frac{1}{2}''$, medium seeds with $\frac{3}{4}''$, and large seeds with $1''$ of peatmoss, leafmold or other moisture-retaining, non-crusting material. A wide trench, says Mr. Farnham, won't fill with seed-smothering soil in spring rains, and the soil in the bottom stays moist longer.

A tip for tiny seeds: single sheets of facial tissue laid in the furrow let tiny seeds show up well for easy spacing with a toothpick. The tissue soon rots away.

To harden seedlings to be planted out, gradually reduce temperature and watering, and increase light — an aluminum foil reflector behind seedlings in a window can be very beneficial. "Mudding" the roots after removal from the flat, by gently pulling them through a thin mixture of soil and water, aids formation of feeder roots.

After setting the plants, give a weak "starter" solution of complete fertilizer high in phosphorus. Then mulch between the rows with half-rotted organic material: this both aids soil warm-up and supplies growth-stimulating carbon dioxide.

Gambit for Direct Seeding

For early bloom or harvest, gardeners start seeds indoors or use plastic mulches and cloches to protect early garden sowings. However, the gardener who hasn't the time or inclination for these measures can gamble — with reasonable odds in his favor — with unprotected seedings made 1 to 4 weeks earlier than is usual for his area, if he uses these ideas:

Avoidance of frost pockets and planting on south-facing slopes are obvious. But just as important is control of soil temperature. Loose, soft soil warms rapidly, hastening seedling emergence and root development. Commercial vegetable growers know that a well-drained, non-crusting, medium- to fine-textured loam high in organic matter is ideal for early direct seeding. This is best achieved by digging the soil in the fall and adding compost material, leaving it bare through the winter, then giving shallow cultivation in early spring.

Secondly, plant deeper than usual — Ohio State University recommends planting corn 1½" deep to keep the growing point below the soil surface for frost protection. And, finally, watering with water that is near air temperature, rather than icy cold from the faucet, avoids root shock. A rainbarrel or tank in the sun, or a tempering device to mix hot and cold water to the desired temperature in the line, are worthwhile.

Holding Operation

When seedlings are ready to go outdoors but the weather won't cooperate, the gardener can hold them in storage for several weeks, says Dr. R. W. Langhans of Cornell University.

A cold cellar, porch or outbuilding is necessary, where as near 35° to 40° as possible can be maintained. A fluorescent fixture containing two 40-watt cool white tubes is suspended 12" above the plants, with the lights on 14 hours a day. They are watered as needed, and a small fan or other provision for ventilation will keep them healthy. The method has proven successful for all but zinnias and coleus. Marigolds, petunias, stocks, geraniums, lobelias, asters, salvias, snapdragons, dianthuses and sweet alyssums can be held at optimum transplanting size for as long as 6 weeks. Ageratum, balsam, cosmos and most vegetables tolerate up to 2 weeks of storage.

Seeding in Situ

Gardeners who would like to sow seeds of trees and shrubs directly where they are wanted — rather than in a seedbed, which necessitates laborious and growth-slowing transplanting — will be interested in the "collar-and-mulch" sys-

A combination of a collar around the seed and a mulch encourages germination and growth by controlling temperature, moisture and weeds.

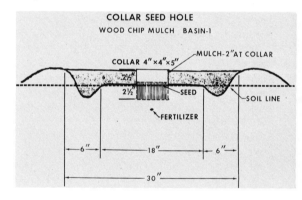

tem developed by Dr. R. W. Harris and others of the Department of Environmental Horticulture, of the University of California at Davis.

A hole is dug about 4" deep and wide, and a pinch of high-nitrogen fertilizer is put at the bottom. Then a collar, 4" wide and 5" deep, is set in place as the soil is replaced, so that 2½" of the collar is below the ground level and an equal length is above it. An open-ended tin can works well, as do milk cartons or cylinders made of kraft or asphalt paper. The seed is planted in the center of the collar, twice as deep as the seed's largest dimension. Then a 2" mulch of wood chips or similar loose material is put down outside the collar, confined by a ring of soil thrown up about 12" from the collar.

The collar speeds germination and growth by increasing the soil temperature in the seed area, and allows easy watering. The mulch controls weeds and reduces moisture loss. A wire cage of ½″ mesh hardware cloth will guard the seedling from birds and rodents until it is several inches high, then can be replaced by a taller poultry wire cylinder left in place for several years. Constant renewal of the mulch, plus frequent deep watering and fertilizing every spring, will result in rapid growth.

Sizable Success

In propagating woody plants, gardeners often take a large number of small cuttings, as insurance against a high percentage of failure to root. But nurserymen who have tested small versus large cuttings note emphatically that larger cuttings almost always root more surely and more heavily — and, of course, a larger plant is produced more quickly.

At England's East Malling Research Station, best rooting is consistently obtained with apple understock cuttings at least 24″ long. A New Jersey nurseryman who regularly uses 12″ cuttings of Hicks yew reports that cuttings double that length have rooted successfully. Another researcher notes that when short cuttings must be used, thicker cuttings will root more vigorously than thinner ones.

Framework for Cuttings

A simple but very efficient frame for softwood propagation has been developed by Alfred J. Fordham, propagator at Boston's Arnold Arboretum.

In a site with bright light but no direct sun, a standard 1′ x 2′ greenhouse flat is plunged into the soil to its full depth. The flat is lined with 2-mil polyethylene, cut to extend 2″ above the sides, and a medium of equal parts of sand and horticultural perlite is added and firmed. Then turkey or utility wire is cut and bent so that it will support a plastic cover about 6″ above the cuttings. Mr. Fordham stresses that this framework must lie flat at the top, so the moisture droplets that condense on the inside of the plastic will fall back evenly on the cuttings and medium — a curved top would "direct them to the side

SOAKING SEEDS PREVENTS "CHILLING INJURY" that reduces plant growth and vigor, reports Plant Physiologist B. M. Pollock, at the Colorado Agricultural Experiment Station (Fort Collins, CO 80521). Lima beans, he found, can be injured by even the moderately low temperature of 59° at the critical time just after the seed begins to absorb water for germination. Soaking the seed 8 hours in room-temperature water before sowing prevented this injury.

walls and down, leaving the center portion of the chamber dry."

Softwood cuttings taken in early morning are cut on a slant and the tips treated with rooting hormone, then inserted into the medium and watered. "The framework is put in place and covered with polyethylene plastic; soil is then mounded over the plastic where it meets the ground. It should be emphasized that with this system of propagation it is imperative that all air leaks be eliminated as they could reduce the very necessary high humidity and cause failure."

When the cuttings have rooted, they are potted and covered with plastic, which is removed at night, for 5 or 6 days, then taken off completely as the plants become accustomed to the less humid normal atmosphere.

Shortcut Cuttings

Simplified propagation of deciduous trees and shrubs by hardwood cuttings is outlined by Ray E. Halward, propagator at the Royal Botanic Gardens in Hamilton, Ontario.

Softwood cuttings root readily in this propagator under a plastic cover supported by a flat wire frame.

water, or by freeze-drying and grinding the cuttings, then extracting the substance with water. When synthesized, these materials should be very helpful in combination with hormones to aid the rooting of many hard-to-root plants.

Healthy, vigorous stems of the current year's growth are taken during a mild spell, the immature top ends are discarded and the remainder are cut into 4″ to 10″ lengths, with a minimum of two nodes on each. Mr. Halward notes that growers have found the old practice of making the final cuts just above buds at the top and just below buds at the base does not improve rooting. The cuttings should be dusted with a fungicide such as captan 50W, and tied in bundles.

Simplest storage method: put moist — not wet — sphagnum moss around the base of the bundle, and seal it tightly in a plastic bag. Keep the bag in a cool room — 50° to 60° — for 8 to 10 days, then put it in the refrigerator.

Plant the cuttings outdoors in sandy soil in very early spring, leaving just the top bud exposed. Water as needed, fertilize early in the season, then transplant and prune the following spring.

A useful basic work on propagation is *"CUTTINGS THROUGH THE YEAR,"* $2 from the *ARBORETUM FOUNDATION (UNIVERSITY OF WASHINGTON, SEATTLE, WA 98105)*.

Rooting Solution

New root-promoting substances, more potent than the rooting hormones now in use, have been discovered at the Ohio Agricultural Research and Development Center at Wooster.

Prof. Makoto Kawase found that cuttings of easily rooted plants such as willow release a strong rooting stimulant when their bases are set in water. When mung bean cuttings were put into the water in which the willows had steeped, rapid and profuse rooting occurred. In comparison tests, the rooting hormone indoleacetic acid aided mung bean root formation only slightly, but a combination of the hormone and the willow water extract produced roots several times more effectively than either material alone.

Professor Kawase has obtained rooting substances similar to the willow extract from softwood cuttings of cotoneaster, euonymus, holly, honeysuckle, ninebark, sweetleaf, viburnum and yew. The strongest substance increased rooting of mung bean cuttings 9 times over control cuttings in water alone. The new rooting stimulators are easily extracted by steeping cuttings in

Mister Versatility

Mist propagation, both indoors and out, has become a widely accepted technique. With misting, almost any woody plant can be propagated at any time of year, and because cuttings under mist are given full sun, much sturdier growth results. The increased photosynthesis and reduced transpiration make rooting rapid and heavy. Misting has also proved an aid to germinating seed.

Does it pay to mist with nutrients? Cornell University's Department of Ornamental Horticulture tested intermittent mist containing a high-analysis fertilizer on hardwood and softwood cuttings. Considerably more growth was noted on the nutrient-misted cuttings during rooting than on cuttings misted with plain water, and following transplanting the nutrient-misted specimens grew up to twice as rapidly and often with double lateral branching.

THE GEORGIA AGRICULTURAL EXPERIMENT STATION (ATHENS, GA 30601) offers a useful bulletin, *N.S. 139, "AN EVALUATION OF VARIOUS EQUIPMENT AND MEDIA USED FOR MIST PROPAGATION AND THEIR RELATIVE COSTS."* Plans for a 6′ x 6′ easy-to-build mist propagating frame are obtainable from Virginia Polytechnic Institute's Agricultural Engineering Department (Blacksburg, VA 24061). *E. C. GEIGER (BOX 27, NORTH WALES, PA 19454)* has free literature on its "Mist-A-Matic" system, and *WHITE SHOWERS, INC. (722 PORTER STREET, LANSING, MI 48905)* offers a booklet, *"BEGINNING WITH MIST,"* for $1. A simple but efficient unit for the garden is the "Mistic Bubble," by *MIST METHODS COMPANY (5612 COURT SOUTH, BIRMINGHAM, AL 35212)*.

An automated indoor-outdoor mist system for propagating — and for evaporative cooling of plants, greenhouse and even the home — is Aquamonitor *(BOX 327, HUNTINGTON, NY 11743)*. Consisting of a sensor, valve and solid state electric power supply, the system can monitor up to almost a quarter acre of seedbed, cuttings, plants or roof. The sensor measures the moisture in the area and applies water whenever it drops below a pre-set level. Either hose or pipe, and mist or sprinkler nozzles, can be used with the system, which operates on 24 volts and is completely portable.

Better by the Bucket

An improvement over the plastic bag "window greenhouse" developed several years ago by the Agricultural Research Service has been devised by Robert Wester, horticulturist at the ARS Plant Industry Station in Beltsville, Maryland.

The plastic mini-propagator does an excellent job of starting seeds, rooting cuttings and even growing some plants to maturity. It uses an ordinary 5-quart plastic bucket and thus is more versatile and easier to handle than non-rigid plastic bags. Four holes are cut with a knife on the bucket's sides to provide drainage, and a second wire handle is attached to the original handle at right angles and hooked onto the lip of the bucket. These form the frame for the "tent," a 15" or 18" plastic bag dropped over the handles and secured with a rubber band under the bucket lip.

The Cornell Peat-Lite Mix (Jiffy-Mix, Redi-Earth) is used for starting seed, and a mix of 2 parts shredded sphagnum or peatmoss and 1 part perlite or sand for cuttings. The plastic bag is removed when the cuttings have rooted or seedlings emerge and are thinned. Mr. Wester reports that chives, cabbage, lettuce, onions, tomatoes, petunias and marigolds have been grown successfully from seed in the mini-propagator, and cuttings have been rooted of azaleas, chrysanthemums, coleuses, hollies and rhododendrons. He notes that even difficult plants like red rhododendrons have rooted readily in 8 weeks.

SPECIAL TECHNIQUES

Cold Facts

Until recently, cold hardiness has been a neglected field of horticultural research. Now there is an Institute of Low Temperature Research in Japan, and a new laboratory for study of plant hardiness has been established by the Horticultural Science Department of the University of Minnesota directed by Prof. Conrad J. Weiser. Professor Weiser reports some interesting conclusions:

Water freezing within a plant cell invariably causes the death of the cell. When the temperature declines gradually, permeability of the cell membrane increases and water moves out of the cell, giving the cell a lower freezing point. But when the temperature drops rapidly — as when a plant in sun is suddenly shaded by a building or other object — water cannot move out of the cell

fast enough. American arborvitae (*Thuja occidentalis*) resisted $-125°$ of slow freezing (9° per hour), but was killed at 15° when freezing was rapid (18° per minute).

Sunshields — burlap on frames, snow fence, reed mats or evergreen boughs — are therefore very important to protect many evergreens, particularly young plants. Winter burn on one-year-old arborvitae, the researchers proved, was due to rapid temperature changes rather than desiccation, and was eliminated by shading. Rhododendrons in Minnesota survived $-35°$ when shaded.

Shading, however, must not be applied early: maximum light is necessary through fall for the plants to accumulate sugars through photosynthesis. Plants shaded in October suffered severe winter injury; those shaded in December were comparatively unharmed. Professor Weiser notes, "The common practice of shading newly rooted cuttings to harden them off after mist propagation limits their already depleted carbo-

The Agricultural Research Service is testing an insulating foam that will protect young vegetable plants overnight against frost.

hydrate reserves and probably reduces their capacity to acclimate to cold."

As for mineral nutrition, a high level of nitrogen and, in some cases, of phosphorus increases winter injury, while potassium reduces it. Feeding late in the growing season thus should provide high potassium, little or no nitrogen and phosphorus. Concerning water, Professor Weiser states, "It is doubtful that withholding water is beneficial in hardening most plants and may actually interfere with natural hardening. Probable exceptions to this are plants which do not go into rest in the fall and need unfavorable conditions to stop their growth . . . Caution is called for in withholding water except in special cases."

A new combination growth stimulant and frost retardant, available in aerosol cans, is Frosbar (GROSTIM CORPORATION, BOX 555, MERIDIAN, ID 83642), a patented non-toxic formulation of 36 nutrients and other substances. It is recommended for weekly use on both indoor and outdoor plants to promote vigorous healthy growth. Applied for frost protection in early spring at 2- to 5-day intervals, Frosbar is said to enable tender vegetation to withstand at least several degrees of frost. Two applications to flower buds of fruit trees provide protection for from 5° below freezing point for flowers of Jonathan apples to as much as 18° in the case of pears. In the fall, weekly use is said to harden tender plants so they will stand early frosts, and toughen hardy plants so they can endure more cold. Users report that tomato plants have survived temperatures as low as 20° in autumn when sprayed with Frosbar.

Another aid to outwitting those scattered early frosts that cut short the life of tender plants is a lawn sprinkler. The method is based on the principle that heat is released as water changes to ice. Some of this heat will be absorbed into the plants and flowers, enough to keep them above the freezing point. Water is sprayed on the plants continuously while the air temperature is below freezing and until rising temperatures have melted the ice. Even distribution of the water is vital, so that each plant is wetted at least once a minute.

Microclimatics

"Hardiness," said the late Ralph Bailey of "House and Garden," "means absolute susceptibility to this temperature or that only about 2% of the time." The other 98% of the time, the many factors of the plant's immediate soil and air environment — its microclimate — are the ruling elements. The most successful gardeners know their gardens intimately, and so can find microclimates hospitable to any plants susceptible to winter cold or summer heat.

Observing snow is very helpful. Where snow melts first, generally in a southern exposure with shrubs or a wall on the north, is the place for the tenderest plants. Conversely, only the hardiest should be located in spots that are swept clean by winter winds. Where drifts form is ideal for broadleaved evergreens, which will benefit from deep snow cover against winter wind and sun.

Since cold air drains downward, low spots must be avoided. At the Arnold Arboretum in Boston, as much as 18.5° differences have been observed between high and low elevations on still nights when there was no wind to mix warm and cold air masses. Tender plants should not be sited where any plant or structure blocks the downhill flow of cold air, trapping it around them. An open eastern exposure is also risky, because precipitous warming of frozen plant cells by the early morning sun can cause severe damage.

For plants sensitive to summer heat, a shaded eastern exposure will avoid subjecting them to midafternoon's blazing heat — delphiniums will do well much farther south than usual if given such a site. An east-facing slope provides both the coolness and perfect drainage essential to alpines. And for winter survival of any doubtfully hardy plant, avoid or correct poorly drained depressions where thaws leave puddles.

Gone With the Wind

Wind control, says Gary Robinette of the American Society of Landscape Architects, is a vital consideration in gardening.

In many areas, wind causes more winter plant desiccation than does sun. Increased transpiration, plus greater cold due to the "wind chill factor" — a 40 mph wind at 20° is as chilling as −10° with a 5 mph wind — injures not only questionably hardy plants, but also many very hardy ones such as forest natives like hemlock and fir which are not adapted to open situations.

In addition, wind-whipped plants may suffer broken roots, and fruit trees do not bear when wind tears off the blossoms. Wind retards growth through increased cold, as seen in the "cold bands" on corn leaves when chilling temporarily halts growth, or through reduction of photosynthesis because less leaf surface is exposed to the sun. The Oklahoma Agricultural Experiment Station found that a 15 mph wind delays maturity of marigolds and reduces their flower size by 50%.

Windbreak plantings can cut wind velocity by 75% or more, for a distance of ten times the height of the windbreak. The best windbreak plants are those that are densely branched to the ground, or multiple-stemmed with rough bark. A curving hedge on the north will turn aside wintry blasts, while in summer it catches and deflects through the garden much-needed cooling breezes. These breezes can also be accelerated by channeling them through openings in south and west plantings.

Windbreaks can also be used to shut off the flow of cold air that occurs on even the slightest slope, preventing its settling at the lowest point to injure plants there. An opening in plantings at the bottom of the slope is also helpful to allow cold air to drain out of the garden.

Limited space in modern gardens has placed a premium on windbreak plants which grow narrow or can be trimmed so. A few, tall-growing but dense to the ground, are suggested by Dr. Donald Wyman: American arborvitae, *Thuja occidentalis;* bolleana poplar, *Populus alba* 'Pyramidalis'; red cedar, *Juniperus scopulorum* and *J. virginiana;* common privet, *Ligustrum vulgare;* fastigiate European hornbeam, *Carpinus betulus* 'Fastigiata'; and tallhedge buckthorn, *Rhamnus frangula* 'Columnaris.'

Where winter winds really rage, select windbreak plants that are hardy for several hundred miles north of your location.

Raising Alpines

The brilliant beauty of alpine plants tempts every gardener. But these gems of mountainsides and high meadows need a special site and climate — they simply will not tolerate high humidity with high temperature. There are, however, three solutions that are aesthetically and culturally effective:

Raised beds, either built up from ground level or in the form of English-style trough gardens, can give that extra degree of drainage and ventilation that allows growing even the marvelous high-altitude primroses, gentians and lewisias. Enclosed with rocks, brick, cinder blocks, or railroad ties laid in dry-wall fashion to a maximum height of 3′, the raised bed should be oriented for morning sun and full exposure to the garden's natural air flow. It may be 4-sided, of formal design or free-form, or built against a slope or structure. All chinks and the inside of this "container" are filled with a mix of 3 parts soil and 2 parts each of leafmold, peat and sharp sand or pea gravel, with several inches of rubble as a bottom drainage layer.

Troughs cast in Hypatufa make handsome replicas of the old stone troughs long favored in England for alpines. Hypatufa is 1 part each of cement and sharp sand to 2 parts dry sifted sphagnum peat, mixed with sufficient water for easy workability. The trough can be shallow and raised on rock slabs, or deep and free-standing. Rocks set on the soil mix should be of varying sizes, firmly bedded and arranged to provide intercroppings with ample planting crevices. An excellent article on making and planting troughs is found in *"HANDBOOK ON MINIATURE GARDENS," $1.25 FROM THE BROOKLYN BOTANIC GARDEN (BROOKLYN, NY 11225)*.

Screes. Some of the choicest alpine plants — certain penstemons, androsaces, aquilegias, *Potentilla nitida, Dianthus alpinus, Campanula saxifraga* and others that provide masses of bloom on tiny plants — need the very specialized conditions of a scree. In nature, a scree is a mountainside pocket of rocky rubble, exposed to icy winds but affording perfect drainage. In the garden, you can duplicate this by excavating an area as large or small as desired, in full sun, to a depth of 30″. Save the topsoil to use in the scree mix, but discard the subsoil. Fill the bottom 18″ of the excavation with small boulders, broken drain tiles, rocks, bricks, etc., using the smallest rubble at the top. Then lay down a thick layer of leaves or inverted sod to keep the drainage from clogging up, and top this with a 2″ layer of vermiculite.

The scree mix is made up of 1 part each of loam, peat and coarse builder's sand to 3 parts of pea gravel, plus a handful each of bonemeal and balanced organic fertilizer per wheelbarrow load of mix. Decorative rock outcroppings or steppingstones may be set on this. The whole area is then topdressed with 1″ to 2″ of pea gravel before planting.

Tidal Marsh Gardening

How to grow tomatoes, hydrangeas and many other plants in a tidal marsh has been demonstrated by Fred Heutte, retired Director of the Norfolk Botanical Gardens.

Mr. Heutte has been gradually extending his two-acre garden into the marsh that edges his property along Virginia's Lafayette River. For 25 years he has thrown all his garden wastes out into the marsh to build humus, and the soil is further enriched by the minerals in the sea water. He states that he never has to water in this enriched area, which extends from about 3′ above the mean high-tide line down to the marsh grass.

The tomatoes are grown in 2′ sections of terra-cotta flue pipe, the hydrangeas in plastic chemical drums with bottoms removed. Water rises readily from the marsh into the soil in these containers. Some hydrangeas are also planted directly in the enriched marsh area, as are daylilies, cannas, cardinal flower, gladioli, sedums and pampas grass. Shrubs thriving in the marsh soil include hibiscus, baccharis, yucca, oleander, yaupon holly, aucuba, magnolia and pittosporum. Several Japanese black pines and fig trees, plus asparagus, Swiss chard and New Zealand spinach have also proved suited. Camellias and rhododendrons have done well when planted 18″ to 24″ above the mean high-water line.

Plants by the Bale

A fascinating idea from England is growing plants on bales of straw. It has proved successful with greenhouse tomatoes and cucumbers, and the Lee Valley Experimental Horticulture Station says, "There seems no reason why the technique should not be tried out with a whole range of crops. It may well provide a method of raising seedlings of bedding plants, and it could be used to create a garden in a concrete backyard."

The basis of the system is fermentation of the straw, which produces heat just as fermenting manure does in a hotbed. A bale, wired to hold its shape, is watered at intervals for 3 days until fully soaked. To induce fermentation, the Station watered in a 21% nitrogen fertilizer, giving 3 applications of 1 pound each at 3-day intervals. At the last application, 4 ounces of magnesium phosphate, 18 ounces of potassium nitrate and 10 ounces of triple superphosphate were added. At air temperatures of 50° or higher, fermentation develops rapidly and in a few days the interior of the bale reaches 110° to 130°. A thin layer of soil or soilless mix is spread on the top of the bale, and the crop is planted in this.

The roots penetrate rapidly into the straw, and "growth has been tremendous," due both to the heat at the roots and the carbon dioxide rising from the decomposing straw. The straw must be kept moist, and the rule is to feed and water the bale as well as the plants. After use, of course, the rotted straw makes a fine soil amendment or mulch.

Immortal Names

Virtually everlasting plant labels — good for 25 years, or even longer — can be made of zinc strips, and hand-printed with ink and equal parts of hydrochloric acid and butter of antimony. The originators of this method, Mr. and Mrs. Stanley M. Rowe of Cincinnati, use strips 7″ x 1¼″, to accommodate the plant's common and botanical names, source, the date acquired and a code number for easy reference to a record book maintained for all their plants. The labels are attached with aluminum wire.

Grow Your Own Stakes

Shrubby willows planted in odd corners or as screens, says English gardener R. W. Sidwell, can provide all the stakes a gardener needs for his beans, dahlias, annuals, etc.

Speaking of *Salix viminalis,* often used for basket-making, Mr. Sidwell says, "When cut back hard, 8′ of young growth is quite possible in the year, but the shoots are very soft, and to provide good runner bean sticks it is best to allow them a second year in which to thicken up. Excellent light sticks of finger thickness and 3′ to 4′ lengths can be obtained from the annual growth." He notes that S. *purpurea* should also be good for this purpose, and other possibilities include S. *caprea,* S. *discolor* and S. *gracilistyla.*

Because willow cuttings root so easily, Mr. Sidwell says the stakes should be cut either in early winter and allowed to dry out, or early in spring just as the leaves appear, and should be left lying around for several weeks before use.

Some sources of suitable willows are GIRARD NURSERIES (GENEVA, OH 44041), ZILKE BROS. NURSERY (BARODA, MI 49101), BACHMAN'S, INC. (6010 LYNDALE AVENUE, MINNEAPOLIS, MN 55423), AND WAYNESBORO NURSERIES (WAYNESBORO, VA 22980).

Bird Gardening

Increasing restrictions on pesticides have put birds into the front line of defense against insects and weeds. And there's another reason for encouraging birds: if you take the ornithological into consideration, you'll have superior horticultural values in your landscaping. This is the theme of the finest book on attracting birds we've seen — "LANDSCAPING FOR BIRDS," edited and beautifully illustrated by Shirley A. Briggs, and published by the AUDUBON NATURALIST SOCIETY OF THE CENTRAL ATLANTIC STATES (8940 JONES MILL ROAD, WASHINGTON, DC 20015; $1.75 PLUS 25¢ POSTAGE).

The accent is on the best design uses of a great many excellent fruiting ornamentals, to provide both beauty throughout the year and continuous food and cover for birds and other wildlife. Virginia creeper, for example, is seen as a quintuple-purpose plant: twining densely on the west side of the house, it air-conditions against hot afternoon sun; it will quickly give a feeling of age to a new house; the fruit is prized by birds; and the crimson autumn leaves supply mulch and compost material when they fall — all in addition to its ornamental value. Also fascinating are the directions for creating miniature woodlands and cliffs, providing wattle hurdles and dusting places, making nesting faggots and utilizing "little ruins" as wildlife homes.

Two birds every gardener wants in his garden are hummingbirds and bluebirds. An excellent list of plants that attract hummingbirds is given in the catalog of wildlife plant specialist Cliff Walters (DUTCH MOUNTAIN NURSERY, AUGUSTA, MI 49012). WAYSIDE GARDENS (MENTOR, OH 44060; CATALOG $2) lists special shrub and perennial hummingbird collections. A useful booklet is "HUMMINGBIRDS — ATTRACT AND FEED," 35¢ FROM WOODSWORLD (600 OLIVE SPRINGS ROAD, SANTA CRUZ, CA 95060), which also offers the SweetServer Feeder for $2.95 plus 40¢ handling, with the booklet included free.

Showmanship

A master exhibitor at the International Flower Show, Stanley F. Bulpitt of Brookside Nurseries (Darien, CT 06820), gives some valuable tips for forcing for shows:

Use light soil mixes that dry rapidly, incorporate phosphate rock to stimulate root growth and feed often with dilute liquid fertilizer. Watering with 100° water will also stimulate growth, as will application of a hormone such as SUPERthrive or Transplantone. Additional warmth and humidity can be provided by enclosing the plants in plastic. To give maximum light, clean greenhouse or window glass regularly, and paint every possible surface white. Supplementing and extending natural light with artificial is also very helpful.

The fourth revised edition of the "HANDBOOK FOR FLOWER SHOWS" (NATIONAL COUNCIL OF STATE GARDEN CLUBS, 4401 MAGNOLIA AVENUE, ST. LOUIS, MO 63110; $4), contains a section on growing for shows, in addition to its chapters on staging, exhibiting and judging. Also useful are special sections on color, and judging fruits and vegetables.

Wildly Edible — or Deadly?

Concerning poisonous plants, Robert F. Lederer, Executive Vice President of the American Association of Nurserymen, writes that "half-truths and myths in much of the material written on the subject work a serious disservice on the general public as well as on the florist and nursery communities."

The constantly repeated — and totally false — story about the deadliness of the poinsettia is one example. Mr. Lederer notes that many other plants have been wrongly accused in the press, partly because until very recently the statistics issued by the National Clearinghouse for Poison Control Centers did not distinguish between actual poisonings (which go from mild allergies to severe indigestion to, very rarely, death) and inquiries about ingestion of harmless plant substances.

He advises these safety measures: know your plants . . . avoid those you don't know — and teach children early to do the same . . . avoid smoke from any burning plant substance . . . don't let children use any part of an unknown plant for playthings or as skewers for food . . . call the local Poison Control Center immediately if an unknown plant substance is ingested.

For those who share the current enthusiasm for edible wild plants, "THE WILD FOOD TRAILGUIDE," BY ALAN HALL (HOLT, RINEHART & WINSTON, PAPERBACK, $3.45), contains a special section on poisonous plants that resemble safely edible ones.

Sleuthing

As a final recourse for plant identification — if your local horticultural society, botanical garden or extension service is unsuccessful — send a specimen to the HERBARIUM, U.S. NATIONAL ARBORETUM (WASHINGTON, DC 20250). Whenever possible, a specimen should include flowers or fruit as well as foliage. It should be heat-dried between layers of newspapers, pressed down and tied securely to keep it flat. Mail between protective cardboards, with a label attached to the specimen giving size of the plant, growth type (tree, shrub, vine, etc.), the date and place of collection and cultural conditions. These directions are applicable for sending specimens to any source of identification.

For researchers seeking to find if a rare plant is grown in the U.S., the PLANT RECORDS CENTER OF THE AMERICAN HORTICULTURAL SOCIETY (MOUNT VERNON, VA 22121) can provide the location of any species or cultivar growing in any major North American botanical garden, park or arboretum, for a minimum fee of $10.

An aid to finding a retail or wholesale source of a plant is the L. H. BAILEY HORTORIUM (CORNELL UNIVERSITY, ITHACA, NY 14850), which has the world's largest collection of current wholesale and retail seed and nursery catalogs. These catalogs have been indexed, and thus form a monumental guide to plant sources. If a plant is commercially available, the supplier can be located through this index. This has not been publicized, probably because increased requests for sources from growers and gardeners would overburden the staff (a charge for this important service would certainly be in order to enable its expansion).

A commercial source service is "PLANTSEARCH" (1328 MOTOR CIRCLE, DALLAS, TX 75207). From its extensive files of catalogs and lists collected over many years and constantly updated, Plantsearch will find one or more sources where any plant, seed or bulb may be ordered, and supply the customer with the retail addresses and prices. The customer is requested to supply both common and scientific names, if possible, and a short description. The fee is $1 per item searched — money is refunded if the search is unsuccessful.

Narrow-Track Tractor

Any gardener with an appreciable amount of land that requires frequent cultivation may find a valuable tool in an unusual tractor recently hailed in a nurserymen's trade magazine.

Made in Germany, the Holder A-15 has been called "the smallest, most powerful 4-wheel drive diesel tractor on the world market." Extremely compact — just over 2' x 3' x 6' — it has a low center of gravity for excellent stability, and its track width is adjustable from 31" to as little as 24", which allows working in very narrow spaces. The 14-horsepower diesel tractor also has the unique ability to "bend in the middle," turning in a very small radius. Like its larger 23 hp and 34 hp companion models, the A-15 has 6 forward and 3 reverse gears, hydraulic lift, 12-volt electrical system, and power take-off independent of transmission. Nurserymen and landscapers have

commented enthusiastically on its ruggedness, maneuverability, exceptional performance and excellent fuel economy.

The exclusive American distributor is TRADEWINDS, INC. (BOX 1191, TACOMA, WA 98401).

Lunar Logic

Does planting by the moon have any scientific basis? This ancient practice is still followed scrupulously by many respected gardeners, who attribute their success in large measure to planting root crops only on a waning moon, and plants that bear above ground on a waxing moon. Weeding and harvesting are other operations best restricted to times when the moon is waning, and pruning and grafting to the waxing phase.

The most commonly held explanation of the moon's seeming effects on plants involves terrestrial water: just as tides are controlled by the moon, so the up and down movements of moisture in the soil may be affected by the moon's "pull," a waxing moon thus providing more moisture for seed and seedlings. A second theory is that the moon's light, even though slight, may aid germination of seeds that require exposure to light. And, finally, electrical forces may enter the picture — Dr. H. S. Burr of the Yale School of Medicine has shown that small but significant increases in electrical voltage occur each month in trees, correlated with the phases of the moon.

Current Experiments

In an age when man visits the moon, an open mind to some of the exotic ways of influencing plant growth may be in order. We refer to the reported responses of plants to electricity, sound, thought waves and touch.

There is a considerable body of scientific research, as well as amateur experimentation, that indicates a rather startling potential for growth stimulation through either harnessed atmospheric electricity or generated direct or alternating current. More rapid germination and faster maturity, greater yields, even improved flavor of food crops have been noted.

For example, English nurseryman G. W. Millard of the Reddiglade Nurseries in Kent, in experiments with electrical fields set up around trees, found that the speed and direction of movement of growth materials within a plant can be influenced by electrical means. Many of these growth substances carry an electrical charge, and

Tin cans, steel stakes, wire trellises and other metallic fixtures may set up growth-stimulating electrical fields, say experimenters with electroculture.

sophisticated electronic instruments have been developed to study how these natural bioelectric potentials are affected by seasonal, cultural and environmental factors. This is giving researchers valuable data on how and when to apply electrical fields to stimulate or retard plant growth. The work so far with trees has demonstrated that intermittent, pulsating direct or alternating electrical fields have the most pronounced effects.

Some fascinating garden experiments and reports of amateur and professional research are found in *"ELECTROCULTURE AND PLANT GROWTH,"* *50¢ FROM RODALE PRESS (EMMAUS, PA 18049)*.

Tactile Tactics

In a report of plants' reaction to touch, P. Landreth Neel of the University of California at Davis observed that "plants are very sensitive to tactile stimuli and/or motion and may react to it by increases in ethylene production, and reduction in cell expansion and/or division . . .

"A gentle stroking of the leaves of *Bryonia dioica* (bryony vine) for a short period each day was sufficient to reduce both leaf size and internode length. Upon chromatographing extracts of the plants, it was discovered that auxin levels in the touched plants were less than in the untouched plants . . . A similar report of reduction in leaf size was mentioned in work on cocklebur . . . Touched leaves were reduced in their growth by some 30% . . . Other reports indicate that respiration rates of plant parts are increased upon handling . . ."

Mr. Neel has also shown that shaking or wind increases the radial growth of tree trunks while decreasing height growth, and that rigid staking results in tall, thin and weak trunks. The same reduction of "muscle" or strengthening tissues when the plant is not subjected to motion has been observed with herbaceous plants such as datura and sunflower.

Most interesting are experiments which demonstrated that tilting tree seedlings in flats at a 45° angle, rotating them one quarter-turn daily, caused increased trunk diameter and decreased height. These findings "indicate a possible nursery technique for growing shorter trees with trunks of larger diameter" — and may even have applications for bonsai!

Notes on Harmony and Theory

From Bach to rock, music has soothed, excited, even radicalized man. In recent years, its effect on other forms of life has been demonstrated in enhanced egg and milk production — and in insect control: Dr. Trenchard Bowelson, an entomologist in Davis, California, has found that rock tunes "bug" termites, spurring them to a suicidal frenzy of activity.

Sonic stimulation of plants may well be a sound horticultural technique. Working with grain crops, tobacco, sweet potato, petunia and other plants, Dr. T. C. N. Singh of Annamalai University in India achieved greatly accelerated and healthier, sturdier growth with daily 30-minute applications of music from violin, flute, tuning fork, female voice and other instruments. Seed germination was speeded up to 300% by ringing an electric bell. Sound percussion transmitted through the earth was also effective: performing the "Bharat Natyam dance without trinkets on ankles" made marigolds grow 60% taller and flower 14 days earlier.

An Illinois seedsman reports that playing "Rhapsody in Blue" gave him higher yields of corn . . . a fruit grower in Australia claims to raise bigger, better-quality bananas by broadcasting a continuous bass note . . . seed of winter wheat grew $2\frac{1}{2}$ to 3 times larger, in experiments in 1968 by Dr. Pearl Weinberger of the University of Ottawa.

Dr. Weinberger and other scientists speculate that sound waves have a resonant effect on the "naturally irritable" protoplasm of plant cells, affecting their metabolism so they synthesize larger amounts of food.

Thought-Provoking

In an even more exotic vein are investigations of the effect of thought waves on plants.

At Oxford, at Annamalai University in India and at the extrasensory perception laboratory of Duke University, experiments seem to show that positive and negative thinking and prayer can favorably or adversely affect plant growth. Most startling is the work of Cleve Backster, a New York polygraph expert, who discovered that his instruments registered a violent reaction in plants when he simply thought about burning a leaf with

Special Techniques   175

a match. A "remembered" threat, Backster says — such as the entrance into a room of a person who had previously harmed another plant in the same room — elicited similar sharp reactions.

At a four-day symposium on forms of psychic energy at Stanford University, Prof. Thelma S. Moss, of the Department of Psychiatry of the University of California at Los Angeles, reported that a special photographic technique reveals an aura, indicative of some form of energy, in and around living tissues. A leaf's aura of tiny bubbles is disrupted when the leaf is injured, but if a person with healing powers or a "green thumb" lays a hand over the leaf for a few minutes, the bubble pattern returns and the leaf's vitality is restored. A person with a "brown thumb," she states, has the opposite effect, hastening the leaf's death.

Dr. Bernard Grad of McGill University reported that water over which a "healer" had laid his hands "made plants grow at express speed." Seed given the treated water consistently outgrew untreated plants and developed greater net weight.

These intimations of a "primary perception" or "cellular consciousness" in plants are being increasingly accepted by scientists. Concerning memory, for example, Dr. Fergus Macdowall of the Plant Research Institute in Ottawa has said, "As biological organisms we share some biochemical mechanisms as well as cell structures with plants and other forms of life. . . . It is reasonable to conclude that plants have developed memory to a greater degree than is commonly realized."

The possibilities of emotional and extrasensory capacities recently prompted Dr. C. K. Youngkin, writing in the "American Orchid Society Bulletin," to wonder if plants to be divided should be given an anesthetic. This may not be so fanciful: Sir Gagadis Chunder Bose, a plant physiologist knighted in 1917, reportedly used chloroform to successfully transplant very large trees.

Landscaping

Capital Assets

How much is really good landscaping worth compared to "average" landscaping? Quite a bit more than you might think, real estate agents report — one estimates that a beautifully landscaped house can bring 25% more than the same house with nondescript planting. Nurserymen, garden centers and landscape designers are beginning to realize this, and to upgrade and promote their products and services accordingly.

Avant gardeners must let new gardeners know that a great many plants improved in form and color for multi-season beauty with reduced maintenance are available to replace the obsolete silver maples and Pfitzer junipers still widely sold. Basic principles of artistic use of these are not all that difficult to impart to novices — anyone can learn to meet the needs of privacy and outdoor

activity areas with some attention to form, balance and other plant and structural qualities and relationships. Original costs are minimized by planting small sizes, and developing the garden slowly.

Setting Your Sites

Landscape designer Betty Ajay has called attention to a long-standing problem coming into new prominence today.

This is the often total lack of consideration, by both home builder and buyer, of the relationship between the house and the land. Indifference to the design and placing of the house in relation to the site's topography can result in lifelong dissatisfaction and decreased property value. No amount of gardening skill can completely compensate for the house that looks out of place in its environment, for large masses of exposed foundation, for loss of natural integration of indoor and outdoor living. These faults may or may not be correctible by costly regrading, but certainly not by plantings. The common resort to overplanting to "tie down" such houses only accentuates the problem.

The remedy lies in educating the prospective homeowner to demand houses designed to relate properly to the land, and to be prepared to have the cost of grading included in the purchase price. Grading at time of building is far less costly than grading later, but builders will not undertake it until buyers make known their realization of its importance.

Designing Aids

A three-dimensional visual aid to the home landscaper is the new Plan 'n Plant Landscape Kit, by W. R. BROWN ENTERPRISES (BOX 429, CLAREMONT, CA 91711; $9.95). The kit provides a green styrofoam base on which the home and other structures, walks, driveway, etc., are easily

~~~~~~~~~~~~~~~~~~~~~~~~~~~~~~~~~~~

ATURAL STONE SCULPTURES cut from caves in ndiana limestone quarries, plus free-form boulers, stone benches, limestone coldframes, and any types of stones for walls, patios and veeering are produced by Victor Oolitic Stone Company (Box 668, Bloomington, IN 47401).

~~~~~~~~~~~~~~~~~~~~~~~~~~~~~~~~~~~

indicated, plus nearly 200 full-color photographic reproductions of mature trees and shrubs, all in $\frac{1}{8}'' = 1'$ scale. The models of the plants, which represent the most useful and popular in almost all growing zones, are simply inserted into the styrofoam wherever desired, and can be moved as needed. The instructions make it easy to create a true picture of a property's landscaping as it will be when the plants are fully grown.

The Homescaping Kit by the AGRICULTURAL EXTENSION SERVICE, UNIVERSITY OF WYOMING (BOX 3354, UNIVERSITY STATION, LARAMIE, WY 82070; $1) supplies every essential for landscape analysis and design, from a scale and drafting paper to stencils of plants.

"OUTDOOR LIVING — PLANNING AND CONSTRUCTION GUIDE," published by Midwest Plan Service and available for $1 from the EXTENSION AGRICULTURAL ENGINEER, OHIO STATE UNIVERSITY (2073 NEIL AVENUE, COLUMBUS, OH 43210), is notable for its clarity and practical ideas.

A handy aid to landscape layout is an optical tape measure which "eyes" distances from 6' to 100', $19.95, from EDMUND SCIENTIFIC CO. (555 EDSCORP BUILDING, BARRINGTON, NJ 08007).

New Dynamics

Today as never before, "we must look at plants in new ways," says a remarkable book published by the National Park Service. "PLANTS, PEOPLE, AND ENVIRONMENTAL QUALITY," BY GARY R. ROBINETTE,

A moon gate frames focal points in the distance, inviting the viewer to enter and explore.

Evergreens dominate this garden, where gently curving lines of plants and plantings create tranquillity.

executive director of the American Society of Landscape Architects Foundation (*$4 FROM SUPERINTENDENT OF DOCUMENTS, WASHINGTON, DC 20402*), puts horticulture in a whole new perspective in the modern world.

Our subjective attitude toward plants — regarding them for their "gardenesque," i.e., purely aesthetic and emotional value — must become more objective. Plants can be objectively evaluated and quantified, says Mr. Robinette, and must be used for the functions they are capable of performing — functions which make the environment more livable and more desirable.

The section on architectural uses of plants comprises a superb course in landscape design. Mr. Robinette shows how to use plants as space articulators and mood delineators, how to apply techniques such as pooling and enclavement, how to create "view-step dichotomy" (fascinating, and not nearly so technical as it sounds) and a great many other ways to bring beauty and excitement to small and large planted areas.

The engineering and climatological uses of plants, involving control of sound, glare, erosion, pollution, temperature, solar radiation, wind and precipitation, are similarly detailed and magnificently illustrated. How plants can ameliorate unfavorable environmental conditions — indeed, how they can go far toward making an ideal "comfortable microclimate" for man — is covered here as it has never been before in such a wealth of detail and practical application.

The Park Setting

A major trend in the design of small suburban gardens in England is the creation of a "park" setting. The aim is twofold: to achieve beauty with minimum maintenance, and to give a natural look to the home landscape to counteract the stark artificiality of the modern development.

Paradoxically, this may call for the use of more plants than the standard lawn-and-borders approach. On one or more edges or corners of the property, a miniature woodland effect is sought, employing small to medium trees "understoried" by shrubs and herbaceous plants. Around the home, curved beds of low shrubs, stressing beauty of form and contrasting foliage tones, are the rule, with additional interest from columnar material and herbaceous interplantings. The transitional area between house and woodland can vary, from mainly grass with scattered, open plantings of single or grouped compact trees or shrubs, to inclusion of more elaborate rock garden, alpine meadow or groundcover treatments. Formal hedges and — except in front of the house — sweeps of lawn are avoided.

This concept has, of course, long been practiced in some form by many fine gardeners, but it deserves much wider encouragement among novice gardeners to avoid the monotony of form and content that characterize so many new gardens.

Border Blends

The mixed or hardy border, advocated by the great English gardener, Gertrude Jekyll, at the turn of the century, is coming into its own. Lack of space and desire for low maintenance have made the pure perennial border impractical for many gardeners. So the mini-landscape idea has evolved, breaking down the artificial segregation of herbaceous and woody plants to follow nature's "layer" system of integrated groupings.

Thus small trees, dwarf to medium evergreen and flowering shrubs, perennials, bulbs and groundcovers are increasingly seen in border and island plantings. All the plants are permanent, long-lived and deep-rooted. Overall beauty of design is the primary object, with season and length of bloom the most important secondary consideration. Admittedly, this takes a great deal of planning!

Some useful suggestions are given by Mrs. John Parsons in the *"BULLETIN" OF THE HORTI-CULTURAL SOCIETY OF NEW YORK (128 WEST 58TH STREET, NEW YORK, NY 10019)*. For an 8' border, flowering trees and shrubs such as crabapples and lilacs are best kept to 10' height and 5' width, so they will not cast too much shade. If an open-growing groundcover like *Vinca minor* is used, small bulbs and many wildflowers will come up through it readily, as will the larger later-blooming bulbs. Clematis is very fine on any fence or low wall that exists on one side of the border.

Expanding Vistas

How to make a small plot look bigger is a universal suburban problem. Some suggestions, from an English specialist in the design of small gardens:

Use false perspective — bring shrubs and trees closer together as they recede from the main viewing point, or plant progressively smaller specimens to give a feeling of distance . . . keep focal objects such as statuary in the far background . . . use fencing rather than a hedge on a portion of one boundary, and bring the lawn right up to it . . . all other plantings, as well as paths and the terrace or patio, should have flowing curved lines . . . tight-knit sweeps of one color or shades of it carry the eye farther afield than mixed colors in flower borders . . . tall flowers in small clumps surrounded by much lower ones give an effect of space . . . blue flowers add distance . . . use container plants lavishly on patio, walls, steps . . .

Contrast rounded trees with fastigiate or weeping ones . . . provide changes of level through raised beds and sitting areas and banks . . . use bold-textured plants in the foreground, with compact, small-leaved types in the distance . . . extend a shrub or flower border out into the garden, and recess a small pool or other "surprise" behind it . . . plant climbers and espaliers on walls and fences . . . underplant a tree in a distant corner with shrubs, groundcover and wildflowers for a miniature woodland effect . . . the most important design principle: avoid all "fussy" undulating curves — smooth sweeps of line are vital for unifying the different features of the garden.

Shadow and Structure

Two oft-ignored but vital points in landscape design are emphasized by Dr. Joseph E. Howland of the University of Nevada in *"THE GREEN THUMB" (FIRST MEN'S GARDEN CLUB OF DALLAS, 5545 PARK LANE, DALLAS, TX 75220)*.

"Shadow-exploiting is the most neglected subject in garden design today. Shadows provide beauty of motion — a constantly new scene, and they double the number of elements in each composition. Without cost! Captured imaginatively, shadows produce beauty possible in no other way. No fence or garden wall should be built until its usefulness for shadow-catching is studied . . .

"The structure of more important plants — how they grow — needs to be evident. Prune away the 'spinach' that masks branch patterns; create 'living sculpture.' It's neither necessary nor desirable to prune away all the side branches, only the ones that keep you from appreciating the structure. You ought to be able to see how the branches go together to make up the tree you see. Most people are too fearful when pruning — or too knife-happy. Either way, they substitute 'de-horning' of perfectly good branches instead of removing the unimportant branches. The plant responds by producing a plethora of unwanted branches that further obscure the structure."

Just Around the Corner

Distinguished contemporary foundation plantings are far from commonplace, and usually the most poorly conceived areas are the plantings at the house corners.

For these problem areas, Ray Rothenberger, Extension Horticulturist, University of Missouri, suggests groupings of plants with "irregular and informal growth habits, to develop a natural feeling in the landscape." Also, corner plantings can control the apparent size of the house: "A short house will appear longer if the planting is extended well beyond the corner. A long house can be made to appear shorter by extending the corner planting more in front of the house and less to the sides. When house proportions need no apparent change, the largest plant is placed to the front and out to the side at approximately a 45° angle . . ."

Small trees may be suitable in corner plantings for large homes, but smaller homes need shrubs "that do not grow more than ⅔ the distance to the eaves." He recommends "3-tier" plantings of large, medium and small shrubs and groundcovers, of varied textures and forms, and stressing horizontal lines and masses, which are "more restful than vertical lines."

Winning Entries

The late great Garden Editor of "House and Garden," Ralph Bailey, often remarked, "What we need is more dooryard gardens!" Very recently, we've seen indications that the more imaginative gardeners and landscape designers are heeding his call.

The sterile and uninviting lawn-hedge-foundation planting stereotype is being replaced with a vibrant new concept. It embodies a largely naturalistic treatment of the areas to the side and rear of the house — with the gardener's special interests and entertainment areas "naturalized" into these — while the front yard is given the designer's best efforts for greatest excitement, color, four-season interest.

This is, of course, entirely logical from the "viewpont" of passersby as well as the homeowner. It is also a considerable challenge. The dooryard garden, as Mr. Bailey also said, can be simple or elaborate, a virtuoso performance of flowering material, or a neat scheme utilizing the patterns, proportions and textures of non-flowering plants. The latter, a wise choice for the gardener seeking ease of maintenance, can be as stunning as the former. But essential to both is a basic, organized design, and every plant must be weighed for its contribution to the unity of the picture.

Two helpful books are "HOW TO PLAN AND PLANT YOUR OWN PROPERTY," BY ALICE RECKNAGEL IREYS (BARROWS, $7.95), and "ENTRYWAYS AND FRONT GARDENS," A SUNSET PUBLICATION (LANE BOOK CO., $1.95).

Sanctuary

The walled garden of yesteryear is re-appearing — but in new guises, prompted by new needs. Dictated by desire for a feeling of privacy on the small property and for at least the illusion of being secluded from the furor of modern life, the intimate enclosed garden — of Scottish origin, by the way — is being interestingly adapted with modern materials.

Instead of high brick walls for definition, we see attractive combinations of low brick walls and tall hedges, or simply head-high borders of evergreens or densely planted mixed deciduous material. Fences of solid or woven wood or fiberglass are also common, perhaps alternated with tall plantings. Newest trick is the vertical-louvered fence, useful for ventilation, as is the baffle fence of widely spaced boards on both sides of a frame, staggered so that the gaps on one side are covered by the boards on the other. Today's walled gardens, incidentally, are seldom totally enclosed unless lack of a suitable vista on one or two sides or considerations of privacy make four "walls" necessary.

A patio is almost invariably a component of a contemporary walled garden, but often this is the only area where brick is used. Paths are of washed gravel, bluestone, the new colored stones or even tanbark, confined by plastic or metal edging. An important feature is a fountain or pool — the latter generally informal in style, and often made by simply lining an excavation with heavy plastic sheeting in a double layer.

The design of the interior plantings is also usually quite informal. Totally absent are straight-sided beds and borders. "Island" plantings are the order of the day. Finally, container gardening in pots, tubs, hanging baskets and all manner of raised planters is widely practiced in this new, completely American style of garden design.

Plants Before Flowers

The greatest challenge in gardening, a landscape architect once observed, is to achieve beauty without bloom. The average gardener tends to think, perhaps even subconsciously, of flowers first, and plant and foliage form last. Outstanding gardeners do just the opposite.

Even the so-called green garden, of course, has some flowering trees, shrubs, vines and perennials. But green is its overwhelming basis, and the blendings and contrasts of various "weights" of green and of plant shapes and textures give it its supreme sophistication. The secret is to evaluate all plants for their textural and color weights: silvery and yellow-greens are light, deep greens and blue-greens are heavy and a small-leaved plant of open form, such as a willow, is light in comparison to a rhododendron or other big-leaved or dense-growing plant. The most vital

SOURCES OF THE FINEST CONTEMPORARY HANDCRAFTS for the garden, from one-of-a-kind ceramic vases and pots to imposing avant-garde sculpture, are supplied by The American Craftsmen's Council (29 West 53rd Street, New York, NY 10019).

point to remember in designing is that a medium-heavy plant can appear very heavy and coarse if placed near one of extremely light color and texture — use strong contrasts sparingly, only where emphasis is needed.

Admittedly, the blending of plant textures is more of an art than a technique. But it is perhaps more easily achieved in today's informal gardens than in yesterday's formal landscapes. And its rewards include not only beauty in all seasons but also a superb restful quality, both for the viewer and for the gardener who will appreciate its low maintenance requirements.

Cotoneaster's tiny leaves make lighthearted contrast to bold brick walls and heavy pines.

Gardener's Palette

We see increasing emphasis in many gardening publications on plants with colorful foliage. Their value for beautiful contrast effects with green plants is undeniable, though often their proper use requires even more discerning an eye than does designing for textural interest. Some suggested plants, with sources for the less common ones:

For brilliant, multicolored foliage, there are crotons, caladiums and coleus, and amaranths

Rock outcroppings don't call for dynamite, but a frosting with alpine plants and wildflowers.

such as Joseph's coat, *Amaranthus tricolor splendens.* Less often grown is the handsome "crinkled coleus," *Perilla frutescens crispa,* bold dark red leaves with a bronze sheen (GEO. W. PARK SEED CO., GREENWOOD, SC 29647).

In more subdued tones for broader accents, consider many hostas with yellow-green to blue-gray foliage, and the heaths and heathers in hues of gold, red, gray; *Dianthus plumarius,* bluish-gray; ground ivy, *Nepeta mussini,* silvery gray, fine for edging; white-woolly silver sage, *Salvia argentea;* silver-gray lavender cotton, *Santolina chamaecyparis;* the unusual lamb's ear, *Stachys lanata,* soft white downy foliage; or the 18" silver-blue mounded *Ruta* 'Blue Beauty' (WAYSIDE GARDENS, MENTOR, OH 44060; CATALOG $2).

Then there is that always dependable but much-confused group, the dusty millers: *Artemisia stelleriana,* A. 'Silver King' and A. 'Silver Mound' (WAYSIDE); *Centaurea gymnocarpa* and *C. candidissima* (*C. cineraria*) 'Diamond,' 'Silver Dust,' 'Hoar Frost,' etc.; *Lychnis coronaria;* and *Senecio cineraria.*

Ornamental grasses include fountain grass, *Pennisetum ruppelii cupreum,* with coppery foliage; blue fescue, *Festuca ovina glauca;* and *Arundo donax variegata,* with white-striped, gray-green leaves (WAYSIDE).

Choice in deciduous trees and shrubs is somewhat limited. Besides Japanese maples, note the silver linden, *Tilia tomentosa,* and white poplar, *Populus alba nivea,* both with leaf undersides white, and the silvery-leaved forms of eleagnus. The range of evergreens, however, is much wider, including golden privet, *Ligustrum vicari;* blue spruces, *Picea pungens* varieties (BRIMFIELD GARDENS NURSERY, WETHERSFIELD, CT 06109; CATALOG $1); blue and golden Atlas cedars; the numerous blue, golden and variegated junipers; silver and gold forms of chamaecyparis and golden arborvitae (GIRARD NURSERIES, GENEVA, OH 44041).

A gardener suggests that even rhododendrons, rarely chosen for anything except their flowers, offer considerable variety in foliage that a discerning eye can use to influence the beauty of a planting.

A few examples: dwarf *Rhododendron yakusimanum,* with woolly beige new growth . . . *R. bureavii,* leathery leaves with thick orange-red felt beneath and silvery new growth . . . *R. laetevirens,* pieris-like foliage . . . 'Ramapo,' tiny blue-green leaves . . . *R. ovatum,* egg-shaped leaves . . . 'Noyo Chief,' superb glossy foliage . . . 'Vulcan,' very pointed leaves . . . *R. williamsianum,* small round bronze-tinged leaves . . . long- and drooping-leaved *R. maximum* . . . 'Arthur J. Ivens,' heart-shaped leaves, red-bronze new growth . . . Guyencourt Hybrids, long, narrow, hairy foliage . . . 'Moser's Maroon,' bright red new growth . . . P.J.M. Hybrids, leaves turn bronze-purple in winter . . . 'Queen Souriya,' misty blue leaves . . . *R. racemosum,* tiny leathery foliage, silvery beneath.

The excellent HANDBOOK 66, "RHODODENDRONS AND THEIR RELATIVES," BY THE BROOKLYN BOTANIC GARDEN, BROOKLYN, NY 11225; $1.50), lists many more with unusual foliage values and also gives a fine list of sources.

"FOLIAGE PLANTS," BY FREDERICK A. BODDY (DRAKE PUBLISHERS, $6.95), describes over 1000 garden plants with distinctive shades of green or tinted, evergreen, textured, aromatic, variegated or fall-colored foliage — a most useful book.

A picket fence with climbing roses, plus the eye-catching arch of climbers over the door, "disguises" the tininess of this suburban front yard.

Color Guards

A noted landscape architect says that the most difficult flower colors to work with are the pinks. Most can be classified as either yellow-pink or blue-pink, and one of the most important rules is never to use them too close together. Only pale to golden yellows combine pleasingly with salmon-pinks, while all but palest yellow clashes with rose-pink.

Where a rose-pink peony will look "dirty" near a brilliant yellow iris, it is enhanced by juxtaposition to pink or blue lupines — the pink of the lupines has a tinge of blue in it, and the blue lupines have some red in their blue. Salmon-pink phlox go beautifully with pale to deep yellow daylilies, whereas rose-pink phlox would cause a distinct color clash. Red flowers also require care: only scarlet-reds, which have some yellow in them, can be used near salmon-pink flowers . . . only blue-reds — maroon and crimson tones — near rose-pinks.

To help plan next year's color combinations, it's a good idea to pick flowers from this summer's garden and hold them together to see how they blend. Do this outdoors, for bright sun will intensify some strong colors while weakening paler ones, making them look much different from the same grouping in an indoor arrangement.

White flowers, of course, are marvelous buffers between unsociable vibrant hues, as are light blues and pinks to some degree, and silvery-foliaged plants. Strident tones of red or blue can be tempered with tints and shades of the same color. Magenta's harshness disappears if white, blues to purples, or traces of soft yellow are added.

Master Strokes

"Casual sophistication" is a vital garden art, says a veteran horticulturist, remarking that the true gardener practices it instinctively, others never learn it.

What is this mysterious art? It's simply the knack of using a single plant or small group of plants in just the right spot where it will look totally natural, growing there by design of nature rather than of the gardener. This strategic placement can attract greater attention than masses of the same plant in a border or other formal grouping.

Some examples: a single clump of daffodils at the base of a boulder in the lawn . . . a few diminutive hostas or primroses under a water spigot . . . creeping *Ranunculus repens* at the edge of a hedge bordering the sidewalk . . . one fern or a wildflower peeking from a hollow stump . . . wild ginger springing up in the corner crevice of a bottom step . . . a clump of *Dianthus barbatus* at the base of a birdfeeder or clothespole . . . an artemisia 'Silver Mound' at the outer corner of a patio . . .

The possibilities are endless for supremely effective use of surplus or volunteer plants, or plants grown specifically to tuck into that odd nook or corner where they will be "just perfect."

Landscaping with Mosses and Lichens

"Cultivated" mosses deserve an important place in American gardens, says Dr. William Campbell Steere, President of the New York Botanical Garden.

Dr. Steere notes the beautiful moss gardens of Japan, where the ground is completely carpeted with many-hued varieties. The value of mosses for naturalistic garden effects is rarely appreciated here, even in the Pacific Northwest where high humidity allows them to thrive. However, the recent invention of mist and fog devices makes it entirely feasible to grow mosses almost anywhere.

Dr. Steere suggests that hundreds of species can be used for magnificent texture and color effects in the garden. Particularly recommended are the woodland species, *Leucobryum glaucum,* the pincushion moss, and *Dicranum,* broom moss, and mat-forming types such as *Thuidium,* the fern moss, and *Hypnum.* Mosses are easily transplanted from the wild if conditions of shade, soil mixture and pH are duplicated. Or you can sprinkle rocks or wood with dilute molasses — a fine "culture medium" for moss spores alighting from the air.

Lichens, those curious partners of algae and fungi, also offer intriguing possibilities, says Dr. Roger A. Anderson. Their colors are even more varied than those of mosses, ranging from white and yellow to green, orange and black. Unlike mosses, they must have dry conditions.

Lichens that live on rocks in exposed places are the most adaptable, so Dr. Anderson suggests "transplanting" such rocks to the garden, giving them the same orientation to the sun as they had in the wild. Lichens on rocks will also keep their color and form indoors for years, provided they are not watered or fertilized.

VIEWPOINTS

"On Gardening," by Gertrude Jekyll (Scribner's, $6).

"Garden Design," by Sylvia Crowe (Hearthside, $8.95).

"The Tropical Gardens of Burle Marx," by P. M. Bardi (Reinhold, $15).

"Your Private World — A Study of Intimate Gardens," by Thomas Church (Chronicle Books, $9.95).

"Modern Gardens and the Landscape," by E. B. Mock (Museum of Modern Art, $5.95).

"The Wild Gardener in the Wild Landscape," by Warren G. Kenfield (Hafner, $7.50).

"Room Outside," by John Brookes (Viking, $6.95).

"Modern American Gardens," by James C. Rose (Reinhold, $16.50).

"Spot Gardens," by Robert E. Atkinson (McKay, $9.95).

"Imaginative Small Gardens," by Nancy Grasby (Hearthside, $7.95).

"Color for Your Yard and Garden," by Elda Haring (Hawthorn, $12.95).

"The Complete Book of Garden Ornaments, Complements and Accessories," by Daniel J. Foley (Crown, $9.95).

"The Use of Water in Landscape and Architecture," by Susan and Geoffrey Jellicoe (St. Martin's, $12.50).

"The World of the Japanese Garden," by Lorraine Kuck (Walker/Weatherhill, $17.50).

"The Art of the Japanese Garden," by Tatsuo and Kiyoko Ishimoto (Crown, $3.95).

GARDEN CONSTRUCTION

Thoughts on Materialism

The use of garden building materials has become so popular that in some areas, such as southern California, plantings are often overpowered by expanses of wood and stone. While the form and texture of construction materials are important ingredients in garden design, careful selection and — except for the Japanese garden — sparing use are essential to preserve the spirit of a garden.

Wood is a fine blender with plants and with other building materials. Anything from a rustic look to highly modernistic design is possible with wood in fencing or structures. Bark or chip mulches, tree trunk "rounds" for paving, and railroad ties as steps, edging or retaining walls give naturalistic effects. Stone is similarly versatile, offering picturesque boulders, fieldstone for walls and paths, and many types of gravel. The last-named requires restraint, although the monotony and artificiality of large areas of gravel can be relieved by island plantings and stepping stones, or even mixing in some contrasting gravels.

Brick is another universal harmonizer, adaptable to every sort of horizontal pattern and vertical construction. A useful tip: for a formal effect in paving, lay bricks close together with smooth joints; make the joints deep and wide for an informal effect. Concrete's versatility can be enhanced by the amount, type and exposure of stone aggregate in the mix, and vertical masonry grillwork can be chosen in patterns that give intricate and airy or massive effects. Rigid plastics used for screening need their unusual texture complemented by wood framing and perhaps gravel or coarse aggregate concrete flooring and plants in sizable wood or clay containers.

The ingredients for this floating island are a raft of styrofoam, soil, plants and an anchor.

"BUILDING BEAUTY WITH COMMON MATERIALS" is explored by EDWARD H. STONE, chief landscape architect of the forest service, in *"OUTDOORS USA," THE YEARBOOK OF AGRICULTURE, 1967 ($2.75 FROM SUPERINTENDENT OF DOCUMENTS, WASHINGTON, DC 20402).* Mr. Stone suggests that inexpensive byproducts or used materials obtainable from wrecking companies, salvage yards, mills and shops, can, with imagination, be transformed into useful works of garden art. Such materials as railroad ties, telephone poles, piping of many types, weathered planks, even broken pavement or curbing have some challenging potentials for creating natural beauty.

Territorial Rights

The world's greatest water pollutant is not sewage, but sediment. Erosion causes huge losses of topsoil, necessitates much dredging, and the nutrients carried in sediment induce algal growth which degrades water quality. The chief culprit today, says the Soil Conservation Service, is urban and suburban construction work, which can cause 1000 times the annual average 50-tons-per-square-mile soil loss that occurs on cultivated land.

Gardeners, too, should be aware of every practice that will reduce soil and water loss. Minimum tillage and maximum cover — plants and mulch — prevent erosion on level to slightly sloping ground. However, as slopes become steeper, contouring or terracing may be necessary.

To measure the degree of slope, lay a carpenter's level on a 2″ x 2″ board 5′ long. Hold the board with one end against the slope and the other pointing straight out, level it, then drop a plumb line from the outer end. Measuring the length of line from the bottom of the board to the slope below will give the percent of slope: 6″ = 10%, 2′ = 40%, etc. As a general rule, planting on the contour should be considered for slopes over 20%, terracing for grades above 30%.

"GARDENING ON THE CONTOUR," HOME AND GARDEN BULLETIN 179 (10¢ FROM SUPERINTENDENT OF DOCUMENTS, WASHINGTON, DC 20402), tells how to find the contour line. Using a level mounted on a 2 x 4, "begin about the center of the slope. Lay the 2 x 4 along the slope and move one end up or

down until the bubble on the level is centered; mark the spot with a stake. Repeat this process across the slope to establish the contour guideline. Plant the rows parallel to this line." For decorative terracing on short slopes, the bulletin suggests: "Beginning just below the top of the slope, place flat stones on edge in the soil to make small benches 2′ to 4′ wide depending on the slope. Each bench should slant slightly toward the original slope . . . Slightly irregular stones are more attractive than bricks or blocks, which can be pushed out of line easily by frost action."

IF YOU USE RAILROAD TIES for landscaping, buy only pressure-treated ties, which last 15 to 20 years — dip-treated last only 3 to 5 years in the ground, says Michigan's Department of Natural Resources.

Horticultural Steps

Providing strong horizontal and vertical lines, steps are a counterpoint for the plant forms around them. So they should be designed to enhance them, to make a "horticulturally valid" as well as easy transition between garden levels.

Brick steps, of course, are out of place in all but highly formal situations — as part of a terrace wall flanked by rose beds, for example. At the other extreme, risers of railroad ties, round or roughly squared logs, or 2″ x 8″ planks (held upright by deep stakes at each end), give a naturalistic effect when grass is used for the tread, a more formal effect with gravel treads. Logs or utility pole sections set on end make fine steppingstone stairs — but can be very slippery in damp areas. Flags and similar stones usually need to be set in concrete with footing to below frost level. Stacked layers of stone "pavers," set dry on a deep gravel base, are more modernistic. So are concrete rounds or wedges, the latter narrower at the rear of the tread than at the front, which gives recesses for interesting plantings.

Outdoor steps may be straight or curved, and generally are more attractive and useful when made wide enough for two persons. Good proportion also calls for lower risers and wider treads than are used for indoor stairs. Risers should never exceed 6″, and a good rule is to decrease the riser 1″ to each 3″ increase in tread width

— 5″:15″, 4″:18″, etc. For gradual slopes, ramp steps a full one or two strides deep may be used. Sometimes steps can be given dramatic shadow interest by having the treads deeply overhang the risers.

Rules for Retainers

Any slope exceeding 30° usually calls for a retaining wall — not a difficult project if these rules from Iowa State University Extension Service are followed.

Proportions: height, not over 4′; top, not less than 12″ thick; base width, about one-third the height. If the stones or other building materials are unequal in size, put the largest at the bottom. Always avoid long vertical joints.

For dry walls, a foundation of concrete or large stones must extend 18″ below ground to resist sliding. The front face of the wall should slope back 3″ to every 12″ of height. Walls laid up with mortar require a foundation to below the frost line — at least 36″ in most northern states — and backward sloping of 1″ for each vertical foot. Mortared or solid concrete walls also must have good drainage to reduce pressure: use a layer of gravel or cinders behind to within a foot of the wall's top, plus 2″ weep holes of pipe or tile through the wall at 6′ intervals.

For mortar, use a mix of 3 parts sand, 1 part Portland cement, with sufficient water to give workable consistency. A concrete mix should be composed of 2½ parts sand, 3 parts crushed rock or gravel and 1 part Portland cement, with no more than 5 gallons of water per sack of cement.

"THE FORGOTTEN ART OF BUILDING A STONE WALL," a 64-page manual by Curtis P. Fields, has become a surprise best seller, says its distributor Walter F. Nicke (Box 71, Hudson, NY 12534) who offers it at $2.50 per copy, plus 75¢ handling or two for $4.50.

Rock Festival

Natural stone, a landscape contractor tells us, is much less difficult to cut than is usually realized. Like wood, stone has a "grain," along which it can easily be split to size and shape for walks, terraces and walls.

With a broad-bladed "blocking" chisel and a hammer weighing at least 3 pounds, make a groove with light blows across the narrow edges, then across the top following the grain as much as possible. A few heavy blows will then make a clean fracture. Trimming across the grain requires more patience, and the use of short, chipping cuts. Proficiency can be developed by practicing first on less desirable rocks.

Pandemic Paving

Soil-cement paving has long been used for roads and airfield landing strips, yet few gardeners know of this valuable technique for garden paving, patios, even parking areas.

The formula is simply 1 part cement to 9 parts sandy soil. Soil that is higher in organic matter and clay requires 1½ parts of cement. Test your soil by mixing small amounts of the ingredients in a pan. Let dry a week, then if an icepick does not penetrate, enough cement has been used.

After marking off the area to be paved by sinking a spade around the edges, dig up the area 4″ deep, remove all stones and as many roots as possible and pulverize the soil. Then spread the cement — about 1 sack per 2 square yards gives a 1:9 ratio — and blend it in thoroughly to the 4″ depth. Rake smooth, and moisten well to 4″ deep with a fine spray. Handfuls of the mixture when squeezed should mold without crumbling or dripping. Use a garden roller, or tamp the paving with a flat board to make it smooth and dense. Keep all traffic off the paving for at least a week.

Rainy-Day Diversions

Unless diverted, the downpour from the downspout in a rainstorm can be damaging to foundation plantings and the home. Prefabricated plastic splash pans or homemade ones of brick, concrete, tile or fieldstone are helpful for dispersing the flow, as is the roll-up perforated hose that attaches to the downspout and unrolls under pressure of the water. Also useful is a square conductor pipe, attached horizontally along the foundation wall or siding a foot or so above the ground and soldered into the downspout; 3/16″ holes drilled every 6″ along its outer side will convert roof runoff into a gentle shower all along the wall.

Where the roof area is large and rainfall heavy, however, a dry well connected to each downspout is the most efficient answer. Cellulose fiber piping, easily cut with a saw and fitted to the spout with an elbow, is buried in a trench 1′ deep and sloping 1″ for each foot of length. This leads into the dry well itself, which should be at least 15′ from house walls. The well is simply a pit lined with brick, stone, an open-ended metal drum, 3′ or wider sections of clay or concrete piping, or concrete blocks laid on their sides. This is filled with gravel or broken rock and covered with a wood or concrete slab, which should be at least 6″ below ground level to allow grass growth.

The subsoil into which the dry well drains must be porous. A dry well generally should be a minimum of 3′ wide and 4′ deep to handle the volume of water from most roof drains.

CEMENT ASBESTOS FLEXBOARD, 4′ x 8′ and ⅛″, 3/16″, and ½″ thick, is rot-proof, easy to work, and can be painted or decorated for planter boxes; from lumber and building supply dealers.

Housing Project

The lath house is once again becoming an essential feature of fine gardens. But it's appearing in new forms, and is often multi-functional. Originally a simple shelter for summering indoor plants, it now may be an elaborate "outdoor living" structure, a combination conservatory and recreation center.

On smaller properties, the lath house adjoining the patio or attached to the home, garage, greenhouse, wall or fence, is an aesthetically pleasing as well as space-saving solution. So are the "half-and-half" designs, with part lath and part solid roof, or roofed with alternating wide and narrow lath. A lath house may become a greenhouse in winter, especially if it is attached to the home, so an open door or window can supply at least enough heat for cool-growing plants. Polyethylene sheeting, or sash covered on both sides with plastic, is tacked on in the fall.

Some tips on design and construction: standard 1½″ to 2″ lath, spaced a lath width apart, gives ample shading for many plants, with bamboo or reed shades or vines to provide more if needed . . . a concrete foundation is best for permanence in larger structures, plus a cement, stone or gravel floor that can be damped down for humidity-loving plants . . . quite a few woods will serve for corner posts, studs and beams when treated with wood preservative . . . use 2′ x 4′ or larger for joists if you plan to hang plants . . . roof beams can be steamed into curved shapes for a contemporary design . . . a roof overhang will provide midday shade for a foundation planting.

Finally, use unusual materials. We once saw a stunning lath house with a "sun wall" of concrete blocks cast with a central open cloverleaf design, and another roofed very attractively with spent fluorescent tubes spaced ¾″ apart — being vacuum tubes, these insulate and so give extra coolness.

Wood Treatment

For preserving wooden greenhouse benches, hanging baskets, lath structures, etc., Celcure (*AMERICAN CELCURE WOOD PRESERVING CORP., 1074 EAST 8TH STREET, JACKSONVILLE, FL 32206)* is both highly effective and attractive, says F. B. Schmitz, in the "American Orchid Society Bulletin."

Celcure gives more resistance to rot than copper naphthenate, and also does not cause the color variations which result when the latter is applied to light and dark woods. Nor is it toxic to plants as are creosote and pentachlorophenol, which many gardeners have found to their dismay are very herbicidal. Dipping in Celcure gives a mellow silvery gray-green color after several weeks' drying. Mr. Schmitz reports that his Celcure-treated pine lath house has resisted rot and insects for 20 years, and the wood is extremely hard.

Floating Island

Not as famous as Babylon's hanging gardens, but almost as old and just as fascinating are Mexico's chinampas or floating gardens. As far back as 1000 B.C., the Aztecs and others grew vegetables on rafts anchored in Lake Texcoco. This "reverse irrigation" — bring the crops to the water, instead of vice versa — was practiced until the lake was drained only a few decades ago.

The idea has been spectacularly revived at Sterling Forest Gardens in Tuxedo, New York, where a 30′ x 40′ garden floats about on International Lake. Supported by 10″ x 18″ x 16′ styrofoam logs, its wooden understructure of 2′x

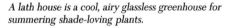

A lath house is a cool, airy glassless greenhouse for summering shade-loving plants.

6's and 2'x12's is covered with plywood. Boulders and soil sink this giant "floating flower box" to water level. Each spring a weeping willow, rhododendrons and other shrubs are planted on the island, and in the fall it is pulled ashore and the plants are removed and heeled in for winter.

Illuminating Guides

Garden lighting has reached a point of sophistication where its value in all seasons is recognized. Subtlety, of course, is the key to heightening interest in plants and design for winter nighttime enjoyment as well as summer. Recent innovations

— especially l-v (low-voltage) fixtures which permit all sorts of flattering low-key effects — assure achievement of this aim in any garden. L-v systems are inexpensive and simple to install, and provide glareless illumination which features the effect rather than the source, even in lighting designed primarily for safety or security.

Some excellent publications are *"LIGHT FOR LIVING OUTDOORS,"* FREE FROM INQUIRY BUREAU, GENERAL ELECTRIC COMPANY (NELA PARK, CLEVELAND, OH 44112); "ADD CHARM TO THE NIGHT WITH OUTDOOR LIGHTING," FREE FROM RESIDENTIAL LIGHTING DEPT., WESTINGHOUSE LAMP DIVISION (BLOOMFIELD, NJ 07003); and the fine SUNSET BOOK, "OUTDOOR LIGHTING," $1.95 FROM LANE MAGAZINE & BOOK CO. (MENLO PARK, CA 94025).

New Dimensions

Versatility and design and space-stretching advantages have prompted a spectacular rise in popularity of container gardening.

Container cultivation of large woody plants is receiving special attention, and we note some interesting ideas. Santa Barbara, California, has solved the problem of poor growth of trees in planters on its streets by combining container and direct planting: the city uses a bottomless planter, so that the tree's roots can go down into the soil below. With increased root room and better drainage, the trees are healthier and longer-lived. An adaptation of this is the "dropped-in" plant container, sunk into a deck, patio or terrace. This can provide the depth of soil needed for trees and shrubs, without the obtrusive effect of a large, high planter set on the surface.

"Mini-trees" — hardy shrubs grafted on standards — add an exciting new dimension to container gardening. They thrive in relatively small planters and provide dramatic, elegant formal

effects. Some of the best tree forms, offered by *WAYSIDE GARDENS (MENTOR, OH 44060; CATALOG $2):* Euonymus radicans vegetus, evergreen bittersweet, which can be sheared to a ball shape; 'Golden Vicary' privet, for a striking color effect; heavily berried cotoneaster 'Sealing Wax' and *C. apiculata;* and for spectacular flowers, the dwarf Korean lilac (Syringa palibiniana), Viburnum juddi, Prunus 'Hally Jolivette' and Hydrangea paniculata grandiflora.

Planter Guidelines

Peat and other humus materials should be used very sparingly in soil mixes for trees and shrubs in planters, says William Flemer III of Princeton Nurseries in New Jersey.

These organic materials are broken down by soil organisms, and as they disappear, the soil compacts. It loses the vital porous structure that admits air to the roots and facilitates drainage. A

Container Gardening   189

Year-round container plants of all types adorn the courtyard and even the roof of this southwestern home.

ball when planting it in the container.

More points for successful growth: except in warm climates, planters for trees must be a minimum of 2′ deep and 5′ wide . . . cement blocks or bricks under the root ball will prevent the plant from settling too deep in the soil . . . if the container has no drain holes, the gravel drainage layer (separated from the soil by fiberglass matting) should be one-quarter the depth of the soil, and a siphon tube to the surface can be used to remove excess water . . . a 2″ organic or gravel mulch will greatly reduce watering . . . "watering wells" — gravel-filled cardboard or wire cylinders — aid distribution of moisture to the roots . . . roots and the biological life of the soil will be healthier and more active if shielded from extremes of heat and cold, so it is becoming standard practice to line the side walls of wood, metal and other thin-walled planters with 1″ to 2″ styrofoam sheets or flexible glass wool (fiberglass) insulation.

Zoning for Planters

Mr. Flemer also stresses the importance of ecologically sound plant selections for large permanent planters. His criteria for choosing trees and shrubs for this purpose apply to selecting species for in-the-ground planting, too, wherever rigorous growing conditions are encountered, or where the gardener seeks trouble-free plants requiring minimum maintenance.

First choices should always be the "ecological pioneers," those shrubs and trees that are the first to appear on land that has been cleared. These will stand the exposed conditions and limited soil volumes of containers far better than the later or "climax" species that follow them in the natural plant succession. Thus, Mr. Flemer states, a hawthorn would be a better choice than a stewartia, and an amur maple more suitable than a striped maple.

The rule is to use plants which are rated hardy at least one zone north of the area in which the planter is located: in USDA Plant Hardiness Zone 6 (−10°), use plants hardy in Zone 5 (−20°), or better yet, plants hardy in Zones 3 or 4 (as low as −40°).

small amount of humus is necessary to stimulate root growth in the early stages, but the bulk of the humus usually used should be replaced by porous inorganic materials like calcined clay and perlite.

Mr. Flemer recommends a mix of 45% sandy loam, 10% coarse sphagnum peat, 25% horticultural perlite and 20% calcined clay (such as Turface). Also, to provide mycorrhizal fungi which promote root growth and nutrient absorption, place a few chunks of root-filled humus, taken from the woodland floor, against the root

Cold Facts

Hardy plants in planter boxes, tubs and other containers need the same winter protection as their counterparts in the ground — and then some.

These are essentials for plants in both situations: avoidance of growth-stimulating nitrogen feeding after midsummer . . . thorough watering until the soil begins to freeze, and again in winter thaws (and don't let algae on the surface persuade you falsely that the soil is moist below) . . . a 3" to 4" mulch of wood chips, pine needles, coarse peatmoss, etc., after hard freezing to lessen temperature fluctuations that heave plants . . . antitranspirant sprays to reduce moisture loss from plant tissues . . . and screens of burlap, boughs or slats around evergreens as "vertical mulch" to reduce sharp temperature changes caused by sun or wind.

In addition, plants in containers need the insulation of bales or slabs of straw or hay packed all around the sides of the containers. Where feasible, remove container plants from the drip-line of eaves, or build sloping shelters over them. Tie the branches of multiple-stemmed and wide-limbed evergreens so they will not be broken apart by the weight of snow and ice. Snow should always be brushed off gently. Burlap or other shields can be eliminated if the containers can be moved to areas free of sun and wind — but do not put them in low spots which are extra-cold pockets, or near walls or other surfaces that reflect sun heat during the day. Good drainage is, of course, essential in containers, for root injury due to heaving is much more common in water-logged soil.

The most vulnerable plants can be encircled, container and all, in a chicken wire enclosure filled with hay, shavings, dried leaves or needles and provided with a waterproof cover. Finally, do not be hasty in removing winter protectors early in spring, as much winterkill occurs when balmy days are followed by very cold, windy nights.

Window Dressing

Window boxes are making a comeback — on windowsills, fences, walls, balconies, porch railings. And the great variety of plants grown in them today to spectacular effect is a credit to gardeners' horticultural and artistic talents.

Proper engineering of the boxes is vital. Wood is still the best material, 1" thick, or use ¾" exterior plywood reinforced with 1" battens down the inside corners. Minimum inside dimensions are 8" wide and 8" deep. Use brass screws to assemble the box, and treat with Cuprinol wood preservative if the box is not to be painted; if painted, give one coat inside, two outside. Boxes that will be in full sun are best insulated inside on the front with a ½" styrofoam slab.

Provide ½" drainage holes 6" apart, in two alternating rows. Cover these with mesh or crock, then put in 1" of cinders, gravel or broken brick. Over this, lay a fiber-glass mat (such as Weed-Chek, by BRIGHTON BY-PRODUCTS CO., BOX 23, NEW BRIGHTON, PA 15066) to prevent soil filtration. The best general soil mix is equal parts of loam, peatmoss or leafmold, and vermiculite or perlite.

Newest Hang-Ups

Outdoor hanging baskets have become as popular and varied as their indoor counterparts, according to a growers' magazine. Whereas petunias, fuchsias, achimenes and tuberous begonias once made up the bulk of basket sales, more than 150 plants are now being grown in baskets for the retail market. Today almost any flowering or foliage plant, of mounded, cascading or even upright habit is considered a basket candidate, with size the only limitation.

The newest vogues are vegetable and herb baskets, and hardy hanging plants. Chives, parsley, mints, rosemary, thymes, other herbs, strawberries, sweet potatoes, dwarf non-vining cucumbers, squashes and green beans, even miniature tomatoes are excellent subjects, says Prof. P. B. Pfahl of Pennsylvania State University. For permanent baskets, creeping juniper (*Juniperus horizontalis*) is superb, especially 'Bar Harbor' and 'Wiltonii.' Other trailing types, such as *J. procumbens* and *J. conferta*, are also suitable, as are many hardy low-growing azaleas, the vine-like Sasanqua camellias, trailing evergreen cotoneasters and vinca. Numerous groundcovers can be considered. In winter, the baskets should be set on the ground in an area free of sun and wind, mulched and watered in thaws.

An inmate in Florida State Prison — which has a unique Ornamental Horticulture Training Program — gives a valuable tip for good growth in summer. He fills the bottom third of the basket with 1½" smooth riverbottom stones, with just enough sphagnum moss to hold in the soil. Drainage is rapid, and the plants have "cool feet" even at 100°.

Robert Dingwall of the Missouri Botanical Garden suggests "total planting" for hanging baskets. He uses an open wire basket lined with sphagnum moss and filled with soil, firmed and watered well. After draining, a board or tray is laid over the top, and the basket is turned upside down. Small rooted trailing plants are then easily planted by poking holes between the wires on the sides and bottom. When these have become established, the basket is turned right side up and the board removed so the top can be planted. The result is a basket completely covered with plants, beautiful from every angle.

Pillow Paks

An unusual and versatile container is the Cornell pillow pak. Developed by Drs. J. W. Boodley and Raymond Sheldrake, of Cornell University, pillow paks are tubes made by folding over and stapling the edges of a polyethylene sheet, then filling with the Cornell peat-lite mix or a commercial version such as Jiffy-Mix *(JIFFY-POT CO. OF AMERICA, BOX 338, WEST CHICAGO, IL 60185)* or Redi-Earth *(ZONOLITE DIVISION, W. R. GRACE & CO., MERCHANDISE MART PLAZA, CHICAGO, IL 60654).*

The tube is stapled tightly shut at the ends, and plants are inserted into slits cut in the top. The paks may be placed in window boxes, on patios, in the garden or indoors — anywhere an "instant garden" is desired.

Instead of laying the pak down horizontally, gardener Cornelius Ackerson hangs it vertically to make a pillow pak pillar. One of his handsomest pillars was a 2″ pak, 6′ long, planted to bonsai-type chrysanthemums. To assure ample water as the plants grew large, he inserted several short lengths of ½″ plastic hose through which water is easily poured from a watering can. Mr. Ackerson says his tests show that, given proper light, virtually any soil-growing plant will thrive in pillow paks in any position.

CONTAINER GUIDES

"Container Gardening Indoors and Out," by Jack Kramer (Doubleday, $6.95).

"Outdoor Gardening in Pots and Boxes," by George Taloumis (Van Nostrand, $5.95).

"Window Box Gardening," by Henry Teuscher (Macmillan, $3.95).

"Hanging Gardens: Basket Plants Indoors and Out," by Jack Kramer (Scribner's, $5.95).

Six months of pruning, training and pinching produced this exquisite bonsai chrysanthemum.

Training Plants

Shape Up

"Ornamental pruning" — the arts of topiary, espalier, pleaching, pollarding and other plant sculpture — used extensively in formal European and American Colonial gardens, is surprisingly well suited to the small contemporary garden, if employed with restraint and limited to special situations.

Pollarded trees make exciting accents, hedges and alleys. Pollarding is the annual pruning back of tree limbs to form a globe at 5′ to 12′ height. The most often pollarded tree is the dwarf umbrella catalpa, *C. bungei (C. bignonioides nana)*, but other suitable subjects are alders, beeches, European plane, hornbeams, lindens, poplars and willows.

Pollarding can keep large trees in scale in restricted space, and can lend interest in city gardens where the round shape contrasts with the straight lines of buildings. Pollarded trees in containers are handsome on patios. In all cases, "flat-topping" should be avoided.

Best treatise on ornamental pruning is the handbook by the BROOKLYN BOTANIC GARDEN (BROOKLYN, NY 11225), "TRAINED AND SCULPTURED PLANTS," $1.50.

Vaulted Trees

A famous horticultural sight is the magnificent golden chain tree arbor at Bodnant Gardens in North Wales, England. While Americans limit arbor or archway plantings to vines, European gardeners use flowering trees with marvelous effect. Best, of course, are those with pliable branches and showy pendant flower or fruit clusters. Many small trees, plus woody vines such as wisteria, offer possibilities for this technique in even fairly small gardens. Prof. Clarence E. Lewis of Michigan State University suggests the silk tree *(Albizzia julibrissin)*, redbud *(Cercis canadensis)*, tree clethra *(Clethra barbinervis)*, dove tree *(Davidia involucrata)*, mountain ash

(Sorbus), European white birch *(Betula pendula)* and fringe tree *(Chionanthus virginica)*.

Other plants, such as holly or azaleas, should be included at intervals to provide additional seasonal color or texture interest. Occasional openings in the branch pattern are important to avoid a tunnel effect. The supporting structure can be simple in design, with a squared form rather than an arc. Metal may be used, but cypress or redwood gives a more natural effect.

Experiment with Espalier

Gardeners are reviving the medieval art of espalier in delightful new forms. The many narrow areas in today's gardens call for adornment with plants trained to a flat plane, and the concept is being extended from the usual against-a-wall training to free-standing espaliers as garden dividers, screens, path liners and enclosures, and even to portable espaliers in containers.

Design rules, too, have been liberalized: modern espaliers are formal or informal to almost every degree, from casually free-form to intricately geometric. Best of all, imaginative gardeners are using a far greater variety of plants for espalier. Besides hardiness, exposure needs and "fit-ability" to the site, the only criteria for plant selection are suppleness and not too rapid, multi-stemmed, or twiggy growth.

A fine basic text is HAROLD O. PERKINS' "ESPALIERS AND VINES FOR THE HOME GARDENER" (VAN NOSTRAND, $6.50).

Treesonable Shrubs

Resist the urge to summarily transplant or discard a shrub that has grown too large — instead, consider transforming it into a tree.

Among those agreeable to this treatment are English and Portuguese laurels *(Laurocerasus officinalis* and *L. lusitanica);* Japanese snowball or doublefile viburnum *(Viburnum tomentosum sterile)* and several other viburnums; *Photinia serrulata, Euonymus japonicus, Arbutus unedo, Magnolia soulangeana,* lilacs, some rhododendrons and cotoneasters such as *Cotoneaster franchetii* and *C. parneyi.*

Best choices are shrubs that have a few heavy stems rather than many thin ones. Remove all but the strongest upright stem and all side growths to the height desired, then brace with a strong stake. Plants trained as trees will grow taller than if grown as shrubs.

Cascade chrysanthemums start with rooted cuttings in spring and end with this fabulous display in autumn.

Deck the Walls

"Curtain plants," English gardeners call them, and any retaining wall will benefit if these trailers are planted along the top, says gardener and author George Taloumis. They soften the barrenness of stone or concrete, and add texture and interesting light and shadow patterns in all seasons.

For a tall wall, Mr. Taloumis recommends weeping forsythia *(Forsythia suspensa),* planted 2 to 3 feet apart. Equally useful for medium to high walls are Virginia creeper *(Parthenocissus quinquefolia),* lace vine *(Polygonum auberti),* Japanese honeysuckle *(Lonicera japonica)* and climbing roses. For low walls, English ivy, big-leaved wintercreeper *(Euonymus fortunei vegetus),* bearberry *(Arctostaphylos uva-ursi),* trailing cotoneasters *(Cotoneaster microphylla, C. horizontalis)* and prostrate junipers *(Juniperus horizontalis* and its varieties *douglasii, procumbens,* 'Wiltonii') are ideal.

Many vines which do not naturally hang — bittersweet *(Celastrus scandens),* Dutchman's pipe *(Aristolochia durior* or *A. sipho),* akebia *(Akebia quinata)* and wisteria, for example — can often be trained to drape over walls.

Topiary Ivies

For indoor or outdoor decoration, portable topiary ivies are tops. Gardeners make them in the shapes of animals, birds and all sorts of objects, including avant garde abstract forms.

Buying the frames for topiary ivy has been a problem. Two firms offer an excellent selection: SPAETH DISPLAYS, INC. (149 WEST 24TH STREET, NEW YORK, NY 10011), and BINYON FLORAL DISPLAYS (BOX 24, CEDAR GROVE, NJ 07009). For homemade frames, Ernesta Drinker Ballard, President of the Pennsylvania Horticultural Society, forms heavy galvanized wire into spirals of varying diameters, twisted or curved into the shape desired. To brace the spirals, "ribs" are attached at right angles with tape and light wire.

These frames can be filled with sphagnum moss and rooted cuttings planted directly in them, or the frame may be supported in a pot in which the ivy is planted. Mrs. Ballard prefers small-leaved ivies, and achieves unusually interesting effects by using variegated types or varieties with different leaf shapes and sizes.

Body-Building for Vines

As fascinating as ivy on forms, are "framed" flowering vines.

A master gardener, Mrs. Sidney Keith, trains these and others to spectacular effect: bower

A simple wire frame to which the stems are bent and tied is used to train chrysanthemums into a spreading cascade.

fabulous, unusual doorstep or patio highlight, and varieties can be chosen for muted tones or spectacular color mixes.

It takes about a year to produce a topiary coleus, starting in early spring with rooted cuttings in 4″ pots. These are transplanted as needed and staked, and side shoots are removed constantly so that heads are allowed to form only where wanted on the "trunk" and at its top. The top is pinched when the plant reaches the height desired. Frequent pinching of the shoots making up the heads produces tight, bushy heads. Occasional light pinching after they are fully formed will keep them well rounded.

Longwood's plants are wintered in a greenhouse, but home gardeners should be able to hold them over successfully in a sunny window or porch at 65°, with reduced feeding and water.

plant *(Pandorea)*, canary creeper *(Tropaeoleum)*, cardinal climber *(Quamoclit sloteri)*, cat's-claw *(Doxantha unguis-cati)*, clematis, cup-and-saucer vine *(Cobaea scandens)*, firecracker vine *(Manettia)*, hoyas, *Jasminum stephanense, Lamium galeobdolon, Maurandia,* moonflower *(Calonyction)*, morning-glories, *Passiflora caerulea* and yellow orchid vine *(Stigmaphyllon)*.

While hoyas are especially handsome trained around an oval or circular form, and morning-glories and other very vigorous growers are best suited to a simple pyramid of stakes, a spiral or "whirl" form unquestionably gives the finest display of many flowering vines. Mrs. Keith uses No. 8 aluminum wire, bending several inches of it straight and taping this to the end of a curtain rod, which is then sunk into the soil in the center of the pot. Then the wire is spiraled up, making the circles as wide as desired, and attached to the rod's top.

Florist's string is used to tie the vine as it grows, always tying behind a node or leaf axil to avoid interfering with growth. When the vine reaches the top, it is turned and trained down.

Topiary Coleus

At Pennsylvania's Longwood Gardens, a triple-headed topiary coleus in a 10″ tub makes a

Herb Trees

Herbs are not often considered subjects for training, and certainly herbs grown in tree form are a rarity. Indeed, when the distinguished gardener, Mrs. Paul Mellon, began growing herbs as standards some years ago, her collection was quite possibly unique in America.

Almost any woody, small-leaved herb is suitable — myrtle, rosemary, santolina and thyme are among the best. Mrs. Mellon says it takes about two years to grow an herb tree, beginning with a rooted cutting tied to a firm stake. All side branches are removed as they appear until the plant nears the desired height, which can vary from about 10″ to as tall as 36″. Then the top is pinched to stimulate side branching. Thereafter, constant vigilance is required to form the head of the tree, each new shoot being pinched when it is no longer than 2″ to induce full and balanced growth.

Important to healthy growth are several hours of sun daily, excellent drainage in the container, and frequent feedings of very dilute fertilizer through spring, summer and fall. Once the head is fully developed, root pruning annually during the dormant period will keep root and top growth in balance. Repot in the same size container, adding fresh soil as needed.

Cascade Mums

Those marvelous cascade chrysanthemums that are becoming such a highlight of autumn greenhouse displays and shows are not difficult to produce, a professional gardener tells us.

Cuttings can be started in January, or rooted cuttings purchased in spring, of suitable cultivars. These are grown with full sun, 62° minimum temperature and regular feeding, and repotted into larger containers every 4 to 5 weeks. The final repotting is done by August 15, usually into an 8″ to 10″ tub, and the plant is allowed to become potbound.

In May, when the plant is about 2′ tall, the frame is made by inserting a 12-gauge wire into the soil next to the trunk and bending it over at a 45° angle about 6″ above the soil. Additional 12-gauge wires are similarly bent, inserted and taped to the far end of the first wire to "spread" the frame to the width of the plant. Thinner wires are used for cross members. The plant is bent to fit the frame and tied to it. All laterals are tied diagonally across the frame at a 45° angle to the leader, and pinched to 5 or 6 pairs of leaves; thereafter all new growth except the leader is pinched whenever 2 pairs of leaves are produced.

When the buds start to show color, the pot is raised high, and all ties and the frame are removed. A heavy wire 12″ to 15″ long is bent to the curve of the main stem and inserted in the soil at its base to brace it. Another wire is placed horizontally across the plant in back, about two thirds of the way to its top, and all stems are tied to this to keep the plant spread apart. From the start of training until flowering, the plant should be positioned facing south.

Many cascade varieties — some blooming for 6 weeks — are offered by SUNNYSLOPE GARDENS (8638 HUNTINGTON DRIVE, SAN GABRIEL, CA 91775).

Bonsai Mums

Exacting, but giving exquisite results — this describes the new art of growing bonsai chrysanthemums. A fascinating aspect is that each year a new style of training can be used on the same plant, retaining only the ever-thickening stump of the "trunk." The number of suitable cultivars — dwarf-growing, heavily branched, with short internodes — is growing (a special list is offered by SUNNYSLOPE GARDENS, 8638 HUNTINGTON DRIVE, SAN GABRIEL, CA 91775).

Two expert practitioners of the art, Mr. and Mrs. Charles D. Webster, give the training schedule they follow:

On May 5, a rooted cutting is potted in a 4″ bulb pan, in a light soil mix high in leafmold, and kept in full sun and fed weekly with one-quarter-strength soluble fertilizer. Training begins in mid-May, personal choice dictating the selection of upright, slanting or cascading styles. The branches are directed and shaped by small weights hung from them, wire hooks coming up from the soil, or copper wire coiled around them. Frequent pruning allows air circulation and light throughout the plant, and periodic pinching of ½″ of the tip and main branches controls the height of the bonsai.

On June 20, July 25 and August 31, the plant is removed from its pot, one third of the bottom of the root ball is trimmed off, and it is repotted in a slightly larger pan. Training and pinching continues all summer, with secondary branches pinched back to 2 leaves when they have grown 4 or 5 leaves. No pinching is done from September 6 to 20, then the plant is given an overall pinch, removing ¼″ of every growing tip. Water is reduced, and the plant is grown as cool as possible.

October 1 is the date for the final root trimming. On November 1, the plant is potted in a decorative show container, and the blooms are thinned to one on the end of each branchlet. Bloom should hold for at least 30 days.

Housebound Bonsai

In true Japanese bonsai, only hardy outdoor plants are used. "Indoor bonsai" — using tender or semi-hardy plants that do not require annual dormancy — appears to be an American adaptation. A worthy one, we think, that promises to achieve great popularity, for it brings this superb blending of art and horticulture to ornament the home and greenhouse all year long.

The best plants are those of naturally dwarf or slow-growing habit and small leaves — but almost any indoor plant with "picturesque prospects" may be worth trying. Some suggestions: ivy, podocarpus, gardenia, citrus, olive, myrtle, acacia, mimosa, miniature roses, rosemary, carissa, serissa, mistletoe fig *(Ficus diversifolia)*, dwarf pomegranate *(Punica granatum nana)*, golden bamboo *(Phyllostachys aurea)*, *Corokia cotoneaster, Oxalis hedysaroides rubra, Malpighia coccigera, Daphne odora, Polyscias fruticosa, Sedum multiceps* and *Sarcococca rustifolia.*

Two sources of plants for indoor bonsai are ARTHUR EAMES ALLGROVE (NORTH WILMINGTON, MA 01887; CATALOG 50¢), and EDELWEISS GARDENS (ROBBINSVILLE, NJ 08691; CATALOG 35¢).

BONSAI BRIEFINGS

"Bonsai Handbook" by the Brooklyn Botanic Garden (Brooklyn, NY 11225; $1.25).

"Bonsai Techniques," by John Yoshio Naka (Bonsai Institute of California, Box 78211, Los Angeles, CA 90016; hardcover $25, paperback $12.50).

Circular 338 of the Florida Agricultural Extension Service (University of Florida, Gainesville, FL 32601; single copies free).

Interior Plantscaping

Living Blooms with Plants

Indoor gardening has a new image. No longer is it an unassuming adjunct to outdoor gardening. Today it is dramatic and vital.

Recognition of interior plantscaping as a horticultural art has come from travel, which has exposed more of us to the Europeans' lavish use of plants in every room and nook in the home . . . from contemporary architecture, with its large glass expanses which both provide light for plants and urge their greater use to enhance viewing pleasure from the exterior as well as the interior . . . and the new environmental consciousness, as the ever-growing presence of steel, concrete, and asphalt stirs longings for contact with nature.

So we are seeing the return of many old concepts in home design, as well as the development of new ones. Gardeners are persuading architects to include atriums or interior courtyards, bay windows, skylights and glass walls in their homes. On small properties, the sunporch, giving all-year enjoyment of plants, is replacing the patio in favor. Office and home designs include built-in wells and raised planters, and many a traditional or modern building features one to several window greenhouses that literally bring outdoor space indoors.

The Ceiling's the Limit

"Interior plantscaping" is garden landscaping brought indoors, with much the same objectives, and embodying similar principles of design and operation. The interior plantscaper thinks in terms of accent plants, naturalistic groupings, borders, mass and screen plantings, even "house trees."

Instead of miscellaneous windowsill collections of plants often unrelated in form, origin or interest, the aim is the creation of a true garden setting indoors. Plants compatible in design and habitat are collectively displayed to their and the home's best decorative advantage.

This has inspired new popularity for terrariums, dish and tray gardens, hanging gardens and deep-container gardens in tropical, desert, oriental and many other motifs. These may be simply "planting pockets," or they are often the dominant feature of a room. A trend in commercial buildings is to landscape entire large offices, substituting plantings for partitions. At Maryknoll College in Ossining, New York, a stunning spatial effect has resulted from extending a large rock garden "through" a glass wall into the college's library. The concept is carried farthest in the Ford Foundation building in New York City, where an enclosed courtyard 200′ square and 156′ high has been made into an imposing garden of flowers, shrubs, vines and towering trees.

Designing with Plants

The interior plantscaper also employs decorating principles. Basic are those factors professionals call "plastic elements":

Texture, as in the delicate quality of compound leaves or the bold effect of large ones; color, including hue — glossy dark-green foliage reflects coolness, light-hued plants give richness and warmth — plus value or depth of color, and the chroma or relative brightness or dullness of a plant; form, the horizontal and vertical elements that modify the dimensions of a room, such as short dense plants used to increase horizontal spaciousness; and line, the softening or enhancing of the lines of a room or its furnishings by the lines of a planting and its container.

Consideration of these is important, and we suggest as an aid the excellent KANSAS AGRICULTURAL EXPERIMENT STATION BULLETIN 493, "INTERIOR DECORATION WITH LIVING PLANTS" (free from the DEPARTMENT OF HORTICULTURE, KANSAS STATE UNIVERSITY, MANHATTAN, KS 66502). It keys many plants by their "plastic element" values, and shows how to apply these in open areas, room dividers, screening, structural accents. Also helpful is "USING TROPICAL ORNAMENTALS IN GARDEN ROOMS, ENCLOSED PATIO AND POOL AREAS," free from the AGRICULTURAL EXTENSION SERVICE, UNIVERSITY OF FLORIDA (GAINESVILLE, FL 32601).

The great variety of containers available today — plus the gardener's ingenuity in adapting many designed for other purposes — adds a special dimension of excitement, one not common in outdoor gardening. The principles above apply in large measure to selection of the planters as well as plants, and also to accessories such as statuary, fountains and decorative mulches.

A "fine arts" garden on a sun porch displays topiary ivy, bonsai, citrus trees and an international collection of foliage and flowering plants.

Home Microclimates

Beyond design features, success depends on matching plant to growing conditions. Veteran indoor growers stress that there is no substitute for knowledge of the climatic characteristics of any species' native habitat, with special attention to two factors: light and temperature. Of all the influences on plant growth, these are the most limiting, and also often the least amenable to modification in the average home.

This might appear to restrict choice to plants of similar environmental origin, until you observe the microclimate variations of possible plantscaping areas. In any given room, there may be any number of microclimates, ranging from cool and bright at the windows to dim, dry and warm in corners. A thermometer and a light meter (such as the direct-reading General Electric Footcandle Meter, available from the HOUSE PLANT CORNER, BOX 810, OXFORD, MD 21654) can be helpful to avoid much experimentation and frustration.

Choice of plants, then, is based on evaluation of a microclimate, and feasible modification of it, and culture. The aim, however, is not necessarily to achieve best growth, but rather the type of growth you want. With foliage plants, for example, it is often most practical to strive for healthy but quite slow growth, so they will not get out of bounds or proportion.

If asked to give one unbreakable rule for plants indoors, we would say this: Where light is at the lower levels a plant will tolerate, three actions are vital to maintain it in good condition: (1) keep the soil on the dry side, watering only frequently enough to prevent wilting; (2) give only sufficient fertilizer to prevent hunger signs; (3) keep the air temperature as cool as your own comfort will permit.

These are fundamentals of the "sun-food ratio" rule, which states that the more light a plant gets, the higher levels of nutrients, moisture and temperature it can utilize.

House Trees

Tropical trees are in such demand, Florida growers are hard put to it to supply them, we're told by Kent Hunter, manager of Terrestris, Inc. in New York, a leading indoor-outdoor landscaper.

He notes that they are generally easier to care for than small plants. Growth can be held to convenient 4' to 8' heights by the minimal light-food-water technique, and in many cases (palms excepted) by top and root pruning.

Both dedicated and budget-minded indoor gardeners, incidentally, will find a challenge and unique rewards in growing unusual tropical trees and shrubs from seed. A leading proponent of this idea is Mr. W. J. Brudy (JOHN BRUDY'S RARE PLANT HOUSE, BOX 1348, COCOA BEACH, FL 32931; CATALOG $1), who supplies seed of many exotics. He states: "The dwarfing of many trees and shrubs may be successfully achieved by starting them from seed and maintaining them in restricted quarters, producing a plant which has elegance of form, smaller structure throughout, and surprising endurance."

Liberal Art

Interior plantscaping can be as simple or as elaborate as the home and personal inclination suggest. A single select form of ivy or *Cissus discolor* cascading from a pedestal . . . a large specimen of the remarkable gnarled and spiny elkhorn euphorbia (*Euphorbia lactea cristata*) . . . the elegance of *Hoya carnosa* 'Exotica' framing a window . . . an espaliered fatshedera against a wall . . . a hanging basket of *Hyprocyrta radicans* — any of these can add drama to a room.

Two cautions should be stressed: Ideally, flowering plants should have interest when not in bloom — the temptation of a spectacular or intriguing flower must be tempered by consideration of the plant's other contributions to the total picture. Secondly, the oft-forgotten "size at maturity" factor is frequently just as important a consideration to the indoor plantscaper as to the outdoor landscaper.

SPECIALTIES OF THE HOUSE

Bottling Plants

New plastic and glass containers are bringing a new look to terrarium and bottle gardens. Any clear container with ventilation capability can be used — we've seen exquisite bottlearia of perfume bottles planted with tiny ferns and evergreen seedlings. And for the craftsman who wants to make his own, there are bottle-cutting kits.

Design in plantings, too, has left the traditional. Emulating the gardener's and flower arranger's arts, these gardens in glass may suggest or represent natural scenes or be abstract in the extreme (which doesn't mean "enhancing" with little plastic mice or gnomes, however!). The principles of design that guide landscape and floral arts apply equally to the modern terrarium — proportion, balance, line and a focal point established through form, color or texture of a single plant or massed plants. Plantings can be set at varying levels, and trailing plants as well as perpendicular and spreading ones should be utilized.

With compatibility of culture and rate of growth as the prime criteria, plant choices are wide. Gesneriads such as African violets or the charming miniature gloxinias and *Sinningia pusilla*, miniature orchids, small ivies and tropical or woodland ferns, bromeliads, tropical foliage plants of all sorts, palms, strawberry begonia, baby's tears — opportunities to achieve marvelous effects are endless. Many plants can be tailored to terrariums by trimming their roots and tops, and the restricted quarters of the container aid in dwarfing. Rocks, gravel, bark and driftwood are useful complements.

Experts say drainage material, consisting of 2 parts small gravel to 1 part ground charcoal, should be $\frac{1}{8}''$ to $\frac{1}{4}''$ deep for every inch of growing medium. Recommended media are equal parts of soil, sand and peat, or the new soilless mixes. The rule for depth of the medium is $\frac{1}{4}''$ for each $1''$ of container height. In larger glass gardens, plants may sometimes be left in their pots.

After planting, mist-spray the plants, water lightly and cover. Thereafter, watering should be infrequent and fertilizing rare. Ventilate on hot days, or when moisture appears on the glass. Bright light rather than direct sun is best, and 14 to 16 hours per day of fluorescent light is excellent.

Dish Gardens with a Flair

Contemporary dish gardens are changing greatly from the original concept of a miniature scenic garden of slow-growing foliage plants. The plants are still chosen so they will not outgrow their surroundings, but now the idea is to create a mood rather than "Snow White and the Seven Dwarfs" scenes. The effect to strive for is freer, to achieve beauty by combining plants in still life, fountain, cascade and similar designs.

Pothos is one of many plants that will root and grow in blocks of florists' foam.

This trend has been initiated by a few truly imaginative gardeners, and it is being stimulated by the wide variety of containers available. Even Victorian stone urns are being reproduced in lightweight materials which can be made more attractive by toning or antiquing. Besides commercially available containers, dish gardeners are seeing new possibilities in all sorts of crockery, metal and glass containers, wood boxes and small tubs, shells, rocks — practically anything that will hold sufficient planting medium. For variety, the dish garden that sits in one planter today can be given a new look by being set in another container tomorrow, if it is planted in a "liner."

With the one proviso that plants must be culturally compatible, the dish gardener can employ a great diversity of material. Some of the spectacular bromeliads, for example, combine stunningly with small succulents such as sedums, haworthias and sansevierias.

As in designing terrarium plantings, use tall and upright plants in combination with spreaders and trailers . . . consider unusuals such as grasses, herbs, groundcovering plants, even seedlings of slow-growing hardy dwarf trees and shrubs . . . follow flower-arranging principles of line, proportion, balance to achieve sophisticated designs . . . late winter is a good time to start, as increasing light helps overcome transplant shock.

Hang It All!

The term "hanging basket" has been expanded to include virtually any plant in any container that can be hung, and this concept is enlarging the scope of the indoor garden by adding a third dimension to it.

Some unusual ideas: a kitchen-window hanging garden of miniature plants in measuring cups, funnels, soup ladles, gelatin molds; window boxes hung in tiers; a latticework room divider hung with potted plants attached with decorative cord; a wooden ladder with plants hanging from some rungs and others standing on planks used to widen the rungs; and mobiles and "trees" of epiphytic orchids and bromeliads wired to trunks, branches, logs or driftwood.

In containers, there's the standard mesh basket — we wish they came in smaller sizes — of metal, plastic or wood. Two useful variations are the English half-round wall basket (from WALTER F. NICKE, BOX 71, HUDSON, NY 12534; CATALOG 25¢), and the water-reservoir Easy-Does-It (GEO. W. PARK SEED CO., GREENWOOD, SC 29647). Besides these and other available or adaptable containers, ingenious gardeners use coconut shells, even sea shells, and strawberry jars.

More ideas: a fisherman's swivel at the hanger top allows easy turning of the container . . .

HANG-IT suspends pots, terrariums, anything up to 25 pounds; consists of a transparent nylon cord, Plexiglas plate and clear ring; from House of Hints Corp. (G.P.O. Box 730, Brooklyn, NY 11202).

fluorescent tubes mounted vertically supply light to tiers of hanging plants . . . mesh baskets with flowering plants set in the sides and bottom so they hide the entire container make beautiful "living bouquets" . . . dried flowers and foliage brighten foliage-plant hanging gardens.

Swiss Planter

Vertical "moss-wall" gardening, as yet practiced by only a few connoisseurs — although the idea originated 25 years ago in Switzerland — offers marvelous dramatic effects. Versatility, portability and striking beauty characterize this type of container gardening.

A moss-wall container may be almost any shape: cylindrical, half-round, square, oblong, crescent, etc. It may be free-standing, hanging or attached to a wall, post or fence. It consists simply of a frame of rot-resistant wood such as cypress, cedar or redwood, with a solid bottom and, if it is to be attached, a solid back. All open sides are covered with 1″ or slightly larger wire mesh, fastened with heavy staples. Then the container is lined with sphagnum moss or osmunda fiber and filled with a soilless mix (some gardeners fill the entire container with sphagnum or osmunda).

Rooted cuttings or vigorous seedlings are set in the mesh openings, at an upward slant. They should be planted close together, as they will not spread out as they would in horizontal beds. Water thoroughly after planting, and keep the container in a sheltered spot for a week or so. Thereafter watering is necessary whenever the moss lining starts to feel dry, and a complete fertilizer should be given every 10 to 14 days, at half the strength recommended for house plants.

Virtually any compact plant suited to the light conditions available should do well. Small annuals, colorful foliage plants, even herbs, strawberries, mints and watercress have thrived in these containers. Ingenuity will suggest other unusuals: miniature orchids, for example, would be stunning.

VENTARAMA, by Ventarama Skylight Corp. (174 Main Street, Port Washington, NY 11050), is a plastic-domed skylight which can be installed in most types of roofs to provide more light for interior plantscaping in any room of the house.

On the Waterfront

The trend to soilless media has prompted a revival of interest in growing plants in plain water. A great many foliage plants and some flowering ones can be grown hydroponically in any clear or opaque container, of either ceramic or glass.

Dr. Henry M. Cathey, horticulturist of the Agricultural Research Service, says that sanitation is the vital requirement for success. Containers must be scrubbed well with soap and rinsed thoroughly before use, then cleaned the same way once a month thereafter. The plant stems and leaves should also be wiped and rinsed whenever the container is cleaned. When ½" of roots form, biweekly feeding with a complete fertilizer is begun, at one-quarter the strength recommended for house plants.

Some excellent subjects are African violets, aglaonema, acuba, begonias, cissus, coleus, dracaena, fatshedera, fuchsia, gardenia, geranium, hibiscus, impatiens, ivies, myrtle, nephytis, oleander, peperomia, philodendrons, pothos, sansevieria, tradescantia and zebrina. Plants lacking long stems can be supported over the water with wide wire mesh.

The best "water planters" feature combinations of unusual foliage colors and forms — try the variegated *Aglaonema pictum*, bronze-leaved *Philodendron micans*, or tradescantias with gold, silver or wine leaves, and many others.

Dr. Cathey's latest inspiration is potless-soilless planting. Blocks of florists' foam — Oasis — are cut into any desired size and shape, cuttings are inserted into the foam, and the block is watered and fertilized as usual for the plant. Ivy, ficus, pothos, peperomia, Chinese evergreen, bromeliads and cacti are some that thrive well in foam blocks. The blocks, of course, may be set in any container, a variety of plants can be grown in combination in a block, and cut foliage and flowers poked into the foam will add decorative effects for special occasions. Dr. Cathey recommends fertilizing with a 20-20-20 formula, 1½ teaspoons per gallon of water.

A self-contained hydroponic unit for home gardening is the Hydropod, by BURWELL GEOPONICS CORPORATION (BOX 125, RANCHO SANTA FE, CA 92067). Available in redwood, fiberglass and mahogany paneled models, from 1½' x 4' to 2' x 6' and in kit form for up to 2' x 12', Hydropods include a growing bed with gravel aggregate, solution reservoir, pump, timer and pre-mixed nutrient formulas. Once the apparatus is set for the number of feeding-waterings desired daily, biweekly changes of nutrient solution are the only care required.

"HYDROPONIC GARDENING," BY RAYMOND BRIDWELL (WOODBRIDGE PRESS, 11440 ACACIA STREET, LOMA LINDA, CA 92354), is an up-to-date primer on soilless culture for indoor, backyard and greenhouse growing.

Indoor Aqua-Tactics

Indoor pools have a special appeal. A friend gives these directions for a handsome, easily built small pool:

Have a tinsmith make a galvanized tray in the desired size and shape, but no deeper than 5", to accommodate a 3" depth of water. He can also install a watertight bottom "window" of colored glass or Plexiglas, so a floodlamp on the floor below will send up beams of light. A drain plug in one side will facilitate changing the water. The tray should be given two coats of a suitable paint, inside and out. Then set the tray on a platform of wood, concrete blocks or bricks to hold it about 12" above the floor, and cover the outside of the tray and platform with cork bark or other decorative material.

Plants for the pool include many dracaenas and philodendrons, Chinese evergreen, cissus, ivy, pothos, tradescantia, maranta, nephthytis, podocarpus and many others. Set them on heavy needle holders, raised on stones if necessary so only the roots are submerged, and use pebbles to conceal these. Change the water weekly for the first month, then every 10 days; charcoal will help to keep it clear.

Contemporary see-through plant pools are easily made with Plexiglas. A useful booklet is "DO IT YOURSELF WITH PLEXIGLAS ACRYLIC SHEET," 25¢ FROM BOX 4470, PHILADELPHIA, PA 19140 . . . or send for the catalog of CORTH PLASTICS (532 HOWLAND STREET, REDWOOD CITY, CA 94063).

Indoor Groundcovers

Creeping and trailing plants are as necessary to the interior plantscaper as to the outdoor gardener. Diminutive groundcovers add the perfect finishing touch for many pot plants, bonsai, dish gardens and terrariums.

Terrarium specialists provide useful groups of mosses and lichens, and of course there is the popular "baby's tears," *Helxine soleirolii*. Two other fine carpeters are miniature creeping fig, *Ficus pumila minima*, and gill-over-the-ground, *Nepeta hederacea variegata*. The tiny peppermint, *Mentha requienii*, is a creeper with little mauve flowers. Several miniature pileas are also excellent — *Pilea repens, P. involucrata, P. depressa* and the artillery plant, *P. microphylla*, which "explodes" its pollen.

The little-known genus *Pellionia* offers *P. pulchra*, with blue-gray, black-veined leaves, plus the so-called trailing watermelon begonia, *P. daveauana*. And among the mossy-ferny selaginellas we find several gems: the peacock moss, *Selaginella uncinata*, with metallic blue foliage; *S. kraussiana*, a bright clear green spreader; and *S. kraussiana brownii*, which forms a perfectly circular green mound like cushion moss.

These and others are available from ARTHUR EAMES ALLGROVE (NORTH WILMINGTON, MA 01187; CATALOG 50¢), EDELWEISS GARDENS (BOX 66, ROBBINSVILLE, NJ 08691; CATALOG 35¢), LOGEE'S GREENHOUSES (DANIELSON, CT 06239; CATALOG $1) and MERRY GARDENS (CAMDEN, ME 04843; CATALOG 25¢).

HOUSE PLANTS

Strategy for Strangers

Most house plants today are produced in the South, under very high light and high humidity, and even though northern retailers provide some degree of conditioning by holding them in a less bright and damp environment, still the change to a much darker and more arid home atmosphere can be a shock. An abrupt change will result in rapid yellowing and loss of some leaves, an alarming symptom to which too many gardeners react by doing just the wrong thing — pouring on water and fertilizer.

A new acquisition should be given bright light (sun if it is a plant requiring high light intensity) in a window or under artificial lights, for at least the first two to three weeks. Cool temperatures and gentle air circulation are also important, but be especially careful to avoid cold drafts or the hot, dry air currents from heating systems. Mist foliage several times a day, water enough to keep the soil moist but never soggy, and withhold fertilizer. Then, over the next month or so, the plant can be moved gradually from the window or lights to areas of lower light and higher temperatures, and can be misted less often.

Tactical Tips

For safe and easy moisture control, double-pot whenever practical, setting one container in another wider one, filling in between them with horticultural sphagnum moss kept moist to slow drying . . . in a large planter without drainage holes, use a dip-stick in a tube to check the water level in the gravel drainage layer, and never allow this layer to become water-filled . . . use room-temperature or warmer water at all times.

Many self-watering pots and moisture-regulating systems are on the market. Some of the best are: Water Wick (MARDON GARDENS, 182 SHERBURN DRIVE, HAMBURG, NY 14075); Riviera self-watering

No matter how ideal their indoor environment, all house plants benefit from a summer vacation outdoors.

pots and planters (THE GREATEST POT, 1214 LEXINGTON AVENUE, NEW YORK, NY 10028); Plantender (PLANTAMATION, SEAMAN, OH 45679); and Ecology King self-watering planters (GREEN ISLAND INTERNATIONAL, BOX 1369, WINTER GARDEN, FL 32787).

Potted Water

A new water-retaining material, Hydrogel (UNION CARBIDE CORP., 270 PARK AVENUE, NEW YORK, NY 10017), can greatly reduce watering needs.

In experiments with potted tomatoes and coleus, Prof. J. W. Boodley and John Vlahos of Cornell University found that Hydrogel mixed into the soil made it possible to maintain good growth with one-sixth to one-eighth the usual frequency of waterings. The most effective rate was 12 ounces of Hydrogel per cubic foot of soil mix, which consisted of 2 parts of sphagnum peat to 1 part each of sand and perlite.

When planting in fresh soil mix is not feasible, cores of Hydrogel mixed with soil can be inserted into holes made in the soil around the plant. Four of these cores, with the Hydrogel at double the rate used when it is incorporated into a planting mix, proved as effective as the incorporation method.

Quality Soil

If you collect soil, the best source is the root zone of a long-established pasture or hay field. Soil from frequently cultivated plots such as flower beds or the vegetable garden will have less humus.

It's wise to avoid the packaged potting soils offered in many stores. Some come from inferior sources, and often muck is added to give a "rich, black" color. Even the better types are so finely sifted their vital granular structure is destroyed.

Periodic heavy watering with plain water is important for all potted plants, to flush out accumulations of fertilizer salts which can kill a plant by drawing fluids out of its roots. One final important caution: don't collect roadside, woodland or cultivated soils on which herbicides have been used.

Clean Soil

For a soil free of weeds, diseases and insects, sterilize it. Actually, pasteurize is the more exact term, for complete sterilization would destroy the soil structure and release toxic substances.

Soil can be sterilized without mess or odor in oven cooking bags. A gardener recommends a "Brown-in-Bag," turkey size, adding ½ to 1 cup of water to the loosely packed soil, and cooking it "as per instructions for cooking the turkey." For large volumes of soil, use an electric soil pasteurizer (SOIL KING CORP., BOX 3066, SAN MATEO, CA 94403, has models under $200), or sterilize with chemicals. Formaldehyde (formalin, from drugstores), 1 cup to 3 gallons of water, used as a drench, destroys many fungi and bacteria and some weed seeds. Chloropicrin and methyl bromide are trickier to use and require extensive precautions, but the newer Vapam (STAUFFER CHEMICALS, 299 PARK AVENUE, NEW YORK, NY 10017) can be simply sprinkled on the soil. With any chemical sterilant, all instructions and warnings should be scrupulously heeded.

Always important with any method of sterilization: avoid recontamination of the soil with disease organisms by frequently sterilizing all tools and equipment with a solution of Clorox or a disinfectant such as LF-10, (LEHN & FINK PRODUCTS, 225 SUMMIT AVE., MONTVALE, NJ 07645).

Soilless Media

Difficulties in obtaining clean soil of known quality have brought a switch to soilless mixes. They offer numerous advantages: the principal cause of failure — disease caused by soil organisms — is eliminated; materials are easy to obtain and inexpensive; the fertility of the mixes is known and controllable; they are lightweight, free of weed seeds, easy to mix and store, and their physical properties are better than those of topsoil.

Best known is Cornell's Peat-Lite, available in two commercial versions, Jiffy-Mix (JIFFY POT CO. OF AMERICA, BOX 338, WEST CHICAGO, IL 60185) and Redi-Earth (W. R. GRACE & CO., CHICAGO, IL 60654). With these mixes, seed is sown about twice as deep as in soil. They should be watered daily the first week after sowing or planting, and thereafter handled just like soil. Slow-release fertilizers work well with them.

Many other materials are used in potting and propagating media. Joe M. Woodard of the First Men's Garden Club of Dallas, Texas, reports that a screened medium of composted pine bark proved more successful in starting African violet leaf cuttings than a sterilized growing mix or coarse sand. Horticultural (unmilled) sphagnum moss, an ingredient in many soilless mixes, is also an excellent medium used alone.

In the windows of the Horticultural Society of New York, plants from African violets and ferns to giant dracaenas have thrived for 20 years without soil, in trays only 2″ deep. These are the famous tray gardens developed by R. B. Farnham, the Society's former Executive Secretary. Mr. Farnham's trays are simply four 1″ x 2″ pieces of lumber nailed to form the sides, then covered with heavy plastic fabric which also serves as the bottom. Coarse vermiculite (insulation grade) is the planting medium.

PUCCI, the famous fashion designer, says that people are beginning to seek satisfaction from sensations and feelings rather than objects and possessions — hence the greatly accelerating trend toward flowers and plants in the home.

The fascinating tropical pitcher plants, Nepenthes, and other carnivorous plants, need very high humidity and warmth, so are best grown in enclosed cases.

CONNOISSEURS' HOUSE PLANTS

Foliage Plants for Low Light

Aglaeonema, Chinese evergreen — *A. roebelinii*, with silver-mottled leaves and long-lasting berries, is one of the finest plants for very low light; *A. treubii* is a smaller form; *A. marantifolium tricolor* has white stems, feathery leaf markings; *A. pseudobracteatum* has white stems; also many handsome variegated cultivars of *A. commutatum*.

Araucaria, Norfolk Island pine — *A. heterophylla (A. excelsa)* is widely sold; *A. bidwillii*, the Australian bunya-bunya, has irregular twisting branches; *A. heterophylla albo-spica* has silvery new growth tips.

Asparagus — *A. sprengeri* is popular for its delicate arching cascades of greenery, but more elegant is *A. meyeri*, whose dense fronds form a solid hemispherical rosette of rich green.

Aspidistra elatior, cast-iron plant — the old-time parlor plant, with bold dark green leaves; excellent for very dim light.

Aucuba japonica, gold dust plant — a handsome shrubby plant, the thick glossy leaves speckled with gold in *A. j. variegata*, or splashed, centered or margined with gold in other varieties.

Calathea — best known is *C. makoyana*, peacock plant, with lovely feathery designs on olive-green leaves, but worth seeking are tiny-leaved *C. micans*, striking green-and-pink-striped *C. roseo-lineata*, and new *C. insignis*, feathered yellow-green, deep red beneath. A calathea relative, *Ctenanthe oppenheimiana tricolor*, has narrow upright leaves in bright tones of green, pink, cream and rose.

Dracaena — most common are the handsome dragon tree, *D. marginata*, and corn plant, *D. sanderiana*, but also useful are such recent additions as the spotted-leaf shrubby *D. godseffiana* 'Florida Beauty,' stunning silver-banded *D. goldieana* and striped-leaf *D. deremensis warnecki* 'Roehrs Gold.' *D. terminalis*, ti plant — more correctly, *Cordyline terminalis* — has striking coppery-green and red leaves in varieties such as 'Firebrand' and 'Eugene André.'

Fatshedera lizei, tree ivy — a hybrid (*Fatsia japonica* x *Hedera hibernica*) with large leathery star leaves on wiry upright stems.

Ferns — a wonderfully diverse group useful in low light, but generally requiring very high humidity — a notable exception is *Asplenium bulbiferum*, a mother fern which thrives on much drier soil and air. Many dwarf ferns are now available: "table" ferns like *Pteris ensiformis* 'Victoriae,' silver-lace, or *Adiantum bellum*, little Bermuda maidenhair; a 3″ Boston fern, *Nephrolepis exaltata* 'Mini-Ruffle' has just been patented. The many selections in larger ferns range from the feathery rabbit's-foot, *Davallia fejeensis*, with creeping furry rhizomes, to unfernlike species such as button fern (*Phyllitis scolopendrium*), bird's-nest (*Asplenium nidus*), staghorn (*Platycerium*) and holly (*Cyrtomium*) ferns. Really unusual are stout-trunked tree ferns — *Alsophila australis* and *Cibotium scheidei* have feathery fronds, while *Blechnum brasiliensis* and compact *B. moorei* have dramatic stiff fronds. The climbing fern, *Lygodium scandens (L. japonicum)*, can climb 10′ and has typical feathery fern foliage, but needs full sun in winter.

Ficus — a few suggestions from the many available: variegated *F. elastica doescheri* is the handsomest rubber plant . . . for a sizable shrub or tree, grow *F. benjamina* 'Exotica' or the Indian laurel, *F. retusa nitida* . . . the unusual dwarf mistletoe fig, *F. diversifolia*, has succulent leaves and numerous yellow fruits . . . rare shrubby *F. parcellii*, clown fig, has cream-marbled leaves . . . striking 3′ to 5′ fiddle-leaf fig, *F. lyrata (F. pandurata)*, has quilted violin-shaped leaves with yellow-green veins . . . in trailers, there are *F. radicans variegata* and tiny-leaved creeping *F. repens pumila*.

Fittonia verschaffeltii — a beautiful low grower, almost creeping, with rosy-veined olive leaves; *F. v. argyroneura* has silver veins.

Ligularia kaempferi aureomaculata, leopard plant — dwarf, round green leaves spotted gold; rare *L. k. argentea* has white-margined bluish-green leaves, pinkish when young.

Maranta — much like *Calathea* and as diverse; excellent are yellow and green *M. arundinacea aurea*; *M. bicolor*, feathered silver-green, maroon beneath; chocolate-blotched *M. leuconeura kerchoveana*, prayer plant; and the new red-veined *M. l. massangeana* 'Voster's.'

Pandanus, screw pine — *P. veitchii* has long arching green and white leaves, *P. sanderi* is gold-banded, *P. pygmaeus* is a dwarf.

Peperomia — a few of the best of the dozens available are woolly-leaved *P. incana*; *P. griseo-argentea* 'Blackie,' darkest copper-green; velvety, red-stemmed *P. bicolor;* rare waxy-leaved *P. pericatti;* silver and copper *P. metallica;* red-edged *P. clusiaefolia;* and tiny-leaved creeping *P. rotundifolia.*

Philodendron — this indispensable is available today in vining, self-heading (bushy) and tree types, with foliage from ferny to elephant-ear, in every leaf color and texture. Superb new ones include self-heading green-gold *P. warscewiczii* 'Golden Selloum,' vining silvery 'Burle Marx's Fantasy,' leathery maroon-green 'Burgundy.'

Sansevieria, snake plant — at least a dozen fine varieties are sold today, such as low-growing bird's-nest *S. trifasciata* 'Hahnii' in silver- and gold-banded forms, sword-leaved *S. laurentii* 'Bantel's Sensation' with white and cream stripes, and the tall but compact steel-blue, white-edged *S. ehrenbergii.*

The ponytail, Beaucarnea recurvata, is an unusual foliage plant with a woody bulbous base, excellent in bright light.

Foliage Plants for Bright Light to Full Sun

Alocasia — huge elephant-ear or lance foliage prominently veined. Rare *A. watsoniana* has 18″ leaves, hybrid *A. amazonica* is glossy-leaved, and several other species and hybrids have olive-green to purple leaves with red to silver veining.

Boweia volubilis, climbing onion — a twining plant for a small trellis, growing a feathery green plume from a succulent green bulb.

Brassaia (Schefflera) actinophylla, Australian umbrella tree — a handsome "house shrub," with a slender trunk and glossy, richest green palmate leaves.

Carex morrowi — a pretty little tufted ornamental grass.

Chamaeranthemum — several species of this little creeper or trailer have velvety green or brown leaves, red- or silver-veined.

Cissus, grape ivy — fine trailers or twiners, including little bronze-leaved *C. striata;* silver-and-red-leaved *C. discolor;* the foolproof kangaroo vine, *C. antarctica,* with saw-toothed foliage; felt-leaved *C. capensis;* and pink-leaved *C. adenopodus.*

Codiaeum, croton — indispensable for true tropical splendor, the brilliantly multicolored leaves may be long and narrow or broad, often wrinkled or corkscrewed.

Cycads — one of the most ancient plant groups, with dramatic leathery palm-frond foliage. Among the best for house culture are the Sago palm, *Cycas revoluta; Dion purpusii,* with numerous narrow pinnae on stiff stems; *Ceratozamia mexicana,* a short trunk and many-leaflet leaves; and *Zamia floridiana,* shining deep green fronds.

Dieffenbachia, dumbcane — one of the best for dry air, with long broad leaves splashed, speckled, ribbed or veined white or cream. Especially striking leaf patterns are found in 'Arvida,' *D. hoffmanii, D. jenmanii, D. bowmannii.*

Dizygotheca elegantissima, finger aralia — a very artistic cut-leaved shrub, the leaves rust-brown, leathery and mottled.

Elaeagnus pungens — sometimes called arbutus shrub, the variegated-leaf forms make excellent "house shrubs."

Eucalyptus — many eucalypts will grow as shrubs or trees in pots; particularly good are silvery-blue-leaved *E. cinerea* and *E. citriodora,* the latter with strongly lemon scented foliage.

Euonymus — some suggested for indoor culture are *E. japonicus* 'Silver Queen' and 'Gold Queen,' tiny-leaved *E. japonicus microphyllus* and trailing *E. fortunei minimus.*

Fatsia japonica (Aralia sieboldii) — big and bold, with glossy, deeply cut leaves; 'Moseri' grows more compactly.

Geogenanthus undatus (Dichorisandra mosaica undata), seersucker plant — a charming low grower with broad oval leaves striped silver and black, purple beneath.

Gynura, velvet plant — besides the royal-purple-leaved *G. aurantiaca*, try *G. bicolor*, serrated green leaves, purple beneath; and *G. sarmentosa*, a deep purple trailer for baskets.

Mikania terenata (M. scandens), plush vine — a fast grower with purple leaves, resembling miniature grape ivy.

Musa cavendishii (M. acuminata, M. nana), dwarf banana — a trunk-like stem and long broad leaves, producing many small edible fruits if given much sun.

To flower the Easter cactus, Rhipsalidopsis, near Easter, a night temperature of 50° in winter is essential.

Myrsine — *M. africana* is the handsome dwarf African boxwood, and *M. nummularia* is a creeping version of this easily grown shrub.

Nicodemia diversifolia, indoor oak — an arching vine with glossy blue-green leaves resembling those of English oak.

Olea europaea, olive tree — beautiful silvery leaves, will stay small in pots.

Oplismensus hirtellus vittatus, ribbon grass — pretty grassy foliage, striped pink and white.

Palms — these adapt marvelously to rigorous conditions: single-stem types — *Caryota urens*, fishtail; *Chamaedorea elegans (Neanthe bella)*, parlor palm, a dwarf to 18″; *Howeia (Kentia) belmoreana* and *H. forsteriana*, sentry palms; *Licuala grandis*, a small fan palm; *Livistona chinensis*, Chinese fan palm; *Phoenix roebelinii*,

the very graceful pigmy date palm; the red-fruited Christmas palm, *Veitchia merrillii* . . . multi-stemmed types — *Caryota mitis*, clustered fishtail; *Chamaedorea erumpens*, bamboo palm, and other species; *Chamaerops humilis*, dwarf Mediterranean fan palm; *Chrysalidocarpus lutescens*, butterfly palm; and *Rhapis excelsa* and *R. humilis*, lady palms.

Pilea — numerous creeping to bushy species: shrubby *P. cadieri*, aluminum plant, has silver-sheened leaves; *P. microphylla* is the pollen-discharging artillery plant; *P. involucrata* 'Moon Valley' has chocolate leaves overlaid with green. Good creepers are *P. cadieri minima*, *P. repens*, *P. nummulariaefolia*.

Podocarpus macrophylla maki, African pine — actually Chinese, this dense shrub is prized for its dark yew-like foliage; easily pruned.

Polyscias — unusual shrubs with ferny *(P. filicifolia)*, "parsley" *(P. fruticosa)* or "spinach" *(P. balfouriana)* foliage.

Rubus reflexus — an unusual trailer, the large leaves velvety, green with gray variegations, chocolate beneath.

Scindapsus (Pothos, Rhaphidophora), devil's ivy — dependable climbers with heart-shaped leaves; best are *S. aureus* 'Marble Queen,' white-mottled, and 'Tricolor,' gold-blotched, and the silver-spotted *S. pictus argyraeus*.

Selaginella — related to ferns but resembling mosses; good for baskets and groundcovers in pots are *S. kraussiana*, *S. emmeliana*, and *S. uncinata*. A fine erect grower is *S. martensii*. *S. lepidophylla* is the resurrection plant, which curls up in drought.

Syngonium (Nephthytis) podophyllum — arrowhead leaves to 6″ long; 'Emerald Gem,' 'Green Gold,' 'Imperial White' are the finest.

Flowering Plants for an East or West Exposure

Abutilon, flowering maple — blooming all year, the many new cultivars of *A. hybridum* have tissue-thin bell flowers in white, yellow, pink and red; 'Savitzii' and 'Souvenir de Bonn' also have variegated foliage. Yellow-variegated *A. striatum aureomaculatum* bears apricot flowers. *A. megapotamicum variegatum* is a fine trailer.

Acalypha — chenille plant or red-hot cattails, *A. hispida*, bears fluffy pendent red catkins and stands neglect. Showy foliage is found in numerous cultivars of *A. wilkesiana*, copperleaf; the finest is 'Ceylon,' deepest maroon with crimson serrated edges.

African Violets — biggest news are the miniatures and semi-miniatures, blooming as lavishly as standard types but in 2½″ to 3″ pots, and the brand new trailing African violets such as the single-flowered 'Violet Trail,' double 'Blue Border' and double pink 'Mysterium,' all with 1½″ flowers, and the 2″ double pink 'Seventh Heaven.'

Anthurium — numerous useful species from the dwarf everblooming *A. scherzerianum* with teardrop leaves and 2″ orange spathes, to the lacy begonia-leaved *A. pictamayo*, *A. crystallinum* with 10″ bronze-green silver-veined leaves, and climbing *A. scandens* and *A. warocqueanum*.

Aphelandra, zebra plant — spectacular broad silvery to emerald-green white-veined leaves and waxy-bracted yellow, orange or scarlet flowers in fine cultivars of *A. squarrosa* — 'Diana,' 'Louisiae,' Brockfeld' and 'Uniflora Beauty.'

Aristolochia elegans, calico flower vine — a lovely twiner with heart-shaped leaves, producing its 3″ white, purple-veined flowers when only 3′ to 4′ tall.

Begonias — not only are new varieties constantly appearing in the popular semperflorens, beefsteak, angel-wing and other old-favorite types, but there are dwarf and miniature rex begonias in striking color combinations, and many new "eyelash" rhizomatous *B. boweri* hybrids with fabulous marbled and speckled foliage. Most exciting are the Rieger elatior begonias, crosses of winter-flowering hybrids of *B. socotrana* with summer tuberous types. These vigorous, large-flowered plants which bloom most of the year do best with full sun in winter. Important to remember with begonias is that flowering kinds need more light, while foliage types require higher humidity.

Bulbs — indoor gardeners are going beyond the usual amaryllis, forced hyacinths, tulips, daffodils, freezias, etc., and growing caladiums, dwarfs such as *C. humboldtii* or some of the over 2000 varieties of big-leaved standard and lance-leaf types . . . showy *Clivia miniata*, now in selections with extra-bright orange flowers . . . *Eucomis*,

pineapple lily, with an umbrella rosette of leaves topping its flower spike, ranging from the 1′ *E. bicolor* to the new gigantic *E. pole-evansii* with 3′ leaves and 4′ flower stem . . . *Haemanthus*, blood lily, fantastic white, orange or red flower heads . . . *Eucharis grandiflora*, Amazon lily, blooming several times a year, the narcissus-like blooms white and fragrant . . . *Moraea*, the fabulous long-blooming South African peacock moraeas (often sold as *Dietes*) . . . *Veltheimia*, rosy tritoma-like flowers over a whorl of green leaves . . . *Watsonia*, long spikes of rose or white flowers resembling gladiolus . . . *Sprekelia formosissima*, Jacobean lily, glowing mahogany-red lilies from bare bulbs . . . *Lachenalia*, Cape cowslip, strap leaves and multicolored flowers . . . *Vallota speciosa*, Scarborough lily, clusters of scarlet amaryllis-like blooms . . . *Zantedeschia*, calla lily, now in low-growing varieties like 'Little Gem' and unusual colors like the apricot Sunrise Hybrids . . . and even lilies, with precooled bulbs making forcing possible for almost any time of year, and the new miniature lilies like 'Gold Coast' and the Little Rascal Strain well suited to indoor growing.

A SURE CURE FOR MITES, thrips, etc., is immersing the plant in 110° water containing 3 tablespoons of Fels Naptha per gallon, reports Mrs. Peter Crocker in "African Violet Magazine" (Box 1326, Knoxville, TN 37901).

Cacti and Succulents — a vast minimum-maintenance group ranging from miniatures with breathtaking flowers to "maxi-cacti" of incredible form for sculptured accents. Often within any one of the more than 100 genera there is tremendous diversity: *Euphorbia*, for example, varies from the flowering dwarf crown of thorns, *E. bojeri*, to the stunning gnarled crested elkhorn euphorbia, *E. lactea cristata*. Pincushions, *Mammillaria*, and chin cacti, *Gymnocalycium*, are but two of the easiest windowsill cacti — also recommended are *Notocactus*, *Parodia*, *Echinopsis* and *Rebutia*, all small and free-flowering. Other succulent plants leading the list for compatibility with varied home conditions are *Gasteria*, *Haworthia*, *Echeveria*, *Kalanchoe* and some aloes. With a little more attention to needs, sedums, mesembryanthemums, the fantastic stapeliads and lithops, epiphyllums or orchid cacti and many others can adorn the home. Remember that desert cacti and flowering succulents in general need much higher light than jungle types. An excellent introduction is the "HANDBOOK ON SUCCULENT PLANTS," $1.50 from the BROOKLYN BOTANIC GARDEN (BROOKLYN, NY 11225).

Carissa grandiflora, Natal plum — *C. g. nana* 'Boxwood Beauty' and 'Bonsai' are handsome dwarf shrubs with dark waxy leaves and white flowers followed by 1″ red fruits.

Clerodendrum — well known is *C. thomsonae,* glory bower vine, but also excellent are the shrubby red-flowered *C. speciossimum,* shrubby blue *C. ugandense* and white *C. fragrans,* which can be pruned to make a shrub.

Cyanotis — charming little trailers; *C. kewensis,* teddy-bear vine, has furry leaves, while *C. somaliensis,* pussy-ears, has silvery-downed foliage and violet-blue flowers.

Gardenia — more compact and so better for limited space than *G. jasminoides* are species offered as *G. j. veitchii, G. radicans, G. stricta nana.* New research shows temperature is critical to bloom: gardenias must have 70° nights for buds to form, then 65° nights for buds to open without dropping.

Gesneriads — next to gloxinias — now in dwarf types which bloom in 3″ pots — best known are *Achimenes,* summer-blooming rhizomatous gesneriads; *Episcia,* flame violet, erect or trailing plants having beautifully patterned shining or velvety foliage and brilliant bell flowers (give full sun in winter); *Columnea,* superb basket plants; and *Streptocarpus,* Cape primrose, large flowers on single-leaved to bushy plants (these need cool night temperatures). But also charming are the mini-miniature *Sinningia* hybrids; lipstick vines, *Hypocyrta* and *Aeschynanthus;* temple bells, *Smithiantha,* with racemes of exquisite nodding flowers, and the somewhat similar *Kohleria;* and for especially stunning foliage, *Rechsteineria* and *Nautilocalyx.*

Hoya, wax plant — one of the finest climbers; numerous new species and cultivars with varied leaf forms and colors and striking umbels of fragrant waxy star flowers, such as tricolor-leaved, pink-flowered *H. carnosa variegata* 'Krimson

Queen'; *H. compacta regalis* 'Hindu Rope,' with tightly curled leaves; miniature *H. bella* and *H. lacunosa,* very fragrant; and *H. darwinii,* pink-spotted silver leaves and deep pink flowers.

Hypoestes sanguinolenta, polka dot plant — soft, downy pink-spotted foliage and mauve flowers, easy to grow.

Ixora — many new species and cultivars of this old favorite with glossy leaves and heads of starry flowers, such as dwarf *I. colei,* big pure white blooms; very floriferous red 'Superking'; bright pink 'Angela Busman'; compact yellow 'Frances Perry'; 'Trinidad Red,' 7½″ flower heads; and 'Helen Dunaway,' free-flowering deep orange.

Lapigeria rosea, Chilean bellflower — a very handsome vine with leathery leaves and 4″ waxy rose flowers.

Malpighia coccigera, miniature holly — stiff little spiny leaves, and flat fringed pink flowers; *M. glabra,* Barbados cherry or acerola, grows taller and has pink bloom and edible red berries.

Myrtus — *M. communis,* the old-time myrtle, with shiny boxwood leaves and fluffy fragrant white flowers, is available in tiny-leaved and variegated forms.

Neomarica, apostle plant — shining sword leaves in fans, and fragrant flowers, white and violet in the strong-growing *N. northiana,* white and brown in compact *N. gracilis,* blue in *N. caerulea.*

Ochna multiflora, bird's-eye bush — a little African shrub with yellow primrose flowers in early spring, then jet black seeds.

Orchids — two of the most beautiful and longest blooming are the lady's-slippers, *Paphiopedilum,* and moth orchids, *Phalaenopsis.* Many dwarf and miniature orchids also do well with less than full sun.

Oxalis — some of the finest are upright, feathery-foliaged *O. hirta,* with large rosy flowers; shrubby *O. ortgiesii,* gold bloom, olive-maroon foliage, *O. cernua flore pleno,* fragrant double Bermuda buttercup; trailing red-leaved *O. siliquosa,* yellow

AN AVOCADO PLANT that is growing too tall can be made "weeping" simply by pinching out the top and tying down the branches — new branches will sprout up from the bent ones to produce a bushy plant.

blooms all year; and the firefern, *O. hedysaroides rubra*, a tiny tree with little red leaves and glowing yellow flowers.

Punica granatum nana, dwarf pomegranate — a charming little twiggy and glossy-leaved shrub bearing red blooms and orange-red fruits.

Ruellia — trailing *R. makoyana* has dark silver-veined leaves, carmine flowers, erect *R. coccinea* has red flowers, shrubby *R. macrantha* has long leaves and large rose-purple blooms.

Saxifraga sarmentosa, strawberry begonia — a fine pot or basket plant, with silver-veined reddish leaves; var. *tricolor* is pink-edged, and 'Maroon Beauty' has large, darker red leaves.

Setcreasea purpurea — a very adaptable trailer with silver-striped, deep purple leaves, bearing lavender-pink blooms in bright light.

Spathiphyllum — able to stand dim light, these are the most free-flowering aroids. Best dwarf is S. *floribundum* with wide velvety leaves; rare S. *cannaefolium* has 8″ white spathes; 'Mauna Loa' is a taller large-spathed hybrid.

Tradescantia, wandering Jew, inch plant — many varieties, from diminutive fern-leaved *T. multiflora*, with white flowers, to green-purple, lavender-flowered *T. blossfeldiana*, giant *T. albiflora albo-vittata* with blue-green and white foliage, and fabulous gold-leaved forms of *T. fluminensis*.

Flowering Plants for a South Exposure

Bougainvillea — can be kept thriving in a 5″ or 6″ pot by summer pruning. Many fine varieties, such as glowing pink 'Texas Dawn,' double golden 'Tahitian Gold'; *B. harrisii* has variegated leaves.

Bromeliads — grow in pots, on slabs of wood or tree fern, or on branches as "living mobiles." Practically indestructible, surviving darkness and dry air, but producing marvelously colorful stiff foliage and spectacular very long lasting flower spikes when given high light. Widely available are species of *Aechmea, Billbergia, Cryptanthus, Guzmania, Neoregelia,* and *Vriesia*.

Brunfelsia calycina — a glossy-leaved small shrub with a profusion of rich violet flowers that fade to white, blooms all winter.

Campanula — for a bright, cool window, *C. isophylla* is a fine trailer with starry blue flowers; also the white-flowered form, and furry-leaved *C. i. mayi* with larger blue flowers. Rare *C. elatines flore pleno* and *C. e. alba plena* have double flowers.

Cestrum nocturnum, night jessamine — a long-blooming, glossy shrub with white flowers fragrant at night. Prune to keep small. Other species have red or day-scented flowers.

Citrus — unsurpassed for handsome foliage, fragrant creamy flowers and decorative fruits are the Otaheite *(C. taitensis)* and Calamondin *(C. mitis)*

Lithops, the fascinating "living stones," have translucent "window" tops and fragrant flowers.

Full sun, heavy feeding and cool night temperatures are the key to spectacular bloom with miniature cymbidium orchids.

oranges, Meyer and Ponderosa lemons *(C. limonia)* and Persian lime *(C. aurantifolia)*. For larger pots and tubs there are the myrtleleaf orange *(C. aurantium myrtifolium)*, mandarin orange *(C. nobilis deliciosa)* and citron *(C. medica sarcodactylis)*.

Coffea arabica, coffee tree — a handsome glossyleaved tree that can be kept small by pinching; fragrant white blooms, red berries.

Corokia cotoneaster, ghost plant — fascinating, with rigid and twisted growth, black bark, tiny leaves which are silvery beneath and little yellow star flowers.

Crossandra infundibuliformis — very shiny gardenia-like leaves and salmon flowers on a 1′ shrub.

Dipladenia amoena, pink allamanda — a climber with big crinkly leaves and rosy morning-glory flowers.

Feijoa sellowiana, pineapple guava — a shrub with silvery leaves, camellia-like white and red flowers and edible green guava fruits; it is easily kept small by pruning.

Gelsemium sempervirens, Carolina yellow jessamine — a twiner with very fragrant tubular yellow blooms.

Grevillea robusta, Australian silk oak — a fine little tree with ferny foliage and racemes of orange flowers. *G. wilsonii,* the fire wheel, has open racemes of red and yellow flowers.

Heterocentron — showy panicles of white or rosy star flowers in profusion on a small shrubby plant.

Hibiscus — some of the best for south windows are *H. rosa-sinensis cooperi,* small scarlet flowers, leaves splashed red and white; *H. huegelii,* deeply lobed leaves, purple flowers; and *H. schizopetalus,* pendulous orange-splashed flowers with recurved petals.

Jacobinia carnea — shrubby, to 2′, the leaves large, dark green and glossy, and 2″ tubular pink flowers in conical trusses. Brazilian fuchsia, *J. pauciflora,* is more compact and has nodding gold-tipped scarlet flowers.

Jasminum, jasmine — deliciously fragrant flowers on twining or shrubby plants, including *J. gracile magnificum,* royal jasmine, shrubby and white-flowered; *J. parkeri,* a dwarf with yellow blooms; *J. officinale grandiflorum,* double white; *J. sambac* 'Maid of Orleans' and 'Grand Duke,' single and double whites.

Jatropha podagrica — a fascinating, slow-growing little house tree with a squat barrel-like trunk, huge rosette of leaves and long-lasting brilliant orange-red flower clusters.

Lantana — weeping *L. montevidensis,* for baskets, has lavender flowers; shrubby *L. camara* has white, yellow, rose flowers all year.

Mahernia verticillata, honeybell — ferny foliage and fragrant, nodding golden bell flowers, a good trailer for baskets.

Medinilla magnifica — a handsome slow-growing shrub, worth growing for its glossy, leathery blue-green leaves alone, but bearing long pendulous trusses of raspberry-pink-bracted flowers in summer.

Murraea exotica — a small shrub with dense light green foliage and waxy orange-scented bell flowers several times a year.

Orchids — the gardener with a south window or a 4-tube fluorescent set-up can enjoy species and hybrids from at least 100 genera. For the beginner, some of the most dependable are found in *Epidendrum, Brassavola, Cattleya, Brassia* and *Laelia.* Multigeneric hybridizing has produced smaller versions of strong-growing types — "cocktail" orchids such as *Epicattleya, Ascocenda, Renantheropsis, Potinara.* Virtually all orchids demand high humidity, and a cool-vapor humidifier is an invaluable aid to these as well as to many other plants.

Osmanthus — *O. ilicifolius variegatus,* false holly, has small cream-edged holly leaves; sweet olive, *O. fragrans,* has tiny, fragrant, creamy flowers all winter. Prune to keep small.

Passiflora, passion flower — many fine vines for bright windows, such as blue-flowered *P. alatocaerulea,* red *P. racemosa,* pink *P. mollissima;* and for foliage, *P. coreacea,* with silver-centered butterfly leaves and *P. trifasciata,* satiny, silver, bronze and purple.

Pelargonium — hundreds of cultivars of miniature, dwarf and semi-dwarf zonal geraniums *(P. hortorum)* are offered by specialists. Equally popular are the scented and fancy-leaved types, and some fascinating novelties are the cactus-flowered, carnation-flowered, bird's egg and rosebud hybrids. Only the Martha Washington *(P. domesticum)* and trailing or ivy *(P. peltatum)* geraniums are difficult, requiring lower temperatures and higher humidity.

Pentas lanceolata, Egyptian star cluster — new dwarf varieties of this shrub bear clusters of white, pink, purple or rose flowers all winter.

Pittosporum tobira, Australian laurel — shrubby, with thick laurel-like leaves, and fragrant greenish-white flower clusters.

Reinwardtia indica, yellow flax — fine for pots or baskets, easily kept compact, with large yellow flowers all winter.

Russellia equisetiformis, coral or fountain plant — square arched stems carry clusters of red flowers all year; fine basket plant.

Senecio — *S. mikanioides,* German ivy, is a pretty, bright green climber; *S. confusus,* orange glory vine, bears orange flowers in winter.

Streptosolen jamesonii — a many-branched shrub for baskets, with wrinkled leaves and clusters of orange-red flowers in winter.

Thea sinensis, tea plant — shiny foliage and fragrant white camellia-like flowers; can be pruned to any size.

Thunbergia erecta, bush thunbergia — shrubby, to 2′, with blue-violet flowers.

Tibouchina semidecandra, glory bush — silvery foliage and large purple flowers; can be kept to 2′ height.

Trachelospermum jasminoides, Confederate jasmine — a twiner that can be pruned to make it shrubby, with small leathery leaves and very fragrant white star flowers; also a variegated-leaf form.

Waterlilies — two miniature waterlilies for indoor pools or aquariums in a sunny window or under lights are 'Margaret Mary' and 'Dorothy Lamour.'

HOUSEPLANTER'S LIBRARY

"The Complete Book of Houseplants," by Charles Marden Fitch (Hawthorn, $9.95)

"Ferns and Palms for Interior Decoration," by Jack Kramer (Charles Scribner's Sons, hardcover $6.95, softcover $3.95)

"Flowering House Plants" and "Foliage House Plants," by James Underwood Crockett (Time-Life Encyclopedia of Gardening, $6.95 each)

"Garden in Your House," 2nd ed., by Ernesta Drinker Ballard (Harper and Row, $6.95)

"House Plants," by George Elbert and Edward Hyams (Funk & Wagnalls, $7.95)

"House Plants for City Dwellers," by Alys Sutcliffe (E. P. Dutton, $3.95)

"House Plants for the Purple Thumb," by Maggie Baylis (101 Productions, hardcover $7.95, paperback $3.95)

"How to Grow Beautiful House Plants," by T. H. Everett (Fawcett, paperback, $1.25)

"Making Things Grow," by Thalassa Cruso (Knopf, $6.95)

"Nothing Grows for You?" by Frances Tenenbaum (Charles Scribner's Sons, $6.95)

HOUSEPLANTSMEN

General:

Alberts & Merkel Bros., 2210 South Federal Highway, Boynton Beach, FL 33435; catalog 50¢

Edelweiss Gardens, Box 66, Robbinsville, NJ 08691; catalog 35¢

Logee's Greenhouses, Danielson, CT 06239; catalog 75¢

Merry Gardens, Camden, ME 04843; Pictorial Handbook and price list, $1.25

Norvell Greenhouses, Box 73, Greenacres, WA 99016

Sunnybrook Farms Nursery, 9448 Mayfield Road, Chesterland, OH 44026

African violets, gesneriads:

Buell's Greenhouses, Eastford, CT 06242; catalog 25¢ plus 20¢-stamped self-addressed No. 10 envelope

Fischer Greenhouses, Linwood, NJ 08221; catalog 15¢

Kartuz Greenhouses, 92 Chestnut Street, Wilmington, MA 01887; catalog 50¢ (also begonias, geraniums)

Lyndon Lyon, 14 Mutchler Street, Dolgeville, NY 13329; stamp for list

Tinari Greenhouses, 2325 Valley Road, Huntingdon Valley, PA 19006; catalog 25¢

Bromeliads:

Plaza Nursery, 7430 Crescent Avenue, Buena Park, CA 90620

Seaborn Del Dios Nursery, Route 3, Box 455, Escondido, CA 92025 (also cycads, palms)

Bulbs:

P. de Jager & Sons, South Hamilton, MA 01982

International Growers Exchange, Box 397, Farmington, MI 48024; catalog $2

Cacti and succulents:

Davis Cactus Garden, 1522 Jefferson Street, Kerrville, TX 78028

Grigsby Cactus Gardens, 2326 Bella Vista, Vista, CA 92083; catalog 50¢

Carnivorous plants:

Armstrong Associates, Box 127, Basking Ridge, NJ 07920; catalog 25¢

Epiphyllums:

Beahm Gardens, 2686 Paloma Street, Pasadena, CA 91107; catalog 25¢

Over 500 species of peperomias are known, providing many fine foliage plants for dim, dry interiors.

Fuchsias and geraniums:

Carobil Farm, Church Road, R.D. 1, Brunswick, ME 04011

Orchids:

Margaret Ilgenfritz Orchids, Box 665, Monroe, MI 48161; catalog $2

Jones & Scully Orchids, 2200 N.W. 33rd Avenue, Miami, FL 33142

Fred A. Stewart Orchids, 1212 East Las Tunas Drive, San Gabriel, CA 91778

Seed of tropical trees, shrubs, vines:

John Brudy's Rare Plant House, Box 1348, Cocoa Beach, FL 32931; catalog $1

Hurov's Tropical Tree Nurseries, Box 10387, Honolulu, HI 96816

Waterlilies:

Three Springs Fisheries, Lilypons, MD 21717; catalog 50¢

LIGHT GARDENING

High-Voltage Hobby

The life essential present since before the earth was born is coming under the gardener's domination. In the past 20 years, light has been synthesized and harnessed for horticulture, and phytoillumination has become a byword for better indoor gardening.

The gardener who relies on man-made light, of course, eliminates all of natural light's variations and limitations due to season or weather. This year-round uniformity in the quality, intensity, duration and even the plane of light confers remarkable benefits in growth. Some of these are only beginning to be realized: for many tropical plants, for example, dormancy — in nature, a protective reaction to seasonal periods unfavorable to growth — is eliminated under lights, so that growth and often flowering are continuous.

Electrifying Advances

The technology of light gardening is surging ahead, given tremendous impetus by the new "accelerated growth" and "total environmental control" concepts. At the Agricultural Research Service's Phyto-Engineering Laboratory, growth of seedlings or cuttings of annuals, vegetables and

Light Gardening   215

"MIRACLE PLANTS UNDER LIGHTS," a publication of the Indoor Light Gardening Society of America (35¢ from Mrs. R. D. Morrison, Corresponding Secretary, 5305 S.W. Hamilton Street, Portland, OR 97221), describes over a dozen plants "that bloom in the winter for several months at a time — or all year."

many foliage and woody plants has been increased 10 to 50 times by giving them at least 16 hours a day of up to 4000 footcandles of light from cool white fluorescents and incandescent lamps, with temperatures at 85° day, 75° night and 65% minimum humidity. The air was enriched with up to 2000 ppm of carbon dioxide and kept moving at 35 to 40 feet per minute. A 20-20-20 fertilizer was applied every 4 to 6 hours.

Petunias flowered from seed in 5 weeks, lettuce grew to harvestable size in 25 days. Moreover, the favorable influences of this "head start" treatment carried over when the plants were removed from the chambers, and they continued to be superior in size, appearance and performance.

These findings are being applied to indoor gardening, and realization of the ideal "combination of ingredients" which comprise the optimum environment for house plants is not far off. High-intensity lamps, plus a variety of devices to supply all the other growth factors in controlled amounts, are already available or rapidly being developed.

Gloxinias thrive from seed to flower under a 1:1 combination of cool white and warm white fluorescents.

Dynamics

The basics of light are now well understood. Light is only a small part of the electromagnetic spectrum, which ranges from gamma and x-rays, through ultraviolet, visible or light rays, and infrared, to radio and electric waves. A standard unit of measurement for the wavelengths of all these forms of radiant energy is the angstrom — about one 25-millionths of an inch. Light energy extends from 3800 to 7600 angstroms.

The most important finding of recent research is that people and plants do not "see" light in the same way. The human eye is most sensitive to yellow-green wavelengths in the 5000 to 6000 angstroms region, while plants react mainly to energy in the red (6300 to 7600) and blue (3500 to 5000) regions.

The SED — spectral energy distribution — of a light source, therefore, is extremely important. For normal growth, light must be provided in the ranges, proportions and amounts effective for every activity of a plant from its vegetative to its reproductive stages. Photosynthesis, the basic food-manufacturing process, has high red and blue light energy requirements, but there are also certain low light energy processes which require small amounts of light in a very special color range.

These involve the plant pigment phytochrome, which is the master control for such responses as stem length, leaf size, germination of light-sensitive seeds, flower bud initiation, tuber and bulb formation, foliage and fruit coloration and dormancy of woody plants. Phytochrome is photoreversible — red light at 6600 angstroms will make it stimulate a process such as leaf expansion, while far-red (near-infrared) at 7300 angstroms will change the phytochrome to its opposite form which inhibits leaf expansion. Unless the artificial light source, like sunlight, has a fairly even balance of red and far-red wavelengths, many processes cannot occur normally.

Light Switch

Phytochrome also operates in photoperiodism, the reaction of many plants to the relative lengths of night and day. In darkness, the form of phytochrome active under light is slowly reversed, bringing about the opposite effect. But if light in the red and far-red ranges is supplied during the dark period (the plant will respond to whichever it is most sensitive), the process that was taking place during the light period will continue.

Thus, if short days are lengthened by giving this light — in many cases, very small amounts for very short periods — during the night, plants such as tuberous begonias that need long days to flower will initiate buds. Conversely, flowering is inhibited when short-day plants like chrysanthemums and poinsettias are given a lengthened photoperiod.

Commercial growers use this mechanism to time the blooming of many plants or otherwise "tailor" them by manipulation of their growth processes. But since most ornamental plants are day-neutral (insensitive to photoperiod), the indoor light gardener need only keep in mind that if a plant fails to bloom when all its other needs are met, the reason may be incorrect length of the dark period.

However, for gardeners who would like to experiment with forcing and tailoring plants, the BROOKLYN BOTANIC GARDEN'S HANDBOOK 62, "GARDENING UNDER ARTIFICIAL LIGHT" ($1.50 FROM THE GARDEN, BROOKLYN, NY 11225), details the applications of photoperiodism for numerous plants.

The Light Approach

Adequate growth of many plants can be achieved with a great many kinds and combinations of lamps. For the average light gardener growing a diversity of plants, the all-around best choice is a 1:1 combination of cool white and warm white fluorescent tubes, says George A. Elbert, President of the Indoor Light Gardening Society of America (128 West 58th Street, New York, NY 10019).

The "plant growth" tubes (Sylvania's Gro-Lux, Westinghouse's Agro-Lite) are advertised as superior because they emit some red/far-red rays, but they are notably low in total light output. The warm white, however, has a much higher output and produces considerable red rays, and teamed with cool white gives close to balanced light to support compact, sturdy growth and long flowering of many plants. Also, says Mr. Elbert, these tubes cost less, and are available in high-output types for plants, such as some orchids, cacti and bromeliads, that need high light intensity (cacti and bromeliad growers, incidentally, praise the Vita-Lite and Natur-escent Tubes by DURO-LITE, FAIR LAWN, NJ 07410). For general growing, incandescent bulbs are unnecessary, and give too much heat and too little light for their wattage.

Actually, Mr. Elbert says, most disappointments in light gardening are due not to incorrect lighting but to imperfect culture. Poor growing methods can cancel out the benefits of light that is ideal in both quality and quantity.

The last point may be debatable for some plants that require high light, and for seedlings. No fluorescent lamp produces sufficient far-red rays for optimum growth of these, says the ARS Phyto-Engineering Laboratory, which uses a combination of cool white fluorescents and incandescent bulbs in its growth rooms. Generally 1 watt of incandescent to each 5 watts of fluorescent light is recommended. Where the heat from incandescents would be a problem, industrial "extended service" bulbs can be used — rated at 130 volts, they burn cooler, and a 25-watt bulb will not injure a plant placed only an inch from it.

For very high light requirements, or where the light source must be far from the plants, the new bulb-type high intensity discharge (HID) lamps are promising. When the problems of glare and heat output can be mastered, these undoubtedly will have an important place in at least some phases of home light gardening. Reports of use by commercial growers with vegetable seedlings, roses, chrysanthemums, African violets, geraniums and other plants show that Lucalox, a high pressure sodium lamp (GENERAL ELECTRIC CO., NELA PARK, CLEVELAND, OH 44112) when used alone is an excellent growth-promoting supplement to natural light. For growing entirely under artificial light, a 1:1 combination of Lucalox and a metal halide HID lamp, such as Multi-Vapor (GENERAL ELECTRIC) or Metalarc (SYLVANIA ELECTRIC CO., SALEM, MA 01970), has proved successful. While HID fixtures and lamps are more expensive than fluorescents, the lamps use much less power and last longer.

Another step forward is the new Fluomeric lamp, by Duro-Lite. A combination mercury vapor incandescent fluorescent lamp for use in ordinary household sockets, the Fluomeric emits intense white light very close to the sunlight spectrum. It needs no external ballast, lasts up to 20 times longer than incandescent bulbs and delivers more light at lower cost. Fluomerics are now available in white, reflectorized and narrow-beam types, in wattages up to 1250 for indoor and outdoor use.

Radiant Culture

As experience with accelerated culture has shown, plants will attain their best growth — maximum size, fullest form, most flowers — under the highest intensity of balanced light they can utilize, provided all other growth factors are supplied in proportion. As light is increased, so must moisture, carbon dioxide, nutrients, etc., be correspondingly increased.

Light gardeners should give constant feeding, as commercial growers do. A small amount, as little as one-eighth the manufacturer's recommendation, of a high-analysis soluble fertilizer, is given in each watering. An occasional flushing with clear water will prevent build-up of chemical salts. Since watering is more frequent under lights, a highly porous medium that will not waterlog is essential. The new soilless media fill this requirement admirably.

Frequent misting, the tray and gravel method, and enclosing the growing area in plastic all help to raise humidity. But the best solution is probably the cool-vapor humidifier, preferably a short-range type whose output can be restricted mainly to the light garden so the rest of the room does not suffer from peeling paint.

A slow-moving fan will help in dissemination of carbon dioxide, and a window opened in an adjoining room whenever possible aids in maintaining carbon dioxide at the normal atmospheric level. Several times this, however, is necessary for optimum growth. Some growers report excellent results from misting with carbonated water, but probably the best method is burning wood alcohol or ethanol alcohol in a kerosene lamp. CO_2 should be given, of course, only while the lights are on.

Finally, temperatures 5° to 10° higher than those generally considered best for the plants being grown are advisable. At night, the temperature should drop about 10°. Water temperature is also important. The growth-slowing root shock that occurs when cold water is used in watering is avoided when water at or near 90° is used.

In growing plants from seed for the garden, remember that accelerated culture greatly shortens the time needed to produce plants ready to go outdoors, so seed for spring planting can be sown later than usual. Good seedlings of many plants may be raised under the usually recommended set-up of two 40-watt fluorescents with two 25-watt incandescents, but growth gets proportionately better and faster as one approaches the conditions used in the ARS Phyto-Engineering Laboratory.

Many light gardeners maintain special propagation areas, where they start annuals for the garden in March, perennials in June, house plants and softwood cuttings of shrubs in midsummer and hardwood cuttings in late fall. Plants started under accelerated culture, incidentally, are not overly succulent, as might be feared. They harden off easily and stand up well when transplanted outdoors.

Power Ploys

The great variety of lamps becoming available is making the task of designing a light garden much easier. For example, while fixtures for fluorescents or both fluorescents and incandescents are obtainable, there are also high-intensity iodine quartz spot and flood lamps, which can be installed a considerable distance from the plants. Foliage can be maintained in good condition for long periods under these.

Then there are high-output fluorescents. These give almost 30% more light in the same tube length. They include General Electric's Power Groove, Duro-Lite's HO Natur-escent, and Sylvania's HO and VHO Wide Spectrum tubes. Also useful are the slender internally reflectorized tubes, which can be mounted close together to give up to 50% more light than un-reflectorized tubes.

The three-lamp circular fluorescent fixture often used in kitchens will give high and balanced light if the outer tube is replaced with a high-output circular 40-watt tube, and an incandescent socket is mounted in the center. Or the light gardener can use the new Cool White Panel Fluorescent by General Electric, 80 watts but only 12″ square. Handsome light gardens made with banks of these are described in the USDA publication, *"INDOOR GARDENS WITH CONTROLLED LIGHTING" (HOME AND GARDEN BULLETIN 187, 30¢ FROM SUPERINTENDENT OF DOCUMENTS, WASHINGTON, DC 20402).* Iodine quartz lamps can be mounted outside these to provide incandescent light, or the long, slim incandescents called Lumelines could be installed between the panels.

Other means of increasing light intensity include mounting tubes on the sides of the growing area as well as above it, and reflectorizing every possible surface with aluminum foil or white paint. Light gardeners recommend flat white paint of the whitest white — super or decorator white — plus white stones beneath the pots. To reduce heat where many lamps are used, the ballasts can be removed from the fixtures and set up outside the growing area, or a sheet of plastic may be installed between the plants and the lights.

Worth experimenting with is Lifelite Reflector (*LIFELITE, INC., 61 AVENIDA DE ORINDA, ORINDA, CA 94563*), a bluish-red plastic film that is attached to fluorescent lamp reflectors. It intensifies the blue and red rays and to some extent the far-red.

Tips for the Light-Headed

Both ready-made and home-built light set-ups can be exciting. On the market are all sorts of table-top units, multi-tiered plant stands and carts, and enclosed cases from terrariums to intricate growth chambers. But the ingenuity and craftsmanship of light gardeners knows no bounds — we've seen marvelously handsome light gardens in homemade cabinets, shadow boxes, bookcases, room dividers, stands made of prefabricated metal shelving, old television cabinets, even delicatessen cases!

Often the space available dictates the light that can be provided. Always use the longest tubes possible, as output falls off toward the ends of the tubes. Sometimes it helps to remember that longer duration of light can compensate for low intensity. Keep all lamps clean, and replace fluorescent tubes every 6 to 8 months, for both their color balance and intensity change with age. In modifying any electrical equipment, the services of an electrician are essential.

Light gardeners are often concerned about measuring the light they use. However, only very complex instruments can measure the light from many of the tubes now in use. It is more practical to follow the rule of supplying a minimum of 20 watts per square foot of growing area for low-light plants, to 40 or more watts for high-light plants, and adjusting the intensity by raising or lowering the lights or plants.

This brings us to the all-important matter of knowing your plants. Research their natural habitats: the closer you can approximate these — and even "improve" on them — the quicker plants introduced into your light garden will acclimatize and continue to grow normally or better than normally. Then learn to evaluate their reactions. The light gardener knows that success so often is only a matter of changing a plant's "habitat" in the light garden by moving it a few inches — up, down or sideways.

ENLIGHTENING SOURCES

"The Indoor Light Gardening Book," by George A. Elbert (Crown, $10.95)

"Fluorescent Light Gardening," by Elaine Cherry (Van Nostrand, $6.95)

"Gardening Under Lights," 2nd ed. by F. H. and J. L. Kranz, (Viking, $7.95)

"The Complete Book of Gardening Under Lights," by Elvin McDonald (Doubleday, $4.95)

"Lighting for Plant Growth," by Elwood D. Rickford and Stuart Dunn (Kent State University Press, $16)

. . . and many bulletins from the lamp manufacturers.

Tube Craft, Inc. (1311 West 80th Street, Cleveland, OH 44102) — FloraCart lighted plant cart

Environment/One (2773 Balltown Road, Schenectady, NY 12309) — Phytarium growth chamber

Lord & Burnham (Irvington, NY 10533) — Solar Plantarium lighted case

Famco, Inc. (300 Lake Road, Medina, OH 44256) — 8' Portable Lighting Unit

Shoplite Co. (650 Franklin Avenue, Nutley, NJ 07110; catalog 25¢) — lamps, fixtures, etc.

Floralite Co. (4124 East Oakwood Road, South Milwaukee, WI 53172) — standard and special fixtures

GREENHOUSES

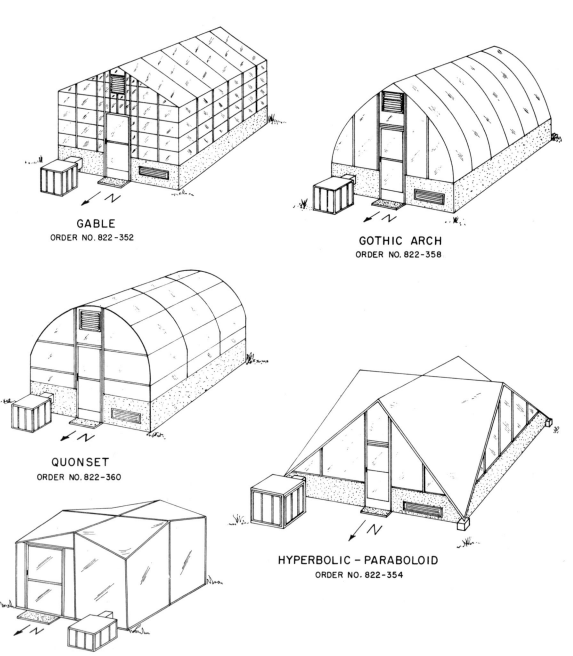

GABLE
ORDER NO. 822-352

GOTHIC ARCH
ORDER NO. 822-358

QUONSET
ORDER NO. 822-360

HYPERBOLIC – PARABOLOID
ORDER NO. 822-354

HYPERBOLIC – PARABOLOID
ORDER NO. 822-362

Pennsylvania State University offers plans for several unusual greenhouse designs it has developed and tested. R. A. Aldrich, Pennsylvania State University

The Golden Age of Greenhouses

Advances in greenhouse design and function in the past decade have been little short of fantastic —and it's high time the greenhouse came out of limbo.

For almost 2000 years, since Pliny described the first greenhouse — a mica-glazed pit used to grow flowers and vegetables for Tiberius Caesar — greenhouses could be said to have "just happened." They were neither designed as efficient solar collectors, nor notable, except in rare instances, for architectural beauty.

But suddenly we are seeing dramatic changes. Made possible by new materials and mandated by new basic knowledge of plant requirements, the newest designs not only provide considerable improvement in function, but also make the greenhouse a truly ornamental "garden room," a natural and integral part of the home and landscape.

Types and Prototypes

So far, this revolution has been most visible in commercial and institutional installations, but the more progressive designs and equipment are starting to appear in custom-designed, owner-built and even manufactured home greenhouses.

Biggest news is the geodesic dome. Buckminster Fuller's invention has reached its ultimate horticultural application in the magnificent Climatron at the Missouri Botanical Garden. Covering more than half an acre, this dome has a skin of Plexiglas panels set in metal frames suspended from a hexagonal skeleton of tubular aluminum. The geodesic dome affords the largest possible interior volume for the surface it occupies, is one of the strongest shapes known, requires no interior supports and provides maximum light transmission.

The first geodesic dome home greenhouse is now being marketed — the Greendome, by DOME EAST (325 DUFFY AVENUE, HICKSVILLE, NY 11801). Gardeners are also designing and building their own, with provocative aids such as "DOMEBOOK ONE," BY LLOYD KAHN (PACIFIC DOMES, BOX 1692, LOS GATOS, CA 95030; $3) and "GEODESICS," BY EDWARD POPKO (UNIVERSITY OF DETROIT PRESS, 4001 WEST MCNICHOLS ROAD, DETROIT, MI 48221; $4).

Dome kits, parts and plans are available from DYNA DOME (22226 NORTH 23RD AVENUE, PHOENIX, AZ 85027) and POPULAR SCIENCE (355 LEXINGTON AVENUE, NEW YORK, NY 10017) offers plans for its Sun Dome greenhouse for $5.

Several other designs are attracting much attention. The Boettcher Memorial Conservatory at the Denver Botanic Gardens is a vaulted-arch greenhouse designed on the principle of the catenary curve, of cast concrete arches with plexiglass panes that vary from square at the top of the house to diamonds at the base. The three new dome conservatories at Mitchell Park in Milwaukee are conoid or "beehive" in form, with a framework of reinforced concrete covered by an aluminum and glass skin; the panes are in hexagonal, diamond and triangular shapes that give a geometric flower pattern effect.

The more elaborate of these designs, of course, offer only limited possibilities for adaptation to home greenhouses. But the vision and inventiveness that produced them is also producing valuable new features in standard hobby greenhouse designs, as well as totally new garden glasshouse forms — the Gothic arch, A-frame, Quonset, barrel vault, circular, improved sunpit, gazebo, hyperbolic-paraboloid.

Some of these are already available in prefab form, such as Sturdi-built's circular and A-frame models, Gothic styles by Maco, Reimuller, Texas and Trans-Sphere, and Gazebos from Allgrove, Lifelite and Mid-America. Those not yet "packaged" by manufacturers are obtainable as plans.

Dream Greenhouses

The gardener desiring a greenhouse thus has an unprecedented range of styles to choose among. So the question of which style best enhances home and garden is added to size, site and cost considerations. Since a greenhouse is usually a

An ideal energy-saving, minimum-maintenance greenhouse is the sun pit, which uses earth-stored heat.

lifetime investment, thorough planning is vital, beginning with study of the catalogs of every manufacturer.

Two tips: anticipate needs far into the future — the old saw that "a greenhouse shrinks as the owner's plant interests expand" is incontrovertible; and "plan and order in winter, erect in spring, stock in summer" is a schedule that insures ample time for invaluable consultation with suppliers.

The current trend is the greenhouse-cum-almost-any-other structure. The opportunity to live intimately with plants is provided by attached greenhouses that, by removal of a section of house wall, become extensions of the living, dining or family room, or even the kitchen. Both the solarium and the atrium or skylighted interior court are being revived, and recently we heard of an entire walled city garden that was covered with an aluminum and glass greenhouse roof.

Sunporches and breezeways glazed and roofed with plastic or glass become permanent greenhouses. A patio, terrace or lath house which converts into a greenhouse in winter by enclosure with glazed panels or plastic film is a versatile arrangement. Other ingenious ideas are window greenhouses built into the full length of a house wall, and greenhouses erected over cellarways and around enlarged basement window wells.

Updated sun pits are another new dimension. Actually a large, deep, walk-in coldframe, the sun pit uses earth-stored heat as its sole or main source of night warmth, held in by an insulating cover. Cool-growing plants thrive even when outdoor temperatures dip below zero, while tropicals can be grown with the addition of a minimal heating system.

Cinder block and sash were formerly the standard materials for constructing sun pits.

Modern versions use anything from concrete and stabilized earth to railroad ties and conduit for foundation and framing, and film and rigid plastics for glazing. One of the handsomest pits we've seen is a prefab aluminum lean-to built into the side of a hill. Highly imaginative designs have been devised by an architect, KEN KERN (SIERRA ROUTE, OAKHURST, CA 93644). His Kern-Form pits use a pipe frame or pre-cast concrete cantilevered units that combine framing and benches, a rounded roof of earth-insulated concrete layers and fiberglass on the south side. An 8' x 21' Kern-Form pit greenhouse of the pre-cast type can be amateur-built for about $300.

Best text on sun pits is the new edition of *"WINTER FLOWERS IN GREENHOUSE AND SUNHEATED PIT," BY KATHRYN S. TAYLOR AND EDITH W. GREGG (CHARLES SCRIBNER'S SONS, $7.50).*

Structuring and Glaziery

A bewildering array of materials is available today for constructing and glazing greenhouses, and new combinations are constantly being tried by commercial growers. The home gardener, too, should evaluate each possibility for appearance, purpose and permanence.

For framing, aluminum or galvanized steel are popular for their strength, design flexibility, low maintenance and lack of light-blocking bulk. Redwood is prized by many for its beauty and durability, and common woods such as pine and fir, often laminated or pressure-treated, are still used for both glass and plastic houses. Very inexpensive construction-grade fir is usually adequate for film and fiberglass houses. Ingenious

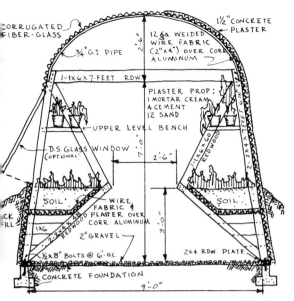

The following labels appear on the diagram:

CORRUGATED FIBER-GLASS
1½" CONCRETE PLASTER
¾" G.I. PIPE
12 ga. WELDED WIRE FABRIC (2"×4") OVER CORR. ALUMINUM
1-1×6×7·FEET·RDW
PLASTER PROP: 1 MORTAR CREAM 4 CEMENT 12 SAND
UPPER LEVEL BENCH
D.S GLASS WINDOW (OPTIONAL)
2'-6"
SOIL
WIRE FABRIC & PLASTER OVER CORR. ALUMINUM
SOIL
1×6 REDWOOD
2" GRAVEL
½×8" BOLTS @ 6'·OC.
2×4 RDW PLATE
CONCRETE FOUNDATION
9'-0"

Kern-Form home-built pit greenhouses have a combination frame and bench structure which is prefabricated on the ground and set up as a complete panel unit.

growers are adapting other materials: a new low-cost idea is the use of thin-walled electrical conduit for framing film-covered houses (detailed in literature on Copolymer houses from DBB COMPANY, DRAWER 8, DAYTON, OH 45401).

The all-aluminum, glass-glazed greenhouse is the most permanent and maintenance-free type, and in general the costliest. At the opposite end of the scale in all respects are the plastic films. Rigid plastics range widely in between.

Standard polyethylene films have a life rated in months. The new ultraviolet-inhibited copolymer film, Monsanto 602, lasts in good condition 2 years. Weatherable vinyl films such as Eskay-Lite and Amerex U-V come in heavier gauges and last about 4 to 5 years, and are proportionately more costly than polyethylene. For winter covering of porches and similar structures, and for simple houses used for wintering plants or producing vegetable and bedding plants for spring, poly and vinyl offer economical, easily applied glazing.

Two layers of film — 4- to 6-mil outside, 2- or 4-mil inside, spaced 1" to 2" apart — give a 40% saving in fuel, and actually provide more light than one layer because condensation is greatly reduced. Wood strips can be used as spacers, but Dr. Raymond Sheldrake, Jr., of Cornell University, has developed a time-saving technique of using air pressure from a small blower to separate the layers. Totally air-supported "bubble" houses have proved practical in tests at Oregon's North Willamette Experiment Station (Aurora, OR 97002) and at Washington State University (Pullman, WA 99163).

In rigid plastics, corrugated polyvinyl chloride (PVC) is not favored because it lacks structural and impact strength and durability. Much better are acrylic plastics (plexiglass) and fiberglass-reinforced plastic (FRP). Acrylic is as costly as glass, but is unexcelled for glazing arches, and has twice the impact strength of glass. FRP is also stronger than glass, can be used flat or curved, and gives reduced heat and diffused light that aids plant growth.

FRP is being hailed as the greenhouse glazing of the future, but it is important to buy only the finest quality for best results and long life: clearest grade, 6- to 8-ounce, with a guarantee that states clearly the number of years it will remain in top condition without refinishing. The best types need cleaning and recoating only every 15 to 20 years. Incidentally, "hybrid" glazing — glass walls and fiberglass roof, or fiberglass set on angle irons above a glass roof — is useful to lower summer heat without reducing winter light. And for "portable" use, fiberglass panels (KELLY KLOSURE SYSTEMS, BOX 443, FREMONT, NB 68025) are a worthy idea.

Plastic houses to date are well detailed in "PLASTIC GREENHOUSES," CIRCULAR 905, COLLEGE OF AGRICULTURE, UNIVERSITY OF ILLINOIS (URBANA, IL 61801). The future holds possibilities of "self-shading" glazing — a glass-plastic that darkens when hot is made by Eberspacher Glass Company of Esslingen, Germany . . . colored plastics that control light wavelengths to improve growth (LIFE-LITE, INC., 1025 SHARY CIRCLE, CONCORD, CA 94520) . . . and very lightweight fabric-plastics are under study by the Lightweight Construction Center of Washington University (St. Louis, MO 63130).

ALWAYS HANG UP THE HOSE after watering in the greenhouse, a horticulturist warns: hose left lying in a muddy puddle can spread fungus disease organisms all over the greenhouse the next time it is used.

Ways and Means

Dr. Joseph E. Howland, Natural Resources Development Specialist at the University of Nevada might well be called horticulture's "motivational researcher." His investigations into why people garden — and why they don't — have produced intriguing insights that could profitably be studied by all who serve gardeners. Recently he looked into the misconceptions that keep people from owning greenhouses:

Costs too much to operate — not true if properly oriented, and wise choices made on what plants to grow . . . doesn't enhance the beauty of the home — add as a room rather than a commercial greenhouse "hung" on the house (extra room adds value in selling house; regular greenhouse likely to lower value to all except someone looking for it) . . . ties you to the house — not if you provide even minimal automatic watering and ventilating controls; allows once-a-week attention even in summer . . . danger from poisons getting into the house — not true if you keep a circulating fan operating 24 hours a day: insects and disease then are so little a problem that experience has shown that a single bug "bomb" is enough for all the spraying you'll do in 12 to 24 months . . . takes too much space — can be as small as a 12″ space outside a window, though an attached room about 10′ x 20′ is the easiest to care for because smaller volumes of air change temperature too quickly . . . requires a really green thumb for success — nonsense: anyone who can care enough to grow a tomato plant in the backyard can succeed handsomely, and enjoy every minute of it!

Dr. Howland recommends buying "a series of glass doors to provide superb dual advantage: 1) complete floor-to-ceiling glass on north, east and south sides of your greenhouse room, and 2) screened ventilation for free circulation needed for warm weather cooling" . . . a non-transparent roof in areas where the summer sun is very intense . . . artificial soils, and clay rather than plastic pots, with seedlings and cuttings started in peat pellets . . . pots, planters and multi-tiered carts instead of benches, for greater flexibility . . . concrete flooring for disease and nematode control . . . completely submerging new acquisitions in water for an hour "to float away any hiding insects and to make diseased leaves conspicuous by their water-soaked appearance and softness."

Varishading

A permanent variable greenhouse shading which transmits more light in winter than in summer is produced by SOLAR SUNSTILL, INC. (SETAUKET, NY 11733), makers of Sun Clear, a no-drip coating for plastic houses.

Varishade applied to the interior of a glass or plastic house is transparent when kept wet by winter condensation. In summer, when no condensation occurs, it is dry and opaque. The amount of Varishade coating applied determines the degree of shading. It can also be used on the outside of the glass, where rain will make it transparent, or a water spray on either inside or outside coatings will reduce its shading when more light is desired. Varishade is non-toxic, and will repeat its wet-dry cycle indefinitely.

New Heating System

An infrared vacuum gas heating system called Co-Ray-Vac offers extremely even heating, low cost and space-saving advantages. Consisting basically of a small, easily installed overhead burner connected to 2½″ infrared heat-emitting pipe, it operates on natural or bottled gas. The invisible infrared rays radiate in divergent straight lines to all surfaces, while convective transfer from the heated surfaces warms the air. The system fires under vacuum, and vents outdoors.

Combustion efficiency is 92%. Hobbyist James Wyrtzen of Floral Park, New York, reports that it heats his 20′ x 12′ x 10′ high Mylar-and-fiberglass greenhouse for $60 to $70 a season. He states that temperature 3½′ from the pipe is 62°, at 4″ above the floor it is 56°.

Co-Ray-Vac is a product of ROBERTS-GORDON CORPORATION (44 CENTRAL AVENUE, BUFFALO, NY 14206).

Pot-Cap Pads

Capillary watering, wherein potted plants are set on a tray or bench of sand and take up moisture through the drainage holes by capillary action, has been advanced by the CORNELL CAP PAD SYSTEM.

Developed by Dr. Raymond Sheldrake, Jr., and others at the Department of Horticulture, Cornell University, the system replaces the sand with 12″ x 18″ pads of ½″ expanded polystyrene. These eliminate the heavy weight of sand and its requirement for an absolutely level bench. Each pad holds approximately three pints of water, which can contain liquid fertilizer. In commercial greenhouses, the water is supplied by a CHAPIN LEADER TUBE (CHAPIN WATERMATICS, WATERTOWN, NY 13601), and completely automatic watering and feeding is achieved by placing the pad on a moisture scale which turns on the water when a set weight loss is reached. Roots will not grow into the pads as they will into sand, and there are no algae or crusting problems.

Tuffy Cap Pads, made by TUFFLITE PLASTICS, INC., are available from HENRY F. MICHELL CO. (KING OF PRUSSIA, PA 19406).

Fuel Conservers

Fuel shortages bring these tips on conserving fuel and saving money on greenhouse heating from the Task Force on Energy and Agriculture of Cornell University.

1. Tight houses are essential — attach bar caps if needed to prevent glass slippage (aluminum glass clips are $7 per 100, $30 for 500, from STUPPY GREENHOUSE SUPPLY, 120 EAST 12TH AVENUE, NORTH KANSAS CITY, MO 64116).

2. In plastic houses, a double layer of film gives up to 40% savings in fuel.

3. Reflect heat from the pipes back into the greenhouse by hanging aluminum-reflectorized tarpaper between the pipes and wall (leave an air space between the tarpaper and wall so the wall won't freeze and crack).

4. Check boiler, burner and back-up systems to insure peak operating efficiency, repair or replace the insulation on the boiler and pipes leading to the greenhouse and check all automatic valves for proper operation.

5. Check thermostats for accuracy; thermostats housed in aspirators respond more quickly to temperature changes, so are more efficient.

6. Black cloth systems used at night both reduce the critical heating area and cut radiation heat losses to the sky.

7. Attach polyethylene or fiberglass on the inside gable ends for insulation to produce a thermopane effect (but do not line the roof, as this could cause snow to pile up on it).

Cultivating Energy

Scientists and gardeners are coming up with novel ways of using solar energy and conserving fuel to help in the energy crisis.

Dr. Aden Meinel of the University of Arizona (Tucson, AZ 85721) has developed a solar heater that can be home-built in half a day for $100, and which should be most useful in sunny southern and coastal areas. His system uses polyethylene tubes and a poly bag which is set on the roof or on the ground. A fan takes air out of the house or greenhouse to the bag, where it is heated by the sun and returned to the building. The sun will raise the air temperature as much as 90° above the outside temperature. For $100 more, Dr. Meinel states, a storage unit can be added to hold heat for night use.

A gardener suggests that water, circulated by a pump, could be used instead of air in the tube-and-bag system: in tests at the Idaho Agricultural Experiment Station, water-filled mulch bags heated by the sun have proved useful in the garden to keep vegetable seedlings warm on cold spring nights.

An even more efficient system has been developed by Dr. Maria Telkes of the new Energy Conversion Institute at the University of Delaware (Newark, DE 19711). Dr. Telkes captures solar heat in salt hydrates contained in $1\frac{1}{2}''$ flexible plastic tubing. These compounds melt during the day under the sun's heat, then solidify and release their stored heat at night. Different hydrate mixtures with varying melting points will give temperature control in any range from 20° to 200°; Dr. Telkes has found that one that works at 65° is excellent for greenhouses. In Delaware, she reports, midwinter sunlight can provide up to 77% of the heat needs of a greenhouse, more for south-facing attached greenhouses.

Dr. Telkes has also developed new heat-saving glazing — an inexpensive double-layer plexiglass that cuts heat losses in half, and a flexible "bubble" plastic which reduces heat loss 80%. And for summer cooling, she has found hydrates which freeze at night, then release their cold during the day.

Two methods of insulating to reduce heat loss have been developed by commercial greenhousemen. A trade magazine says that an interior "tent" of single-layer aluminum foil laminated to kraft paper — the sheets simply taped together and hung over wires — can reduce a greenhouse's nightly heat requirement by 50%. Tents of polyethylene or the black cloth used for photoperiodic control of flowering are also effective. In another method, sheets of polyethylene are taped together to make a huge plastic bag that conforms to the roof, and the walls as well in very cold areas. This is tied over the greenhouse with ropes, and kept inflated with an inexpensive squirrel-cage fan at one end (a source of these fans is W. W. GRAINGER CO., 355 MULBERRY STREET, NEWARK, NJ 07102). Finally, a dense evergreen planting to windward of a greenhouse is an excellent insulator against heat-stealing winds.

"Building Hobby Greenhouses," Agricultural Information Bulletin 357, 25¢ from Superintendent of Documents, U.S. Government Printing Office, Washington, DC 20402

"Home Greenhouses," Circular 879, free from Agricultural Information Office, 112 Mumford Hall, University of Illinois, Urbana, IL 61801 — the best bulletin on designs, equipment, costs, with sources of plans and publications

"Greenhouse Handbook," Brooklyn Botanic Garden, 1000 Washington Avenue, Brooklyn, NY 11225; $1.25

"Greenhouse — Place of Magic," by Charles H. Potter (E. P. Dutton, $5.95)

"The Flowering Greenhouse Day by Day," by Elvin McDonald (D. Van Nostrand, $5.95)

"Greenhouse Gardening for Fun," by Claire L. Blake (Barrows, $6.95)

"Gardening Under Glass," by Jerome A. Eaton (Macmillan, $8.95)

"Commercial Flower Forcing," 7th ed., by Laurie, Kiplinger and Nelson (McGraw-Hill, $14.95) — despite its title, an indispensable construction-and-plants manual for the amateur

BLUEPRINTS

A Gothic Greenhouse for Town and Country Homes, Circular 892, Virginia Polytechnic Institute, Blacksburg, VA 24060

Home Greenhouse Plans, Johns-Manville Corporation, 22 East 40th Street, New York, NY 10016

A-Frame Home Greenhouse, Plan 210, Agricultural Engineering Department, University of Connecticut, Storrs, CT 06268

A Low Cost Portable Panel Greenhouse, Building Materials Department, Union Carbide Corporation, 6855 West 65th Street, Chicago, IL 60638

10' x 16' A-Frame Greenhouse, Plan 48-6, Louisiana State University, Baton Rouge, LA 70803

Plastic-Covered Greenhouse, Building Plan 73, Oregon State University, Corvallis, OR 97330

A Simple Rigid Frame Greenhouse for Home Gardeners, Circular 880, Information Office, 112 Mumford Hall, University of Illinois, Urbana, IL 61801

Experimental Greenhouses: Dome, Plan 822-350; Gable, 822-352; Multibarrel Vault, 822-356; Gothic Arch, 822-358; Quonset, 822-360; and two Hyperbolic-Paraboloid, 822-354 and 822-362; $1 per plan, Extension Agricultural Engineer, Pennsylvania State University, University Park, PA 16802

Kentucky Rigid Frame Greenhouse, Plan 771-8, 75¢, Department of Agricultural Engineering, University of Kentucky, Lexington, KY 40506

The Cornell "Twenty-One" Plastic Greenhouse, $2, Department of Vegetable Crops, Cornell University, Ithaca, NY 14850

Slant-Leg Rigid Frame Plastic Greenhouse, Plan 139, 15¢, Agricultural Engineering Department, Rutgers University, New Brunswick, NJ 08903

Note: The Cooperative Extension Service in each state — at your state college or university — has bulletins and often plans for home greenhouses. Also, when ordering any of the above, request a listing or copies of any other greenhouse literature that may be available.

MANUFACTURERS AND SUPPLIERS

Arthur Eames Allgrove, North Wilmington, MA 01887

Aluminum Greenhouses, Inc., 14615 Lorain Avenue, Cleveland, OH 44111

Geo. J. Ball, Inc., West Chicago, IL 60185

Brighton By-Products Co., Box 23, New Brighton, PA 15066

Filon Corporation, 12333 South Van Ness Avenue, Hawthorne, CA 90250

Florist Products, Inc., 780 West Oakton, Des Plaines, IL 60018

E. C. Geiger, Box 285, Harleysville, PA 19438

Greenhouse Specialties Co., 9849 Kimker Lane, St. Louis, MO 63127

Ickes-Braun Glasshouses, Inc., Box 147, Deerfield, IL 60015

Life-Lite, Inc., 1025 Shary Circle, Concord, CA 94520

Lord & Burnham, Irvington, NY 10533

Ludy Greenhouse Manufacturing Corporation, Box 85, New Madison, OH 45346

Maco Products, Box 3312, Salem, OR 97302

Mid-America Greenhouse Company, 10907 Manchester Road, St. Louis, MO 63122

Modern Greenhouse Manufacturing Company, 2511 Jackson Street, N.E., Minneapolis, MN 55418

National Greenhouse Company, Box 100, Pana, IL 62557

J. A. Nearing Company, 10788 Tucker Street, Beltsville, MD 20705

Porta-Green Company, 41 Fornof Road, Columbus, OH 43207

Redfern's Prefab Greenhouses, Mt. Hermon Road, Scotts Valley, CA 95060

Peter Reimuller, Greenhouseman, Box 2666, Santa Cruz, CA 95060

Rough Brothers, 4229 Spring Grove Avenue, Cincinnati, OH 45223

X. S. Smith, Red Bank, NJ 07701

Stearns Greenhouses, 98 Taylor Street, Neponset, Boston, MA 02122

Stuppy's Greenhouse Supply Co., 120 East 12th Avenue, North Kansas City, MO 64116

Sturdi-Built Manufacturing Company, 11304 S.W. Boones Ferry Road, Portland, OR 97219

Texas Greenhouse Company, 2717 St. Louis Avenue, Fort Worth, TX 76110

Trans-Sphere Trading Corporation, Box 1564, Mobile, AL 36601

Trox Manufacturing Company, 18 Angell Street, Battle Creek, MI 49016

Turner Greenhouses, Box 1620, Goldsboro, NC 27530

Winandy Greenhouse Construction, Box 597, Richmond, IN 47375

Horticultural Education and Therapy

Bringing Up Gardeners

The need for trained personnel in horticulture grows more critical each year, with shortages of qualified people in plant production, retailing, floristry and landscape design, and in every field of plant science from research and plant breeding to tropical biology. The "skilled plantsman gap," as it has been called, has reached crisis stage.

Recently, however, some outstanding programs have come into being to stimulate interest in horticulture both as vocation and avocation. Without question, the finest horticultural education program in America on the elementary school level is offered by the Cleveland Public Schools. This program, reports its Directing Supervisor, Peter J. Wotowiec, includes practical gardening activities in science classrooms for every child from kindergarten to twelfth grade,

Every crop from every plot in Garden Hilltop is weighed and recorded at "The Work Spot."

home and tract garden projects which now involve over 20,000 pupils, an outstanding Children's Garden Fair and vocational horticulture classes for high school students. A 56-acre Horticulture Education Center is being developed, and a post–high school Horticulture Technology program is now in operation.

Details on how to establish similar programs in any school are available from Mr. Wotowiec (Horticulture Division, Room 400, Cleveland Public Schools, 1380 East 6th Street, Cleveland, OH 44114). Mr. Wotowiec will also supply at cost to any school system the excellent printed materials used in his program. The Horticulture Division, incidentally, achieves all its remarkable work with less than .5% of the Cleveland Public Schools' annual budget.

Another organization making a fine contribution to horticultural education is the National Junior Horticultural Association. Operating at local, state and national levels, the NJHA works to inspire and train young people 14 to 21 years old, helping them "to obtain a basic understanding and to develop skills in the ever-expanding field of horticulture." The only youth organization that restricts all its activities to horticulture, the NJHA emphasizes practical education and vocational and professional opportunities in the field.

More than 200,000 young men and women have participated in its programs over the past 30 years. The NJHA is supported entirely by contributions. For further information on its activities, write the NJHA (Box 603, North Amherst, MA 01059).

Garden Hilltop

Garden Hilltop, a unique combination of children's gardening program and teacher education outdoor laboratory, celebrated its 25th anniversary. Originated 25 years ago by Dr. Barbara Shalucha of the Department of Botany of Indiana University, it is sponsored by the University, the City Department of Parks and Recreation and the Bloomington Garden Club.

On a hilltop acre at the edge of Bloomington, Hilltop is a world of horticulture in miniature. Within its borders are flower, fruit, rose, herb and woodland gardens, ninety-five 9′ x 9′ vegetable plots, a pool, shrub border, compost pile, greenhouse, coldframe, library, laboratory, even a tiny amphitheater. Here the city's children and teachers learn together in a remarkable program encompassing every aspect of indoor and outdoor gardening. "Hilltoppers" also take nature walks,

aid in community beautification projects and compete for achievement awards, and the "teaching interns" conduct research seminars in addition to their in-service leadership training.

Dr. Shalucha continues to direct Hilltop, and dreams of "Garden Hilltops in countless neighborhoods across this great land of ours. A boy, a girl, can truly know what it is to love and protect this land when each actually works with nature . . ." Write Dr. Shalucha at the University (Bloomington, IN 47401) for a brochure and sample program.

"SCHOOL SITE DEVELOPMENT FOR CONSERVATION AND OUTDOOR EDUCATION," an invaluable guide for every community planning to build new schools, is available free from the Pennsylvania Department of Education (Box 911, Harrisburg, PA 17126).

"A Child's Garden"

A remarkable book, "A CHILD'S GARDEN — A GUIDE FOR PARENTS AND TEACHERS," is offered free by the ORTHO DIVISION, CHEVRON CHEMICAL COMPANY (200 BUSH STREET, SAN FRANCISCO, CA 94120).

An outgrowth of Ortho's Children's Adventure Garden at the University of California in Berkeley, it reveals more about making horticulture a vital part of the learning process than any other book we've seen. The first part yields a tremendous number of insights invaluable to anyone seeking to solve horticulture's most pressing problem: how to inspire the young to a lifelong interest in gardening and nature.

The remainder is an intensely practical capsule course in gardening, covering growth processes, soil, nutrients, organic matter and vegetable gardening. An astonishing amount of information useful to every gardener is presented, with excellent illustrations and sources of further data and plants. A special chapter describes outstanding children's gardening programs throughout the country.

Training Plantsmen

There is wide agreement among educators that the most valuable vocational training is given in two-year, post–high school programs. To implement this concept for horticulture, educators and industry members have cooperated with the Office of the Department of Health, Education and Welfare to produce a guide, *"ORNAMENTAL HORTICULTURE TECHNOLOGY: A SUGGESTED CURRICULUM" ($1.75 FROM THE SUPERINTENDENT OF DOCUMENTS, WASHINGTON, DC 20402).* Curriculum areas covered are landscaping, nursery operation, floriculture, turfgrass management and arboriculture, with course outlines, texts, facilities and equipment detailed for each.

ARTS AND SCIENCES

The following list of correspondence courses was compiled by Dr. Norman F. Childers of Rutgers University for the American Society for Horticultural Science. Unless noted, the courses cover general horticulture.

University of Florida, Department of Correspondence Study (805 Seagle Building, Gainesville, FL 32601) — forestry, fruit crops, soils

University of Guelph, Independent Study (Guelph, Ontario, Canada) — home gardener's course, nursery management, parks, turf, landscaping, floriculture, etc., with a 3-year course leading to the Ontario Diploma in Horticulture

University of Missouri (Columbia, MO 65201)

Pennsylvania State University (202 Agricultural Education Building, University Park, PA 16802) — twenty excellent courses in all branches of horticulture

Utah State University, Extension Service, Independent Study (Logan, UT 84321) — design, fruits, vegetables, soils

Brigham Young University (Provo, UT 84601)

Washington State University, General Extension Service, Bureau of Correspondence Courses (Pullman, WA 99163) — general, entomology, turf, vegetables, soils

National Arborist Association (1750 Old Meadow Road, McLean, VA 22101) — Home Study Program covers a general introduction to commercial arboriculture, anatomy and physiology, soils, pruning, identification and selection, and fertilizing and watering.

Blooming Therapy

With little fanfare in either the medical or horticultural worlds, horticultural therapy has become a highly respected and widely practiced discipline. Since World War II, gardening has proved its worth in rehabilitating the physically handicapped and the mentally ill. Therapist *ALICE W. BURLINGAME,* co-author with *D. B. WATSON* of *"THERAPY THROUGH HORTICULTURE" (MACMILLAN, $4.95),* uses the motto, "A Hoe Instead of a Cane" in hospital work, noting that gardening "gives the patient renewed confidence, a feeling of achievement, and the drive to do just a little more the next time."

An excellent review of current knowledge and practice is *"HORTICULTURE AS A THERAPEUTIC AID,"* by *HOWARD D. BROOKS* and *CHARLES J. OPPENHEIM,* $2 from the *INSTITUTE OF REHABILITATION MEDICINE (400 EAST 34TH STREET, NEW YORK, NY 10016).* Notable programs of horticultural therapy are conducted at the Institute, at the Menninger Foundation (Topeka, KS 66601), where an arboretum is being developed by the staff and patients, and at Florida State Prison (Raiford, FL 32083), in cooperation with the Florida Federation of Garden Clubs.

A unique institution, the Melwood Horticultural Training Center (5606 Dower House Road, Upper Marlboro, MD 20870), is demonstrating its remarkable value in aiding the mentally retarded.

Started in 1963 with a tent and 7 acres of land, Melwood now has extensive classrooms, greenhouses, nursery facilities and a flower shop. More than sixty boys and girls, with an average I.Q. of 60 to 70, are currently enrolled in a program that embraces every vocation and work experience in horticulture. The aim is development of basic skills, responsibility and employability, and the results achieved at Melwood are gaining national attention, with Melwood graduates sought by horticultural firms and institutions, and even by unrelated industries. Youngsters with apparently extremely limited abilities have been found to be highly productive and creative — witness Marie, who for 5 years in another institution did not progress beyond putting plastic spoons into plastic bags, but after a year at Melwood became a competent floral designer.

The Center has acquired a 100-acre tract where it will establish a Horticultural Training-Residential Facility. And the new National Council for Therapy and Rehabilitation Through Horticulture is headquartered at Melwood.

A different but very inspiring operation is the unique commercial greenhouse–vocational training–social service home for delinquent youths created by retired construction executive Edward R. Timbello in upstate New York (New Haven, NY 13121). His "La Bergerie" was supported only partially by funds from the New York State Department of Corrections, so Mr. Timbello, who had been a florist many years ago, decided to make it self-supporting by establishing a green-house range. Two 28′ x 103′ greenhouses have been erected by the boys and now produce an extensive line of cut flowers and house plants, which are sold at wholesale to florists.

The business has not only proved profitable, but is being acclaimed for its success in making troubled boys into trained workers sought by growers, florists, even botanic gardens. As a judge commented, "Timbello's Home for Boys has an excellent, even outstanding, reputation for helping young people."

The Gardener and the Living Environment

The Phyto-Psyche Factor

Suddenly, gardening has become a front-rank defense against ugliness, waste and the destruction of the environment. The gardener, amateur and professional, is being asked to bring his skills to bear upon a major challenge of the times: restoration not only of our poisoned air, soil and water, but also of an environment aesthetically and psychologically polluted by an ever-increasing dearth of the open space and greenery essential to enrichment of the human spirit.

Scientists are now seriously investigating the idea that plants are basic nourishment for both senses and soul. Dr. Hugh Iltis, Taxonomist at the University of Wisconsin, believes that man is "genetically programmed" to require living plants in his surroundings, and he is researching this theory through a grant from the Horticultural Research Institute of the American Association of Nurserymen.

Seattle's Operation Triangle creates vest-pocket parks wherever street intersections leave "useless" odd-shaped plots.

SEED MONEY — to be matched by community funds — for a wide variety of environmental restoration and improvement projects is available to garden clubs and other local groups from the non-profit America the Beautiful Fund (806 15th Street, N.W., Washington, DC 20005).

Everett Conklin, a leading commercial interior plantscaper, has noted that "research in human behavior seems to indicate a symbiotic relationship" between man and plants, and quotes a doctor as saying that "not only do plants need man's care to develop best, but man also requires direct contact with plants to develop and retain a mental wholeness." He cites the long-recognized healing value of horticultural therapy, the improved morale and production in "landscaped" offices, and the remarkable effect on blighted areas of such planting programs as those of the Philadelphia Neighborhood Garden Association and the New York Housing Authority.

Philadelphia Story

An outstanding urban beautification project is the garden block program of the Neighborhood Garden Association of Philadelphia (3723 Mount Vernon Street, Philadelphia, PA 19104). A grass roots program involving the participation of residents, it has transformed more than 450 city streets with window and planter boxes, frontyard gardens and community and 4-H Club gardens. The Demonstration Garden — actually a whole array of model gardens — at the Association headquarters is a center of information on community improvement through horticulture.

Not only has the program arrested urban blight, but it has brought a new and vital spirit of friendship, civic responsibility and inter-ethnic understanding and cooperation to over 150,000 residents. The Association is generous in sharing its experience, and under its guidance similar projects have been initiated in numerous cities and several countries.

The program is detailed by its founder, the late Louise Bush-Brown, in her book, *"GARDEN BLOCKS FOR URBAN AMERICA"* (CHARLES *S* RIBNER'S SONS, $10).

Seattle's Blueprint for Beauty

Universally useful plans for urban beautification are rare. An outstanding one is the *"OPERATION TRIANGLE" PROGRAM KIT ($2 FROM THE SEATTLE CHAMBER OF COMMERCE, 215 COLUMBIA STREET, SEATTLE, WA 98104).*

Operation Triangle was conceived in 1965 to bring garden beauty to Seattle's many "triangles," odd parcels of public land formed by sharp-angled street junctions. Vest-pocket parks of often remarkable attractiveness have been created on these sites through the cooperative efforts of the city's Engineering Department, the Seattle Beautiful Operation Triangle Committee — composed of landscape architects, horticulturists and businessmen — and local communities, usually represented by a garden club or civic organization.

This highly successful working partnership has met every problem posed by the essential requirement of minimum maintenance, the complexities of funding, traffic engineering standards and the urban rigors of polluted air, poor soil, vandalism, etc. Perhaps most noteworthy is the system of investigation-planning-implementation applied to each site and assuring minimum cost and no failures due to improper design or plant selection.

VITAL STATISTICS: A minimum of 48,750 square feet of healthy turfgrass or 78 mature trees in active growth are necessary to convert to oxygen the carbon dioxide produced daily by one American through his breathing, household use of electricity, home heating, driving, garbage incineration and production of goods by burning fuels.

Boston — The City Is the Park

One city has a marvelous program dedicated to the ideal of "20% to 25% living cover" required for a healthy landscape, cited by Paul Sears in *"WILD WEALTH" (BOBBS-MERRILL, $20).*

In the words of Joseph E. Curtis, Commissioner of Parks and Recreation, in Boston "a new order has arrived! . . . The massive planting of city trees, the purification of inland streams, brooks, ponds and city lakes, the psychological return to the soil of urban gardeners and horticulturists, the acknowledging that filth and poison injected into the soil will likely go directly back into our bodies — this is illustrative of the action needed . . ."

Boston has passed strong laws to protect existing trees in the city, has begun a "Plantree" program to double its tree inventory in 3 to 5 years, is rehabilitating its parks and has mobilized public and private agencies of all kinds to plant extensively on their grounds. Standards for plants sold in Boston are being updated to insure higher quality. A master park plan is being drawn up for decades ahead, to "move the city forward toward the goal of park-like living for all." As Mr. Curtis says, "This simple yet bold concept is a thrust never attempted in any other major American city."

An especially interesting part of the program is a proposed revision of the Building Codes to require that all roofs "be constructed to have the strength, accessibility, and proper design controls, in order to accommodate roof gardens or similar landscaped areas."

Commissioning Beauty

Organized beautification through tree planting, care and control is the province of the shade tree commissions.

New Jersey's system has long served as a model. Operating under special state laws, one of every four of its municipalities has a shade tree commission, consisting of three to five residents appointed by the mayor and unsalaried. These commissioners are responsible not only for planning and planting new trees, but also for maintaining existing public trees. Financed by the municipality, the commission may use consultants or hire arborists to direct its working staff.

The most progressive shade tree commissions devote great effort to public educational campaigns, in cooperation with garden and civic clubs, on tree selection and care, thus extending their good works to private land. Many commissions maintain their own nurseries to insure a low-cost source of the best new cultivars. Detailed bulletins to aid any town wishing to establish a commission are obtainable from THE NEW JERSEY FEDERATION OF SHADE TREE COMMISSIONS (COLLEGE OF AGRICULTURE, RUTGERS UNIVERSITY, NEW BRUNSWICK, NJ 08903).

Also notable is New York City's new Street Tree Match Program. When a block association or other group contributes $200 toward the cost of planting 4 trees in its neighborhood, the Parks Department matches this with 6 more trees. Pruning and spraying are taken care of by the Parks Department, while the group is responsible for watering, feeding and guarding the trees from vandals.

Lots of Parks

The National Commission on Urban Problems reports that more than 20% of the land in 106 American cities of over 100,000 population is vacant. The idea of vest-pocket parks on this land is catching on, and now there is an excellent handbook.

"A LITTLE ABOUT LOTS," free from the PARK ASSOCIATION OF NEW YORK CITY (LOTS BOOK, BOX 600, NEW YORK, NY 10010), presents designs for mini-parks ranging from gardens for tots and sitting areas for oldsters to teenagers' recreation areas. Also discussed are problems such as acquisition, fund-raising, vandalism, insurance and maintenance.

Another fine idea, for sites where construction is delayed, is the "portable park," developed by the Little Rock Housing Authority (Little Rock, AR 72201). Easily moved to any location as needed, the park includes grass, trees, benches, bus shelters and gaslights.

Methods of building parks over blacktop are being tested at a 3-acre site at the John H. Eader Elementary School in Huntington Beach, California. Because it would have been prohibitively expensive to remove the blacktop and replace the soil, Landscape Architect Richard Bigler spread gravel for drainage, then installed a series of raised planters filled with a soil mix graded from 2' to 6' to give the effect of rolling land. The soil mix consisted of redwood sawdust, mushroom compost, sand and ammonium sulphate.

Lawns have been planted, and ivy is used extensively for groundcover. Over 100 mature trees are being planted by an unusual method: the root balls are enclosed in plastic bags, which will protect the roots while they adjust to the unusual transplant. As they grow, they will break through the plastic covers.

Mr. Bigler believes his planter-park concept will be useful for developing mini-parks in such areas as large parking lots, where tearing out the pavement to permit landscaping would be too costly.

Odd-Lot Gardener

Municipal real estate auctions, says New Yorker Jack Gasnick, are an unusual and virtually unknown avenue to gardening for apartment dwellers.

For from $25 to $300, Mr. Gasnick has purchased numerous vacant properties, ranging in size from 10' x 128' to 23' x 62', in three boroughs of New York City. He finds the most desirable by scouting the offerings described in booklets issued by the city in advance of the auction, and his main expense after purchase is fencing the properties. From some he has harvested apples, grapes, even figs, and others he maintains in shrubs, ferns and wildflowers, as oases for wildlife.

City-owned odd-lot parcels of land abound in municipalities of any size, and usually are offered at auction at regular intervals. For individuals and garden clubs, these would seem to offer an ideal opportunity to own urban vest-pocket gardens and wildlife preserves at low cost.

Nature Parks

"It's a whole new ball game," says a prominent parks director. "The trend is to nature areas, and even in big cities the idea of formal parks is being replaced by these re-creations of undisturbed ecosystems."

Greenacre Park in New York City is an outstanding vest-pocket park, an oasis of beauty and serenity in a business district.

A nature park may be many acres, or as small as a vest-pocket park or a corner of a school backyard, commercial site or home yard. An outstanding example is Walden Park in Madison, Wisconsin. To prevent a vacant lot from becoming a parking lot, residents of an adjoining University of Wisconsin women's dormitory consulted the University's Department of Landscape Architecture for aid in making it into a park. A student developed a plan for a natural area, a mini-restoration of Wisconsin prairie and deciduous and coniferous woodlands. Businessmen donated money for grading and topsoil, wood chips and rounds for paths were supplied by a utility company and the Madison Park Department, and plants came from gardeners, the University's Arboretum, and volunteer seed collectors. Volunteers did the planting and helped the seedlings through the difficult first year. A bank has provided funds for the minimal maintenance required over the next 10 years.

Now in its third year, there is magnificent bloom in the prairie section, and the woodlands are beginning to show the character and diversity of the native forests. Butterflies, bees and birds throng the park. It is a place to enjoy, to learn, to escape the lifeless asphalt-steel-concrete environment — and it is readily accessible for thousands of people.

Excellent aids for anyone desiring to establish a nature park are the *"NATURE ENJOYMENT AREAS"* leaflets available free from the ENVIRONMENTAL IMPACT OFFICE, UNIVERSITY OF UTAH (SALT LAKE CITY, UT 84112). Local offices of the FOREST SERVICE, SOIL CONSERVATION SERVICE, NATIONAL PARK SERVICE and STATE EXTENSION SERVICE can also offer much help.

Open-Space Savers

In the last few years, individual and organizational efforts to preserve open space have increased enormously — and so have development pressures against such preservation. Economic considerations are paramount, and the success of a project or program may depend more on land acquisition costs than on all other factors combined.

A community Christmas tree recycling project converts a usually wasted resource into mulch for residents' gardens.

The non-profit "land trust" technique, whereby a group of citizens forms a non-profit corporation to receive tax-deductible contributions of land, in many cases offers the most inexpensive solution. The method is detailed in "PROPERTY POWER" BY MARY ANNE GUITAR (DOUBLEDAY, $6.95).

An "open space conservation amendment" to the New Hampshire constitution demonstrates a new approach to preserving wild land. It allows legislation valuing land on "actual purpose" uses rather than on purposes for which it might be used if developed. Thus an owner wishing to keep his land in its wild state would not face higher taxes when land values skyrocket around him because of development. This relieves him of a powerful pressure to develop his own land.

Several states are finding "scenic easements" very useful for preserving natural beauty. These involve purchase of a landowner's right to do anything that would mar the landscape — erect billboards, deforest, etc. Many landowners have donated scenic easements free of charge.

California and New York are states which provide favorable tax treatment for land in "agricultural preserves." The land must be limited by contract to agricultural uses for at least 10 years. Commercial horticultural operations come within the scope of these statutes.

The Land Heritage Program of the National Wildlife Federation (1412 Sixteenth Street, N.W., Washington, DC 20036) aids landowners who want to make present or future gifts of their land to public or private nature preservation organizations.

Some helpful publications: "OPEN SPACE, ITS USE AND PRESERVATION," 20¢ from the SUPERINTENDENT OF DOCUMENTS (WASHINGTON, DC 20402); "PRIVATE APPROACHES TO PRESERVATION OF OPEN LAND," $12 hardcover, $10 softcover, from the CONSERVATION RESEARCH FOUNDATION (13 WOODSEA PLACE, WATERFORD, CT 06385); and "OPEN LAND FOR URBAN AMERICA," by DR. JOSEPH J. SHOMON (JOHNS HOPKINS PRESS), $7.50 from the NATIONAL AUDUBON SOCIETY (1130 FIFTH AVENUE, NEW YORK, NY 10028).

Garden Development

A unique "garden community" is coming into being at a famed horticultural showplace in North Carolina. Francis W. Howe, owner of Clarendon Gardens, has announced the opening of a 166-acre land development as "a new concept in garden living."

Lots 150' x 200' are offered in the attractive Sandhills area, and the development "has been landscaped and designed on gently rolling terrain, so that each home will have the most advantageous garden location." The homes will be situated amid mature long-leaf pines, and complete landscaping service is available for home grounds, as well as propagating beds for residents' use. And in addition to enjoying the plant collections at Clarendon Gardens, homeowners can take advantage of the excellent horticultural lectures and classes at Sandhills Community College.

For information, write MR. AND MRS. FRANCIS W. HOWE, CLARENDON GARDENS (BOX 1071, PINEHURST, NC 28374).

Chip-In

Here's how to plan a Community Christmas-tree recycling program, following the highly successful project organized by the New York State University College of Environmental Science and Forestry in Syracuse.

A weekend about two weeks after Christmas is a good time. The location, an open, easily accessible area such as a parking lot, should be publicized in the local news media, and ample volunteers should be on hand to direct traffic, unload the trees and bag the chips. A local arborist firm or a utility company will usually supply the chipper, and the only cost of the program is paying the operator of this machinery — at the College a student-organized waste-paper recycling project has generated some money that was used to pay the operators, in a sort of environmental chain reaction.

Participants should be urged to bring their own containers, such as shopping bags, and each person is given an amount of mulch approximately equal in weight to the tree or trees he brings. An important part of the project is giving each participant a sheet of instructions for using the organic mulch in his garden. Often people who live in apartments and so have no use for the mulch bring trees anyway, and the surplus chips that result are used to mulch plantings on public grounds. At the college, a free lunch was provided by a food concessionnaire — an inducement not considered essential to the success of the project but one which added greatly to the community spirit of the program.

Rewarding Beautification

Young people are being recognized as a vital force in the re-greening of America. One of the best ways to encourage their participation is through the President's Environmental Merit Awards Program, administered by the U.S. Environmental Protection Agency (4th and M Streets, S.W., Washington, DC 20460).

Of special interest to horticulture is the "Community Service Projects" section of the PEMA program. This includes landscaping, planting of trees and flowers, and other beautification projects, as well as anti-litter and recycling work. Students in some 110,000 public and private schools, 11,000 summer camps, and all youth organizations are eligible to participate. Details are available from the national or regional EPA offices.

Air Conditioning

While acute injury to plants from sudden and severe air pollution is generally obvious, the effects of chronic low levels of pollution have only begun to be revealed. A leading expert on the subject, Dr. Marlin N. Rogers of the Department of Horticulture, University of Missouri (Columbia, MO 65201), reports that these include destruction of chlorophyll, disruption of membrane permeability and thus interference with transfer of nutrients, increased respiration and alteration of important enzyme activity.

This "invisible injury" causes suppression of growth, and often general debilitation which results in lowered resistance to insects, disease, drought and other adversities.

Edward P. Hume of Southern Illinois University notes that improved vigor through feeding, mulching, watering, pruning and removal of competing plants aids resistance to pollutant stress. Fertilizing, however, should be moderate: succulent growth caused by excessive nitrogen feeding is more susceptible to damage. Soil drainage should be improved if necessary, and lime applied to counteract acidity caused by sulfur dioxide precipitation. In buying plants, always select the strongest, cleanest specimens, purchasing them if possible in an area subject to pollution so their tolerance of it is demonstrated. Dr. George S. Avery of the Brooklyn Botanic Garden states that injury is often least severe on young new leaves, so it is wise to use plants that grow continuously through the season.

New Dual Threat

Two deadly and widespread pollutants, herbicides and salt, are as injurious to plants as air pollution.

Much damage is laid to 2,4-D, mainly through drift and especially when the highly volatile ester formulations are used. However, arborists say that far more injury is due to dicamba (Banvel D), contained in feed-and-weed lawn preparations.

Since it can be absorbed by plant roots, dicamba must not be applied over tree or shrub roots — which often extend several times the branch spread of the plant. Leaching into the soil, it is quickly taken up and translocated through plant tissues, causing leaf distortion, elongation of new growth, dieback and death in severe cases.

An effective antidote, if applied to the soil immediately after dicamba is used, is Activated Charcoal (WITCO CHEMICAL CORP., 277 PARK AVENUE, NEW YORK, NY 10017). Watering and foliar or soil fertilizing will aid in restoring vigor to

MANUAL OF TRANSIT PLANNING," a 64-page handbook describing plants for the urban environment and showing how to use them, is designed to aid public transportation officials in "greening up" transit facilities; $3 from the American Horticultural Society (Mount Vernon, VA 22121).

injured plants. Recent research, incidentally, indicates that maintaining a continuous supply of organic matter in the soil speeds herbicide degradation by microbes, and that eventually it may be possible to nullify herbicides by applying "microbial broths" containing strains especially suited to breaking down these chemicals.

The second killer is salt used for de-icing. A nurseryman who recently drove across the Northeast and Midwest tells us of hundreds of miles of highways where virtually all trees, shrubs and turf are dead or dying up to 30′ back from the roadway, and the problem is no less serious in the cities and suburbs.

Salt injury may not show up for months. Grass and evergreens directly hit by salty slush will show "burned" foliage in early spring, caused by the salt withdrawing moisture from the leaves. Sodium chloride washed into the soil burns the roots, resulting in moisture stress in summer that shows as leaf scorch and dieback. Growth is stunted as sodium is absorbed in place of minerals such as potassium and magnesium, and vital soil structure is also destroyed by the sodium. A heavy attack by salt can kill shrubs and trees in a single season, or they may die in several years from repeated small doses. Often by the time symptoms are seen, the plant is too severely injured to be saved.

Substitutes for salt that give traction without melting are sand, ashes, cinders or the granite dust and grits commonly used on roads in the Alps. Sawdust and Kitty Litter are also effective and do not "scour" floors. Where removal of snow and ice is necessary, remember the Salt Institute of America's advice that only 10% of the amount required to completely melt ice is enough to soften it so it can easily be pushed away. Or use calcium chloride, which is somewhat less harmful to plants, or a mixture of salt and potassium chloride, to lessen soil and root damage due to excessive sodium.

The best solution, however, is urea fertilizer. It is as effective as salt in melting ice, it has far less corrosive effect on concrete and car bodies and of course its fertilizer value is beneficial to plants. Urea is now being sold specifically for de-icing — as Tred-Spred, available at hardware and auto supply stores.

Some more answers to the salt pollution problem: copious watering in spring will leach out much salt . . . gypsum applied to the soil will aid root recovery by restoring soil structure . . . antitranspirants give foliage some protection against splashed salt . . . black coloring matter, such as a black humus product, spread on sheet ice will speed its melting by solar heat absorption . . . plant salt-tolerant plants along roadways: in grasses, 'Fylking' bluegrass, 'Norlea' rye, and tall fescue; in trees and shrubs, avoid sugar maple, white pine, hemlock, balsam fir, spruce, elm, birch, barberry, euonymus, spiraea — choose instead Norway maple, oaks, hawthorn, honey locust, ash, red cedar and Russian olive.

Purer Water

The reduction of phosphates in detergents, the building of more sewage treatment plants and strong action against industrial polluters of streams have started the nation on the long road to purifying its waters.

The Gardener and the Living Environment   237

Gardeners can help to reduce water pollution in several ways: work fertilizer into the soil so it doesn't run off into streams and sewers . . . never flush away coffee grounds, tea leaves or any other vegetable wastes that can be composted . . . use pesticides that do not harm aquatic life, and don't dispose of unwanted hazardous pesticides in the water system . . . reduce your consumption of electricity so power plants will discharge less heated water into streams and rivers.

"Polluted rain" is a new problem. Dr. Gene E. Likens, Cornell University (Ithaca, NY 14850), warns that the rainfall in New York and New England has become "surprisingly acid." While distilled water has a pH of 5.7, and the records show that rainfall in New York 50 years ago was actually alkaline (above pH 7), precipitation today gives pH readings of 3 to 5. This increasing acidity is due to growing levels of sulfur and nitrogen oxides in the air — from vehicular and industrial pollution — which combine with moisture to make acid solutions.

Dr. Liken warns that in addition to damage to buildings — already a world-wide problem — the acid rain "has serious implications for ecological systems." Acidification of the soil and accompanying changes in nutrient availability will alter natural plant communities, and make it necessary for gardeners to check and modify the soil reaction in their gardens much more frequently to grow plants successfully.

Plant Solutions for Noise Pollution

Using plants for sound control is a relatively new science, but a rapidly progressing one. Reduction of noise pollution is now recognized as a matter of survival: 80 decibels (downtown or expressway traffic) cause a rise in blood pressure, while 130 decibels (a jet taking off) induce physical pain.

Inclusion of specifications for sound-engineered plantings is becoming commonplace in the design of commercial buildings. No longer are wide expanses of lawn and a shrub or tree here and there considered adequate landscaping, for even low levels of land and air traffic and activities such as mowing are now known to "distract subliminally" and lower productivity.

The degree of sound absorption depends on depth and density of a planting. Grass, for example, is an efficient sound absorber, but a thick, deep groundcover is better. A dense and

Small curbside parks change the whole atmosphere of a bleak business street in Lake Wales, Florida.

wide deciduous hedge can be as effective in winter as a narrow evergreen one. Surprisingly, a dense vine covering a building wall can reduce noise penetration as effectively as tall foundation plantings — even espaliered plants are useful.

Best of all, of course, is the massed planting that forms a deep barrier from ground level to considerable height. But a "solid wall" effect is neither aesthetically desirable nor necessary: the plantings can be spaced out, graduating from low to high as they approach the building. Thus a groundcover, fencerow planting strip or low hedge near the sidewalk traps ground-level noise, while low trees, shrubs or "island" plantings in the lawn area act as intermediate height baffles, and tall trees near the house blot upper-story sound waves.

A final, seldom-considered rule: hard surfacing does not absorb sound — so use tanbark and similar materials for walks, and deep, loose organic mulches.

Going Native

Plant species endangered by pollution and progress undoubtedly number in the thousands. What gardeners can do to save them is suggested by GEORGE E. ALLEN IN "THE GARDENER" (MEN'S GARDEN CLUBS OF AMERICA, 5560 MERLE HAY ROAD, DES MOINES, IA 50323).

Mr. Allen practices individual or "Johnny Appleseed" conservation. This is conservation by garden use, rather than by preservation of wild habitats. Mr. Allen observes that many native trees, shrubs and other plants "found growing under minimal conditions may, when planted out as specimen plants and treated with the tender

loving care you would give an exotic plant from Timbuktu or Tibet, suddenly become exotic, ornamental, conversation pieces." He urges gardeners to seek out scarce plants, learn to propagate them and use them in the garden, then make them available to others. Many plants he has "rescued" were given to his county's nursery and now grace public parks and rights-of-way. Others, donated to garden club plant sales, are garden highlights.

Several organizations and institutions are taking up this idea. The Rare Plant Group of the Garden Club of America (598 Madison Avenue, New York, NY 10022) has members all over the country, each seeking out and propagating rare, unusual and exceptionally meritorious plants in her specialty. These plants are made available to members at meetings of the 12 Zones of the GCA. The program and its educational and beautification impacts are growing, and dedicated plantsmen and arboretums are sharing their rare plants with the group.

In California, the 20-acre Theodore Payne Foundation Nursery (Sun Valley, CA 91352), managed by volunteers from among the foundation's 300 members, has two aims: to preserve plants native to California which are in danger of extinction, and to encourage the use of native plants in gardens. Although it is still in the process of development, the nursery already has for sale more than 220 varieties of native plants and over 100 kinds of seeds. Considerable literature on the uses and culture of native plants is produced and distributed by the members.

THE MONTANA AGRICULTURAL EXPERIMENT STATION (BOZEMAN, MT 59715) has published an invaluable listing, "NATIVE MONTANA PLANTS WORTH GROWING IN GARDENS" — a project that should be duplicated in every state and many localized areas. THE BOERNER BOTANICAL GARDENS (HALES CORNERS, WI 53130) is known for its excellent "PRAIRIE PROPAGATION HANDBOOK" ($1.25), which describes 300 prairie plants and how to grow them. And commercial nurseries that handle solely native plants, such as THE SHOP IN THE SIERRA (BOX 1, MIDPINES, CA 95345; CATALOG 50¢), are beginning to appear.

THE URBAN LAND INSTITUTE (1200 18th Stree N.W., Washington, DC 20036) offers a fr 28-page environmental guide for the land deve oper, to aid him in controlling pollution an maintaining environmental quality.

Even botanical gardens are going commercial. Hawaii's OLU PUA GARDENS (BOX 518, KALAHEO, HI 96741), one of the great tropical botanical gardens of the world — established by Bettie and Ray Lauchis, amateur horticulturists from Cleveland, Ohio — sells rare plants, seeds, cuttings and dried material. Near Elizabeth City, North Carolina, Frederick Heutte, retired Director of the Norfolk Botanical Gardens and founder of schools of horticulture at Norfolk and at Sandhills Community College (Southern Pines, NC 28387), is establishing a botanical garden which will propagate and sell worthy species and cultivars from its collections.

Planting with Nature

Choosing plants for their ecological fitness is the theme of a brilliant book by William Flemer III, of Princeton Nurseries.

"NATURE'S GUIDE TO SUCCESSFUL GARDENING AND LANDSCAPING" (THOMAS Y. CROWELL COMPANY, $8.95) is a marvelously practical work on a "new" horticultural science, that of applied ecology. In his initial chapter, "The Garden Is an Ecosystem," Mr. Flemer shows how basing the garden on locally adapted plants, sited in suitable microclimates, results in unusual beauty and minimum maintenance.

He examines the ecology of open-land, woodland, wetland, desert, city, rock and wall gardens, and describes hundreds of plants which can be grown with optimum success and minimal care in each of these environments. A great deal of advice is given on specific problems encountered in these settings, and on "propagating with nature" and controlling pests with natural weapons.

Honor the Earth

The new outlook on gardening and its relation to man and his environment has never been more perfectly expressed than in these words by Henry Beston, America's great naturalist-ecologist, from *ESPECIALLY MAINE: THE NATURAL WORLD OF HENRY BESTON FROM CAPE COD TO THE ST. LAWRENCE," EDITED BY ELIZABETH COATSWORTH (STEPHEN GREENE PRESS, BRATTLEBORO, VT 05301; $6.95):*

"The ancient values of dignity, beauty and poetry which sustain [a human life] are of nature's inspiration; they are born of the mystery and beauty of the world. Do no dishonor to the earth lest you dishonor the spirit of man. Hold your hands out over the earth as over a flame. To all who love her, who open to her the doors of her veins, she gives of her strength, sustaining them with her own measureless tremor of dark life. Touch the earth, love the earth, honor the earth, her plains, her valleys, her hills and her seas; rest your spirit in her solitary places. For the gifts of life are the earth's and they are given to all . . ."

BASIC BOOKS
FOR ENVIRONMENTALISTS

"Design with Nature," by Dr. Ian L. McHarg (Doubleday Natural History Press, hardcover $19.95, paperback $5.95)

"The Inland Island," by Josephine W. Johnson (Simon and Schuster, $5)

"Working with Nature," by John Brainerd (Oxford University Press, $15)

"In Defense of Nature," by John Hay (Little, Brown, $4.95)

"Consider the Process of Living," by William H. Eddy, Jr., Gonzalo S. Leon and Robert C. Milne (The Conservation Foundation, 1717 Massachusetts Avenue, N.W., Washington, DC 20036; $5.95)

"A Sand County Almanac," by Aldo Leopold (Oxford University Press, $6.50)

Appendix—
Books for Avant Gardeners

The Basics

The serious gardener needs certain standard reference works that provide detailed identification of plants, and information on their use and culture. The first six books on the following list are considered the best for this purpose, while the others are either basic texts on plant growth and function or general books which supply a great deal of information on many aspects of gardening.

"Wyman's Gardening Encyclopedia," by Donald Wyman, 1971, Macmillan, $17.50

"Encyclopedia of Gardening," by Norman Taylor, 1961, Houghton Mifflin, $15

"Standard Cyclopedia of Horticulture," 3 vols., by L. H. Bailey, 1900, Macmillan, $65

"Hortus Second," by L. H. and D. Z. Bailey, 1941, Macmillan, $14.95

"Manual of Cultivated Plants," by L. H. Bailey, 1949, Macmillan, $19.50

"Royal Horticultural Society Dictionary of Gardening," 2nd ed., edited by Chittenden and Synge, 1956, Oxford University Press, $60

"Introductory Botany," by Arthur Cronquist, 1961, Harper, $9.25

"Plants of the World: The Higher Plants," 2 vols., by H. C. D. deWit, 1967, Dutton, $17.50 per volume

"Horticultural Science," by Jules Janicek, 1966, Freeman, $8.50

"Fundamentals of Horticulture," 3rd ed., by Edmond, Senn and Andrews, 1964, McGraw-Hill, $8.95

"10,000 Garden Questions Answered by 20 Experts," 3rd ed., edited by Marjorie Dietz, 1974, Doubleday, $10.95

"America's Garden Book," by James and Louise Bush-Brown, 1958, Scribner's, $8.95

"The Complete Illustrated Book of Garden Magic," 2nd ed., by Biles and Dietz, 1969, Doubleday, $9.95

"The Complete Gardener," by Lois Wilson, 1971, Hawthorn, $12.95

Classic Revival

Two publishers have specialized in the reprinting of facsimile editions of classic references. Dover Publications (180 Varick Street, New York, NY 10014) lists such eminent works as the four-volume Britton and Rose "The Cactaceae." Stechert-Hafner, Inc. (31 East 10th Street, New York, NY 10003) has reprinted the three-volume Britton and Brown "Illustrated Flora of the United States" and others.

An antiquarian bookseller, Augustus M. Kelly (Box 458, Sakonnet Point, Little Compton, RI 02837), who is also an avid gardener, has launched a series called Theophrastus Reprints. These are high-quality reprints, offered at very reasonable prices ($8.50 to $12.50), of rare and widely sought gardening classics which are valuable not only for the fame and stylistic accomplishments of their authors, but especially because they still provide substantial information for the gardener who wants to grow unusual plants. Theophrastus Reprints include Murray Hornibrook's invaluable "Dwarf and Slow-Growing Conifers" (2nd ed., 1938), Reginald Farrer's "My Rock Garden" (1907) and "In a Yorkshire Garden" (1909), Frank Kingdon Ward's "The Land of the Blue Poppy" (1913), E. A. Bowles' "My Garden in Spring" (1914), and Ira N. Gabrielson's "Western American Alpines" (1932).

Books from Abroad

A source of British and Canadian gardening books, as well as government bulletins from these countries, is Pendragon House (899 Broadway Avenue, Redwood City, CA 94063).

Like our USDA, the British Ministry of Agriculture, Fisheries and Food publishes numerous bulletins on horticulture (a list is obtainable from Her Majesty's Stationery Office, P62, Atlantic House, Holborn Viaduct, London, E.C.1). These range from the comprehensive, such as "Fruit Tree Raising," to the highly technical.

Another excellent source is Daniel Lloyd ("Heather Lee," 4 Hillcrest Avenue, Chertsey, Surrey, England). Mr. Lloyd's catalog of out-of-print garden books is highly commended by librarians and collectors. He can also supply all new English garden books, and it is usually less expensive to buy them direct than from American sources.

Source Guides

In recent years, several very helpful guides to sources of information, plants and supplies have appeared.

"The Directory of American Horticulture," published by the American Horticultural Society (Mount Vernon, VA 22121; $5) is updated every 3 years. It lists over 600 sources of information and assistance, from libraries, plant societies and agricultural extension offices to educational institutions and public gardens.

Marion Schroeder's "The Green Thumbook" (Valley Crafts, Box 99, Cary, IL 60013; $2.95) is an excellent guide to 503 sources of seeds, plants and supplies, and 424 inexpensive publications on all aspects of gardening, plus information on plant societies, garden magazines, the USDA and State Extension Services.

HHH Horticultural (68 Brooktree Road, Hightstown, NJ 08520) annually publishes a "Hardy Plant Finder" and a "Tender Plant Finder," guides to over 500 U.S. and foreign retail mail-order nurseries, plus such data as a basic reference book list, plant society popularity polls, and a list of horticultural publications and services.

"1200 Trees and Shrubs — Where to Buy Them," Handbook 63 of the Brooklyn Botanic Garden (Brooklyn, NY 11225; $1.50), gives pithy descriptions of each species, cultivar and hybrid, keyed to lists of wholesale and retail nurseries.

Book Search Services

Able Book Finders, 200 West 20th Street, New York, NY 10011

Antaeus Books, Box 153, Granville, MA 01034

Books-On-File, Union City, NJ 07087

Hunt Search Service, Box 130, New York, NY 10003

. . . Also the list of dealers from the Antiquarian Booksellers Association, 630 Fifth Avenue, New York, NY 10020

Booksellers

G. A. Bibby, 714 Pleasant Street, Roseville, CA 95678 — gardening and natural history

Edward C. Fales, Box 56, Salisbury, NH 03268 — gardening, cookery

Garden Way Research, Charlotte, VT 05445; catalog $1 — gardening and country living

Marian L. Gore, Box 433, San Gabriel, CA 91775 — gardening, herbs

K. Gregory, 221 East 71st Street, New York, NY 10021 — books and prints

Lew Heymann Books, Box 6448, Carmel-by-the-Sea, CA 93921 — mushrooms, grasses, weeds, ferns, mosses, lichens, mycology

HHH Horticultural, 68 Brooktree Road, Hightstown, NJ 08520 — the largest mail-order list of recent garden books

Hilltop House, 1 The Loch, Roslyn, NY 11576; catalog $1 — many rare, out-of-print works

Horticultural Books Inc., 219 Martin Avenue, Stuart, FL 33494 — fine list of gardening books for warm climates

John Johnson, R.F.D. 2, North Bennington, VT 05257 — botany, birds

Nada Kramer, 927 15th Street, N.W., Washington, DC 20005 — botany

Eric Lundberg, Ashton, MD 20702 — botany and insects

Pomona Book Exchange, 33 Beaucourt Road, Toronto 18, Canada; send stamp for list — from new to antiquarian books

Santa Paula Books, Box 384, Santa Paula, CA 93060 — many old and rare works, also special rose book list

S. J. Singer Co., 1133 Broadway, New York, NY 10010; catalog 25¢ — rare antiquarian garden books

Sportshelf, Box 634, New Rochelle, NY 10802 — old and new works

Elizabeth Woodburn, Booknoll Farm, Hopewell, NJ 08525 — probably the largest stock of recent to antiquarian gardening books anywhere

Zimmer's, Inc., 1244 Santa Fe Drive, Denver, CO 80204 — new, unusual books

A mother and child pose for a photo after participating in the planting of a vest-pocket park in Harlem.

PICTURE CREDITS

INDEX

PICTURE CREDITS

INDEX